T0354686

THE COMING
TYRANNY

THE COMING TYRANNY

How Socialism Will Lead to Civil War in the United States

David A. Herrera

THE COMING TYRANNY
HOW SOCIALISM WILL LEAD TO CIVIL
WAR IN THE UNITED STATES

iUniverse books may be ordered through booksellers or by contacting:

iUniverse
1663 Liberty Drive
Bloomington, IN 47403
www.iuniverse.com
844-349-9409

ISBN: 978-1-6632-2099-8 (sc)
ISBN: 978-1-6632-2100-1 (hc)
ISBN: 978-1-6632-2098-1 (e)

Library of Congress Control Number: 2021911841

Print information available on the last page.

iUniverse rev. date: 06/29/2021

To my wife Patricia, my family and friends, and all present and future generations of patriotic Americans who want to keep America great, and the leader of the free world; to police departments across America who are the first line of defense against injustice; to all veterans who served our country well with sacrifice and honor and defended the freedoms that we have today; and to our present active duty military whom we trust to defend our constitutional freedoms domestically and serving in remote places around the world to protect our country from all foreign enemies. God bless you all.

CONTENTS

LIST OF FIGURES AND TABLES

TABLES

FIGURES

INTRODUCTION

The Coming Tyranny is about Democrats who gained control of the White House and both houses of Congress, who have passed presidential executive orders and congressional legislation to insidiously redistribute the wealth of Americans and corporate America and shift the power of conservatives to Democrat leftists. The shift in wealth and power to Democrat elites and their cronies, will enable them to transform the United States into a socialist country whose policies will oppress freedom-loving Americans, leading to a civil war between oppressed patriotic Americans and a tyrannical socialist government.

The Coming Tyranny begins with Democrat leftists under the Obama Administration who insidiously attempted to bribe Vatican officials to change Catholic Church doctrine and align it with leftist political morality regarding homosexuality and abortion so people could view each favorably and enhance Democrat political power. Examples of socialist policies of former President Obama and his nefarious scandals are presented. Socialist policies of 2016 Democrat presidential candidates are presented to show how they all want to remake America and how Democrats are mismanaging their cities and states with their misguided policies. The goal of all of them is to shift wealth and power away from conservatives and from corporate America to leftist Democrats and their supporters so they can attain perpetual power.

In 2020, a frail old leftist Democratic presidential candidate was elected to office in an election highly suspected of being riddled with fraud. Democrats also gained a majority in the Senate, and now have a majority in both houses of Congress. A dysfunctional US Supreme Court refused to hear any evidence of election fraud from any investigators, witnesses, or states who filed suit to present election fraud evidence.

State supreme courts of key states and the Supreme Court of the United States refused to hear evidence obtained from investigators and key witnesses with sworn affidavits that they observed voting fraud. This is the biggest historical failure our federal and state justice systems that over 74 million Americans have ever seen; the court system refused to hear evidence on the biggest instance of election fraud in United States history. Evidence points to the idea that election fraud was the concerted effort of corrupt Democratic officials at the federal, state, and local levels of government, along with a contracted election computer company, ballot counters, election officials, and mail carriers. Our court system is dysfunctional. President Trump, who delivered on his promises and who created the best economy in US history with record job growth and job opportunities, and made the United States the world leader in oil and gas production, was cheated out of a sure win, angering seventy-five million Trump voters. Joe Biden was sworn in as president on January 20, 2021, amid the biggest show of force—protection by police and National Guard troops—in US history, all because of a Democratic-concocted fear that Trump terrorists might assassinate the new president.

No Democratic Party in history has ever been as far to the left as the Joe Biden administration, with many leftists selected by Joe Biden as his vice president and his White House staff. Several Democratic members of Congress are socialists who support socialist policies to remake the United States. The Biden administration is only the beginning of turning the United States into a socialist nation. Leftist Democratic policies will encroach upon the United States; the leftist government is hell-bent on remaking the United States into a tyrannical, oppressive socialist state, which ultimately will lead to a second US civil war. As of March 9, 2021, Joe Biden has signed sixty executive orders. Source: An article in MarketWatch by Victor Reklaitis and Robert Schroeder entitled, *"All of President Biden's key executive orders — in one chart"*, dated 03/09/2021 at website: https://www.marketwatch.com/story/all-of-president-bidens-key-executive-orders-in-one-chart-2021-01-21. He issued executive orders that have sidestepped the two legislative houses of Congress to avoid debate, delays, embarrassments, and the possibility that the issues would be rejected by members of Congress. Some of Joe Biden's executive orders are unconstitutional and destructive to Americans. Joe Biden is ruling by dictatorial powers and legislating from the White House.

Leftist policies began in the Obama administration. The Obama administration was very progressive. Obama weaponized his agencies to oust world leaders. Before leaving office, the corrupt Obama administration weaponized his agencies to spy on candidate Trump to rig the 2016 election for Hillary Clinton. The objective was to fish for crimes candidate Trump may have committed, particularly, his alleged collusion with Russia to win the 2016 election, in order to disqualify him from the presidency and relegate the presidential throne to Democratic candidate Hillary Clinton. Hillary Clinton and the Democratic National Committee (DNC) used the biased Democrat-run news media as a war machine against candidate Trump.

President Trump was elected, much to the chagrin and shock of Democrats. Then leftists in the corrupt FBI, DOJ, CIA, and State Department continued to spy on President Trump for over three and a half years to remove him from office, continuing to use the unverified Russian dossier. House Democrats, driven by mixed progressives and socialists in the Democratic Party, tried to impeach President Trump as a coup to remove him from office, but to the shocking dismay of the House Democrats, the Mueller investigation, consisting of pure anti-Trump Democrats, found no evidence of Russian collusion as alleged by House Democrats.

In their greed for power and control, radical members of the Democratic Party, supported by their fake news media, have led their party closer toward socialism. Domestic terrorist organizations such as Antifa and Black Lives Matter (BLM), which Democratic Congress supports, have hijacked peaceful protests and turned them toward revolution, anarchy, rioting, and antipolice violence. We faced multiple threats from Marxist revolutionaries in some cities across the United States. Most of the presidential candidates who ran in 2020 are socialists, and more extreme than at any other time in US history.

Socialism in the United States has developed with concurrent Marxist principles and leftist reform strategies funded by nefarious New World Order (NWO) sources of power. President Trump stood in the way of the NWO cabal as they tried to aid and abet leftists in the United States to destroy and rebuild our institutions; reform government policies, reform our schools, law enforcement agencies, churches, and religion; weaken or diminish our constitutional laws, our public safety protocols, our elections, and our immigration system. As seen on TV during the 2020 Democratic presidential debates, the majority of the Democratic presidential candidates presented themselves as socialists who advocated the transformation of the United States from a nation with the best economy in the world to a socialist United States of free health care for all, including immigrants; open borders; reparations for descendants of historically oppressed blacks; free tuition; and forcing income equality for all by raising taxes on corporations and on rich white people who allegedly, "oppress their victims." Democratic socialists want all Americans to be dependent on big government.

Socialist activists are actively trying to destroy, reform, or rebuild the institutions and revise the history that made the United States a great country. Activists want to rebuild the United States into their own leftist utopia by means of violence and terrorism. Unruly mobs took over parts of Democrat-run cities without opposition from police or Democratic city administrators. US Institutions are being attacked that include churches, national monuments, and statues of Jesus and Mary have been vandalized or destroyed. Businesses in riot areas were attacked because they are symbols of capitalist America. Sanctimonious House Democrats did not call out Antifa for any of their rioting or violence. Democrat leaders of badly managed cities failed to keep the peace and allowed their cities' businesses to be looted, burned, and vandalized. Some Democrat-run cities have reduced their police budgets.

After the 2020 election, Democratic members of Congress indicated that the seventy-five million Trump voters needed to be "reprogrammed." Other Democrats said that the children of Trump voters needed to be put in reeducation camps. High-tech companies have joined the leftist Biden administration to censor Trump voters. Twitter canceled the account of President Trump and the accounts of other conservative leaders, and Facebook is notorious for censoring the personal posts of conservatives on its website. Nancy Pelosi and other House Democrats hurriedly impeached President Trump a week before he left office, and social media are still demonizing him even though he has gone from office. Out of fear, vindictive Democrats sought to prevent Donald Trump from ever running for president again.

Strategies are planned, and coordinated efforts by leftist groups are being made, to force reforms to our existing US institutions. The socialist-leaning Biden Administration wants to build and maintain greater power. As socialism develops, naive Democratic socialists are promising a utopian dream to end racism, force income equality, and redistribute wealth from the wealthy to the supposedly disenfranchised and oppressed. Democrats will seek to impose high taxes on rich white capitalist oppressors. These oppressors include the working middle class and those who own successful businesses. High taxation on wealthy Americans and corporations is a necessary strategy, as argued by big government socialists, to achieve economic justice and serve the common good.

We are once again facing tyrannical reforms from big government and violent demands from leftist domestic terrorist groups within our own country, aided by foreign NWO elites, to achieve a socialist United States. *The Coming Tyranny* predicts scenarios for how the United States will become a socialist tyrannical country, a country that again will fight against the tyranny that our country's forefathers originally rejected and escaped from. Conservatives from the Republican Party know well that those who ignore the historical mistakes of socialist governments of the past are bound to repeat them. Conservatives believe that through initiative and hard work, individuals will "be all they can be" to achieve success, prosperity, and the American dream. Republicans win the hearts and minds of the American people with economic success and integrity. Socialists, on the other hand, oppose the US Constitution and seek to weaken, rewrite, or replace it; they believe fair and economic equality for all comes from big government. Socialists believe in big government over individual rights and in redistribution of wealth. They rig and steal elections, depose US and world leaders from office, and team up with violent domestic terrorist groups and the biased propaganda-broadcasting news media to bash conservatism. Socialists seek to change culture, reform institutions, rewrite US history, and destroy the United States' current capitalist system of success, prosperity, and leadership. In short, Democrats want a complete transition of wealth and permanent power and control into a one-party socialist system of government in which no other political party can ever be elected to office.

Socialists invented a "new morality" aligned with political liberalism in order to morally justify the idea that big government knows best what all human beings need and that everyone should share the wealth for the common good—that is, income equality for all, including sharing our wealth with immigrants from all over the world. It is highly suspected that the Obama administration, with the funds of George Soros, lobbied the Vatican to retire Pope Benedict and replace him with Pope Francis, a more liberal pope, and groom him to be the voice of progressive morality before his September 2015 visit to the United States; more details follow in *The Coming Tyranny*.

Individual prosperity made possible by extraordinary ability and hard work is a capitalist economic system rejected by socialists. Democrats see it as evil and unfair that "rich oppressive white guys" have so much wealth; most of their wealth should be confiscated by big government and given to all "oppressed victims" who rightfully deserve other people's money. Worse, socialists want open borders in order to remake the United States by bribing illegal aliens with promised government handouts to draw them in for amnesty, to get their votes. Advertised government handouts are strictly for illegal aliens, while neglecting many homeless Americans and US veterans, but these handouts are all at US citizen taxpayers' expense. Does this make any sense?

Socialists plan to exploit illegal immigrants for cheap labor. These immigrants may replace US citizen workers who may have been dismissed from their good-paying jobs and were once accustomed to prosperity. Socialist politicians want to remake the United States with a combination of foreign migrants and existing leftist US citizens to overwhelm the conservative population and thereby win elections forever. Once in power, socialists aim to pass laws that will give illegal immigrants amnesty to ensure their own power will never end.

The intent of *The Coming Tyranny* is to provide analysis that leads to the conclusion that tyranny intensifies in order to establish a socialist government in the United States. It describes what socialism is, the socialist agenda, the strategic development of socialist power in the United States, the deceptive and corruptive practices of socialist politicians and their supporters, and their consequential efforts to deprive Americans of the freedoms that our country's founders won. Socialism will not work in the United States. *The Coming Tyranny* explains why.

Since the election of President Trump and before the COVID-19 pandemic, the United States became prosperous for all people: blacks, Hispanics, Asians, and everyone else. The economic message was that choosing wisely and seeking good training begets good opportunities for jobs, and the individual becomes successful through hard work to achieve the American dream. Blacks held on the "Democratic plantation" in neglected, poverty-stricken cities, riddled with crime, threw off their chains by seeking the increased jobs and opportunities made available by President Trump's policies. The United States has been made great by President Trump's policies, with little or no help from the Democratic members of Congress, who wasted much time trying to impeach and remove President Trump since he was elected president, because he had been so successful and they feared he would be reelected in 2020.

The Coming Tyranny predicts that creeping socialism will encroach upon the United States. As socialists increase their power, their oppression and tyranny will intensify. Socialists will develop a police state filled with preferred amnesty migrants, who will enforce Democratic laws without hesitation. Socialists will also groom the military to defend the socialist government against coups, insurrections, and Trump voters, whom Democrat liars now call white supremacists.

Democratic politicians already anticipate that freedom-loving Americans will oppose their tyrannical laws and fear they will fight or die rather than give up their freedom and constitutional rights. Socialists will enact laws to severely restrict firearms and will confiscate some of them from law-abiding gun owners. The police state will assist with enforcing gun laws, and the military will put down any rebellions arising from the confiscation of citizens' guns. Banning guns or enacting heavily restrictive gun laws may likely trigger a secession of states that oppose the socialist government's stance on gun control. State residents will be unhappy about losing their constitutional rights. If states secede, they will form their own state militaries and take over any US military bases in their states. Seceding states will recruit soldiers and mobilize their troops to defend their states. Scenarios are presented to expose the strategies that elected socialists will use to tax-oppress the wealthy, take guns away from law-abiding citizens, and enforce the taking of the wealth of the rich and redistributing it to illegal aliens, the poor, the unemployed, unskilled blacks, and amnesty migrants – all likely Democrat supporters. The economy will likely fail, driving middle-class Americans into poverty or homelessness. Poverty and crime will increase, and a civil war will likely occur when Americans find themselves unable to oust incompetent and oppressive elites from power. Unless immigration is curbed, the United States will reinforce tyrannical socialists with more power, thereby making the United States a socialist country. Tyranny will be used to enforce laws passed, driving patriotic, freedom-loving Americans into a second US civil war, a war between the red states and the blue states, but more so between leftists and constitutionalists. If states do not secede, opposition to tyranny will still gain varying momentum. In some states, state leaders who support tyranny will be pressured out of office and replaced by conservative leadership.

A last likely prediction is presented to explain that a third civil war will be coming to the United States. Socialists under the Biden administration have already gained practical control of the federal government, and *if* socialists win the second US civil war, Muslims who partnered with socialists against conservatives in the United States will be betray socialists, who naively allowed Muslim immigrants to enter the United States from all over the world to overpopulate and control parts of the United States. A scenario is presented to explain that the third civil war in the United States will be between Muslims and non-Muslims. As Muslims gain more control of the states they heavily populate and more control of the socialist federal government, they will use the aid of Muslim countries in the civil war against non-Muslims.

The United States will likely be split up into two countries, one Muslim, the other non-Muslim, as a result of a United Nations-negotiated peace settlement. The result: The old United States as we knew it, may never return.

Since the election of 2020 was stolen from President Trump, the Biden administration has begun showing its wrath by spending like socialists, a prelude of the coming tyranny. We will see our individual rights and freedom diminished, and likely the last hope for a great America will fade. Calls for secession will increase. We can likely expect two potential bloody US civil wars before the end of the twenty-first century.

PART 1

PROGRESSIVISM AND THE SOCIAL ENGINEERING OF THE UNITED STATES

1

WHAT IS PROGRESSIVISM?

The Meaning of Progressivism in the United States: Progressivism = Liberalism

Progressivism, synonymous with liberalism, is increased government control of the citizenry to advance social and political leftist ideology or reforms. Progressive issues include massive government spending, social justice reforms, racial reforms, reform and promotion of LGBT ideology, industrial and labor reforms, abortion rights, economic reform, and a persistent drive to maintain power and control in government, even by corrupt or by unethical means. Progressivism is watered-down socialism. It rejects a traditional the United States and its long-held customs and traditions, that is, the status quo, and seeks to replace these customs and traditions with New Leftist social norms and moral behavior in line with a purely leftist partisan agenda. Progressivism carried out to the extreme leads to totalitarianism, such as socialism, communism, fascism, or a dictatorship, where the power resides with the state, not with the individual. World history is full of cycles of totalitarian governments that oppressed their citizens, resulting in incidents of violence, suffering, poverty, starvation, or genocide.

Progressivism in the United States is not change that amounts to the type of progress that achieves success, benefits Americans, or promotes respect and unity in the United States. Rather, the progressivism of the United States is pure leftist partisan culture change, designed to achieve a new world order. It is social engineering of our moral values, our justice system, our system of government, and our way of life. Progressives think big government knows better what is good for all individuals, rather than believing that individuals know what is good for themselves. Progressives have a history of changing long-established sick and abnormal behaviors into "acceptable behavior" that should now be a new norm, and if it is not accepted, those opposing the new norms are accused of racism or intolerance. Progressive new norms were considered sick and freaky before, but now leftists want everyone to tolerate the people who behave in sick ways as if what they're doing is normal and acceptable. Progressives think that things previously considered to be sick, such as homosexuality, should not only be protected but also should be promoted to children in all schools across the United States without the consent of parents. Progressives are "change agents" who want to radically change or destroy the status quo of the United States. Progressives seek to social engineer culture for their own benefit with no regard for those who support the status quo. By increasing their numbers through immigration and open borders, progressives or socialists will have an easier time pushing their agenda of social reforms with little or no opposition from conservatives. Progressives are hypocrites, are typically intolerant of the status quo, and often utilize nefarious means to increase their own power and control.

Progressives use word tools, divisiveness, and partisan politics to enact laws that may diminish, weaken, or even take away our individual freedoms. Progressives seek bigger government to limit or deny our freedom of choice based on their oppressive leftist politics. They are trying to reduce or destroy our natural inclination toward God, traditional family values, and pride in our great country. In contrast, our country as led by conservatives has always recognized individual rights and has always followed traditional social norms. The only social norm that conservatives expect of a citizen in our constitutional republic is that you love and respect your country and stand up for your fellow citizens.

Americans need not be lectured or belittled by sanctimonious, hypocritical liberal buffoons who suggest that the majority of "intolerant" Americans should conform to their social engineered norms. Progressives succeed when conservative Americans do little or nothing to block their freakish "hope and change" social agenda or their leftist tyrannical government mandates. Freedom-loving Americans should have the responsibility to block all social and political reforms if they weaken or deny our basic individual rights as laid out in the Constitution.

We don't need politicians or people from colleges or universities lecturing us, forcing their new norms on us, belittling us, cancelling us, attacking us, or destroying us if we don't accept them. We need only to respect and love our diverse civil society. Progressives use words such as *racist* and *intolerance* as tools to shame us for refusing to conform their social norms and oppressive laws, thereby eliminating our freedom of choice to live in the communities we desire. Americans will always have the right to choose friends in communities they prefer without being forced to do otherwise by oppressive progressive laws opposing our choices. Life experiences and our own wise personal choices determine our way of life and where we choose to live, not controlling politicians, the PC police, or progressive partisans.

Tools of Social Engineering Used by the Progressive Left

Progressives have divided this country into "oppressors" and "victims" and have used words as tools so as not to offend protected victims. The "oppressors" should always be politically correct when referring to liberal-defined oppressed victim groups. If an oppressor is not politically correct when referring to a class of victims, then liberals trot out more words to describe them: *racist, sexist, homophobic, xenophobic, Islamophobic*—you name it. Hillary Clinton used such words during her campaign to describe the "basket of deplorables" who would vote for candidate Donald Trump. The problem with progressive/ liberal politicians is that they give these victimized groups much lip service in every election year in order to get their votes, but once they get elected, they neglect their districts and constituents that they are supposed to be representing.

Progressive politicians snookered many black progressives in their districts into becoming a "victimized class" and enraging them with anger and bitterness. But these victims should ask of their leaders, "What have you progressive liberals done for me to better my district? to get me out of poverty? to put food on my table? to eliminate crime in my district? to keep drugs out of my district? to stop the gang violence? to provide me and my family jobs and opportunities for prosperity and a better life?" These questions were never asked of John Conyers, a Michigan congressman for more than fifty years, of Congressman Elijah Cummings from Maryland who served for twenty-three years, or of Maxine Waters, who served in the House of Representatives for twenty-eight years and is serving another two-year term. Why did these incompetent fools bamboozle their constituents and not improve their districts?

Progressives have made our country more secular and more disrespected, stifled free speech and our religious rights, disrespected our flag and country, and permitted violent terrorist groups such as Antifa to commit violence against people they disagree with. Partnering with and using the pro-Democrat hate-filled media and radical Muslim members of Congress, Democratic progressives have incited leftists to be divisive, disrespectful, vulgar, and intolerant. Universities used to champion free speech on campuses during the Vietnam War, but in the twenty-first century, most liberal college campuses do not allow conservative protests or free speech and will not protect conservative demonstrators or conservative speakers against violence from crazed liberal mobs. Liberal states guilty of silencing speech are California, Oregon, Washington, Illinois, and New York. Most liberal, socialist, and communist professors and college administrators on liberal campuses agree with silencing conservative speech.

Characteristics of Progressivism

"Why is progressivism bad?" you might ask. The answer is as follows:

- Progressivism has led, and will continue to lead, the United States into moral decay.
- It has led to an increase in secularism and atheism.
- It has led to an increase in violence and lawlessness.
- It has established once abnormal behavior such as sodomy, homosexuality, and same-sex marriage as normal behavior that should be tolerated, protected, and promoted.
- Progressivism has allowed corruption within government agencies so progressives may enrich themselves in pay-to-play schemes, quid pro quo schemes, and lobbying activities.
- It allowed collusion with billionaire Gorge Soros, and others in Europe, to bribe the Vatican in Rome, oust a conservative pope, and install a new pope more amenable to socialist progressive ideas in the hopes of changing Catholic doctrine to accept abortion and homosexuality as "moral human rights," which would win favor in the United States with "progressive Catholics" and be in complete alignment with the new progressive morality advocated by Barack Obama, Hillary Clinton, Joe Biden, Tim Kaine, and other progressive Democratic politicians. *Note:* Had this blasphemy happened, the Catholic Church would now be split up into conservatives and progressives, or else Catholicism would be destroyed as a religion. The result: God saved his church, and progressives failed.
- Progressivism has allowed "crony capitalism" corruption in which government allocates tax revenues strictly to progressives and to businesses and corporations that donated campaign money to progressive candidates and progressive causes and that enriched other progressive friends and countries.
- It has allowed the IRS to target conservative individuals, Christian churches, and conservative organizations for any violations of tax law. Christian churches were threatened with

losing their tax-exempt status if they expressed favor for a conservative political candidate for office or for conservative policies, or if they expressed political opposition to progressive policies or candidates, as directed by former president Barack Obama.

- It has allowed a progressive president (Barack Obama) to weaponize federal agencies and resources to target conservatives, contract with foreign intelligence agencies to spy on an opposition candidate (Donald Trump), and leak vile and negative propaganda about the opposition party to the liberal media so they would broadcast it with the aim of destroying presidential candidate Donald Trump, all to rig the election in favor of the progressive candidate (Hillary Clinton).

- It allowed a group of holdover progressives from the Obama administration known as the "Deep State," who opposed the election of Donald Trump and his policies, to spy on the duly elected president to seek out any crimes he may have committed and to try to impeach him with a series of false hoaxes manufactured by the Left-controlled House of Representatives, which is made up of a majority of corrupt, inept, progressive Democrats. As one hoax fails, progressives go to another hoax and fish. After that one fails, they continue to fish for crimes— more hoaxes. The goal was for the progressive leftist House of Representatives to try to impeach the president for any reason, lie about what they were doing, and make it a distraction during the election year, hoping they could remove the president from office with the help of the pro-progressive, hate-Trump media with their fake anti-Trump propaganda. Otherwise, aside from election fraud, President Trump certainly would have been reelected as president for four more years.

- Progressivism will lead to socialism with spending plans coming from socialists running for president who cannot compute or refuse to compute the accumulated cost of their spending plans, and who will not say whom they will tax or state how much they will tax individuals and businesses, or how they will enforce collecting such oppressively high revenues to fund their spending scams.

- It will lead to open borders now that a progressive socialist presidential candidate was elected in 2020. This means anyone in the world can enter the United States unchecked with dirty bombs, explosives, illegal drugs, infected with COVID-19, or biological agents to cause more deadly pandemics. This means that terrorists, criminals, drug cartel members, and MS-13 gang members may enter the United States, all potentially causing great harm to the security of the United States and great stress and risk to our economy.
- It will lead to an increase in mismanaged poop cities and homelessness across the United States now that a Democratic progressive president has been elected and Congress is controlled by Democrats.
- It will lead to violent pushback by freedom-loving Americans against oppressively high taxes and confiscation of wealth, which will include taxes on the rich, the middle class, businesses, and corporations. Progressives have no clue how stealing the wealth of many Americans will affect the economy, the stock market, employment, or debt, or if it will drive Americans into poverty or homelessness.
- It will lead to severely restrictive gun laws and the confiscation of firearms from law-abiding Americans, or the banning of firearms altogether.
- It will lead to the silencing of free speech, along with monitoring social media to find those who oppose the progressive government.

If a Far Left progressive or socialist presidential candidate is ever elected and all strategies of socialism are ever implemented in the United States, a bloody civil war will occur. With socialists confiscating guns, channeling food to only blue states, confiscating wealth, instituting taxation without representation, stifling free speech, stifling the Christian religion, and spying on or investigating conservatives, there will be more than enough reasons to begin a bloody revolution.

Who Are the Progressive and Socialist Leaders?

We had eight years of "hope and change" progressivism under the Obama administration, which weakened the US internally and externally but enriched many progressive Democrats in government. Scandals and corruption were rampant among progressives and their crony friends. Americans rejected progressivism and elected Donald J. Trump as president in 2016. Who are these progressives and Far Left socialists of today who ran for president? As of early December 2019, they included the following:

1. Elizabeth Warren—hard socialist
2. Bernie Sanders—hard socialist
3. Andrew Yang—hard socialist
4. Cory Booker—hard socialist
5. Julian Castro—socialist
6. Peter Buttigieg—socialist
7. Amy Klobuchar—socialist
8. Joe Biden—hard progressive
9. Tulsi Gabbard—progressive
10. Marianne Williamson—spiritualist and healer
11. Deval Patrick
12. Michael Bloomberg—progressive
13. Bill de Blasio—hard socialist
14. Eric Swalwell—hard socialist
15. Kamala Harris—hard socialist
16. Kirsten Gillibrand—hard socialist
17. Beto O'Rourke—hard socialist
18. Mike Gravel
19. John Hickenlooper
20. Jay Inslee
21. Wayne Messam
22. Seth Moulton
23. Richard Ojeda
24. Tim Ryan
25. Joe Sestak

All failed presidential candidates were eliminated because of a lack of funds, a lack of support, or inability to compete, or they withdrew, except for Joe Biden. They were all bad candidates, but the hard socialists were the worst. Socialists are ranked worse than progressives. The dropouts were rejected for good reasons, particularly candidates 13–17.

The Democratic Party of Today

Today, the Democratic Party is the party of mismanagement, empty ideas, and socialism who stand with freeloaders, illegal aliens, and open borders. The judge who stopped Trump's asylum law is from San Francisco, a stinky poop sanctuary city full of liberal judges and liberal city administrators who are all Trump haters. Many of the city administrators are Trump-hating homosexuals. In his decision, the partisan judge, legislating from the bench, reaffirmed that Democrats want open borders and are opposed to anyone, including ICE, preventing illegal aliens from entering the United States illegally.

Democrats in Congress established a sexual harassment slush fund in 1997 and paid $17 million in sexual harassment lawsuits up to 2017. Who authorized Congress to create this taxpayer-funded slush fund to protect sexual predators who harass workers they employ? We may never know; the list of named predators has never been released.

Some socialist presidential candidates in the 2019 debates on TV clearly stated they would confiscate wealth from the rich 2 percent only. Socialists like Elizabeth Warren wanted to place a wealth tax on all rich people; Andrew Yang wanted to give every adult US citizen $1,000, including every adult illegal immigrant who entered the United States. Other socialists proposed a graduated tax scheme that would tax the middle class, in addition to wealthy individuals and businesses, to pay for their own spending schemes. The odd thing is that Democratic socialists never address certain things, such as the following:

(1) how willing are taxpayers having their wealth confiscated by socialists to accommodate their spending gigs, particularly, giving their money away to illegal aliens?

(2) how will socialists enforce oppressive taxes—by resisting taxpayers who refuse to be robbed by the socialist government?

Socialists never care to ask or conduct a survey to find out whether they have the gleeful permission or support of taxpayers to give up a large portion of their wealth for socialist spending scams and giveaways, nor do socialists indicate to wealthy individuals or businesses how the tax monies they surrender will be spent to represent their interests. Socialists don't care about the opinions or permission of taxpayers when they tax them. Spending taxpayers' money without their input is a major problem with the current Democratic Party. They don't care what taxpaying American citizens think.

The Democratic Party of today offers nothing to benefit American citizens, other than shamefully offering "free" government handouts to lazy freeloaders and illegal aliens, who are prioritized above US citizens, at taxpayer expense. It appears that a political clan from the area around the most liberal city in the United States, San Francisco, has represented and governed the state of California for several decades. Some incompetent political buffoons from the "Frisco clan" who have ruined or continue to ruin California include Dianne Feinstein, Eric Swalwell, Nancy Pelosi, Barbara Boxer, and Gavin Newsom, in addition to other California State Democratic lawmakers. Democratic city administrators and California state lawmakers have allowed San Francisco and Los Angeles to have a massive homeless problem with the associated feces, urine, and trash that breeds rats and fleas and could start a bubonic plague in California and spread to other states. California may soon be significantly populated by so many illegal aliens that one day Hispanics may regain control of California. However, California and all local governments are so badly mismanaged, one can make the prediction that California politicians will declare bankruptcy one day and beg the federal government for a bailout for their mismanaging of the state. In 2021, California has already received bailout money, along with all other blue states.

2

THE EVOLUTION OF CULTURE IN THE UNITED STATES

Colonization of the Americas by Europeans

England, France, and Spain colonized the Americas and fought and killed Native Americans who stood in their way, or else drove them out of their settlement homes. The Natives would certainly regard colonists (early settlers) as illegal immigrants because they invaded their land and took it over by force for their own benefit.

But the early settlers kicked English rule out of North America via the American Revolution. English colonists and their descendants formed the USA, the Constitution, and the three branches of government. American politicians then purchased the Louisiana Territory from Napoleon Bonaparte in 1803 without permission from the American Indians who had long lived there. Then, after Spanish Conquistadores colonized Mexico and killed many Indians in doing so, the remaining early settlers (Mexican colonists) kicked out Spanish rule from parts of the United States and Mexico in 1821.

The United States was well settled for generations as it began accepting immigrants. Immigrants today enter the United States seeking a better life, but they should come into the US legally, not illegally. We would want to filter out criminals and terrorists, and we don't want people who hate our culture and refuse to assimilate into it.

US taxpayers cannot afford to take in everyone in the world who wants to enter the United States. With the homeless problem in states like California, tax monies are going toward cleaning up after the homeless, arresting criminal illegal aliens, and incarcerating them. Taxpayers also pay for the health care provided to illegal aliens at no charge.

Culture Change in the United States from the 1950s to the Present

How did our culture get to where we are today? US culture has changed from the 1950s to the present. About 50 percent of today's millennials are a lost people in trouble. Democrats have become extremely progressive and secular. Moral behavior that was considered unacceptable and abnormal in the 1950s has been "social engineered" and is now acceptable. Free speech was something demanded by progressives in the 1960s and 1970s, particularly on college campuses in the 1960s, when it was used as a form of protest. Now certain speech is to be silenced if it's disagreeable to liberal students on campus. We respected our leaders in the 1950s, but now, we express our respect for our leaders in Hollywood stage plays calling for the assassination of the president, by holding a president's look-alike decapitated head on TV (which one woman did), and advocating that a child of the president should be kidnapped by pedophiles, as done by one Hollywood actor. "God bless America" was once a phrase proudly said in song and prayer in Christian churches. On May 7, 2008, a reverend of a black Christian church attended for years by Barack and Michelle Obama politicized "God Bless America" by changing it to "GD America." Football and soccer games used to be fun to watch, but Democratic progressives have politicized these sports after players refused to sing or stand for the national anthem and instead kneeled while it played; now many fans don't care about either football or soccer as they used to.

Displaying "In God We Trust" in public schools is about undoing the destructive liberal Democratic social engineering of our culture in order to bring common sense, morality, and God back into our culture. Look at some of our youth today. Many millennials no longer respect our flag, our country, or the value of life and our laws, and have abandoned God. We need to shed this sick culture and bring back God, healthy customs and traditions, healthy relationships, respect for others, respect for life, patriotism, respect for our flag and national anthem, and our Christian values. Hypocritical Democrats in Congress often quote the Bible to support their allegedly moral liberal agenda, but they stifle religion, take away Bibles from the classroom and from military institutions, remove crosses from public buildings, and remove the Ten Commandments from government buildings. They only use the Bible when it suits them in political speeches for gain, yet they prohibit God and the name Jesus Christ from being spoken in public school graduation speeches, and for a while under Barack Obama's administration, the greeting "Merry Christmas" was prohibited from being said. Hillary Clinton wanted to continue with Obama's legacy had she been elected. God has a way of intervening to protect his people. Unfortunately, the Biden Administration is Obama's "Hope and Change" Part II on steroids.

The United States was not founded on Islam as liar Obama claimed; the United States was founded on Christianity, plain and simple. There is ample evidence of God being mentioned in our Constitution and other founding documents written in the early era of the United States. No matter how people worshipped God, Jesus Christ was worshipped by Catholic France and Spain, while England was Christian Protestant; these three nations were the only European countries to significantly colonize the Americas.

Muslims migrate to this country and demand imposition of sharia law in the United States; their goal is to Islamize the USA, as they are trying to do in Europe. Americans must reject this encroachment upon our culture. Our laws allow freedom of religion, but we must reject the bashing and stifling of Christianity. Groups responsible for the rejection of Christianity, the social engineering of Christianity to fit it to liberal political morality, and the marginalization of Christianity are Muslim immigrants, atheists, and leftist Democrats.

Since the 1950s, we've allowed disgusting and undesirable agents of change to social engineer our culture, leading to the socialist-leaning Democratic Party of today. Weak Republican politicians have allowed

Liberal Democrats to reform our Christian morals. In political speeches, liberals preach their own progressive political morality, which they use to win elections and to promote their agendas. We have allowed school administrators to hire liberal teachers who indoctrinate our young kids with progressivism and with disrespect for our laws, US history, our country, our flag, and traditional American values.

Most recently, our culture has changed to allow some schools to teach the historical accomplishments of homosexuals, along with tolerance of cross-dressers and transgender people, as if homosexual history were vitally important to the education of children and the practice of teaching it should be applauded and adored. The fact that there are pedophiles who commit crimes by forcing sex acts upon little girls is irrelevant here; it is already illegal and immoral. The topic here is male homosexuality, *not* the promotion of pedophilia—adults performing sexual acts with underage girls or boys—or lesbianism. The question as to whether homosexuality is linked to pedophilia or not is irrelevant. The real question that should be asked is: Does introducing homosexuality in school classrooms for kids who *do not want or need any civil rights help* from LGBT promoters violate *their* civil rights or stir up any curiosity (not interest) about homosexuality among the naive kids in the classroom? Answer: Yes, of course it does.

Using logic and common sense, it's easy to understand where gay promoters and pedophiles are going with this. They want to introduce homosexuality in public schools to legitimize homosexuality as normal behavior and to promote curiosity in some young kids' minds about homosexuality. Of course, not all pedophiles are gays and not all pedophiles are child molesters, but most pedophiles and some homosexuals would prefer to meet boys who would have consensual sexual relations with them. Why do gay men want to introduce homosexual education into the classroom for young students? Answer: Homosexuals argue that they want to help LGBT students, fight for tolerance, fight against LGBT discrimination, and fight for equal rights for LGBT kids. Ironically, gay men do not dare mention three following elephants in the room.

The first elephant in the room is that gay proponents want to expand and promote homosexuality for kids at an early age regardless

14

of what the kids' parents say. It is my strong belief that Joe Biden and his LGBT lobbyists clearly plan to pass off homosexual education for kids in states as a civil rights issue *and* prevent parents from having any voice in the promotion of homosexual education in the classroom for their kids.

The second elephant in the room is that homosexuality is Biblically immoral, as stated in several verses of the Bible. So why would homosexual promoters push teaching homosexuality in schools to little kids that goes against their religious beliefs and their religious upbringing by parents? It is shamefully immoral.

The third elephant in the room is that there are statistics showing there are bad mental and physical repercussions for kids who become homosexuals.[1]

Introducing homosexuality to kids in the classroom behind a facade of protection of civil rights is one strategy gay men use to promote tolerance to homosexuality among youths. Note that gay lawmakers proposed and approved those laws without any input from parents. Do Americans want homosexual education in the classroom for kids in the fifth or sixth grade? It depends on who you ask, but most conservative parents *do not want* homosexuality taught in the classroom to their young kids. That is, parents don't want *any* kind of perverted sex education for young kids in public schools or at home. Most conservatives are against it, but almost all liberals are for it.

I am not writing *The Coming Tyranny* for fear of offending homosexuals, teachers, or the LGBT promoters. I am writing *The Coming Tyranny* for God-fearing Americans who want to raise their kids with Christian morals and without physical or mental disorders. I do not support *sexual perversion* being taught to little kids in school classrooms for the benefit of gays or pedophiles! Homosexuals will not like any part of *The Coming Tyranny* anyway; they are not my intended audience!

Securing and controlling the southern border of the United States was supported in the last part of the twentieth century, but now Democrats want unsecured borders and refuse to provide funds to secure the border. Instead, Democrats are currently attracting illegal aliens like

---

[1] Frank Joseph, "Everyone Should Know These Statistics on Homosexuals," Tradition in Action, accessed February 24, 2021, https://www.traditioninaction. org/HotTopics/a02rStatistcs.html.

a magnet to enter the United States illegally by offering foreigners from all over the world government handouts such as free health care and free college tuition. In some states and cities, Democrats protect illegal alien criminals who have been released from prison from being deported by ICE. The leaders of this abhorrent progressive culture change have been liberal Democratic politicians with their shameless Hollywood friends, partnering with the leftist hate-filled fake news media.

Even worse, we are now fighting for the survival of this country. How is that possible? Answer: In early 2021 we have a massive border crisis – owned and perpetuated by President Joe Biden and supported by Democrats in both houses of Congress. We are fighting the socialism that has taken over the Democratic Party. We are fighting to preserve the First, Second, and Fourth Amendments of the Constitution. We are fighting for economic prosperity in the United States to eliminate economic inequality. We are fighting violence that stifles free speech on campuses, in malls, in restaurants, and in Democrat-run cities. We are fighting for the right of law-abiding people to bear arms. We are fighting Democrats in Congress to protect the safety of Americans by trying to eliminate the smuggling of illegal drugs across the border and by preventing criminals and terrorists from entering the United States. We are fighting against illegal aliens who may have COVID-19, are not all tested for it, and may be spreading it to whatever communities they are being transported to in the US. We are fighting socialists who may soon mandate cops to illegally enter the homes of law-abiding citizens to confiscate their weapons. We are investigating crimes committed by the Obama administration, which weaponized government agencies and abused its power in order to rig an election for the Democrats' preferred candidate, Hillary Clinton. We are fighting to prevent the confiscation of wealth from US citizens and businesses with unacceptable massive taxation oppression. All these events are happening now under the Biden Administration (in early 2021) who now control the Federal government. Social engineering reforms by socialists in the Democratic Party pose even more danger to the United States than liberal reforms, *if* we let this social engineering happen.

Culture Wars and Social Reform in the United States

Liberal Democrats have social engineered our US culture over the course of decades in ways that have conflicted with conservative values and divided us. Never before in US history has there been so much hate spread from the halls of Congress by Democrats or hateful propaganda spread by liberal news media against a successful president who loves the United States. Now we have homosexuals and cross-dressers again in the military, thanks to Joe Biden. We have rich professional athletes refusing to stand for our national anthem; we have students in schools who refuse to say the Pledge of Allegiance; we have protesters who hate police officers and commit violence against them; we have liberals who stifle free speech by using violence against people they disagree with at colleges and universities; we have members of Congress who give racist speeches against Jews and white people without being reprimanded or censured; we have members of Congress who advocate socialism for the United States; we have members of Congress who hate the present United States and want to make it a Muslim country; we have lawmakers in California who want to introduce young children to homosexuality in public schools in order to promote pedophilia; and we have Democratic politicians who wanted to change church doctrine as a basis for a "new morality" to justify and coincide with progressivism. We have sanctimonious politicians lecturing us on morality and Christian values to justify their liberal agenda whenever it suits them, or who still criticize the character of President Trump even though he is a private citizen, but at the same time they stifle Christianity and religious freedom, and ban Bibles and religious objects from public schools, public buildings, and military installations. Liberal politicians are on a quest to confiscate firearms from law-abiding citizens or ban them altogether.

Progressives are notorious for being the "thought police," who attack conservatives for merely thinking or expressing that homosexuality or abortion is wrong. When we merely express our conservative thoughts in colleges and universities, liberal millennials become more than the thought police; they shout down a speaker, prevent a speaker from speaking, or violently attack the speaker. That is not a "live and let live" or respectful philosophy. If a conservative speaks on a campus, what are hateful liberals afraid of? Are they afraid the speech they disagree with is going to indoctrinate the crowd listening? The psychological explanation for liberals stifling free speech is that they are fragile, are insecure about who they are, are arrogantly selfish with a strong sense of entitlement, and have no adequate defense mechanisms against conservative speech that hurts their feelings, so they attack or stifle the speakers.

The future appears to be even more chaotic with socialist Joe Biden's executive orders and the House's policies on immigration advocating free borders, advertising free health care for illegal aliens, protecting criminals released from jail from being deported, and allowing people from all over the world to come into our country to get the free government handouts that socialists are offering and advertising. A massive number of illegal aliens are already flooding the US border after Joe Biden stopped Trump's wall from being built and welcoming foreigners into the US; the whole world knows about it and millions more are coming to America from all over the world.

<new paragraph>

More chaotic and irresponsible are their socialist plans to spend trillions of dollars on a Green New Deal; trillions of dollars on climate change; trillions of dollars by giving one thousand dollars per month to every adult in the United States, including foreigners, to combat poverty; and trillions of dollars for reparations to blacks and homosexuals. Democrats will likely pack the US Supreme Court with socialists and communists, eliminate the Electoral College and the Senate if the US Supreme Court dares to reject one socialist law passed by Congress or an executive order from the president as being unconstitutional. Democrats will likely eliminate all or part of $1.5 trillion student college debt, and finally, oppress the rich, the middle class, small businesses, and large corporations with high taxes that will lead to another American revolution if socialists ever get in power.

The Failures of Conservatism in Culture Wars

Why haven't conservatives been able to prevent leftists from social engineering the United States since the 1960s? We have reached this point in 2021 because the radical left has been winning the social erosion war on our traditional, conservative US culture. Leftists have used successful social engineering tactics such as violent protests, feminist protests, and gay parades. BLM and Antifa thugs have rioted, beating up conservatives and attacking police, and have made leftist speeches at colleges. Democratic politicians such as Congresswoman Maxine Waters have urged Americans everywhere to deny Trump supporters of their civil rights by denying them service in restaurants, at lunch counters, and in malls to let them know they are not welcome in any businesses. This sounds exactly like how blacks were treated in the South in the 1950s.

Leftists produced lists of businesses that supported or donated to President Trump and urged Americans to boycott those businesses, harass them, or destroy them. Ex-convicts and serious criminal illegal aliens are now protected from deportation by sanctuary cities. Then after their release, many commit more crimes, such as shooting cops, raping women, or molesting children. Cops have been attacked with objects or had bags of urine thrown at them while on duty, and liberal organizations like Black Lives Matter (BLM) urge the killing of cops. Liberal city and state governments do little or nothing to prevent this.

Politicians are now redefining and reinterpreting the Christian religion right under the noses of conservatives. They are falsely interpreting the Bible to support, justify, and reinforce their own liberal political philosophy and policies. Liberal politicians now preach their supposedly superior morality from the leftist political pulpit, such as in fake news media locations where they are interviewed, giving them the opportunity to preach their social engineered superior morality. Only a few twisted charlatan preachers and reverends preach this nonsense from what they falsely consider to be a church and a holy pulpit, yet prayer was taken from schools; Bibles have been banned from public school classrooms, US military installations, and government buildings; and the name Jesus Christ is currently forbidden from being mentioned in graduation speeches in most public high schools in the United States. Who is responsible for allowing all this hypocrisy? Answer: liberal Democrats. Who is responsible for not preventing this atrocious hypocritical behavior? Why have conservatives allowed this to happen?

After the miraculous election of Donald Trump, it appears the Left is extremely upset and angry at Trump for having opposed all social engineering accomplished in modern times. He stood in their way. Social engineering has been the job and the role of the leftist liberal media since the 1960s. It's gotten worse. Our president can only do so much with his power; Congress with an elected majority of conservatives can only reverse the social erosion of our culture by doing things within their power, granted to them by the Constitution. But any laws to reverse liberal social engineering will always be challenged by liberals in the courts, and that will take time. Now that Democrats control the Federal government, it will be unlikely that any of the destruction brought about by social engineering is irreversible.

Segregation in the South (the Evolution of Discrimination/Racism; History of Racism and Discrimination)

Prior to the 1960s, the United States was predominantly a segregated nation, particularly in the southern states, which include Florida, Georgia, Alabama, Mississippi, Louisiana, and Texas. Most of us born during or after World War II recall housing and school segregation. Blacks lived in their own segregated neighborhoods and went to black schools in those neighborhoods. Places of businesses, such as restaurants, barbershops, theaters, bars, transportation services, and doctors' offices, were also segregated. Hispanics in many southern states were also segregated and went to almost all-Hispanic schools.

According to Britannica.com, on May 17, 1954, the US Supreme Court ruled in a 9–0 decision that public school segregation violated the Fourteenth Amendment of the Constitution in the landmark case *Brown v. Board of Education of Topeka*. The Fourteenth Amendment prohibits states from denying equal protection under law to all state residents. The

Supreme Court ruled that separate schools for white students and black students were unequal, thus rejecting the "separate but equal" doctrine regarding the use of public facilities that justified racial segregation in the Supreme Court decision of *Plessy v. Ferguson* in 1896. This is one of the most important decisions made by the US Supreme Court. The ruling applied only to public school facilities, but it implied that public use of other facilities was also unequally allocated, thereby giving impetus to the civil rights movements of the next two decades.

According to Britannica.com, "*Brown v. Board of Education of Topeka* (II), argued April 11–14, 1955, and decided on May 31 of that year, Warren ordered the district courts and local school authorities to take appropriate steps to integrate public schools in their jurisdictions 'with all deliberate speed.' Public schools in Southern states, however, remained almost completely segregated until the late 1960s."[2]

From my personal experience as a nine-year-old student in Texas, white elementary public schools in Texas began to admit Hispanic students in 1956, but blacks were kept in segregated schools. I passed the second grade in June 1955 at an all-Hispanic school (Guadalupe Elementary School in San Angelo, Texas) and went to third grade in an all-white school (John H. Reagan Elementary School) in September 1956. There were also a few other Hispanics enrolled in that school. I noticed we Hispanics assimilated well in classrooms and got along well with white students, including competing in school sports, without any bias. However, not one black student was admitted to the school up to the sixth grade.

From further experience in Texas in 1953, I observed that some white elementary school students attended a mostly Hispanic elementary school from grade 1 to grade 6 at Ben Milam Elementary School in San Antonio, Texas, and got along well. In Corpus Christi, Texas, less than a handful of blacks attended Ella Barnes Jr. High School in 1959, a mostly all-Hispanic school.

In the early 1960s, governor of Alabama George Wallace was an ardent racist politician who campaigned on segregation and state's

---

[2] Brian Duignan, "Brown v. Board of Education of Topeka," *Encyclopedia Britannica*, May 10, 2020, https://www.britannica.com/event/Brown-v-Board-of-Education-of-Topeka, accessed February 19, 2021.

rights for Alabama. He worked to prevent desegregation ordered by federal law, including blocking two black students from enrolling in the all-white University of Alabama. President John F. Kennedy ordered National Guard troops to Alabama to ensure enrollment of the two black students. On June 11, 1963, Governor Wallace attempted to block the two black students from entering the halls of the university, but was told to step aside or be arrested by National Guard troops; he complied with their orders, and the two black students entered the hall of the university.

While George Wallace was governor of Alabama, civil rights activists were allegedly killed by racist Alabama state troopers. In another racially motivated attack, four little black girls were killed by a bomb placed under the steps of the Sixteenth Street Baptist Church by a Ku Klux Klan member, exploding on September 13, 1963; this was outright domestic terrorism. The act bothered the conscience of white Americans. George Wallace ran a failed run for the presidency in 1968, but in 1972 he ran for president again. A white man attempted to assassinate him on the campaign trail. Wallace was shot multiple times, which left him paralyzed from the waist down for life. Later in life, he admitted to regretting the words he had used in his speech of "segregation now and segregation forever" to a crowd in Alabama when he ran for governor.

Through the tireless efforts of Martin Luther King Jr. marching from Alabama to Washington, DC, in the early 1960s, the United States and the world saw on television how blacks were experiencing the cruelty and violence of bigoted police officers in the South, who attacked them with dogs and batons as they peacefully marched and protested. This was a turning point in US history in my opinion. Continued attacks on peaceful blacks led by a Christian man, Martin Luther King Jr., shocked the conscience of Americans; something was not right. The consciences of many white Americans, including white politicians, were awakened, causing them to realize the outright bigotry of police in the South oppressing peaceful blacks who were just marching in unity for freedom. The conscience of white Americans beheld the truth, namely that past Jim Crow laws had truly oppressed blacks even after the Emancipation Proclamation by Abraham Lincoln.

Such laws had prevented them from gaining economic opportunities to achieve the American dream as whites were able to do. The 1964 Civil Rights Bill proposed by Republicans and opposed by Democrats passed, guaranteeing blacks their right to be served in public establishments and opportunities for work. The 1964 Civil Rights Bill was based not on **outlawing** racism; instead, the impetus behind it was that refusing to serve blacks was a violation of interstate business law and a detriment to the economy. Voting rights for blacks were reinforced, and any state refusing to deprive blacks of their voting rights was in violation of federal law. This had been a common practice of white bigots in the South. President Lyndon Baines Johnson (LBJ) signed the legislation.

The Legacy of Dr. Martin Luther King Jr.

On December 10, 1964, Martin Luther King Jr. was awarded the Nobel Peace Prize for his leadership in the civil rights movement and his tireless efforts to achieve racial justice through nonviolence and civil disobedience. No person thus far has been able to fill his shoes or do as much as he has done for the African American community. In contrast with former president Barack Obama, who also received the Nobel Peace Prize, Martin Luther King earned his peace prize, Obama did not. Instead of promoting peace and bringing people together, Barack Obama and his administration, through his "Hope and Change" agenda, social engineered US culture to divide the races.

Dr. Martin Luther King Jr., a man of peace who rejected black violence and militancy, was tragically assassinated by a white hit man in 1968. Since then, riots have flared up in Los Angeles, California; Baltimore, Maryland; Ferguson, Missouri; Minneapolis, Minnesota; Atlanta, Georgia; and other places. No man of peace, no man of God, and no black man who has the power to change the hearts and minds of white people and bring people everywhere together has emerged since 1964. Instead, we still have "No justice, no peace" rioting mobs and violent domestic terrorist groups such as Antifa, BLM, and the New Black Panther Party. We have death and destruction in black neighborhoods, and we see Democratic House leaders getting millions of dollars in donations because of the rioting and deaths. The black cause for peace and unity has been flushed down the toilet by all these Democrats, 100 percent supported by the evil fake news media. Even young white millennials who were bamboozled by their socialist teachers in public classrooms into hating the United States joined destructive blacks in destroying businesses and beating up or killing shopkeepers. If blacks or whites think this will enhance the black image, win black respect, or help them win their cause, they are miserably mistaken. It will do the opposite. The world, which watched blacks rioting on TV, assaulting and beating up shopkeepers, burning businesses, smashing windows, and attacking police, will consider them nothing more than uncivilized savages who should be incarcerated by the criminal justice system for the crimes they committed. The same goes for the young white millennial men and women who participated in rioting—mere opportunistic thieves who looted and burned businesses; these are sick, lost millennials. Obama, Eric Holder, and Al Sharpton did more to destroy MLK's dream of peace and racial unity than any other black has since MLK's assassination—with the support of Obama's buddy racist Louis Farrakhan, socialist members of the House Democratic Party, and the fake news media.

LBJ and the Great Society (LBJ's Great Society and the Goal to Put Blacks on a Democrat-Controlled Plantation)

LBJ said what Democrats today are saying, but using different words in a private conversation. He said, "I'll have those niggers voting Democratic for the next two hundred years," as he confided with two like-minded governors on Air Force One about his underlying intentions for the Great Society programs. In other words, he expected to keep blacks on a plantation with his Great Society programs, using work programs for pay in return for votes. Note that he never stressed individual initiative or increasing employment opportunities for blacks—because he was a racist from Texas.

Conservative Battles Lost, Progressive Battle Won—Evolution of Culture from the Late 1960s

In the late 1960s, culture changed with expanded drug use, a sexual revolution, Vietnam War protests, lack of discipline at home and in school, the resenting of authority, the abandoning of God, high divorce rates, songs promoting drugs and sex, the rise of pornography promoted by Hollywood and the media, the rise of antipolice sentiment, the rise of antimilitary sentiment, a hippie "do your thing" attitude as a way of life, the lowering of morality, the acceptance of homosexuality as being normal, and reliance on government handouts.

Hippies in liberal cities such as New York and San Francisco were loose, immoral, longhaired dope freaks who opposed the Vietnam War. Many burned their draft cards and refused to serve their country. Nancy Pelosi, Gavin Newsom, Dianne Feinstein, Barbara Boxer, and Kamala Harris are part of this same extreme liberal crowd from San Francisco and the surrounding area. If a war were to erupt, no one knows if they would have enough patriotism to defend the country or would run and hide in Canada.

Democrats from the hippie culture embraced change and made social engineering a political platform to run on. Conservatives utterly failed to prevent and contain this kind of decay of the United States by way of liberal social engineering, which spread like wildfire. We don't have "love children" anymore like the hippies did in the late 1960s and early 1970s, but the arrogant extreme liberals of San Francisco—and New York—continue to ruin California and fail to benefit Americans. Remember, the House of Representatives is led by Nancy Pelosi of San Francisco.

Conservatives have not done well in fighting or resisting a culture of decay in morality, respect, and unity that has been evolving to the present day. The Democratic Party of the 1960s and 1970s evolved into a socialist party even farther to the left. Socialists love freeloaders, and freeloaders love socialists. Both parties, Democratic and Republican, in the 1950s and early to mid-1960s respected law and order. Opposition to the Vietnam War resulted in liberal antiwar protesters who became antipolice and antigovernment. The assassination of Dr. Martin Luther

King Jr. turned the civil rights movement into a black power movement, whose new leaders resorted to rioting, violence, and terrorism to achieve justice. Radical antigovernment and antipolice militants demanded justice through violence, which went directly against what Dr. Martin Luther King Jr. had long fought for. The Black Panther Party and the Weather Underground were two such black organizations leading their members into antipolice violence and into attacking places of business that discriminated against blacks. The slogan of their supporters was "No justice, no peace." Because of the riots, the chief of the Los Angeles Police Department called for the National Guard to assist police in containing the Watts rioters of 1965. The National Guard was also called out for the Detroit riots of 1967, where several blacks involved in violence against police were shot and killed. The late 1960s and 1970s were turbulent times for the country as the state of California and the FBI joined task forces to track and attack militant groups and arrest their members. In the end, black militancy accomplished nothing, but it did prove that violence and terrorism weren't going to change the hearts and minds of Americans in achieving racial equality. Blacks finally realized that blacks could not exist as a single isolated entity fighting inequality and injustice; they had to get along with and work along with white people to achieve equality. But the black power movement, along with Chicano power militants, proved to the United States that they were fed up with racial injustice in the United States, showing that there was still dissatisfaction with racial inequality and that social change was needed to achieve racial equality.

The anti–Vietnam War protests were held primarily in Democratic states such as California, a state with increased drug use, havens for homosexuals, sexual promiscuity, and antigovernment sentiment. Drug-crazed, psychedelic, trip-loving hippies were hedonists and anarchists who could have cared less about war or serving their country. Homosexuals resented the military as they were not allowed to serve in any of the armed forces. Promiscuous "free love" hippies of the 1960s would rather "make love, not war," as their slogan stated.

The use of marijuana and experimentation with other illegal drugs among hippies in the 1960s evolved into today's legalization of marijuana for recreational use in some states, which is still a violation of federal law. There were not enough conservatives to oppose the trend to legalize dope. Any conservatives who disagreed or tried to change the culture were either silenced, ignored, or ridiculed by liberal Democrats. The main reasons for the legalization of marijuana include the increase in drug use by young men and women on college campuses, drug sales and availability in high-poverty and high-crime cities, and dope being transported across the southern border from Mexico. Illegal drugs kill tens of thousands of Americans each year, along with related gun violence from pushing drugs in gang-infested cities across the United States.

Culture change has evolved for the worse, but the war on drugs is still on, fought by law enforcement at the federal and local levels. Stopping drugs from coming across the border was a priority of President Trump to prevent violent drug cartels from transporting their drugs from South America to Mexico and into the United States. Fortunately, President Trump was fighting for border security for Americans in a war with the Democrats, who wanted open borders, refused to fund his border wall, and didn't care about the drugs carried by cartels into the United States at the border. During his term as president, President Trump was fighting progressivism and winning, that's why those of the Left hated him so much.

What is the result of progressive culture change since the 1950s? Answer: Progressivism has led to the following:

- A decay in morality.
- More Americans becoming nonreligious, and atheism increasing.
- An increase in violence and lawlessness, particularly in Democrat-run cities.
- Abnormal behavior such as homosexuality and same-sex marriage, which became normal behavior under the Obama administration, who pushed tolerance of homosexuals, protection of homosexuals, and promotion of homosexual rights, even to young kids in public schools.
- A progressive government that allows corruption within its agencies so government workers may enrich themselves with

contributions from lobbyists and donors and with corrupt foreign pay-to-play schemes.

- A conspiracy by liberal Democrats in the United States and globalists in Europe to bribe the Vatican in Rome into installing a leftist pope they hoped would change Catholic doctrine to accept abortion and homosexuality as moral human rights that would win favor in the United States with progressive Catholics and be aligned with progressive political morality, as advocated by Barack Obama, Hillary Clinton, Nancy Pelosi, Joe Biden, Tim Kaine, and other liberal Democratic politicians. Had this blasphemous conspiracy succeeded, the Catholic Church would have been divided into traditional Catholics and progressive Catholics, or else Catholicism would have been significantly degraded or destroyed as a religion. The result: God saved his church, and progressives failed.

- As directed by President Obama, IRS targeting of conservative Christian churches and conservative organizations for any violations of tax law. Christian churches would lose their tax-exempt status if they expressed favor for a conservative political candidate or a conservative policy, or opposition to progressive policies or candidates.

- President Obama was responsible for directing the weaponizing of federal agencies and resources to target conservatives and contract foreign intelligence agencies to spy on an opposition candidate, then leaking that information to the liberal media to broadcast vile and negative propaganda about the opposition party in order to destroy the presidential candidate, all to rig the election in favor of the progressive candidate Hillary Clinton.

- A group of holdover progressives from the previous progressive administration known as the "Deep State," who opposed the election of a new conservative president and his policies, investigated and spied on Donald Trump to fish for crimes he might have committed in order to impeach him and remove him from office, with the help of the corrupt hate-Trump media. Democrats always feared Trump would be reelected in 2020.

- Socialists who ran for president in 2020 who could not, or would not, compute the accumulated cost of their socialist spending plans and would not explain whom they would tax, to what degree they would tax-oppress the rich, or how they would enforce collecting such oppressively high taxes.

- Open borders under the Biden administration. This means anyone in the world can enter the United States with dirty bombs, explosives, illegal drugs, or diseases. Such people may be terrorists, criminals, drug cartel members, or MS-13 gang members, potentially causing great harm to the security of the United States and great stress to our economy.

- Increased mismanagement of poop cities, along with homelessness, crime, and poverty across the United States, by progressive Democratic mayors and state governors. At the federal level, if a progressive president and a Democratic Congress controlled the federal government, they would merely throw money at the problems without fixing them; this would amount to a massive taxpayer-funded bailout for mismanaged blue states.

- Violent opposition against oppressively high taxes and confiscation of the wealth of the rich, the middle class, businesses, and corporations. Progressives have no clue how high taxes on wealthy Americans will affect the economy, the stock market, jobs, or debt, or if it will drive Americans into increased debt, poverty, or homelessness or, even worse, incite a civil war.

- Banning firearms or confiscating firearms from law-abiding Americans.

- Silencing free speech. Social media giants ban posts on their websites made by people whom they disagree with. These are always conservative posts. High-tech giants from Silicon Valley partner with the progressive government to ban free speech.

- A real possibility of a bloody civil war beginning under the Biden administration. Confiscating guns, channeling food to blue states only, oppressing by way of taxation, stifling free speech, stifling and punishing religion, and continued socialist government spying on conservatives will lead to a bloody revolution.

Real "progress" that benefits the United States is culture change that makes America great—a capitalist America made stronger, more prosperous, and more unified, and creating more opportunities and jobs for Americans to work hard to achieve the American dream. This is what protects our constitutional freedoms, ensures enforcement of our laws, eliminates and prevents fraud and corruption, protects the United States from foreign enemies and unfair trade policies, and protects our customs, traditions, and values.

3

THE DEMOCRATIC PLANTATION
FOR BLACKS

Hillary Clinton and Her KKK
Mentor, Senator Robert Byrd

Hillary Clinton was mentored by former Klansman Robert Byrd, a senator from West Virginia, who talked to her about creating a special plantation for blacks and floated a plan for doing so. Instead of using racial hate-filled rhetoric as used by former governor George Wallace of Alabama, who in the early 1960s openly urged segregation between whites and blacks in the United States forever, thus alienating blacks, Senator Byrd suggested Hillary Clinton use rhetoric to support blacks. He suggested Hillary be smart and become a political champion of blacks in order to get their votes, by riling them up and playing along with their self-victimization caused by racial tensions, flare-ups, discrimination, and their long oppression by white people. Hillary was taught that instead of supporting segregation as Governor George Wallace did in the 1960s, she could pay lip service to blacks, providing them with food stamps and welfare *but no jobs or opportunities*. With this plan, crime and drug use would increase in mixed black and white communities, and those communities would undergo white flight, with businesses also leaving the district. There's the segregation you hoped for—you helped cause it—and black fools in those districts will still give

31

you their votes. Blacks become trapped in those districts with little or no chance of achieving wealth.

If Democrats run these impoverished cities, they will be unable to improve them because their tax base will significantly drop because of white flight and businesses moving out. But if these cities run by Democratic mayors and Democratic city administrators get federal money grants, the mayor and other city administrators will significantly enrich themselves with inflated salaries and pensions, and most of the federal grant money will be absorbed by the fire and police unions for their salaries and pensions, and by the teacher's union to raise their salaries and pensions. The community gets no job opportunities, no businesses to hire people, and no infrastructure money to rebuild the city. Corrupt city officials typically pocket a sizable amount of federal grant money.

Poorly run cities are reshaped by crime, drugs, violence, poor schools, loss of wealthy citizens and businesses, and loss of tax base, becoming segregated ghettos and continuing to be run by incompetent Democrats who will persist in mismanaging or neglecting these centers of crime and poverty for decades, even when billions of dollars are thrown at corrupt city officials. Good examples are Baltimore, Chicago, and Detroit.

Like former KKK senator Robert Byrd, even black congressional politicians pay lip service to their black constituents, verbally supporting their civil rights causes and blaming rich white people as racist oppressors in order to get the black vote. When in power, these black Democrats rely on federal tax subsidies in order to give blacks welfare and other government handouts. This plan keeps black residents at the same poverty level with no opportunities to go outside the plantation. Black constituents are slaves, accustomed to picking welfare checks and food stamps instead of cotton. Segregation works itself out in a natural way. That is, segregation is the automatic result whenever crime, drug use, and poverty increase. The lack of an adequate tax base from individual property and businesses results in abandoned and neglected homes, abandoned businesses, and neglected and dilapidated infrastructure on these go-nowhere plantations. White flight results from what soon becomes a ghetto, leaving segregated blacks with little or no opportunities to advance or move out of the ghetto.

Black Slaves on the Democratic Plantation

In US history classes in public schools, black children learn what their parents or friends had already told them, that their ancestors were slaves bought and paid for from Africa and shipped to the United States and elsewhere to work as slaves, and then that Abraham Lincoln freed the slaves during the Civil War. Racism and Jim Crow laws added to the pain and anger felt by some who developed anti-American sentiment. This must have been degrading to many, making them feel victimized and affecting their self-esteem, even angering some. Today, black and white politicians have become aware that self-victimized blacks tend to blame white people for their misery and poverty. For many decades, especially in every election year, Democratic members of Congress who represent high-crime and poverty-stricken black areas have been playing the race card to victimize and exploit their constituents for votes in these poor plantations. They have victimized their constituents and incited in them anger against racist white people, making them think they deserved and were owed free stuff paid for with someone else's money, without looking for opportunities and working hard. Liberal Democratic politicians running these plantations would quickly cite US history as being full of examples of racial oppression to justify their political rhetoric, claim oppression is still happening, and claim that it will always happen if political power is left to rich corporations and white people. Socialists also support this dogma.

But in reality, "Democratic plantation slaves" were snookered by this lip service from leftist politicians such as the late Congressman John Conyers, Hillary Clinton, the late Elijah Cummings, Al Sharpton, and most of the socialists from the Democratic Party who were running for president in 2020, to get *votes* from these exploited victims. These poor fools were kept on the Democratic plantation and were cared for when they picked welfare checks and food stamps in their ghettos instead of picking cotton. These ghettos lost their tax base because years earlier, white flight occurred, driven by poor city management, high crime, drugs, and poverty. Businesses fled the areas, leaving limited jobs. If a liberal Democrat politician plays the race card, *will that put food on the table?* Answer: No, it does not. Only job opportunities and hard work will put food on the table, enable prosperity, and enable all to achieve the American dream for themselves and their families; this will enable blacks to discard the chains tying them to a miserable life in the ghetto, where they rely on government handouts, and get them the hell off the plantation and into a better life.

The liberal evil fake news media is pushing lie after lie that offers naive Americans freedom from racism and freedom from poverty with socialism, hoping that Saul Alinsky's eleventh rule for radicals, "push a despicable lie long enough, and people will start believing it," is correct, hoping that useful naive idiots will believe the racism garbage, hate Trump, and swallow the false positive media propaganda about Democrats who will give them everything for free and will set them free from racial oppression.

Barack Obama divided the races during his administration. Race agitator Al Sharpton, Nation of Islam racist Louis Farrakhan, and race-baiter Jesse Jackson played the race card for racial division, agitation, and self-victimization and to promote racial anger and civil unrest. Playing the race card repeatedly by black politicians, and by white politicians such as Hillary Clinton, offers nothing beneficial for blacks. The race card will not provide blacks with opportunities for prosperity or put food on their tables. It does nothing but allow the Democratic politicians to exploit poor blacks for their own self-enrichment and power.

Progressives Have Kept Blacks on Democratic Plantations for Decades

Some black congresspeople who represent districts in Detroit, Michigan; St. Louis, Missouri; Baltimore, Maryland; and South Central Los Angeles, and other places, were already aware of this plantation process after the end result. However, these members of Congress failed to fix the problems in their districts. Instead, they continued playing the race card themselves to get reelected in their respective districts. No job opportunities or upward mobility was possible. After more than fifty years of representing a district in Detroit, Michigan, why was House member John Conyers never able to get Detroit out of one of the highest crime rates and highest poverty levels with high numbers of abandoned homes and commercial buildings? After House member Elijah Cummings's district received millions of dollars in taxpayer funds over the course of several decades, why was his Baltimore district neglected, and where did all the money go? These remain unanswered questions.

Aware of the Democratic plantation scheme, former president Barack Obama proposed placing affordable housing for blacks in expensive rich neighborhoods across the United States. That's why Obama always deceptively and dishonestly suggested taxing the top 1 percent or 2 percent, to "redistribute the wealth." His redistribution of wealth included paying for a low-cost housing plan for blacks. States would oppose federal mandates and a proposed law from Congress to selectively fund a racial group. Such a thing would never fly because of high costs and the preferential and discriminatory distribution of wealth. Obama failed to find a way for blacks to leave the Democratic welfare and food stamp plantation, but he was assured to get the votes of blacks because of his lip service.

Democrats Wear Out the Race Card to Keep Blacks on Plantations

Blacks seek prosperity in the United States like anyone else. President Trump enabled opportunities for blacks to get jobs, work hard, and achieve the American dream like everyone else. Wearing out the race card to anger blacks does not offer blacks opportunities for jobs and prosperity. The race card is only designed to keep blacks angry, complaining, and blaming white people for their economic misery. It's also used when liberals can't win arguments. By playing on emotions, Democrats keep blacks on the Democratic plantation with poverty, abandoned buildings, abandoned businesses and factories, white flight, gang activity, and crime. John Conyers of Detroit and Maxine Waters of South Central Los Angeles have done nothing but play the race card for several decades to get reelected. Conyers even proposed free money for blacks under a "reparations for blacks" law, pointing to historical US slavery to get votes. Hillary Clinton, who was mentored by former Democratic senator Robert Byrd, a member of the KKK, played the race card in the 2020 election for votes. She learned that playing the race card instead of playing the southern segregation card wins the black vote—and segregation is still achieved automatically through white flight.

Americans get tired of seeing the race card being played by blacks or white socialists, but these hypocrite black and white socialists never attack or criticize a former member of the New Black Panther Party for killing five Dallas police officers in July 2016; or the racist rants of Louis Farrakhan against Jews who "control everything," or for calling white people "crackers" or the "white devil," or for calling Jews "termites"; or the anti-Jewish racial rants in speeches by House of Representatives members Ilhan Omar and Rashida Tlaib. No Democrats in the Democrat-held House of Representatives have ever leveled attacks against Antifa or Black Lives Matter (BLM) for their 2020 rioting, their attacking of police, or their desire to kill cops. As a matter of fact, House Democrat Jerry Nadler defended Antifa, a terrorist organization, by saying in Congress that Antifa "was a myth."

Reparations for Blacks

Reparations for blacks have been demanded by black politicians for decades during election years. This is done to get votes. Reparations have been preached by Al Sharpton. On TV, the majority of Democrats running for president kissed the ring of Al Sharpton, as they pledged their support for black reparations. Reparations for blacks were promoted by several desperate Democratic presidential candidates who dropped out of the race. They portrayed today's blacks as victims of racism because of the United States' past sin of slavery. To correct the sins of the United

States, socialists in the Democratic Party have demanded reparations for the oppression of blacks. One estimate made by a researcher puts the total between $5.9 trillion and $14.2 trillion. Another estimate is $6.2 quadrillion in reparations that blacks want.[1]

In reality, the blacks demanding reparations are opportunistic freeloaders who are branding themselves as victims because of events that happened beginning in the 1600s. The United States was not even a nation until 1776, yet self-victimized blacks of today want to receive free handouts from people of all nonblack races today who never made them victims.

Note that during election years, Democratic politicians running for office who don't have anything beneficial to offer Americans always resort to playing the race card and bring back the issue of reparations for blacks to get elected. But politicians who are up for reelection get rich from lobbyists who seek their votes. These politicians neglect their districts, leaving them in shambles. Voting for Democratic politicians who play the race card does not put food on the table for their black constituents; these politicians just keep on exploiting blacks in their own plantation districts and never benefit them with good-paying jobs or good schools for education.

Some blacks interviewed on TV argued that they are not victims of white oppression, so why should they be paid reparations? From what nationalities of the white race are black politicians demanding reparations from? Italians? Spaniards? Russians? Irish? English? Germans? White people came from many nations who were not citizens and didn't own slaves. Do these people pay? Blacks were no longer slaves to white people in the last third of the nineteenth century, or in the twentieth or twenty-first century. How about Mexicans who were discriminated against and who are primarily a mixture of Spanish and Native; do they have to pay? How about Native Americans? Should they pay? How about people of mixed race, such as white and Native, or white and Mexican? How about the white immigrants who never owned slaves; do they pay? Can today's blacks prove their ancestors were slaves? I

---

[1] Douglas Main, "Slavery Reparations Could Cost up to $14 Trillion according to New Calculation," *Newsweek*, August 19, 2015, https://www.newsweek.com/slavery-reparations-could-cost-14-trillion-according-new-calculation-364141.

doubt it. Reparations for blacks is the most ridiculous issue Democrats have run on in every election. Every four years, Democratic politicians raise racist issues to stir up anger in the crime-ridden, poverty-stricken cities that they mismanage to get the black vote. After they get the black vote, they ignore blacks in their communities. Examples of these congresspeople are the late John Conyers, the late Elijah Cummings, and today's Maxine Waters, Al Green, and Sheila Jackson Lee, among others.

Black slavery has been a way of life since the world began, and in time it ended. In other words, black slavery was a global practice throughout world history since the dawn of humankind; it wasn't invented in the United States. Muslims owned slaves, both black and white. The Barbary pirates from North Africa captured European ships, kidnapped young white European women, and sold them to rich merchants in the Ottoman Empire as slaves. Blacks also sold their own people in Africa to white people for profit. Even some blacks in the United States owned slaves. During Obama's administration, some African countries apologized to African Americans for their part in promoting slavery in the United States. Why aren't black liberal politicians suing African countries for reparations? Answer: Countries in Africa whose ancestors sold slaves to white people will tell blacks in the US to go to hell. They would say, "You're already living in the richest country in the world, you're fortunate to live there, and some of you are even millionaires. Don't bother us; we are Third World countries."

Without going into detailed history about Jim Crow laws after the US Civil War, I will say that Jim Crow laws oppressed black people's way of life. Blacks were given the right to vote under the Fifteenth Amendment to the Constitution. However, most blacks were still prevented from voting in the South under Jim Crow laws. It wasn't until the Civil Rights Voting Act of 1965 was passed that blacks were freely allowed to vote in the South. But blacks are seeking reparations from all white people; this does not make sense.

Why are blacks the only group seeking reparations for slavery? Irish Catholics are not; Hispanics are not; Unskilled Chinese laborers who were slaves working on the railroads are not. Blacks who owned blacks in early US history and put them to work on plantations are rarely mentioned at all. Why haven't any Democrats ever demanded reparations from blacks in African countries whose ancestors sold blacks from their "stores" to customers from the United States and all over the world?

Regarding Jim Crow laws and discrimination, the Irish were oppressed because of their Catholic religion. Should the Irish and Catholics demand reparations for discrimination as well? Unskilled Chinese laborers were forced to work by the whites building and maintaining railroads. Should the descendants of these people demand reparations too? Mexicans have argued that their land was stolen by the imperialist United States during a planned US-Mexican border conflict from which President James Polk sought to trigger a war with Mexico. Polk urged Congress to declare war on Mexico in 1845. Mexican War battles always occurred in Mexico, never in the United States. Texas, Colorado, Arizona, New Mexico, and California were stolen from Mexico for $15 million because of the debt Mexico owed to the United States. Mexicans in the United States have been discriminated against since the Mexican War, particularly in the South. Should they also demand reparations? Native Americans were conquered and/or driven from their lands as the United States expanded west; some were forced into reservations. Should Natives demand reparations?

Questions: If black politicians demand reparations, when will it end? Is it a onetime demand, or will every black generation to come be demanding reparations? Even the politicians who promote black reparations are hush-hush on this topic. How about reparations for homosexuals, which Elizabeth Warren campaigned on? How does that scam work? How about the Chinese laborers who were forced to work on the railroad in the 1800s? Should all colors of Americans pay reparations to Chinese people in the United States today? How about reparations for Irish immigrants who were discriminated against because of their Catholic religion? How much in reparations shall taxpayers give them? Only liberal and socialist fools are desperate enough to campaign on these scams for votes.

Who exactly will pay the reparations? Will the descendants of whites who never owned or sold slaves still be forced to pay? Will it be necessary to add additional taxes on everyone in the United States? Will Congress collect new taxes, or will the US Treasury print money to pay up to $6.2 quadrillion to blacks for reparations? What people of mixed race will be forced to pay? Will the wealthy have to pay more than the poor? Will descendants whose ancestors owned multiple slaves receive a dollar amount for each slave owned? What about taxpayers who have a slave and also a slave owner in their family history? Why should a select number of people today pay for the sins of previous slave owners in US history? Note that Democratic politicians running for office on reparations never address any of these questions, nor do they say how any blacks today will prove their ancestors were slaves. It's all political rhetoric for the black vote.

It is absurd to pay taxes for slave ancestors and Jim Crow laws to blacks who demand reparations from today's whites and all other nonblack races who had nothing to do with owning, buying, or selling slaves more than one hundred fifty years ago. A Conference of Mayors in mid-July 2020 concluded that reparations for forty-one million black Americans would cost $6.2 *quadrillion* dollars. Additionally, the article states that further research must be done to estimate the following:

1.   the cost of lost opportunities
2.   the cost of the pain and suffering
3.   the costs of colonial slavery
4.   the costs of the racial discrimination that was allowed following the abolition of slavery against the descendants of slaves.

The article says that the interest rates are to be determined by negotiations between the descendants of slaves and the federal government.[2]

If every race and every group who was discriminated against in US history demanded reparations, the US would go bankrupt if socialists allowed such ridiculous reparations demands. Most Americans would

---

[2] Thomas Craemer, Trevor Smith, Brianna Harrison, Trevon Lofgan, Wesley Bellamy, and William Darity Jr., "Wealth Implications of Slavery and Racial Discrimination for African American Descendants of the Enslaved," Sage Journals, June 19, 2020, journals.sagepub.com/doi/10.1177/0034644620926516.

refuse to pay for such foolish Democratic political schemes. Blacks demanding reparations conveniently never mention the 330,000 white Union soldiers who fought in the US Civil War and paid with their lives in blood so that slaves could be free. Reparations have already been paid by whites with their lives. Should white people who are the descendants of those Union soldiers who died on Civil War battlefields freeing black slaves demand compensation from the blacks of today? To the blacks of today, I say, get over it. Go work for a living. You are not a victim. No one today has made you a victim, and no one owes you any money.

The city of Evanston, about 12 miles north of downtown Chicago, is the first city to provide reparations to its black residents for housing through a tax on marijuana sales. On March 22, 2021, the Evanston City Council voted 8-1 to approve a plan to distribute $400,000 to Black residents with ties to the city's Black community between 1919 and 1969. It is considered a reparations model for other cities in the US to follow. Chicago plans to provide reparations for its city using the same model. What was not mentioned is that taxes from marijuana were going for needs and to pay unknown city debts. Now that Chicago received about $2.5 billion out of the $7.5 billion given to Illinois from Biden's $1.9 trillion COVID money, marijuana taxes will now be shifted to pay for black reparations in Chicago. Very sneaky.

Chicago expects approximately up to appropriate $10 million in black reparations over 10 years. It's the Biden Administration's deceptive way to have cities across the US pay reparations for blacks by first bailing out blue states, a state then allocates money to its cities, and its cities reallocate their city taxes collected to pay for black reparations and move the allocated bailout money to fill in for what marijuana taxes were used for. In other words, COVID bailout money allocated to cities may pay certain debts allowed by the COVID relief bill and the taxes cities collect can go to pay for black reparations. What a scam from the Federal level to the city level. Illinois received $7.5 billion out of the $1.9 trillion coronavirus relief package passed by the Biden Administration. Roughly one-third of the direct aid to local governments, nearly $2 billion goes to Chicago.

Source: An article from the Chicago Sun Times entitled, "Evanston passes first-in-nation reparations", by Mitch Dudek and

Fran Spielman, dated 03/23/2021 at website: https://chicago.suntimes.com/2021/3/22/22345860/evanston-passes-first-in-nation-reparations

Obama's "Hope and Change" for Blacks

Barack Obama continued the practice of keeping blacks on the Democratic plantation with little or no opportunities for jobs or for getting themselves out of crime-infested ghettos. No matter how much federal money Obama threw at his hometown of Chicago, he never fixed the continuing gang violence or high crime rate there. The same is true of several other black high-crime cities across the United States. But he made sure the plantation was plentifully supplied with welfare and food stamps, with little or no mention of fraud. Barack Obama was well-known for creating sensationalism and gaining publicity in the media by inciting anger and division after police incidents where white police officers beat up or killed a black suspect. His goal was to divide the country racially by providing the black community lip service about social injustice and the need for police reform. In sensationalizing his hostility for law enforcement, he made things worse; rioting ensued after he sent his "race ambassador" and agitator Al Sharpton to rile blacks in Ferguson, Missouri, and St. Louis, Missouri.

Root Causes of Black Suffering, Crime, and Poverty; Ben Carson Helps Inner Cities

Democratic politicians run plantations where miserable blacks live, where white flight occurred, where high crime, illegal drugs, and poverty frequently occur, where businesses have fled because of high crime, and where the tax base to improve these inner cities has been significantly reduced. Inner cities mismanaged by Democrats became nightmares to live in.

In a debate with the rapper T.I. in September 2019, Candace Owens, a black American conservative commentator and political activist, cited four root causes of black failure in black communities:

1. Liberals support illegal aliens, who are overpopulating the United States, thereby making the black vote insignificant and taking jobs from blacks.
2. Black leaders offer nothing useful to blacks other than playing the race card, providing welfare, and making promises of black reparations.
3. About 74 percent of black children are growing up without a father in the home today.
4. Blacks in black community schools have the highest illiteracy rates.[3]

Black schools are poor and have poor-quality teachers. Most black kids in schools don't want to learn. Plus, crime and drugs affect black schools. People living in these poor communities cannot rebuild them very easily. President Trump and Ben Carson were turning this around by urging investments by *private companies* to provide an infusion of money to go toward rebuilding the infrastructure, building businesses, and bringing job opportunities to improve inner cities. Tax write-offs are just as good in that they are another way to provide the equivalent amount of taxes from local governments that lack tax funds to improve jobs and bring back businesses to these inner cities.

Dr. Ben Carson worked in ghettos as a doctor. He knows well the poverty and misery these people live in daily in their long-dilapidated neighborhoods that have not changed for generations. Ben Carson, who was raised in the ghetto, knows that seed investments help bring back businesses so blacks can help themselves, instead of being put and

[3] Rebecca Diserio, "Rapper TI: America Was Never Great for Blacks; Candace Gives Him Rude Awakening," Mad World News, June 19, 2020, https://madworldnews.com/ti-america-great-blacks-candace/?utm_medium=push&utm_source=onesignal&utm_campaign=onesignal&utm_content=onesignal.

kept on Democratic plantations, relying on government handouts or resorting to a life of crime.

During his term, President Trump expanded the economy and caused job opportunities to grow at a record pace. Residents of inner cities will, as a result, have a chance to seek educational opportunities and get good-paying jobs. Instead of Democrats frequently playing the race card for politics of division in order to make blacks resent the United States and blame white people for their misery, so as to manufacture white oppression propaganda and claim that Democrats are the only party helping poor blacks, Democratic politicians should work with Dr. Carson to promote investment into black communities to fix them so that people in those communities may live better lives. President Trump is a proponent of change to help black communities. He enabled a growing economy and used Dr. Ben Carson to assist in helping underdeveloped communities.

A sad note: As President Trump and Ben Carson tried to invest in and invigorate inner cities across the United States where predominantly blacks live, to improve infrastructure, create jobs, and create a better life for everyone, Marxist Antifa and BLM thugs looted and burned down businesses in parts of these Democrat-run cities after a white police officer was shown on TV keeping his knee on the neck of a black man, who died as a result, in Minneapolis, Minnesota. From June to the end of August 2020, Antifa and BLM terrorists continued to loot and burn businesses in Seattle, Minneapolis, Chicago, New York, Portland, Los Angeles, and Atlanta. Marxist thugs hate capitalism and oppose achieving the American dream, building infrastructure in cities where blacks live, and oppose bringing back businesses and job opportunities so that blacks may attain prosperity. Marxist thugs, who are black, white, and other races, proceed to destroy the businesses, monuments, and churches that strengthen a great America and promote American tradition.

Democratic city leaders are complicit with Marxist rioters and anarchists when they allow their cities and businesses to be looted, destroyed, or burned. To appease rioters, Democratic city officials then significantly reduce police budgets or disband police departments and replace them with counselors or social workers to respond to crimes. What a joke. To make matters worse, Democratic judges dismiss charges and release violent thugs and rioters from prison or jail in some of those cities. The result of these actions taken by city officials and judges is that rioters are emboldened to do more damage and perpetrate more attacks on police, but not be held accountable for their crimes. Marxist thugs set black America back. Members of BLM and Antifa are the worst enemies of blacks. Almost as bad are the clueless whites who help them burn the United States; they also set blacks back. One black female domestic terrorist interviewed on Fox News was heard saying the United States needs to be torn down and rebuilt from the ground up. This rhetoric is similar to that heard during the revolution of Mao Tse-tung, who promoted acts of vandalism against institutions and government, hoping it would catch on and change the hearts and minds of poor people, thereby causing the revolution to significantly increase in size and become enough to go to war with the government oppressors and win.

Who needs more law enforcement protection? Answer: blacks in inner cities where black gang members kill black people, including black children; where drugs are sold; where most black people are poor; where schools are inferior and mismanaged; and where kids can't learn or else refuse to learn in schools. Whites have gotten the hell out before they or their children could become victims of black violence.

Black Support for President Trump

Many blacks came to realize that with Trump's economic policies, they could get an education, find a job, work hard, make a good living, and live the American dream, thereby being able to leave the Democratic plantation far behind. Democratic politicians' failure to provide blacks job opportunities, as President Trump has done for blacks, has awakened many blacks. Many blacks now realize that living on a Democratic plantation was just a scam to get votes because their representatives in Congress could not provide opportunities to improve their lives. Job opportunities in a good economy allow blacks to get out of the ghetto. Playing the race card as a governing policy will only keep blacks on the Democratic plantation, picking welfare checks and food stamps instead of cotton, in a neglected city of high crime, poverty, drugs, white flight, and businesses leaving the city to relocate elsewhere. President Trump's economic policies offered blacks a chance to get off the plantation with opportunities to be all they can be and become prosperous through hard work.

4

THE LEGACY OF BARACK OBAMA

(★★★Note: This chapter was reorganized and revised)

US history books may likely show Barack Obama as the worst president in US history. The Obama administration was one of the most corrupt, dishonest, conniving, deceiving, and scandalous in US history. The corruption of the heads of the agencies "weaponized" by Obama, and the people these leaders worked with, are still being investigated by attorney John Durham (with no results yet).

However, Joe Biden may overtake Barack Obama as an even worse president in US history judged only from his first 62 days as president. Biden's frail mental health: his signs of senility, his poor articulation on interviews and speeches, and his memory loss are not helping him. Biden has a massive crisis at the border and getting worse, gave $1.9 trillion in COVID relief to states mostly as bailout money, and is now considering imposing higher taxes on corporations and on the wealthiest Americans to raise $3 trillion for spending on infrastructure, climate change, and reducing inequities in housing, education and health care. From 2020 to the present, Congress approved about $6 trillion in COVID relief measures. Fox News estimated the national debt will rise to $30 trillion by the end of 2021.

Obama's "Hope and Change" Was
Leftist Social Engineering

When Obama first got elected, people from all over the world thought that he, as the first black president, would unite Americans and become a peacemaker around the world, similar to Dr. Martin Luther King, who wanted all races to walk together, hand in hand, to the promised land. Barack Obama in no way and at no time filled the shoes of Martin Luther King Jr. Quite the opposite. Barack Obama was a community organizer whose goal was to social engineer US culture toward socialism as advertised in his campaign slogan, "Hope and Change." He was mentored as a communist, was raised as a Muslim, and was inspired to join a Christian church headed by Jeremiah Wright, who preached fiery black liberation theology more than he preached the Gospel. Obama attended the Nation of Islam mosque headed by Louis Farrakhan, a racist who hates Jews and calls white people "devils." Obama and Farrakhan became good friends. At his mosque, Farrakhan called Barack Obama the "messiah" in 2009. Obama was also a close friend of convicted domestic terrorist Bill Ayers, and discussed political issues with him socially.

Obama was prematurely granted a Nobel Peace Prize for his "Hope and Change" slogan, which was ambiguous and interpreted in many ways by many. Instead of being a unifier, Barack Obama became an arrogant con artist, a divider of races and also a divider of rich and poor, straights and homosexuals, Muslims and non-Muslims, pro-police people and antipolice people, and men and women. Compared to Dr. Martin Luther King, who received the Nobel Peace Prize for his actions and hard work, Barack Obama received the prize without having done any hard work. Instead, the Obama Administration divided Americans instead of bringing people together. Obama used identity politics to thrash "oppressor" groups.

Former president Obama ended the Iraq War in December 2011, when he withdrew the last combat troops from the country. However, he continued the war in Afghanistan. Obama allowed ISIS to establish a caliphate in Syria, armed partly with US weapons seized by the Muslim Brotherhood in Libya, provided to them by Hillary Clinton to assassinate Muammar Gaddafi, and transported to ISIS in Syria. Obama became a weak-kneed spineless coward who allowed ISIS to behead Christian men and hold Christian women as sex slaves, and Assad to gas his people in Syria, and did nothing about it. Obama went on an apology tour in the Middle East, apologizing for the bad actions of the United States in its conflicts with Muslim countries.

Crony capitalism corruption occurs when government allocates tax revenues strictly to progressives, grants contracts to businesses and corporations that donate campaign money to progressive candidates and progressive causes, and funnels tax revenues to enrich progressive relatives, friends and countries.

Obama's crony capitalism funneled taxpayer money to Muslim countries such as Iran, Palestine, and Afghanistan, and to selective corporations in the form of contracts and tax write-offs in exchange for political donations to his liberal political friends. Obama funded and promoted leftist policies and goals needed to maintain continued growth, power, and wealth for his administration and friends in Congress.

Obama directed his administration before he left office to weaponize his liberal federal agencies to use trusted personnel and government resources to rig the election of 2016. The White House authorized the use of US and foreign intelligence agencies, including the DOJ, White House staff, Congress (certain members), the State Department, the NSA, and the FBI, to rig the election in favor of Hillary Clinton.

Obama saw numerous scandals during his terms, including Operation Fast and Furious, Solyndra, Benghazi, spying on journalists, trying to rig an Israeli election in favor of Benjamin Netanyahu's political opponent, the IRS scandal, the ransom payment for the nuclear deal with Iran, the GSA scandal, the VA death-list scandal, and setting up the spying on candidate Donald Trump at the end of his second term to help Hillary Clinton win the election. To this day, no one knows where the $1 trillion in "stimulus money" went after Obama was celebrated for saving the US economy after his election in 2008. In 2016, the Nobel Prize Commission regretted having awarded Obama a peace prize as he never achieved peace in the world.

In the end, Obama left the presidency with a legacy of little or no economic growth, a divided country, a $10 trillion increase in the national debt within eight years, a weakened military, a flawed Iran deal, a North Korean nuclear threat, an administration full of corruption and scandals, and having let ISIS kill many Christians in the Middle East, caused by his weak-kneed foreign policy. Barack Obama became the most pathetic and blatant liar president in US history.

Former president Barack Obama will be widely known as "the same-sex marriage president" and hero of LGBT communities. It's Obama's love of and promotion of homosexuality, cross-dressers, and transgender people—part of his "hope and change" liberalism—that started these catastrophes during his administration. Democratic policies promoting homosexuality in public schools to young kids are ruining California and New York.

LGBT promoters and atheists are anti-Christian and are opposed to biblical doctrine on homosexuality because several scriptures from the Bible do not fit their immoral homosexual agenda. But there are LGBT promoters who are trying to change Christian doctrine into a "progressive morality" in specific Christian churches that are perfectly aligned with political progressivism. Aligning artificial political morality with Christian biblical morality is absurd because the Bible considers homosexual behavior to be immoral, as is found in several Bible passages. Progressive churches are not real churches; they have accepted political liberal morality as their new morality, which is a progressive moral doctrine concocted by religious cult leaders who cater to the needs of homosexuals. There are several religious cultists and sanctimonious politicians who would prefer to *amend* the Bible to justify their own morality, but they will always fail.

Obama Weakened Our Military

In July 2017, former president Barack Obama amended a directive (Executive Order 13672) to allow transgender people into the military as part of his Hope and Change progressive social engineering. This allowed homosexuals, crossdressers, and transgender people to get hormone shots and/or cosmetic surgery to change their gender. Obama hated the US military, evidenced by the fact that he went on an apology tour in the Middle East to apologize for the war on Islam conducted by the US military. Obama social engineered the US military to weaken it and to force it to tolerate homosexuals and their perversion, which had a negative effect on the military. A man could dress as "Paul" one day and dress as "Paula" the next day, which was an annoying distraction.

Obama fired more generals than any other president in modern times—look it up on the internet. Arrogant con artist Obama was a weak-kneed wimp who ignored Russia's takeover of Crimea; he didn't know what to do about it. Maybe he worked out a deal to let Putin have Crimea in exchange for some unknown benefits. Obama put a red line on Syria that he advised Syrian leader Assad not to cross by gassing his people, but Obama did nothing about it when Assad used chemical weapons on the Syrian people. Instead, Obama cowered. Obama was a con artist, a liar, a coward, and an incompetent commander in chief in managing foreign affairs. Some believe Obama allowed homosexuals, transgender people, and cross-dressers into the military to divide and disrupt it. ISIS, Obama's JV team, took over a large portion of Syria. Obama did nothing about it while ISIS was beheading Christians, crucifying them, and holding women as sex slaves. Obama weakened our military; President Trump had to rebuild it and fund it after he took office.

North Korea's Insults of Hillary Clinton, Barack Obama, and Joe Biden

Barack Obama and other prominent liberals failed to accomplish anything with North Korea. North Korea compared President Obama to a "monkey in a tropical forest" in 2014. North Korea regarded Hillary Clinton as "a funny lady, unaware of elementary etiquette in the international community. Sometimes she looks like a primary schoolgirl, and sometimes a pensioner going shopping."

In November 2019, North Korea called Joe Biden, who was then president-elect, "a rabid dog that must be beaten to death" and "an imbecile and a fool of low IQ." These insults from North Korea appear to be antiliberal, said with candor and without political correctness.

Obama's Corruption and the Iran Deal

There's a reason why Obama and his sidekick John Kerry sent $1.8 billion in cash to Iran: to put part of the $1.8 billion in cash into multiple untraceable secret bank accounts that could be accessed by Obama, Kerry, and other Democrats negotiating the Iran deal for kickbacks. It was kickback taxpayer money going into the accounts of Obama and Kerry, and some of it possibly into the accounts of the rest of the Democrats involved in the Iran deal negotiations. No investigations were made into the likely laundered $1.8 billion in cash from secret banks to Obama, Kerry, and the Democratic members of Congress who helped in the negotiations. Did any of the Democratic negotiators with Iran get kickback money from the untraceable cash given to Iran? We may never know.

President Trump regarded the Iran deal as a bad deal with Iran giving nothing useful in return, a fool's failed negotiation in which Iran snookered US taxpayers out of $150 billion and an additional $1.8 billion in cash. President Trump voided the flawed Iran deal and put strong sanctions on Iran.

Obama invested taxpayer money into Solyndra to use solar energy products to help the environment, but Solyndra went bankrupt after losing $500 million of Obama's DOE's taxpayer investments.

The Pay-to-Play Corruption of Hillary Clinton and the Clinton Foundation

Obama allowed corruption to go unchecked with top leaders of his administration, such as Hillary Clinton, John Kerry, Joe Biden, and Lois Lerner, who were involved in corruption and scandals. Hillary Clinton made corrupt deals that were called "pay-to-play deals" with foreign governments, who paid money in exchange for political action(s). Foreign governments such as Saudi Arabia, and those of other Middle Eastern countries, would stuff cash in her Clinton Foundation as "donations to charity."

Gun Rights Restrictions

Democratic socialists such as Kamala Harris, Cory Booker, and Beto O'Rourke have expressed their desire to severely restrict gun laws for law-abiding citizens or force a mandatory law to buy back assault semiautomatic weapons from the public using taxpayer money. Socialist members of the Democratic Party also wanted to create a special federal police force to confiscate weapons from law-abiding citizens, using deadly force if necessary.

The Second Amendment guarantees us our freedom for self-defense against mentally ill shooters, criminals, and tyrants who would like to transform the United States into Venezuela for total control. The reason socialist lawmakers want to track and severely restrict guns or ban guns is not because they want to prevent people from shooting others, but because they do not want an armed rebellion against socialist elites when they start passing tyrannical laws that take away our freedoms. They do not want armed violence against police agencies trying to enforce the Federal government's mandates on gun laws. Law-abiding citizens will push-back on police agencies trying to enforce unconstitutional Federal gun mandates. Socialists know there will be gunrunning, but they can deal with that by investigating the gunrunners, tracking them, surveilling them, and going after them. But tyrants and their despotic force can't and won't face an armed rebellion of tens of millions who own guns. Reasons **for** justifying gun ownership are as follows:

- A mob of Antifa members beat up a defenseless senior citizen wearing a MAGA hat and a conservative journalist in public; such a thing could happen to any Trump supporter wearing a MAGA cap.
- Black Lives Matter mobs chant that they want dead cops.
- Sanctuary cities release dangerous illegal alien criminals back into communities instead of handing them over to ICE for deportation.
- It takes police on the average five to ten minutes, or longer, to respond to a call when one or more lives are in danger.

- The leftist Biden Administration is proposing future guns laws to register their guns with the Federal government, extend background qualifications on firearm purchases, and plans to outlaw assault-style semiautomatic assault rifles, which they fear most. Democrats also want to ban firearm magazines containing more than nine or ten rounds.
- We can't defend ourselves against violent gangs or criminals who want to invade our homes, rob us at gunpoint, or attack our families.
- Democrat politicians and/or their staff have been known to make public a list of addresses where Trump supporters live so they can be targeted.
- Our gun rights are granted to us by the US Constitution.
- We may see history repeating itself in the United States, in which socialists will kill citizens refusing to surrender their weapons or imprisoning them after taking their guns away, as in Venezuela.

These are all good reasons for all good people in the United States, who understand the value and legality of the second Amendment, to unite and fight these self-serving power-hungry tyrant politicians every way we can. It's a matter of life and death and essential for our survival. It's our right to defend ourselves and our country. We must never give up our guns.

The Biden Administration wants a Federal gun registry so Federal agencies can track every firearm in the US and its location. Federal agents may come like a thief in the night with warrants to search private residences for specific registered guns and may confiscate them. In several situations, law-abiding citizens may even have firefights with Federal agents who want to take away an assault rifle from them. There will be, and there must be, armed resistance against a tyrannical government for the confiscation of semiautomatic weapons, including assault rifles.

Leftist politicians are insensitive to focusing on mentally ill and criminals who can obtain guns illegally. They want to ban semiautomatic assault weapons and magazines that carry more than 10 rounds because these weapons are most effective against fighting tyrannical leftists, where handguns are less effective against a leftist-led military fighting a revolution with tanks, machine guns, bayonets, automatic rifles, and bullet-proof vests. Democrat-passed restrictive gun laws only guarantee that the citizenry will not win an insurrection against a tyrannical US government.

Will Police Departments Enforce Tyrannical Laws?

As the Biden Administration passes more oppressive laws depriving Americans of gun rights and mandatory confiscation of assault rifles, will police departments enforce such unconstitutional laws? Since the Biden Administration control the Federal government, Biden will require police agencies to cooperate and work with DHS, the FBI, and the Bureau of Alcohol, Tobacco, Firearms and Explosives to enforce all Democrat passed gun laws, even if they are controversially unconstitutional, illegal, and oppressive tyrannical laws. If local police agencies will not cooperate with Federal agencies, Biden Administration officials may force city administrators in those counties or cities to order police compliance or fire police officers. One way is to withdraw Federal assistance to the city and/or state to force compliance. There are two ways by which the coming tyrannical laws will be enforced:

1. Leftist Democrats will hire only those willing to enforce tyrannical laws, including amnesty migrants if necessary
2. Biden may use a national security executive order, calling for United Nations Peacekeeping troops on US soil to enforce laws if there is massive resistance to enforcement of their tyrannical laws.

Several states will challenge any unconstitutional gun laws passed by Congress or executive orders signed by the president all the way to the Supreme Court. If the US Supreme Court sides with the Democrats, several states will likely resist the Federal law or secede from the US based due to their firm stance on protecting their second Amendment rights.

Democrat-Run Cities: High Murder Rates and Homelessness

As of July 11, 2019, there were 171 murders in Baltimore. Thirteen of those had happened since the *Chicago Tribune* reported on July 1, 2019, that in Chicago, 1,517 people were shot that year. That was 129 fewer than in 2018; the data is through Saturday, July 27, 2019.

It's going to get worse in a California run by Democrats because of tax oppression of California's residents; rising crime; homelessness; more illegal aliens; more poverty; more homelessness; a shrinking tax base from businesses, wealthy people, and the middle class leaving the state; accumulation of city and state debt; pension at risk at all levels of government; an increase in demand for government handouts; lack of police resources; lack of prisons; and a lower standard of living. Democrats have ruined California, and they will destroy it completely unless they are stopped.

After the George Floyd riots in 2020, Minneapolis, Minnesota, the mayor, and the city council planned to defund the police department. Mayor de Blasio defunded $1 billion from the NYPD, and as a result, New York City is having a tremendous increase in all levels of crime. In Los Angeles, Mayor Eric Garcetti cut $150 million from the LAPD. The city council of Seattle, Washington, is contemplating defunding their police department by 50 percent. Note that these problem cities are all Democrat-run cities. BLM and Antifa learned in 2020 that rioting will cause radical reforms to police departments in Democrat-run cities, so their crimes of looting, burning, and destroying institutions will go unimpeded and will be successful without police around. Liberal Democratic mayors and city councils are complying with demands and threats from Antifa and BLM. Bill de Blasio, a well-known Marxist and mayor of New York City, was seen on TV painting a BLM logo on the street in front of Trump Towers alongside Al Sharpton.

Will a weak and restrained police state run by Democrats still prevail under the Biden Administration? Answer: hell no, since tyrannical laws and executive orders will be passed to stifle conservative speech and religious liberty, to confiscate firearms and greatly restrict their purchase or use, and to tax the living daylights out of the entire middle class.

Democratic socialists will require law enforcement to enforce all their tyrannical laws and arrest anyone using hate speech or committing hate crimes. And all right-wing protests will be labeled as white supremacist protests, with police authorized to use brutal force against white people. Socialists, including BLM, will urge mayors and city councils to arrest white people, because anyone who is white will be considered a white supremacist. BLM will support police brutality and excessive use of force against Trump supporters or white supremacists, the reverse of what they supported under the Trump Administration now. A knee on the neck of a white Trump supporter protester being arrested by a black or white police officer will likely be cheered-on by surrounding mobs, celebrated by BLM, Antifa, and rallied by Democratic politicians and their news propaganda media as true deserved justice.

Another corrupt practice that Obama, Hillary Clinton, and Joe Biden were involved in was trying to bribe the Vatican to change Catholic doctrine to align it with progressivism, using funds from George Soros. Hillary Clinton is a liberal who hates traditional Christianity and, notably, the Catholic Church. Abortion and homosexuality were active social engineering issues for former president Obama. There was much criticism of both from Christian churches, particularly from the traditional Catholic Church. Liberal progressives set plans in motion to send politicians or Obama diplomats to the Vatican to explore ways to have a liberal pope elected after Pope John Paul II passed away. Nancy Pelosi was one such politician who went to the Vatican to try to convince members of the Vatican Council and Pope Benedict to change their views on abortion. They refused, sending pious Pelosi back to the United States with a failed mission. After Pope Benedict resigned, former president Obama sent his VP, Joe Biden, to visit the Vatican to explore whether Pope Francis, Pope Benedict's successor, would be liberal enough to change Catholic doctrine to state that abortion should be a moral and humanitarian right—and the same with homosexuality. Joe Biden and others learned of one member of the Vatican who was homosexual and some bishops in Germany who were tolerant of homosexuality or promoted homosexuality. Even with bribes using George Soros's money, Joe Biden failed to convince Pope

Francis to change Catholic doctrine to coincide with the Left's views on abortion and homosexuality.

Another corrupt scandal in which Hillary Clinton and her husband were involved entailed the sale of uranium to a foreign enemy. With the knowledge of Barack Obama, Eric Holder, Robert Mueller, and people from other government agencies, Secretary of State Hillary Clinton approved the sale of 20 percent of the United States' uranium to Russia for $145 million, donated to her Clinton Foundation by Vladimir Putin, plus $500,000 paid to Bill Clinton as a speaking fee for a speech delivered in Russia. Frank Giustra, a Canadian mining financier, also donated $31.3 million to the Clinton Foundation. Was former president Obama involved in the corruption? Did he receive any money from the uranium deal? All we know is that Obama left the presidency as a multimillionaire. He could never have made that much on his presidential salary.

Follow-up investigations should be made into allegations that Hillary Clinton may have had an assassination slush fund to hire professional assassins to kill a multitude of people who were about to expose her and her husband in the last thirty years. Their possible victims include a number of people who supposedly committed suicide, died in car crashes, got shot in the back by assailants who ran without taking the victim's money, or died mysteriously.

The Clinton Assassination of Gaddafi

Another scandal of Hillary Clinton, with the approval of former president Barack Obama, was the assassination of Muammar Gaddafi of Libya. Some Europeans paid money to the Clinton Foundation to get Hillary Clinton to try to prevent Gaddafi from urging African nations to go to the gold standard, which would cause some European nations to incur huge losses from African debt.

Muammar Gaddafi was killed by the Muslim Brotherhood after Hillary Clinton, working in the State Department, secretly sent sophisticated weapons to the Muslim Brotherhood in Libya to assassinate Gaddafi because he was going to put Africa on the gold monetary standard, with Europe and the United States standing to lose billions of dollars if that were to happen. It is highly suspected that some rich citizens of France, Germany, and other European countries whose banks, including Rothschild, stood to lose a lot of money donated to the Clinton Foundation to have Hillary assassinate Gaddafi as a pay-to-play favor. That appeared to end the gold standard for use in payments of debt from African nations to Europe.

Benghazi and the Muslim Brotherhood

Hillary Clinton as Secretary of State supplied secret weapons approved by Obama to the Muslim Brotherhood in Libya to assassinate Muammar Gaddafi, which they did on October 20, 2011. After the Muslim Brotherhood assassinated Gaddafi, they used Hillary's shipped weapons to take over Libya and attack the consulate in Benghazi, where they killed four Americans. Hillary and Obama ordered the US military to stand down and *not* rescue the Americans in Benghazi. Why? To cover up that secret weapons had been supplied to al-Qaeda and the Muslim Brotherhood in Libya by the State Department, but mainly because Mrs. Clinton wanted to *hush up* that fact that she and Obama both benefited from donations to the Clinton Foundation. Colluding with each other, Obama, Susan Rice, and others invented the preposterous idea that the attack on Benghazi had been carried out by Muslims disgruntled about a video that insulted Islam. But the gold standard where Africans would be paid in gold by European countries and the United States was never implemented, which is what the United States and Europe wanted.

The Muslim Brotherhood gave US State Department–supplied weapons, under the leadership of Hillary Clinton, to al-Qaeda in Libya, which were transported to ISIS in Syria by al-Qaeda and the Muslim Brotherhood; Hillary hadn't thought of that possibility. Terrorist members of al-Qaeda and the Muslim Brotherhood attacked our consulate in Benghazi, Libya, and killed four Americans. Barack Obama, Hillary Clinton, Leon Panetta, or General Petraeus never sent anyone to rescue the Americans being attacked by terrorists in Benghazi after many requests for emergency assistance were made. The ordeal lasted thirteen hours. Additionally, Obama, Hillary Clinton, and Susan Rice lied by falsely blaming the reason for the attack on a Muslim video. This is what happens when corrupt Democratic politicians have no military experience and leave Americans behind to be killed, then try to clean up their own poop with excuses.

John McCain wasn't a war hero as some people thought. John McCain got shot down while on a bombing mission over North Vietnam in 1967. He failed to escape, got captured on the ground, and became a POW in a prison camp for about six years, until the US government negotiated his release on March 14, 1973. He never saved any American lives or accomplished any heroic act that would earn him a medal for any reason.

Hillary Clinton once considered John McCain as her running mate when she ran against Obama, but instead, John McCain also ran for president, won the Republican primary, and faced Barack Obama. During the 2008 presidential debate, Barack Obama, a relative unknown to the majority of the American people, mopped the floor with RINO[1] John McCain.

McCain was involved in a scandal with his friends George Soros and Charles Keating, a savings and loan scandal in which they were trying to bribe certain members of Congress for monetary gain. McCain and Soros had associations with the wealthy, unscrupulous Rothschilds in Europe to control wealth by bribing European politicians who were becoming globalist leaders. McCain was a traitor to the voters of Arizona who thought he would support conservative values. Instead, he voted on the side of Democrats.

McCain disliked Trump and tried to prevent him from becoming president, as McCain had close ties to the Clintons. McCain acquired and provided a version of the dirty Russian dossier about candidate Trump via a courier he had sent to the United Kingdom to retrieve it. It is unknown if McCain's obtained version is the same version as the one for which Hillary Clinton paid to get from British former spy Christopher Steele. McCain provided a copy of the dossier to

---

[1] RINO stands for "Republican in name only."

FBI Director James Comey. Court documents revealed that McCain associate David Kramer shared the unconfirmed dossier with a number of press outlets in December 2017.[2] John McCain passed away on August 25, 2018, from brain cancer.

[2] Chuck Ross, "John McCain Associate Had Contact with a Dozen Reporters regarding Steele Dossier," *Daily Caller*, March 14, 2019, https://dailycaller.com/2019/03/14/john-mccain-dossier-steele-reporters/.

5

THE NEW POLITICAL PROGRESSIVE MORALITY

In their quest for control and power, socialists and other progressives have defined a "new morality" that equates to every change they make to our US institutions and culture. To Democrats, the new morality is not biblical morality but merely their political changes, which they often and conveniently justify by using the Holy Bible. In fact, the Democrats' new morality does not equate to biblical morality, and they never address the conflicts. This chapter will cover how Democrats are trying to reform Christian churches, including the Catholic Church.

"Holier than Thou" Democrat Politicians Define a New Morality

"Holier than thou" phony religious Democrats lecture Americans with their new progressive morality.

Just as socialist leader Adolf Hitler accepted and approved the Christian religion prior to World War II by claiming Jesus Christ was an Aryan and a member of the superior white race, Democrats are using religion as a weapon to justify their immoral, godless, progressive "new morality" in order to support their socialist politics and tyrannical agenda whenever it's convenient. Not only are they religious hypocrites, but also they are anti-Christian, and they can't justify their misaligned new morality by using scripture from the Bible. Democratic politicians like Nancy Pelosi act sanctimonious by promising to "pray for Donald Trump" on TV to the press, but we find that Speaker of the House Pelosi is a staunch advocate of abortion, which is against her Catholic religion, and opposes prayers or Nativity scenes at Christmas in public schools.

Why are socialists like Alexandria Ocasio-Cortez, Bernie Sanders, Elizabeth Warren, Cory Booker, and Beto O'Rourke keeping their mouths shut about the Easter Sunday massacre that occurred in a Catholic church in Sri Lanka? Answer: Socialist phonies don't care about Christians who get slaughtered in US churches, in Africa, in the Philippines, in Asia, or in Europe unless it's a white man killing black people in a black church in the United States for political gain or if Trump can be blamed and defiled in any way.

New Morality Aligned with Political Progressivism Rather than with Biblical Morality

Liberal politicians have defined political progressivism as their own "new morality" to replace the morality of the Christian churches and the Bible. The new morality is aligned with political progressivism rather than with biblical morality. The new morality is just plain leftist politics that liberals claim is morally correct and justified as "humanitarian rights." The problem with liberal Democratic logic is that they intentionally confuse political rights with morality; the two are not the same. Political rights come from the people in the United States and are granted as rights by the US Constitution. Liberals may argue that freedom of choice to have an abortion and same-sex marriage are humanitarian rights, but they are certainly not supported or justified in the Bible and they are not preferred choices of free will.

Progressives considered their new morality of homosexuality and abortion to be humanitarian rights of the individual and personal choices that should be protected by the US Constitution and even promoted in the name of freedom. Nowhere do these moralist progressives cite scripture from the Bible to justify unnatural depraved behavior or the killing of a new life in the womb by abortion. No liberal recalls that that God gave us all free will so that we can choose to do either good or evil. Guess which choice God prefers?

Hypocritical Democratic Politicians Express Their Moral Superiority

For liberals and socialists, "political morality" is their new bible. For example, presidential candidate Kirsten Gillibrand said God gave us free will and, therefore, a woman should have free will or "choice" to terminate her pregnancy. Gillibrand completely misses the meaning of God's free will; it is a choice between good and evil. Yes, Kirsten, a woman can choose to do evil. None of the Democratic or socialist presidential candidates could articulate why they think homosexuality is moral. Presidential candidate for 2020 Peter Buttigieg, who is a homosexual married to another man, says that God is for homosexuals too, just not the GOP. No liberal, including Buttigieg and Kirsten Gillibrand, can quote a Bible verse justifying homosexuality or abortion as moral behavior. But there are several verses in the Bible that consider homosexuality and the intentional killing of a life as immoral.

The New Leftist Progressive Morality Conflicts with Biblical Scripture on Abortion and Homosexuality

In an interview with CNN in April 2019, presidential candidate Peter Buttigieg said that he believes religion should be used as a weapon for personal agendas and to make political points. He, Joe Biden, and Nancy Pelosi have already done this. On homosexuality, Buttigieg believes all marriage, including same-sex marriage, is a blessing and moral. He said that marrying his partner was one the best choices he had ever made, adding that being married to a man has made him a better person and moved him closer to God. Buttigieg rejects criticism of same-sex marriage as divisive and hateful because we are taught God is love and, therefore, people shouldn't criticize homosexuals in love who get married based on "theological grounds." For example, the Bible shouldn't be used to criticize homosexuals; he's upset because of it. Further, Buttigieg claims sex between same-sex couples is an expression of love. It's a good thing Buttigieg didn't write part of the Bible. In mid-March 2021, Pope Francis said the Catholic Church cannot bless same-sex marriages because God "can't bless sin".

Buttigieg is an insecure man who lost his self-esteem by becoming a homosexual. Buttigieg is another bogus holier-than-thou politician who is trying to use religion to conveniently accommodate his sinful same-sex marriage gig in order to further his own political agenda. He should be ashamed of his sick, abnormal homosexual lifestyle and his unholy same-sex marriage. Note that Buttigieg, like all other liberal moralist politicians, never cites biblical scripture to justify abortions or homosexuality. Even the hippies in the 1960s twisted the use of the word *love* to justify their personal agenda of birthing "flower children" out of wedlock arising from freewill loose morals.

Nancy Pelosi Uses Religion as a Political Tool

In an interview with MSNBC on January 2017 reported by the *Washington Times*, Speaker Pelosi said, "I say, this will be a little not in keeping with the spirit of the day of unity, but I say [Republicans] pray on church on Sunday and then prey on people the rest of the week. And while we're doing the Lord's work by ministering to the needs of God's creation, they are ignoring those needs, which is to dishonor the God who made them."[1]

Congresswoman Pelosi is a Catholic gone wrong. She claims Democrats do not wear religion on their sleeves, because they don't want to "exploit" religious issues. That's a flat-out lie. I'll bet at times she has doused herself with holy water to make other people think she's pious or holier than thou, especially when she lectured Trump

---

[1] Douglas Ernst, "Pelosi Says Religious Republicans 'Dishonor' God, Admits Breaking Trump Inauguration 'Unity,'" *Washington Times*, January 20, 2017, https://www.washingtontimes.com/news/2017/jan/20/nancy-pelosi-says-republicans-dishonor-god-admits-/.

supporters on morality in her political speeches. If she is so morally superior, then why does she *ignore the needs* of the homeless population in her district of the poop city San Francisco while bragging on TV about ice cream in her refrigerator in her mansion in San Francisco? Why doesn't she provide leadership on eliminating, preventing, and cleaning up feces, urine, trash, rats, and fleas from her district and all over San Francisco, things that may cause contagious diseases within the population such as typhus, tuberculosis, or the bubonic plague? Why does she support and promote the sins of abortion and homosexuality?

Nancy Pelosi, like many other hypocritical Democrats, uses religion as a weapon to advance her political agenda and when it suits her. As long as these Democrats think that Americans believe the Christian religion aligns itself with the Left's new progressive morality, Nancy Pelosi and other Democrats will use it as a political tool. Traditional Christian thought does not align itself with liberal politics. Democrats silence the voices of true Christianity, stifle it, or wage economic war against it. Examples:

- Democrats sue places of business for refusing to make wedding cakes for homosexual marriages.
- Democrats sue nuns for not passing out free contraceptives.
- Nancy Pelosi demonizes Catholic bishops for their views on abortions, citing women's health issues, but she never addresses nonlife-threatening abortions, the rights to life of the baby with a soul, and abstinence from the irresponsible sex that causes some women to unexpectedly become pregnant.

Like some other Democrats, Nancy Pelosi lectures Americans on morality but never quotes Bible passages to support her immoral agenda. Fake news MSNBC should have asked Nancy Pelosi the following questions:

1. "What Bible verse(s) can you cite to justify your longtime support of abortion, which is the taking of a human life in the womb?"

2. "Do you believe that a baby has a God-given soul in the womb?"

3. "If a woman's health is not in danger, do you still believe it is the mother's choice to abort her baby?"

4. "Under what conditions, if any, do you consider an abortion to be murder?"

5. "Since more black babies are statistically aborted in the United States than babies of any other race, do you think abortions are a form of racism?"

6. "Do you believe that babies just born should be aborted if the mother so chooses?"

7. "Do you think the pope and Catholic doctrine are wrong on abortion?"

8. "To what Bible verses do you turn to justify homosexuality?"

9. "Do you support same-sex marriages? If so, why?"

10. "While you were a congresswoman, did you ever go to the Vatican and speak to a pope at any time to influence him to change his views or to change Catholic doctrine on abortion or homosexuality?"

11. "Did you ever receive funds from George Soros to fly to the Vatican to try to change the Vatican's moral stance on abortion or homosexuality?"

12. "Have you ever been excommunicated or ever been threatened with excommunication by any member of the clergy of the Roman Catholic Church or any member of the Vatican?"

13. "Do you consider yourself a hypocrite when you repeatedly support laws that promote abortion and homosexuality, then go to church to confess your sins, thinking you're forgiven?"

14. "As a Catholic yourself, do you think it's proper to lecture the Catholic Church and other Christian churches while insisting on taxpayer funding for abortions?"

15. "Have you ever been lobbied by any homosexual or abortion lobby during the time you have been in Congress? If so, how many millions of dollars do you estimate you made from that?"

16. "Have you ever had an abortion in your spring-chicken days?"

17. "Have you ever had a homosexual relationship?"

18. "Have you ever been aware that the Democratic Party is laundering taxpayer money and funneling it to Planned Parenthood and that part of that money, involving tens of millions of dollars, is being funneled to the Democratic National Committee as campaign contributions?"
19. "Do you believe in same-sex marriages?"
20. "Do you believe in the worldwide woman's choice to abort babies in the womb in order to slow climate change, as Bernie Sanders expressed to voters?"
21. Why have you and the Democratic Party not condemned Antifa and BLM for the death, destruction, looting, and burning they have caused across the nation to people, monuments, churches, and our other institutions?"

Nancy Pelosi Is Phony Catholic who Thinks She's Morally Superior

Pelosi is a former Catholic who rejected her Catholic catechism taught to her in the Catholic Church. She became a politician who contradicts Catholic teachings—the killing of a baby in the womb with no regrets—and she sidesteps the issue of abortion being the murder of a living baby in the womb.

In September 2008, the *Christian Post* reported that Democratic Speaker Nancy Pelosi agreed to meet with San Francisco archbishop Niederauer privately to discuss Catholic doctrine on abortion, a meeting that Pelosi misrepresented publicly in a *Meet the Press* interview. Pelosi said that, as a Catholic, she believed there were seriously conflicting positions of abortion within the Catholic Church. That drew the ire of many Catholics, including leaders of the Catholic Church, because she does not speak for, nor is she an authority, on Catholic Church doctrine. Pelosi presents herself as a practicing Catholic who said, "Doctors of the church disagree on when life begins," and claimed abortion continues to be an issue of controversy in the Catholic Church.

Speaker Pelosi was reprimanded by Catholic leaders who opposed her opinions, indicating that the Catholic Church has never changed its antiabortion position. Archbishop Niederauer said, "Catholics are not supposed to pick and choose which teachings to follow."

In the same article, it is mentioned that in 2007, as a VP candidate, Joe Biden said in a *Meet the Press* interview that he accepts the Catholic Church's doctrine that life begins at conception but would not impose his religious beliefs on people. At that same time, presidential candidate Barack Obama refused to answer the question "When does life begin, and when does a baby get human rights?" because it was above his pay grade.[2]

On September 2014, according to the *Washington Times*, Vatican cardinal Raymond Leo Burke said in an interview that Nancy Pelosi is an unrepentant sinner who supports and promotes the crime of abortion in government and still calls herself Catholic. Cardinal Burke said Nancy Pelosi has no Catholic right to be granted Communion and that it should be denied to her until she changes her views on and activities related to abortion.[3] However, Pelosi has not been excommunicated by the Catholic Church, according to an article in the *National Catholic Register* entitled "Has the Vatican Excommunicated Pelosi? (8 Things to Know and Share)."[4]

According to an article on CNN's website, Joe Biden was denied Communion at a Catholic church in South Carolina.[5] In 2008, Bishop Joseph Francis Martino of Scranton, Pennsylvania, Joe Biden's hometown, said he would deny Joe Biden Communion in the Scranton diocese because of Biden's support of abortion.

[2] Michael A. Vu, "Pelosi Agrees to Meet Archbishop for Abortion Dialogue," *Christian Post*, September 9, 2008, https://www.christianpost.com/news/pelosi-agrees-to-meet-archbishop-for-abortion-dialogue.html.
[3] Cheryl K. Chumley, "No Communion for Nancy Pelosi: Vatican Court Head," *Washington Times*, September 24, 2013, https://www.washingtontimes.com/news/2013/sep/24/vatican-court-head-no-communion-nancy-pelosi/.
[4] Jimmy Akin, "Has the Vatican Excommunicated Pelosi? (8 Things to Know and Share)," *National Catholic Register*, September 28, 2013, https://www.ncregister.com/blog/has-the-vatican-excommunicated-pelosi-8-things-to-know-and-share.
[5] Eric Bradner, "Joe Biden Was Denied Communion at Catholic Church in South Carolina," CNN, October 29, 2019, https://www.cnn.com/2019/10/29/politics/joe-biden-denied-communion-south-carolina-catholic-church/index.html.

In 2016, Virginia senator Tim Kaine, an ardent nontraditional progressive Catholic, was criticized by several priests because of his pro-abortion stance, his pro–same-sex marriage stance, and his views on gender equality.

Conclusions: It's very interesting that a number of high-ranking Democrats are Catholics whose personal human rights–based "political morality" is supporting and defending abortion and homosexuality. It is also very interesting that top Catholic Democratic leaders, such as Joe Biden, John Kerry, Nancy Pelosi, and Tim Kaine, were denied Communion for supporting abortion and some for supporting homosexuality. So, it logically appears that a revenge strategy was concocted by the Obama administration and the DNC to do the following:

1. Get rid of traditional Catholic Pope Benedict and have him replaced with a more liberal pope.
2. Lobby corrupt vulnerable members of the Vatican to change their interpretation of Catholic doctrine in order to support the pro-abortion and same-sex marriage values of Hillary Clinton and Tim Kaine.
3. Seek lobbying funds to do item#2 above
4. Send the right people to the Vatican to convince a newly installed liberal pope like Pope Francis.
5. Try to convince Pope Francis to change Catholic doctrine to view abortion and homosexuality as moral human rights.
6. Prepare a liberal pope to "legitimize" abortion and homosexuality as basic human rights values before he makes a trip to the United States so then he may give lip service to the Hillary Clinton–Tim Kaine campaign.

Would the Obama–Biden administration collude with 2016 candidates Clinton and Kaine and the DNC to implement these seven steps? See the following pages for further details.

Joe Biden Performed a Homosexual Wedding

On August 1, 2016, Vice President Joe Biden officiated a same-sex wedding, marrying two White House male staffers in the Obama administration, Joe Mahshie and Brian Mosteller, at the vice president's residence in Washington, DC. The two had asked Biden to officiate, the Associated Press reported, adding that the vice president had gotten a temporary license to perform the ceremony from the District of Columbia to make the marriage legal.

Joe Biden claims to be a Catholic, but he violated current Catholic doctrine and biblical scripture by performing a same-sex marriage, not as a Catholic, but as a temporary Justice of the Peace.[6]

Why Hillary Clinton Chose Phony Catholic Tim Kaine as Her Running Mate

Hillary Clinton chose Tim Kaine, a "new morality" progressive Catholic, as her VP running mate to exploit his Catholicism in order to justify Hillary's views on the new morality of homosexuality and abortion supported by the Vatican—if only the Vatican had changed its stance on abortion and homosexuality. Hillary Clinton wanted to reform the Catholic Church in the United States to cause a split with Rome and win a victory for Catholic progressives in the United States. If Hillary Clinton had gotten elected *and* if the Vatican had revised its position on homosexuality and abortion, then the new morality would have led to same-sex marriages in the Catholic Church in the United States. Phony Catholic Tim Kaine would have been exploited to give speeches to LGBT and abortion organizations to celebrate Catholic reforms aligned with the new Soros-and-Obama-created liberal political morality, to be viewed as a blessing. But unbeknown to Hillary Clinton, the Vatican changes would have been considered heresy, and the pope

---

[6] Rachael Revesz, "Joe Biden Marries Two Gay White House Officials at His House," the *Independent*, August 2, 2016, https://www.independent.co.uk/news/world/americas/vice-president-joe-biden-gay-marriage-wedding-home-washington-law-order-episode-cameo-a7168331.html.

and other members of the Vatican who had voted to change Catholic doctrine would be called heretics and be forced to resign by Catholics all over the world. Massive numbers of Catholics would have abandoned the Catholic Church until the heretical issuances were rescinded and the heretical pope and members of the Vatican replaced.

President Trump was elected by way of divine intervention. No one expected him to win the election of 2016, even though the demonic forces of some top leaders of the Obama administration, with funds from George Soros, including the demons of the hate-Trump media, failed to stop Trump from becoming president despite their best efforts. Pope Francis and the Vatican never changed the Catholic doctrine, and Hillary Clinton failed to be elected president. Despite the pope's continuing to insert himself into political matters at times, the Catholic Church was saved from corruption and destruction by evil forces.

The Conspiracy of the Obama Administration to Change Catholic Doctrine at the Vatican

Why did Hillary Clinton select Tim Kaine, a longtime progressive Catholic and a liberal Democrat, as her vice presidential running mate? Answer: It appeared that Hillary Clinton was adamantly seeking Vatican support of the Obama–Hillary liberal political morality or new morality relating to all progressive issues, particularly abortion and homosexuality, using the carrot of millions of dollars provided by George Soros. A changed Catholic doctrine plus a known liberal pope's lip service toward progressive morality in the United States would provide opportunities for Hillary Clinton and Tim Kaine to spread the new Catholic morality in the United States, which would be perfectly aligned with their progressive "moral" policies.

Since 2011, the Obama–Soros plan was one that included Obama's social engineering objectives to reform the Catholic Church to a new morality aligned with leftist progressive political ideas. The mission of the Obama–Soros conspiracy was to influence the Vatican through bribery to obtain public acceptance or modified Catholic doctrine to support Obama's progressive views on abortion, homosexuality, and gay marriage. This influence and support from a socialist-leaning pope would also undermine traditional Catholic teachings on abortion and homosexuality and would permit gay marriage into the Catholic Church in the United States, along with protecting pedophile priests. If Obama and Soros had been successful in obtaining the Catholic Church's support for Obama's progressivism, the traditional Catholic new morality would be considered blasphemy by Catholics all over the world and the Catholic Church would currently be split into two camps: traditional Catholics and progressive Catholics. Former president Obama would indeed seek legalization of same-sex marriage and fund Planned Parenthood to allow abortions in the United States with or without the pope's blessing. However, he could never influence the Catholic Church to allow same-sex marriages without the Vatican's blessing or support. In the United States, Obama and Soros sought to justify their new progressive morality as blessed by the pope in the hopes that it would lead to same-sex marriage in the Catholic Church and to the "blessed" practice of abortion as both a woman's choice and a humane health issue.

A January 2017 article in the *New American* indicated a US-led conspiracy after 2011 by the Obama administration to get rid of Pope Benedict and replace him with a more liberal pope: "Did billionaire speculator George Soros, President Barack Obama, Secretary of State Hillary Clinton, Vice President Joe Biden, and Obama/Clinton adviser John Podesta conspire to overthrow the conservative Pope Benedict XVI and replace him with a radical, Pope Francis? Did they use America's intelligence agencies, and our nation's diplomatic machinery, political muscle, and financial power[,] to coerce and blackmail 'regime change' in the Roman Catholic Church?"[7]

Michael Gryboski's article in the *Christian Post* states, "[Pope] Francis said in the interview that the catechism, or the Roman Catholic Church's official doctrine book, condemns homosexual acts, but he

---

[7] William F. Jasper, "Catholics Ask Trump to Probe Soros–Obama–Clinton Conspiracy at Vatican," *New American*, January 28, 2017, https://thenewamerican.com/catholics-ask-trump-to-probe-soros-obama-clinton-conspiracy-at-vatican/.

called on the Church to love gays and lesbians, who 'must be accepted with respect, compassion and sensitivity.'"[8]

Pope Francis should have a quality control expert in his decision-making because gays cannot be trusted in any position in any Christian church, especially around boys. Reason: As of 2013, the Boy Scouts began admitting openly gay scouts, and in 2015 the ban on homosexual scoutmasters was lifted. More than seven thousand cases of pedophilia had surfaced as of August 2019.[9] The Boy Scouts of America filed for bankruptcy on February 18, 2020.[10] Now there are law companies on TV and on the internet advertising compensation for Boy Scouts who were sexually abused, regardless of age.[11]

Allowing male homosexuals as scoutmasters was a very bad idea; they ruined the Boy Scouts of America, once a great organization for boys. Leftist politicians and lawyers destroyed it.

Allowing gays in church positions around boys and allowing gays into church as priests is a bad idea, one that will open Pandora's box of pedophilia worldwide and financially bankrupt the Catholic Church, destroying it as well. That's what liberals and socialists want. The Joe Biden administration plans to protect gays against discrimination in all religious institutions, which will have very bad consequences. And Joe Biden still calls himself Catholic.

---

[8] Michael Gryboski, "Pope Francis Affirms Church's Views on Homosexuality, Abortion, but Says It Must Accept LGBT with 'Respect, Compassion,'" *Christian Post*, September 19, 2013.

[9] Gail Peterson, "What Went Wrong with the Boy Scouts?," *Human Life International*, August 1, 2019, https://www.hli.org/resources/what-went-wrong-the-boy-scouts-homosexuality/.

[10] David Auro, "Boy Scouts of America Files for Bankruptcy after Sex Abuse Lawsuits," Fox News, February 18, 2020, https://www.foxnews.com/us/boy-scouts-of-america-files-for-bankkruptcy-after-sex-abuse-lawsuits.

[11] Select Justice LLC, a legal website containing a survey and procedure for abused Boy Scouts to file lawsuits against sex abusers, https://selectjustice.com/boy-scouts.

Analysis and Rationale for the Obama Administration Conspiracy to Reform the Catholic Church

The Obama administration became aware that leftist Catholic politicians such as Speaker Pelosi, Secretary of State John Kerry, and Vice President Biden had been denied Communion by US Catholic churches they attended because of their views on abortion and homosexuality. A simple analysis would logically point to an effort by the Obama administration, with President Barack Obama's approval, to dare create a conspiracy to remove traditionalist Pope Benedict and replace him with a liberal pope whose moral views would be more in line with American liberal political values. If a conspiracy could be hatched by the Obama administration to accomplish this, then criticisms by US bishops and cardinals against Catholic Democratic politicians in the United States would stop, and Catholic doctrine on abortion and homosexuality could hopefully be changed, blessed, or anointed by a new, liberal pope as moral human rights. A concerted effort to accomplish this, using the right people, could lead to more leftist social reforms in the United States, such as funding abortions across the United States and promoting or using government extortion methods to eventually force same-sex marriage in the Catholic Church with no more obstacles from US Catholic bishops or cardinals. In addition to these reforms, if they could happen, Hillary Clinton and progressive Catholic Tim Kaine would have a better chance to be elected in 2016.

Such an evil conspiracy to bribe the Vatican in order to oust a conservative pope was hatched by Obama, Hillary, George Soros, Joe Biden, the DNC, and their Vatican inside operative—former chairman of Goldman Sachs International Peter Sutherland, who reformed the Vatican Bank and was also a former attorney general of Ireland. Sutherland's mission was to seek out and bribe vulnerable Vatican officials to select a liberal pope who would inject himself into left-leaning politics and hopefully change Catholic doctrine to suit the Obama–Soros liberal agenda in the United States and thereby benefit Hillary and Tim Kaine when Hillary became president. If elected, Hillary Clinton would select VP Tim Kaine to lead the effort to implement these reforms in the Catholic Church.[12]

Pope Benedict May Have Been Forced to Resign by a Coup Orchestrated by the Obama Administration

According to an article from the Burning Platform website, Pope Benedict was forced to resign because of a coup orchestrated by the Obama administration in concert with George Soros, some members of the Vatican, and European associates of the Vatican.[13] Some ideas to consider on this point are as follows:

- The Obama administration weaponized US intelligence agencies to spy on candidate Trump to rig the election for Hillary Clinton.
- After President Trump was elected, members of the cabal group known as the Deep State attempted to find Russian collusion crimes and to fish for any crime(s) Trump may have committed so as to invalidate his presidency, impeach him, and remove him from office.
- The Obama administration sent taxpayer money to the opponent of Netanyahu totaling $349,276, which went to the One Voice Movement, a joint Israeli–Palestinian organization, to support Netanyahu's opponent in his campaign to become prime minister of Israel.

The effort to use a cabal or Deep State coup to oust a world leader, such as a pope or president, would be very likely. Knowing that the Obama administration used this pattern three different times to oust a world leader, one would think the probability that the Obama

---

[12] Jasper, "Catholics Ask Trump to Probe Soros–Obama–Clinton Conspiracy at Vatican."

[13] "WikiLeaks: Conservative Pope Benedict Was Forced to Resign by 'Deep State,'" February 18, 2018, the Burning Platform, https://www. theburningplatform.com/2018/02/18/wikileaks-conservative-pope-benedict-was-forced-to-resign-by-deep-state/.

administration would again conspire to rig and influence elections in Israel with his weaponized agencies would be high. The probability that the Obama administration using funds from George Soros, in concert with a Soros-operative Vatican banker insider, and lobbying corrupt members of the Vatican Council vulnerable to blackmail to commit a conspiracy to remove Pope Benedict and replace him with Pope Francis was 100 percent. Given that Pope Francis was known to be a more liberal pope who could change Catholic doctrine to appease liberal politicians in the United States with its acceptance of abortion and homosexuality as a moral human right, leading to same-sex marriages in Catholic churches in the United States and potentially destroying the Catholic Church, increased the Obama administration's efforts to plan a coup. Both Hillary Clinton and Barack Obama wanted to exploit the Catholic Church because it conflicted with their extreme liberal political views; they both expected the conspiracy to succeed.

Pope Benedict resigned under mysterious circumstances, and Jorge Mario Bergoglio (who took the name Pope Francis) was elected pope by the Vatican Council on March 13, 2013. Members of the Obama administration and community activist socialists lobbied the church to offer a favorable moral definition of homosexuality and abortion. At the end of Obama's administration, Catholic doctrine remained unchanged, much to the dismay of the Obama administration and particularly to Hillary Clinton, who had been counting on it.

According to WikiLeaks emails, George Soros, Barack Obama, and Hillary Clinton orchestrated a coup in the Vatican to overthrow conservative Pope Benedict in February 2013. Pope Benedict became the first pope to resign since Pope Gregory XII, in 1415, and the first one to do so on his own initiative since Pope Celestine V in 1294. However, a group of Catholic leaders cited new evidence uncovered in emails released by WikiLeaks that claimed the conservative Pope Benedict actually had not resigned on his own initiative but was ousted from the Vatican by a coup that researchers/investigators began calling the "Catholic Spring."

Soros, Obama, and Clinton used the United States' diplomacy, political power, and financial power to coerce, bribe, and blackmail certain clergy members within the Roman Catholic Church to bring about a regime change in the Vatican in order to replace conservative Pope Benedict with Pope Francis, the latter of whom became a surprising advocate of the New World Order socialist left, stunning Catholics around the world. What some Catholic websites indicated, based on WikiLeaks and with corroboration of other evidence, is that the Obama administration showed repeated patterns of abuse of power and lawlessness, using federal agencies involved in a cabal coup to oust some world leaders or political candidates Obama did not like during his eight years in office.

Sidenote on Former President Obama's Pattern of Abuse of Power

On March 19, 2011, then president Obama launched 112 Tomahawk missiles into Libya, without consulting Congress or the UN, to destroy the Gaddafi regime. Obama's excuse was to "protect civilians and rebel forces from Gaddafi," according to the website, Thy Black Man.[14]

But the real reason was to prevent Gaddafi from establishing a gold standard in Africa and thereby endangering the economies of the US and Europe (see the section in chapter 4 titled "The Clinton Assassination of Gaddafi"). This was one of former president Obama's first orchestrated Deep State coups; he weaponized his intelligence agencies to work with al-Qaeda and the Muslim Brotherhood to oust Gaddafi during the Arab Spring, which lasted from December 2010 to December 2012. Hillary Clinton's State Department armed these Muslim terrorist groups with advanced US weapons to capture or kill Gaddafi. US Special Forces captured Gaddafi and handed him over to rebels, who killed him. Muslim rebels supported and armed by Hillary and Obama began the ethnic cleansing of Africans who had defended Gaddafi. Ambassador Christopher Stevens, who was Hillary Clinton's operative in Benghazi, Libya, and three other Americans were abandoned and left to die by Hillary Clinton and Barack Obama to cover up their embarrassing misappropriation of US arms to al-Qaeda in Syria and to the Muslim

---

[14] "Why Did Obama Kill Gaddafi? Part 2," Thy Black Man, January 14, 2018, http://thyblackman.com/2018/01/14/why-did-obama-kill-gaddafi-part-2/.

Brotherhood, and to cover up the Muslim rebels' ethnic cleansing of thirty thousand black Tawergha African tribespeople. Nothing about this orchestrated coup operation was mentioned by Barack Obama, Hillary Clinton, or Susan Rice. The gunrunner who had peddled the US arms to al-Qaeda and the Muslim Brotherhood may have known about the genocide, and Ambassador to Libya Christopher Stevens probably knew about it, but he was abandoned and left to die in Benghazi while requesting urgent help from the US State Department for about twenty-four hours.

Obama's pattern of illegal abuse of power continued as he weaponized his intelligence agencies to gather dirt on Pope Benedict so as to slander him as a pope and worked in concert with George Soros, who financed a New World Order coup, that is, a "Foreign Deep State," which used exploitation operatives to bribe, blackmail, and influence members of the Vatican to install and groom a new pope. After an orchestrated coup to replace a conservative pope with a new progressive pope, the Obama administration continued to work in concert with John Podesta and community organizers to coerce and bribe corrupt members of the Vatican to advise Pope Francis and groom him to become a progressive moral voice of the US liberal agenda; the end goal was to increase the chances of a Hillary Clinton election in 2016.

This criminal pattern of ousting world leaders continued as former president Barack Obama weaponized federal agencies and worked with other Foreign Deep State leaders to organize a coup to oust other world leaders. On July 12, 2016, the Obama administration tried to prevent the reelection of Prime Minister Netanyahu, interfering with the elections of a foreign power by giving the Netanyahu campaign's opponent access to $350,000 in US taxpayer dollars.

As mentioned before, President Obama also weaponized his federal agencies, his White House staff, and his cadre of leftist lawyers to spy on candidate Donald Trump before the 2016 election. Obama's Deep State coup group continued to spy on President Trump after his reelection in hopes of finding something on him to oust him from office. While criminal Obama was involved with enabling and having his federal agencies orchestrate all these illegal activities against candidate Trump, Hillary Clinton paid Christopher Steele millions of dollars for a fake

Russian dossier that no one could verify to leak to the liberal biased media in order to slander and defame candidate Trump and use the dossier to sway public opinion toward the election of Hillary Clinton.

Continuing with the Orchestrated Coup of Pope Benedict

In an article published by the *New American*,[15] we read that WikiLeaks publicly revealed emails from Hillary Clinton and her DNC campaign manager, John Podesta, indicating they conspired to change Catholic doctrine radically to influence public opinion and advance their goals for a Democratic win for Hillary Clinton as president in 2016. The article also states that John Podesta was an operative of George Soros, and in 2011, he and other operatives were working to create a "Catholic Spring" revolution within the Catholic Church. Further, another Soros operative, non-Catholic Sandy Newman, sought advice from Podesta on how to proceed with an effective revolution within the Catholic Church, which he described as a "Middle Ages dictatorship."

Podesta replied to Newman that two newly created Soros-funded Catholic organizations, Catholics in Alliance and Catholics United, were political activist groups seeking to promote abortion rights, same-sex marriage, LGBT education in public schools, women priests, and so on, but they wouldn't work unless there was public support for each from members of the Catholic Church.

Raymond Arroyo, who worked for the Catholic Network (he now works at Fox News), broadcasted that any Catholic Spring political activists who were soliciting changes to the core beliefs of the Catholic Church would not be well received by Catholics.

A January 28, 2017, article in the *New American* reported that a group of concerned Catholics mailed a letter to President Trump asking him to assign someone in his administration to probe what they called the "Soros–Obama–Clinton conspiracy at the Vatican." They alleged that

---

[15] William F. Jasper, "Clinton Campaign's Anti-Catholic E-mails: Will Catholic Voters React?," the *New American*, October 14, 2016, https://thenewamerican. com/clinton-campaign-s-anti-catholic-emails-will-catholic-voters-react/.

George Soros, President Barack Obama, Vice President Biden, Hillary Clinton, John Podesta, and others conspired to overthrow traditional Catholic Pope Benedict XVI and replace him with Pope Francis, a radical leftist. They submitted eight questions to be investigated.[16]

Concerned Catholics indicated that Pope Benedict mysteriously resigned on February 28, 2013, and was replaced by Pope Francis on March 13, 2013, a pope with a foreign leftist agenda. They accused Pope Francis of involving himself too much in politics and promoting the ideological agenda of the Left to Catholics worldwide. They feared that Pope Francis was pandering to the seemingly anti-Christian leftist agenda of Democratic politicians in the United States.

Representing millions of Catholics in the United States, a group of concerned Catholics asked President Trump to investigate and find answers to the following questions:

1. Did the National Security Agency (NSA) monitor the Vatican officials who elected Pope Francis?
2. Were there any secret operations carried out by the US government to assist in ousting Pope Benedict?
3. What members of the Vatican did US government agents contact?
4. Why were international monetary transactions halted with Vatican officials a few days before Pope Benedict resigned? Were there any transactions between US government agencies and the Vatican in these few days?
5. Why were monetary transactions resumed a day after Pope Benedict resigned?
6. What actions were taken by John Podesta, Hillary Clinton, and others in the Obama administration who were involved in the Catholic Spring?
7. What was the reason Vice President Joe Biden and Pope Benedict met at the Vatican on June 3, 2011?
8. What part did George Soros and other financiers who reside in US territories play?

---

[16] Jasper, "Catholics Ask Trump to Probe Soros–Obama–Clinton Conspiracy at Vatican."

George Soros and the Obama administration lobbied the Vatican to change its views on abortion and homosexuality. The acceptance and practice of each conflict with biblical scripture, but lobbyists didn't care about biblical scripture; they hoped the Vatican would revise Catholic doctrine (catechism) to universally accept abortion and homosexuality as being morally acceptable practices in the Catholic Church. Had this doctrine been changed, it would have ignited protests and rebellions by traditional Catholics accusing the pope of heresy and would have significantly damaged or destroyed the Catholic Church, likely leading to the loss of hundreds of millions of its conservative members and perhaps bankrupting the church. Had it happened, I, a longtime Catholic and member of the Knights of Columbus, would have left the church.

Pope Benedict stated that the reason for his decision was his declining health, the result of old age. Cardinal Jorge Mario Bergoglio, archbishop of Buenos Aires, Argentina, replaced him as Pope Francis.

According to an article in *Veritas Vinci International*, Soros, Obama, and Clinton may have been behind the resignation of Pope Benedict XVI:

Leaked Emails Show Political Plot to Oust Benedict

A group of Catholic leaders cite new evidence uncovered in emails released by WikiLeaks that the conservative Pope Benedict did not actually resign on his own initiative, but was pushed out of the Vatican by a coup that the group of researchers are calling the "Catholic Spring."[17]

In January 20, 2017, the group wrote a letter to US president Donald Trump requesting that he launch an investigation into the activities of Barack Obama, Hillary Clinton, and other members of the Obama administration, including billionaire leftist George Soros, all of whom

---

[17] Paul Simeon, "Was Pope Benedict XVI Forced to Resign?," *Veritas Vinci International*, October 20, 2017, https://veritas-vincit-international. org/2017/10/20/was-pope-benedict-xvi-forced-to-resign/.

they alleged were involved in orchestrating the Catholic Spring, which resulted in the replacement of Pope Benedict XVI.

The leaked emails showed that Soros and the Obama administration used US diplomatic connections and resources, political influence, and financial power to coerce, bribe, and blackmail officials in the Roman Catholic Church in order to cause a regime change and replace Benedict XVI with Pope Francis, who since has become an unlikely voice for the international Left, stunning Catholics around the world."

"We were alarmed to discover," their letter notes, "that, during the third year of the first term of the Obama administration your previous opponent, Secretary of State Hillary Clinton, and other government officials with whom she associated, proposed a Catholic 'revolution' in which the final demise of what was left of the Catholic Church in the United States would be realized."

Leaked Emails

"The Letter first directs attention to the notorious Soros–Clinton–Podesta emails disclosed last year [2016] by WikiLeaks, in which John Podesta and other progressives discussed regime change to remove what they described as the 'middle ages dictatorship' in the Catholic Church. Podesta was the former chairman of the 2016 Hillary Clinton presidential campaign."

Given the fact that Obama was involved in interfering in Israel's election, trying to oust Benjamin Netanyahu by providing taxpayer funds to his opponent, and given the fact that Obama weaponized his agencies prior to leaving office so they would spy on candidate Donald Trump in the 2016 election and collude with Hillary Clinton to rig the 2016 election, there is 100 percent probability that members of the Obama administration and Hillary's DNC colluded with George Soros to oust Pope Benedict XVI and have him replaced with Pope Francis.

The Obama administration is suspected of colluding with billionaire George Soros, a Vatican banker insider (Peter Sutherland), corrupt members of the Vatican susceptible to blackmail, and homosexual members of the Vatican, all of whom were involved in a conspiracy to remove Pope Benedict and replace him with Pope Francis. Pope Francis was thought to be a more liberal pope who could change Catholic doctrine to appease liberal politicians in the United States to accept abortion and homosexuality as moral human rights, leading to same-sex marriages in Catholic churches in the United States and potentially destroying or dividing the Catholic Church. Both Hillary Clinton and Barack Obama opposed the Catholic Church because it conflicted with their extreme liberal political views.

The *New American* website indicates that in January 2017, President Obama was suspected of weaponizing the CIA, the FBI, the NSA, and other intelligence agencies to oust Pope Benedict and bring in Francis, who was considered very progressive in his political views. The objective was to orchestrate a Catholic Spring to facilitate replacing Pope Benedict with Pope Francis, which succeeded. This brings into question that if the Obama administration and his weaponized agencies could oust a pope, why couldn't Obama do the same with a presidential candidate like Donald Trump? It has already been proven as fact that Obama weaponized his agencies to spy on candidate Trump.

The website predicts that if the New World Order, that is, the cabal composed of George Soros, the Rothschilds, Peter Sutherland, UN leaders, and the world movement they represent, succeed in blackmail, coercion, extortion, race-baiting, fomenting revolution, and promoting protests and rioting, they will devastate the entire planet.

The investigation that the concerned Catholics are requesting of President Trump should be of interest to more than just Catholics. Peter Sutherland, George Soros, and the world government movement they represent will, if successful, wreak unimaginable havoc and devastation upon the entire planet. The investigation—and prosecutions—cannot begin too soon.

The miraculous election of Donald Trump ended the plot to further the progress of Soros, Peter Sutherland, Obama, Hillary Clinton, Tim Kaine, Nancy Pelosi, Joe Biden, and others in their war against Christianity, to claim victory, and to celebrate the alignment of Catholic morality with their new progressive morality.

The letter sent to President Donald Trump asked for an investigation of high-level US political officials thought to be corrupt, George Soros, and DNC director John Podesta: "WikiLeaks emails revealed that

John Podesta and other 'progressives' discussed ending the 'middle ages dictatorship' in the Catholic Church."

For further details on the letter to President Trump and the investigations requested, see the article in the *New American*.[18]

The Unholy Alliance between George Soros and Pope Francis

An article published on September 3, 2019, on the website Front Lines of the End Times says that WikiLeaks emails revealed George Soros's Catholic Spring revolution to influence the Vatican.

> In 2016, Wikileaks revealed that billionaire George Soros used his funds to shape Pope Francis' visit to the US in September 2015. He lobbied American bishops and members of the Vatican to support Pope Francis. Wikileaks revealed Soros used Cardinal Oscar Andres Rodrigues Maradiaga, a supporter of "People Improving Communities through Organizing" (PICO) and a close friend of Pope Francis, to assist Soros' campaign to undermine the Catholic Church's public moral voice. Soros also urged Maradiaga to advise Pope Francis to promote the liberal/socialist agenda. The website also cites that over 90 members of US Congress sent Pope Francis a letter urging him to focus on liberal agenda. Wikileaks uncovered information from the emails that members of George Soros' operatives viewed Pope Francis as a proponent for their leftist propaganda and exploited him to voice Soros requests to the world.

> Further disclosures from WikiLeaks confirmed the plotting of Democratic officials to infiltrate the Catholic Church in order to "foment revolution" beneficial to

---

[18] Jasper, "Catholics Ask Trump to Probe Soros–Obama–Clinton Conspiracy at Vatican."

their radical causes. In 2012, in the midst of Catholic backlash over Obama's contraceptive mandate, John Podesta received a note from Sandy Newman, president of Voices for Progress.

There needs to be a Catholic Spring, in which Catholics themselves demand the end of a **Middle Ages** dictatorship and the beginning of a little democracy and respect for gender equality in the Catholic church.

In 2013, Francis became Pope and began politicizing the Church exactly as progressives had expected. Podesta would later advise candidate Hillary Clinton to enlist the pope's leftist moralistic views in her campaign. In one Podesta hacked e-mail, he advised that Hillary send out a tweet to Pope Francis to "thank him for pointing out that the people at the bottom will get clobbered the most by climate change."[19]

This is yet another source quoting an excerpt from George Neumayr's book *The Political Pope.*[20]

Pope Francis and members of the Vatican Council temporarily rejected the leftist reformation arguments to change Catholic doctrine regarding abortion and homosexuality. The plot crashed and burned for Hillary Clinton with the election of Donald Trump, also to the disappointment of George Soros, Barack Obama, John Podesta, high-ranking Catholic homosexual clergy in Europe, and phony Catholics such as Tim Kaine, Nancy Pelosi, and Joe Biden. Catholic doctrine was

---

[19] Geri Ungurean, "New Evidence Emerges that the Real Reason Pope Benedict Suddenly 'Retired' Was because of End Times Cabal Headed by George Soros, Barack Obama, and Hillary Clinton," Front Lines of the End Times, September 3, 2019, https://www.nowtheendbegins.com/real-reason-pope-benedict-suddenly-retired-because-end-times-vatican-cabal-headed-by-george-soros-barack-obama-hillary-clinton/.

[20] George Neumayr, "The Unholy Alliance between George Soros and Pope Francis," *American Spectator*, May 3, 2017, https://spectator.org/the-unholy-alliance-between-george-soros-and-pope-francis/.

not changed; however, Pope Francis called for the Pontifical Biblical Commission (PBC) to study scripture in the Bible for a reinterpretation of homosexuality. The PBC was established in 1902 to ensure the proper defense and interpretation of the sacred scripture.

But Pope Francis still supports open borders for the elimination of suffering and misery, climate change policies to protect the earth, and racial equality. He criticized the nationalism that led to tyrannical governments such as that of Nazi Germany, and criticized unregulated capitalism, saying that it would hurt the poor and benefit only the rich.

This evil conspiracy to support homosexuality and no longer interpret it as a sin is heresy and an abomination to God and his church. If Catholic doctrine had been changed, it would have caused a revolution by traditional Catholics against the Vatican and the pope accused of heresy. No person or government today is authorized to change biblical scripture to benefit anyone's political views. The changes that Soros, Obama, Hillary, and some American Catholic progressive groups sought from the Vatican were in direct contradiction to the Holy Bible regarding abortion and homosexuality. The battle was won, but the war on Christianity continues. Corrupt homosexual members of the Vatican are also trying to reform or destroy the church.

It was a miracle that Donald Trump was elected in 2016. *Now more than ever,* I believe that the election of Donald Trump as president was absolutely *divine intervention.* God protected his church and his people. The Obama–Soros conspiracy, aided by Peter Sutherland, was prescribed to benefit Hillary Clinton, whom Obama and the Deep State thought was a shoo-in as president in 2016. If she had been elected, Hillary and her running mate Tim Kaine would have benefited politically from the new morality arising from Vatican corruption, that is, bribes provided by leftist members of the Obama administration and accepted by corrupt high-ranking cardinals and bishops in the Vatican. This would have split up or irreparably damaged the Catholic Church. This conspiracy by the Obama administration should be investigated; those found guilty of bribery should be exposed, and any members of the Vatican who accepted bribes should be removed from their positions forever. If this new morality had been implemented in the United States as a new gospel of Catholic doctrine, it would have been one of the biggest scandals in world history and perhaps would have caused the demise of the Catholic Church.

Liberal millennials have been indoctrinated by their leftist schoolteachers. Now these students are anti-Christian and reject conservative values. These leftist millennials were indoctrinated with Obama's Hope and Change doctrine, with liberals at the time hell-bent on social engineering the morality and institutions of the United States, silencing conservative and religious speech, and destroying their reputation.

The Plot to Align Morality with US Political Progressivism with regard to Abortion and Homosexuality

A shocking discovery I made today about my religion, being a longtime Catholic, was that Barack Obama, Hillary Clinton, and George Soros attempted to bribe members of the Vatican Council, which consists of cardinals, to select a left-leaning pope who would inject himself into politics in line with the Obama–Hillary–Soros liberal agenda to change Catholic doctrine to legitimize homosexuality and abortions and protect pedophilia. The result would be, if embraced, the demise of the Catholic Church.[21]

Pope Francis on Abortion

On April 26, 2014, Pope Francis reiterated his strong opposition to abortion, saying it "compounds the grief of many women" already succumbing to what he called the "pressures of secular culture." Pope Francis denounced abortion as the "white glove" equivalent of the Nazi-era eugenics program and urged families to accept the children that God gives them.

---

[21] Jasper, "Catholics Ask Trump to Probe Soros-Obama-Clinton Conspiracy at Vatican."

Pope Francis on Gay Marriage and Homosexuality

Pope Francis does not attack, condemn, or judge homosexuals, but he has not changed Catholic teaching that homosexuality is "intrinsically disordered," and he opposes gay marriage. He has insisted, however, that Catholics shift their attitude toward gay people to be loving and welcoming instead of judgmental. In answer to a reporter's question about homosexuality, Pope Francis said, "Who am I to judge?"

Despite all the quid pro quo bribery and progressivism of some members of the Vatican, the Catholic Church's views on abortion and homosexuality remain unchanged under Pope Francis. God is the only true Judge of people; we can only identify and expose the injustices of the wicked and what evil people do.

The Attempted Corruption by Obama Administration Officials, George Soros, and Others to Destroy the Catholic Church

The election of Donald Trump as president of the United States, as I mentioned previously, was an act of divine intervention. Thank God for saving his church and for saving the United States. Obama's top "Hope and Change" leaders and European contacts hustled top Catholic leaders to try to get them to make a moral change to Catholic doctrine by offering bribes with funds from George Soros. Barack Obama, Hillary Clinton, John Podesta, George Soros, Joe Biden, Tim Kaine, and Catholic organizations that champion themselves as progressive Catholics would see the Catholic Church destroyed and/or splintered into two groups: traditional Catholics and progressive Catholics. The new morality in the United States, social engineered by progressive politicians, will lead to the following:

- progressive Catholic priests who will gradually allow same-sex marriages;
- liberal lawmakers promoting and protecting pedophilia;

- homosexuals being hired to teach Bible study classes to indoctrinate kids with the new political Catholic catechism;
- taxpayer funding to support the genocide of babies through abortion;
- genderless bathrooms (odd ducks will be found loitering in the same restrooms used by little boys and girls);
- women serving as priests;
- the progressive Catholic Church attracting only freaky churchgoers and the odd ducks of the world;
- a massive number of Catholics leaving the Catholic Church, possibly leading to the destruction and bankruptcy of the Catholic Church;
- massive opposition and protests by traditional Catholics against the Vatican leadership and demands for the pope and all bribed Vatican officials to be fired (in such a case, a new Vatican Council and a new pope would be required to bring traditional Catholicism back);
- Catholics learning that the scandalous Obama administration, with the help of billionaire George Soros and Vatican associates, was responsible for bribing vulnerable Vatican officials.

George Soros Attempted to Take Down Europe and the Catholic Church

Actor James Woods is right in calling George Soros "satanic" for having "undermined the stability of Western democracies." Soros has funded progressive Catholic organizations in the United States that are advocating what he calls "morally correct" (MC) conduct, such as abortion and same-sex marriages. In 2015, Soros funded $650,000 to influence Pope Francis, and he has tried to influence the Vatican to change Catholic doctrine to redefine abortion and homosexuality as morally correct even though to do so goes against biblical scripture. The attempts of Barack Obama, Hillary Clinton, and George Soros to influence the Vatican to coincide with their social engineering Hope and Change agenda crashed and burned when President Trump was elected president. Further information of what Hillary Clinton tried to do to the Catholic Church can be found in the *Remnant* article entitled "A Vatican–Democratic Party Alliance? (Catholics Ask Trump Administration to Investigate)."[22]

According to this article in the *Remnant*, a Catholic newspaper, on August 2016, WikiLeaks released documents hacked from George Soros's Open Society organization indicating that he provided $650,000 to People Improving Communities through Organizing (PICO), which is a radical organization of community organizers embracing the leftist agenda using Saul Alinsky's Rules for Radicals. The funding was for PICO community organizers to travel to the Vatican to discuss leftist strategies in three days of meetings with cardinals in preparation for the 2016 election.

"The WikiLeaks Podesta emails reveal that the Vatican solicited advice from, and collaborated with leftist community organizers to advance the political platform of the Democratic party. Soros strategically funded PICO progressive activists who appear to serve as de facto advance men for the upcoming Pope's U.S. trip in September 2015, by discussing papal site visits and political messaging with key Vatican hierarchy."

George Soros sought to lobby Cardinal Jorge Bergoglio (who later became Pope Francis) and other Vatican officials to support New World Order leftist views, which consist of promoting climate change control, massive immigration, income equality, globalism, and Black Lives Matter, and smearing capitalism. George Soros's community organizers are responsible for advising Pope Francis on environmental reforms supported by the UN's efforts to oversee and promote climate change efforts.

During the three-day meetings, the objectives were to convince/encourage Pope Benedict to echo the agenda of Hillary Clinton and the Democratic Party, voicing the alarm of economic inequality, racial discontent, and economic injustice, and bashing capitalism as a system

---

[22] "A Vatican-Democratic Party Alliance? (Catholics Ask Trump Administration to Investigate)," the *Remnant*, January 22, 2017, https://remnantnewspaper.com/web/index.php/articles/item/3001-did-vatican-attempt-to-influence-u-s-election-catholics-ask-trump-administration-to-investigate.

that oppresses victims, among whom are minorities, homosexuals, Muslims, immigrants, and victims of police brutality. It was to incite anger and energize African Americans to vote for Democratic politicians. These were all political leftist issues that PICO, a self-declared moralistic entity, encouraged the pope to address as moral issues during his visit to the United States. However, PICO community organizers did not mention pro-choice abortionists and homosexuals as oppressed and excluded groups in the United States.

"In our meetings with relevant officials, we strongly recommended that the Pope emphasize—in words and deeds—the need to confront racism and racial hierarchy in the US."[23]

God Saved His Church from the Demons of the Democratic Party

If this article report is true, then George Soros and the Obama–Hillary leftist political machine represented an evil exploitation of the Catholic Church that tempted the Vatican, through its vulnerabilities, to provide lip service as quid pro quo to the Left's new morality, which is aligned with US political progressivism, with the intent to convince Catholics to elect Hillary Clinton as president of the United States.

The election of Donald Trump in 2016 must have been a deep shock to globalists, socialists, community organizers, members of the Deep State, and some members of the Vatican. It must have been a knife struck into the dark hearts of George Soros, Hillary Clinton, Tim Kaine, John Podesta, and Barack Obama.

The reaction of sore-losing Hillary progressives and members of the Deep State was to contest the election of 2016 with allegations that Trump had colluded with the Russians to win the presidency. The demonic forces of the Left continued trying to remove President Trump from office by fishing for crimes he may have committed. On

---

[23] Elizabeth Yore, "WikiLeaks Bombshell: The Soros/Clinton/Vatican Partnership," the *Remnant*, November 4, 2016, https://remnantnewspaper.com/web/index.php/fetzen-fliegen/item/2853-wikileaks-bombshell-george-soros-using-francis-papacy.

December 18, 2019, House Democrats, under the leadership of Speaker Nancy Pelosi, Adam Schiff, and Jerry Nadler, approved articles of impeachment for Donald Trump. All but three House Democrats voted to impeach him. House Democrats had been trying to impeach him for three years, ever since he was righteously elected. Pelosi has refused to submit the articles of impeachment immediately unless another clown show, like the one House Democrats had in the House, was conducted in the Senate, with more witnesses spewing rumors, hearsay, negative propaganda, and partisan rhetoric expressing their hate and unjustifiably accusing Donald Trump of crimes. House Democrats based their impeachment only on the president's "abuse of power" and "obstructing Congress," neither of which absolutely is a case of high crimes and misdemeanors. In a poor theatrical display on TV, House Democrats dressed in dark apparel as if they were going to a funeral, and somberly, many of them gave speeches saying how regrettable and sad it was that they were to vote for the impeachment of President Trump. But in reality, several House Democrats were seen dining, celebrating the impeachment. And Muslim congresswoman Rashida Tlaib was seen grinning and gleeful on TV just before voting to impeach President Trump.

House Speaker Nancy Pelosi delayed passing the articles of impeachment to the Senate because they would have been promptly rejected and dismissed. Senate majority leader Mitch McConnell refused to conduct a clown show as demanded by the House, threatening to dismiss the charges. Never before has the House of Representatives conducted such a parade of clowns to accuse a president of various crimes, which were tossed one day, with new ones being alleged the next day, with no evidence ever provided that such crimes had been committed. Instead, the so-called evidence was based on hearsay, rumors, and gossip.

How sweet was God's intervention! God was the One who interfered in the 2016 election amid all the corruption and plots against Donald Trump. The winning brilliance of President Trump and his staff, with the help of angels, since blessed our country.

David A. Herrera

The Pontifical Biblical Commission at the
Vatican Raises Concerns about Homosexuality

Members of the Vatican's Pontifical Biblical Commission wrote a study on ancient biblical theology that they claim offers Catholic theologians and catechists a new look at progressive views of humankind today and contrasts them with antiquated theology and pontification.

"Composed of four chapters, the study commissioned by Pope Francis and called *What Is Man? An Itinerary of Biblical Anthropology* deals with themes such as man created by God; man in relation to the rest of creation; the relational reality of anthropology (focusing on spousal, parental/filial and fraternal relationships); and the salvific plan of God for humankind."[24]

Particularly noted is chapter 3 of the three-hundred-page study, which is an examination of the morality of homosexual relationships, which, in fact, indicates a heretical progressive movement toward the acceptance of homosexual acts. This means there are modern progressives who think biblical scripture has been interpreted as archaic, historically conditioned pontification that requires reevaluation, with modern interpretations and reforms to present homosexual unions as legitimate conditions of humanity and thereby lead to their acceptance. Those in the Vatican who espouse such things are nothing more than progressive voices of heresy. Lobbyists insinuate that homosexual relationships should not be condemned by biblical scripture because homosexual unions are not clearly or adequately understood as being a worthy expression of human beings, just as ancient people never understood the value of science as we do today.

The *New Catholic Register* further states that progressives in the Vatican conclude, "The Bible says little or nothing about this type of erotic relationship, which is therefore not condemned, because it is often unduly confused with other aberrant sexual behaviors. It therefore seems necessary to examine the passages of Sacred Scripture in which

---

[24] Edward Pentin, "Pontifical Biblical Commission Asks, 'What Is Man?,'" *National Catholic Register*, December 19, 2019, https://www.ncregister.com/blog/edward-pentin/pontifical-biblical-commission-asks-what-is-man.

94

the problem of homosexuality is discussed, in particular those in which it is denounced and blamed."

(In other words, a reevaluation is in order to achieve a more "adequate understanding" of human nature after two thousand years, because homosexuality today is a political hot potato, giving light to the whims of the times. That is, homosexuality needs to be reconsidered and better understood as a value-added and legitimate expression of humanity. Since the Bible says nothing about eroticism being about lust between two men or sexual lust between two women, the study states that it must be allowed and OK as Christ-blessed behavior, right? (Au contraire, my friend.)

It should be noted that the Bible should *never* be revised to please lustful sexual perverts and accommodate their personal temporal whims. The Bible can never be changed. The standard historical biblical interpretations include morals that have stood the test of time and remained in effect for more than two thousand years. The Bible cannot and must not be changed just to please the homosexual mafia and politicians from any country who wish to promote it to win elections. High-level clergy in the Vatican fond of their sexual lusts and desires should be ashamed for even considering or suggesting acceptance of homosexuality as a moral or political right.

Who all is behind this besides homosexual bishops, homosexual cardinals, and their cronies in Rome? Answer: John Podesta of the DNC, billionaire George Soros, Barack Obama, Joe Biden, and Hillary Clinton. The war is continuing. The Catholic Church in the United States has been infiltrated by homosexuals since the 1960s. This is one of the principal sins of Obama, Podesta, Soros, Biden, Hillary Clinton, and others who tried to bribe the members of the Vatican to change the Catholic doctrine and issue a decree to all Catholics that homosexuality is a moral human right and no longer a sin. They claim it's a moral human right, completely aligned with the US Democrats' new political morality used to justify homosexuality. European homosexuals have also infiltrated the Catholic Church for centuries, promoting homosexuals to high-level positions, with these people also having infiltrated the Vatican. There is a good video presentation entitled *The Vortex—the Homosexual Papacy?* on YouTube about homosexuality in the Vatican, found at https://www.youtube.com/watch?v=5vQTtEZenIw&feature=youtu.be.

The infiltration of homosexuals into the Vatican and into dioceses in Western countries that has occurred since the 1960s. Homosexual bishops, cardinals, and priests have been recruited by and ordained in the Catholic Church to promote the homosexual union as a normal one and to promote homosexual behavior as normal behavior, when in reality these homosexual clergy are all dirty perverts trying to satisfy their own needs.

The article goes on to say:

> We do not find in the narrative tradition of the Bible indications concerning homosexual practices, either as behaviors to be faulted or as attitudes tolerated or welcomed" (i.e., nothing was found in the Bible that says homosexuality is to be criticized as perverted or disordered behavior, nor as accepted or favored; that homosexual practices are not viewed as immoral or sinful). This is a heretic interpretation of the Bible designed to lead Catholic activists to promote homosexuality, pedophilia, perversion as a human right, and argue for same-sex marriage, that is now supported by the Catholic Church. These modern studies as written in this document, have not been incorporated into canonical law in the Catholic catechism. These studies on *What Is Man*, by the Pontifical Biblical Commission at the Vatican[,] only arouse controversy about existing Catholic doctrine. They entice false Catholics like Nancy Pelosi to indicate that there is controversy within the Catholic Church on morality she decides to pick and obey, like abortion, as a Catholic. Nancy Pelosi does not speak for the Catholic Church. She cannot pick and choose morality. ...
>
> In conclusion, our exegetical examination of the texts of the Old and of the New Testaments has brought to

light elements that must be considered for an evaluation
of homosexuality in its ethical implications.

That is, the author is considering changing the practices of
homosexuality, traditionally considered to be immoral and sinful, so
they become more acceptable to the modern world as moral behavior
permitted by God as an "ethical value." In other words, let's revise
biblical scriptures on homosexuality to keep up with the whims of the
modern times because such behavior was not faulted in antiquity—and
therefore it shouldn't be condemned in modern times. Additionally,
morals that applied in antiquity don't apply today. That's the kind of
garbage that is written in *What Is Man?*

Certain formulations of biblical authors, as well as the disciplinary
directives of Leviticus, require an intelligent interpretation that
safeguards the values that the sacred text intends to promote, thus
avoiding repetition to the letter that carries with it cultural traits of
that time. The contribution provided by science, together with the
reflections of theologians and moralists, will be indispensable for an
adequate exposition of the problem that is only sketched out in this
document. In addition, pastoral care will be required, particularly
with regard to individual persons, in order to realize the service to the
good that the church has to assume in its mission for humankind (i.e.,
homosexuality has to be reevaluated and the views about it possibly
changed because the Bible is antiquated and the old morality needs to be
reconsidered, as those who wrote parts of the Bible had antiquated ideas
and a lack of understanding of human nature. Our culture is different
now, so the morals of the old culture may not apply today. Therefore,
we must change Catholic doctrine).

In conclusion, what the Pontifical Biblical Commission has done is
to have written a review of Catholic ecumenical liturgy to reevaluate the
morality of homosexuality within a historical and cultural perspective
to determine if it can be made moral or be considered as moral today, in
light of the antiquated culture of the Bible compared to the culture and
personal whims of people today. That is, the PBC seeks to reevaluate
homosexuality to see if it benefits and serves humans today, as compared
to the Bible's view on homosexuality as immoral, and wonders if

Catholic doctrine should be amended or edited to promote acceptance of homosexuality as being for the good of humankind and the mission of the Catholic Church.

What Is Man? is a critique on scripture from the Bible claiming that the Bible is antiquated and saying that morality must change to meet the needs of human beings who lust after members of the same sex. Who are the people behind this conspiracy? They are as follows:

- socialists who give the pope political advice
- Vatican contractors, politicians, and associates who bribe corrupt members of the Vatican
- longtime homosexuals in the Vatican who seek to promote changes to Catholic doctrine as it relates to homosexuality
- homosexuals who infiltrated the Catholic Church and became high-ranking clergy
- billionaire George Soros, who wants to ruin Europe and destroy the Catholic Church
- members of the US Democratic Party who want the morals of the church to be modified to align with their progressivism in order to morally justify their political agenda
- corrupt contractors who do business with the Vatican.

Pope Francis's vision of history is distorted. We all see good and evil happening in the world repeatedly, today and throughout history. But Pope Francis forgets that God gave us free will and, given that God works in mysterious ways, that God has a say in what goes on. Evil does not need to be induced or injected into history to demonstrate brave people of faith fighting evil. God is a Universal Soldier who guides us to stand up and fight evil. People throughout history were evil because of free will, not because God wanted evil to happen. Liturgy should remain unchanged through time and should never be reformed just to suit the whims of the times, personal desires, or the lusts of today's culture. Liturgy should not be changed to contradict biblical scripture for the purpose of picking and choosing prophets and martyrs throughout history to exemplify good and evil.

In an article published by in the Catholic newspaper the *Remnant*, we read the following:

As Pope Francis's Popularity among Practicing Catholics Falls to New Lows, RTV Releases a New Year's Resolution Video, Vowing to Resist Him

As Pope Francis's popularity continues to plummet among faithful Catholics, he has managed to maintain popularity with one demographic: pro-abortion "Catholic" Democrats. A Pew Research poll from last year revealed that the share of Catholics who have a favorable view of the pontiff is 22 points higher among Democrats than among Republicans.[25]

On December 20, 2019, a few days before Christmas, Francis invited UN Secretary-General António Guterres to the Vatican for a joint press conference to talk about migration, climate change, disarmament, and the implementation of the UN's Sustainable Development Goals—all socialist liberal agendas. Abortion was one of the Sustainable Development Goals to be discussed with Pope Francis. Pope Francis wants one world government, leading to the surrender of freedom and sovereignty to international interests.

This is more indication that George Soros's money is influencing the Vatican and the pope to distort Catholic doctrine and to create the new "Chrislam" religion so as to achieve political globalism and world peace for humanity.

---

[25] Michael J. Matt, "The U.N.–Pope: World's Catholics Resolve to Resist Francis in 2020," the *Remnant*, December 30, 2019, https://remnantnewspaper.com/web/index.php/articles/item/4718-the-u-n-shepherd-pope-s-popularity-plummets.

In what many see as an effort to normalize homosexuality in the Catholic Church, the Vatican has released a new book that reduces the sin of Sodom to "a lack of hospitality."[26]

There were a lot of changes in 2019 in the Roman Catholic Church, wrought by the Vatican, with perhaps the biggest two changes being the creation by Pope Francis of the one world religion of Chrislam and the massive preparation to welcome the LGBTQ+P movement into the church. The Vatican even helped fund the Elton John biopic *Rocketman*, complete with the first-ever gay male sex scene in a major Hollywood film. But in order to fully welcome the LGBTQ+P community into the Roman Catholic Church, the biblical account of Sodom and Gomorrah needs to be purged of its convicting truth of the homosexual lifestyle. The Vatican has done exactly that with a release of its document *What Is Man? An Itinerary of Biblical Anthropology*.

The Pontifical Biblical Commission (PBC) of the Vatican succumbed to corruption by George Soros, Barack Obama, John Podesta, Hillary Clinton, Tim Kaine, Joe Biden, and the Vatican's homosexual cronies to support their document *What Is Man? An Itinerary of Biblical Anthropology*, which is an analysis of biblical history regarding homosexuality whose purpose is to consider legitimizing it as acceptable and "blessed behavior" in today's culture, compared to the "anthropological culture" of the past, when the scriptures regarding homosexuality in the Old Testament were written. The authors of *What Is Man?* appear to be biblical history revisionists.

Billionaire Soros, high-level US politicians, and homosexuals in the United States and Europe have been bribing Pope Francis and other members of the Vatican who want to legitimize same-sex marriage. Then they will try to change the Catholic Church's views on abortion. Pope Francis already wants to form a one world religion; he's the first pope to do this. He justifies "Chrislam" in the name of peace and humanity in the world, but never mentions what Jesus Christ

---

[26] Geoffrey Grider, "Pontifical Biblical Commission in the Vatican Publishes New Book Saying that the Sin of Sodom Was a 'Lack of Hospitality' and Not Homosexuality," *Now the End Times*, December 31, 2019, https://www.nowtheendbegins.com/pontifical-biblical-commission-vatican-publishes-new-book-saying-sin-of-sodom-lack-of-hospitality-not-homosexuality/.

would think of the article's content, the revision of history, and or the legitimizing of same-sex marriage. One of the main problems of the Catholic Church is that it has been infiltrated by homosexuals who, over the course of decades, have become priests, bishops, and cardinals who are, together with homosexual communities everywhere, trying to legitimize LGBTQ+P (the *P* stands for "pedophilia"). These heretics all have to be stopped.

Pope Francis opposes Christian evangelists, such as Mormons. Mormons believe in God the Father, Jesus Christ as Savior, and the Holy Spirit as traditionalist Catholics do; Mormonism is not a fake religion. The effect of what the pope is doing is already meeting with resistance among Catholics. The one world religion is being opposed by evangelical Christians in the United States who believe in the Bible literally, not Catholic doctrine revising the Bible to fit the whims of homosexuals, along with their lusts and desires. If the Catholic Church legitimizes homosexuality and same-sex marriage, then it will be split into progressive and traditional Catholics, just as is happening today in the Methodist Church.

With the election of Donald Trump, the new progressive morality in the United States failed to legitimize homosexuality as moral conduct. But George Soros's money continues to successfully bribe homosexual members of the Vatican and Pope Francis. Unbeknown to the Vatican and Pope Francis are three possible predictable events:

1. Based on the continued trend of homosexual corruption in the Vatican, and based on the bad advice the pope is getting from socialists and homosexuals, the Catholic Church on some continents may, in the near future, allow same-sex marriages.

2. If homosexuality or same-sex marriage is declared legitimately moral by the Catholic Church, then the church will lose millions of members and billions of dollars because the change to Catholic doctrine on homosexuality could bring about the destruction of the Catholic Church, which has been a longtime goal of George Soros. Muslims throughout the world would rejoice.

3. The orthodox conservative Catholic Church will fight to replace members of the Vatican and the pope based on blasphemy charges, alleged violations of scripture, and their concocted gift of morality to homosexuals in exchange for Soros's money. The Catholic Church will be split up, one half being orthodox Catholics and the other half being progressive Catholics.

Social Engineering of the Catholic Church and Other Christian Denominations

The Catholic Church and other Christian churches are being social engineered by special interest groups and politicians whose sole purpose is the attainment of power and promotion of their socialist or liberal agendas. Morality is being redefined in churches by specific phony Christian evangelists, by the homosexual mafia, by homosexual lobbies, by abortion lobbies, and by politicians labeling every agenda they are promoting as moral and of benefit to humanity. These politicians tend to be hypocrites and socialists who do the following:

- promote equal rights for all except for themselves, who think they deserve more rights than the everyday individual;
- label intolerance as immoral, except for the social-engineered issues for which they promote tolerance so they can add these to their personal agendas;
- use social justice as an excuse to enforce their tyrannical laws;
- label racism and discrimination as immoral in order to gain support of the citizenry to win elections;
- label those who oppose immigration as racists and Islamophobes in order to gain political power from the massive number of immigrants entering the United States through open borders;
- label rich people as greedy, racist, immoral, and oppressive of the poor in order to gain political power from the poor, freeloaders, lazy people, and disenfranchised citizens;

- enrich themselves—even though they label the rich as greedy and oppressive—through corruption and their power to become very wealthy. They will justify their wealth as well deserved, as they will claim that, because of their super-beneficial government laws and tyrannical agenda, they rightfully deserve high compensation because they know better than the individual what is best for them and have earned it;
- label same-sex marriage as a moral and humane right for all;
- reinterpret and revise the Bible to reject homosexuality as a sin. They will view all passages in the Bible as archaic and coming from an anthropological time and outdated culture that is too far gone and must therefore be revised to righteously apply to today's culture, whims, lusts, and desires, which should be tolerated, humanely permitted, and socially justified.

These politicians are the most intolerant people of all because they fear the opposition to their attainment of power and, like Attila the Hun, they want to weaken, defame, and destroy anything that stands in their way.

Bartholomew Holzhauser (1613–1658) was a German priest and the founder of the Bartholomewites, also known as the United Order, sometimes called Communists, later called the Apostolic Order of Secular Priests. He was a visionary who made the following prediction:

> The fifth period of the Church, which began circa 1520, will end with the arrival of the holy Pope and of the powerful Monarch who is called "Help from God" because he will restore everything. The fifth period is one of affliction, desolation, humiliation, and poverty for the Church. ... These are the evil times, a century full of dangers and calamities. Heresy is everywhere, and the followers of heresy are in power almost everywhere. But God will permit a great evil against His Church:
>
> Heretics and tyrants will come suddenly and unexpectedly; they will break into the Church. They

will enter Italy and lay Rome waste; they will burn down churches and destroy everything.

The homosexuals in the Vatican and their cronies in Europe and the United States are raising concerns about old, outdated ideas on homosexuality and are revising biblical history to make scripture mean what they want it to mean in order to social engineer the Catholic Church and its brand of morality. Evangelist homosexual special interest groups are also reinterpreting morality in the Bible to promote homosexuality as a moral human right, a behavior that should be tolerated by all because progressives label people opposed to it as homophobes who are motivated by hate, which is entirely false. Just thinking, believing, or saying that homosexuality is wrong is something that leftists label as homophobic. Traditional Christians are intentionally accused of hate and of oppressing homosexuals. Nothing could be further from the truth. Just claiming one's First Amendment right by expressing one's personal opinion that homosexuality is a sin is not hatred or oppression. Evangelizing the Gospel and expressing that same-sex marriage is a sin is neither hatred nor oppression. Homosexuals cover themselves with the same civil rights blanket as blacks, claiming they have endured discrimination and oppression for their sick, depraved, disgusting homosexual acts as blacks were discriminated against when they were slaves or lived under Jim Crow laws. Really? These promoters of homosexuality must think people are stupid.

As the homosexual lobby promotes homosexuality in public schools and universities, they have to use their toolbox of new morality tools, such as tolerance, along with their revision of history; rejection of outdated biblical scripture; human rights; rejection of racism, human suffering, and being oppressed victims of unbearable harm; "toxic masculinity"; and income inequality. Usually, socialists become corrupt because they have to do the following:

- Hire people who will enforce tyrannical laws that always lead to oppression.

- Confiscate the wealth of whomever they want, taking as much as they want. They steal from rich Paul to give to lazy freeloader Freddy and to all immigrants coming into the United States from all over the world seeking to claim their "free stuff" from these socialist idiots.
- Legalize drugs so young people can be happy, euphoric, contented, and easily controlled; they will be addicted to drugs and big government.
- Legalize prostitution, pornography, and drugs so young people can be happy and contented, in order to satisfy and easily control people by satisfying their lusts.

If the United States ever becomes socialist, socialist politicians will pass tyrannical laws that will eliminate the tax-exempt status of traditional Christian churches for a variety of reasons, among them being for discriminating against homosexuals, their policies against same-sex marriages, their antiabortion views, and their refusal to hire homosexuals as church parish leaders and leaders of events involving children.

The socialist political agenda will mandate crusades against people who they claim victimize the poor; against immigrants, people of color, and homosexuals; and against people who oppose climate change, green energy, and government-funded health care for all—and this crusade is extended globally. Who wins? It's a win for freeloaders, lazy people, dope addicts, sick depraved homosexuals, the massive number of poor immigrants, low-IQ individuals, and pedophiles. A socialist US government will provide a pacifier to the naive suckers and lazy freeloaders to satisfy their economic baby-bottle-milk needs and their temporal lust and whims, while the socialist government wins by building its phony propaganda machine and exercising its power. On the other hand, rich white people, Christians, freedom-loving Americans, and American patriots favoring the Constitution will lose and become victims of oppression as the socialist government attempts to weaken, stifle, or destroy those who speak out in support of traditional morality and freedom by enforcing its tyrannical laws with its law enforcement, with its military, or with mercenary boots on the ground.

Just as colonists left the countries of Europe to gain freedom from tyranny, Americans once again will be oppressed by a creeping tyrannical socialist government within the United States imposing taxes, restricting gun laws, implementing open border immigration laws, creating sanctuary cities, and depriving Americans of their constitutional freedoms with tyrannical laws. Americans must and will revolt against tyranny in another revolutionary war.

Bartholomew Holzhauser predicted and warned of calamity, poverty, heresy, and corruption for the church in the period beginning in 1520. Today we are faced with heresy from homosexuals who have infiltrated the Catholic and Protestant Churches. International billionaires and European elite organizations would like to see a one world government and a one world religion, and the Bible and traditional Christianity destroyed to be replaced by a new world morality by revising church history and providing a brand-new interpretation of biblical scriptures to fit their social changes and political dogma. The new trend in social evolution would be to interpret biblical doctrine so that it fits with their worldly view and suits their temporal whims. The start of this effort has already begun. The facts are these:

- Homosexuals in the Vatican have been supporting lobbyist changes to Catholic doctrine, particularly on issues of homosexuality, abortion, and immigration. These changes must be justified and discussed in Vatican Council meetings. It is possible that Pope Francis's Pontifical Biblical Commission may raise new concerns and issues to be discussed in a future Vatican Council meeting that would make changes to Catholic doctrine.

- Corrupt members of the Vatican have been suspected of being bribed by billionaires such as George Soros and by homosexual lobbyists from Belgium, Germany, France, and other European countries, some of whose bishops are homosexuals wanting to change Catholic doctrine.

- Members of the Obama administration, such as DNC chairperson John Podesta under Hillary Clinton, Barack Obama himself,

Joe Biden, Hillary Clinton, and Tim Kaine, in collusion with George Soros and Vatican contractors, lobbied the Vatican and tried to use their influence to urge the Vatican to find ways to change Catholic doctrine on homosexuality and abortion.

- As a result of the US political and homosexual lobbies, a study called *What Is Man? An Itinerary of Biblical Anthropology* was written by the Pontifical Biblical Commission to raise the concern that the concept of homosexuality as a sin is archaic and outdated and that biblical scriptures may need a different interpretation to meet the needs of today's people with their lusts, desires, and whims. In addition, biblical history and culture may have to be revised to justify changing the old, outdated sins of those times so they are no longer considered sins within the culture we have today. The Pontifical Biblical Commission does not condone homosexuality, but it does raise the specter of biblical review and reconsideration for change.

- Pro-homosexual evangelism has already reared its ugly head in the United States, its proponents seeking to reinterpret biblical history and social engineer biblical scripture to allow same-sex marriage. Homosexual proponents claim that homosexuality brings peace and love to humanity.

- The United Methodist Church has already planned to split into a traditional church and one that engages in marrying same-sex couples.

- The Presbyterian Church, the Evangelical Lutheran Church of America, and the Episcopal Church in the United States now allow same-sex marriages.

- Hundreds of Mormons are leaving the Church of Jesus Christ of Latter-day Saints because it is opposed to same-sex marriages.

Liberal politicians in the United States continue to lobby corrupt members of the Vatican to revise biblical history and modify "outdated" biblical scripture to suit the lusts and whims of the times. New progressive religious organizations are also lobbying some Protestant churches to change their views on homosexuality and abortion to see them each as a moral human right. Atheists have an agenda to destroy and stifle religion.

Predictions of Jeanne le Royer in the Eighteenth Century

Jeanne le Royer (1731–1798) of Boulot, Fougeres, Brittany, was a nun among the Sisters of the Nativity. She became famous after predicting the French Revolution. The following predictions are loosely translated from the French. About the church, she predicted the following:

"I see that when the Second Coming of Christ approaches, a bad priest will do much harm to the Church."

Speaking about heresy entering the church in the latter days, she said, "It will be like a fire burning underneath, quietly, and be spread gradually. This is even more serious and dangerous, for the Holy Church will not notice these early fires. ... O God! I see the agitation of the Holy Church, when she will realize, suddenly, the increasing size and number of ungodly souls they have drawn into their party! This heresy extends so far that it appears to include all countries. Never any heresy has been so deadly!"

She also said that Jesus told her, "The first two decades of the century in 2000 will not pass without judgment."

To us, Le Royer's "fires" might be the misconduct of priests, too long overlooked. It has cost the Catholic Church dearly, and we're not just talking in dollars and cents. And, from the viewpoint of the first decades of the twenty-first century, the church has not escaped some harsh judgment.

The social engineering of the church from its Bible-based morality to its revisionist interpretations of the Bible by new progressive Catholics, Protestants, and evangelicals, in favor of the new social-engineered morality, will destroy the traditional Christian church. New progressive churches will enjoy new members. In the Vatican, if homosexuality is reinterpreted, moving from a sinful act to a non-sinful act of kindness and love between two people, with the blessings of most Christian churches, then those Christian churches will begin the promotion of an evil morality. Liberal politics will be embraced in the churches as being perfectly aligned with humanitarianism and moral compassion for humankind. The decline of the Christian church follows. Root causes of the decline of the church are:

- allowing immigration in the name of kindness, hospitality, charity, racial respect, tolerance, and "morality" without regard to economic chaos, economic suffering, immigrants with records of horrific crimes entering the United States, social conflicts, a lack of patriotism, increases in crime, disregard for the safety of citizens, or racial conflict;
- allowing same-sex and transgender marriages and weddings in progressive churches; and
- stifling offensive speech or hate speech against any member of the LGBT community.

Among my predictions are that the unrepentant LGBT crowd, including transgender people and cross-dressers, will dominate progressive churches. Traditional Christians will abandon progressive churches and establish a traditional Christian church. Homosexuality in the church will lead to increased pedophilia in progressive churches and public schools. Sexual behavior once viewed as sinful, depraved, and immoral will be viewed as a moral standard and no longer be considered a sin. Cities such as San Francisco, Hollywood, Las Vegas, and New York will become centers and showcases of the type of behavior prevalent in Sodom and Gomorrah in biblical times. Hollywood will produce movies with actors engaging in homosexual acts and will make porn available in homes. Homosexual lobbying organizations will introduce homosexual studies and education into public schools as part of the required curriculum. Sexual depravity may worsen to include the acceptance of incest.

All this sick, evil corruption will be extremely difficult to prevent or stop because leaders of nations in their New World Order, together with their bought-off corrupt church leaders, will have revised biblical interpretations of morality to allow sexual deviants to influence their followers. The sick, depraved sexual deviants, together with lost souls using legalized drugs, will produce creeping immorality, including the worst kind of workers in industry, the worst kind of criminals, the worst kind of child-care employees, the worst kind of schools, and the worst kind of churches, and will result in a lack of incentive for law enforcement officers to enforce laws against sexual misconduct and sexual abuse. No one knows what diseases could be produced from the new liberal morality.

History repeats itself as, in its last days, the Roman Empire destroyed itself from within. Foreigners invaded the Roman Empire from parts of Europe, Asia, and Africa, and from Muslim countries, and the Roman military did little or nothing to defend Rome and its depravity and immoral people. It was said that Nero played the violin while Rome burned. The favorite pastime of the Romans was sponsored by the political leaders of Rome, who fed Christians to the lions in a sports arena for everyone's entertainment. The Romans really knew how to wage war on Christianity. In the last days of the Roman Empire, the leaders of the Roman government viewed Christians as opposing their rule and their depraved Roman culture. Christians were crucified and a spectacle was made of their torment, suffering, and deaths. Jesus Christ was crucified in Jerusalem under Roman rule.

The real Bible is now misinterpreted by leftists to suit the political needs and social whims of the contemporary people. Leftists may one day replace the old traditional Bible with a new revised version with new biblical interpretations containing new morality, reprinting it as the "New Bible." Only evil corrupt church leaders lobbied by LGBT organizations and leftist politicians will be responsible for such biblical history revisionism and new morality as traditional Christians are silenced and ostracized and their numbers diminished. Frequent conflicts will occur between traditional Christians and progressive phony Christians.

House Democrat Alexandria Ocasio-Cortez falsely said that Jesus was a refugee. Leftists say that if Jesus were alive today, he would be a socialist. Leftists and homosexuals allege that Jesus Christ was a homosexual and that same-sex marriages should be blessed by the clergy. Such blasphemous allegations are a joy to the LGBT community and to the secular leftists who support them. Elton John, a homosexual singer and actor, claimed that Jesus was a homosexual. Netflix put out a movie worldwide portraying Jesus as a homosexual. Peter Buttigieg, a homosexual Democratic candidate for president in 2020 who is married to another man, justifies same-sex marriage as love that God would approve of between two humans, saying that God is not just for straight people. This insinuates that same-sex marriage is not a sin. What sins will be left to confess? Perhaps following the agenda of liberal and socialist politicians will shed light on what the new sins defined by the Left may be:

- being anti-immigration—a sin
- being inhospitable to strangers—a sin
- being intolerant; depending on what you're intolerant about—a sin
- being homophobic—a sin
- displaying toxic masculinity—a sin
- being misogynous—a sin
- being racist—a sin.

Leftists will label all comments they disagree with as "hate speech," merely because of people's expressing personal opinions that are not politically correct, that leftists are offended by, or that fragile leftists are hurt by. Leftists will consider hate speech they disagree with as immoral and sinful, something to be remedied by addressing the so-called offenders with censure, ridicule, and even violence. Giving speeches about traditional Christianity will probably be forbidden or met with violence because the *truth* will conflict with liberal/socialist dogma and disagree with new church doctrine. The new church doctrine will be nothing other than political progressivism. Just as the Democratic liberals own the liberal biased fake news media, they will also own the progressive fake church and the pulpits from which the fake news media and the fake church will preach morality to provide favorable propaganda to the socialist or liberal government.

In Nancy Pelosi's meetings with President Trump, each time President Trump berated her, she went on TV afterward and acted like a pious, sanctimonious politician who said to reporters she would pray for President Trump. In reality, Nancy Pelosi is a religious hypocrite, a sinful, phony Catholic who exploits religion for politics' sake as a weapon to destroy a person, elevate progressivism, and attack policies she doesn't agree with. She should be excommunicated by the Catholic Church for her enthusiastic support of abortion.

The Hypocritical Moral Superiority of Chuck Schumer and Nancy Pelosi—Why They Cry

In the United States, liberal sanctimonious Democrats such as Nancy Pelosi claim that building the wall is *immoral*, yet Pelosi never mentions that the murder of Americans and the rape of American women committed by illegal aliens is immoral. Nancy Pelosi and Chuck Schumer have never addressed how US citizens can be made secure from illegal aliens who kill or harm Americans. That is, Democrats don't care about the safety of Americans. Schumer and Pelosi don't pass laws to prevent harm to US citizens perpetrated by illegal aliens. On the contrary, Democratic politicians in several states have adopted "sanctuary cities" or have made themselves "sanctuary states," which protect illegal aliens released from jails and prisons who have committed heinous crimes. Does that make any sense?

Hypocrite Senator Chuck Schumer never cried about children separated from their families who were kept in cages under the Obama administration while he was a senator, yet under the Trump administration, Senator Chuck Schumer would burst into tears on TV about illegal alien children separated by ICE from their families and being kept in cages. But no tears are shed by "Crying" Schumer when an illegal alien kills a police officer who will be forever separated from his wife and kids. Crying Schumer does not shed a tear when MS-13 gang members attack and kill young Americans here in the United States, or when an illegal alien kills a family while driving under the influence of drugs or alcohol, or when American youths die from ingesting illegal drugs smuggled by Mexican cartels across the southern border. Liberal hate-Trump newscaster Rachel Maddow is the same kind of crying fool as Chuck Schumer on TV.

Sanctimonious Buttigieg, Obama, and Biden Redefine Gay Marriage Morality

Buttigieg is just another progressive politician who came out of the closet and declared himself an avowed homosexual. Buttigieg, who is married to another man, preaches Christian progressivism. Because he is homosexual, he justifies his homosexual behavior and same-sex marriage by his own self-defined political leftist morality: that homosexuality is "normal behavior," a "humanitarian right," and "moral." In actuality, the opposite is true. Homosexuality has historically and traditionally been seen as abnormal behavior. It's perversion, not dignified behavior. It is an unnatural act, and it is immoral behavior as mentioned in several places in the Bible. Buttigieg, like Barack Obama and Joe Biden, is in favor of same-sex marriage, not as a freaky or unnatural event, but as a dignified, blessed, normal, and celebrated event.

The Intolerance of the Left

As culture changes, old customs and traditions are insidiously destroyed by the new progressive politicians and their supporters by defining hate and intolerance in ways that align with their own partisan beliefs and values. They do not let Christianity or the Bible get in the way as they try to ignore it, marginalize it, destroy it, and defame it, and redefine and mold its morality and worth into their own new morality, which aligns with their lifestyle, hedonism, and politics. Racism is always used as an argument to support the progressives' ideas of intolerance. Then anyone who disagrees with them, by their own liberal manufactured word definitions, is labeled as intolerant. That is how they censure any conservative free speech they don't like on college campuses or on social media. The Left uses intolerance as a social engineering tool to reject long-held family customs and traditions that they do not tolerate. For example, homosexuals who come out of the closet often turn away from the Bible and accuse straight people of being intolerant of their depraved, abnormal, psychotic, immoral behavior. But homosexuals go beyond just demonizing or complaining about intolerance and discrimination; they also promote their homosexual lifestyle to innocent kids in an attempt to convert them and teach them to tolerate the queer lifestyle as just another "alternative" lifestyle from which to choose. And these sick people are pedophiles who urgently promote the introduction of homosexuality and protection of homosexuals in the classroom for kids as young as grade school age.

6

THE WAR ON CHRISTIANITY

The War on Christianity in the United States by Democratic Politicians and Progressive Christians

Democrats have been waging a war against Christianity from the early 1960s to the present. It began on June 25, 1962, when the Supreme Court took prayer out of schools, declaring prayers unconstitutional in the landmark case *Engel v. Vitale* in New York. The court ruled on the side of Engel, saying that under the Establishment Clause of the First Amendment, "it is not the business of government to mandate official prayers for any group of the American people to recite as a part of a religious program carried on by government." Although it did not rule to ban prayer in schools, it did rule that prayers were not to be sponsored in schools by teachers. But many schools interpreted the ruling to mean that even voluntary prayers or school speeches personally written by students, not teachers, were illegal; this is a clear violation of the right to free speech for all students granted by the First Amendment to our Constitution. The ruling was supported by Muslims and Jews, claiming they were not Christians and therefore should not have to say Christian prayers. Since the United States was founded on Christianity, not Islam or Judaism, this was the reason Christian prayers were justified in the early days of the nation. The result of the ruling was that no prayers from specific religions were required to be school-sponsored, as was the preference under Christianity. That is, public schools could no longer sponsor prayer from any religion, including Christianity.

Ironically, today Muslim immigrants and their supporting organizations, such as CAIR (Council on American-Islamic Relations), demand school-sponsored Muslim prayers in some public schools in the United States. This is a clear violation of the Supreme Court ruling about school administrators and teachers doing this. Charter schools are similar to public schools in that they offer a free education to all students and are publicly funded. They are funded by tax dollars from the state and federal government, similar to how public schools receive their funding. The specific amount of this funding is based on the number of students who attend the school, but these funds are supplemented by other income sources such as donations and grants. Even charter schools are not permitted to teach religious instruction, but they may teach about religion from a secular perspective, that is, without bias for one or another religion. And though charter schools must be neutral with respect to religion, they are allowed to teach civic values.

Some states have private schools funded by vouchers. Vouchers are taxpayer-funded government subsidies for private schools and vendors, with no accountability for results. Vouchers reduce fair access to educational opportunity, weaken rights for students with disabilities, and expose taxpayers to fraud. Only district and charter schools can deliver quality school choice with transparency and accountability in the use of public dollars.[1]

Prayers have the power to create personal religious beliefs that help instill certain values such as humility and discipline in students. Prayers instills ethical values in schoolchildren. Prayers in school encourage students to believe in a moral value system to follow in school. Religious education emphasizes mutual respect among students regardless of their beliefs, race, or social status. But since religion was taken out of the classroom, liberals who have taken over schools as administrators and teachers use "political morality" to teach students to respect one another without religion, that is,, without God involved.

---

[1] Michelle Smith and Bob Popinski, "Act Now for Our Future," Raise Your Hand Texas, https://www.raiseyourhandtexas.org/wp-content/uploads/2018/10/02_ActNow_2019-legislative_one-pager_vouchers.pdf.

In 1980, the US Supreme Court struck down a Kentucky statute that had mandated every classroom in public schools to have the Ten Commandments posted on their walls. Again, liberals, Muslims, and atheists say that this is promoting Christianity in schools, and this is not allowed. It would offend Muslims, Jews, and people of other religions. These reforms to our religious culture and educational institutions were made at the level of the federal government to appease or accommodate atheists and the growing number of diverse non-Christian religious immigrants entering the United States.

The erosion of Christian culture in public schools became far worse. Christian customs and traditions, such as singing Christmas carols, staging Christmas plays, and saying prayers before lunch in school cafeterias, were replaced with problematic secular political morality and activism. For example, teachers indoctrinate kids on the new artificial leftist political morality, which teaches students to be understanding and tolerant of Islam without knowing anything about oppressive sharia law toward women, radical Islam, or homosexuality. Teachers would never teach kids that sharia law is oppressive toward women or that the jihad as mentioned in the Koran is what has justified the genocide and conquest of non-Muslims across the world throughout history.

Some schools in California are sponsoring and promoting homosexuality to pre–high school kids in the name of social tolerance, protection, antidiscrimination, and equal rights, issues that are driven by special interest gay lobbyists trying to inject institutional reform into our public schools again as part of a leftist political agenda. So, the question arises, what is good for the United States, indoctrinating kids by promoting a leftist-biased political agenda, by promoting neutrality, or by promoting a conservative agenda that adheres to biblical scripture and patriotism? My answer is that it's much better to indoctrinate kids to love God, their families, and their country with examples from US history of how the United States is great, rather than to indoctrinate kids by saying they each have the choice to be either a boy or a girl and by accustoming them to gender neutrality, depraved homosexual behavior, activism that promotes the hate or disrespect of the United States, and political protests, or indoctrinating them to ignore God or keep God out of their lives.

It should be considered to make Christian sanctuary schools in some states free from government reform, interference, or tyranny. Sanctuary schools would be approved by parents who support school prayer and the teaching of Christianity as part of an individual's civil rights. Just as some counties or states declare sanctuary cities to protect heinous criminals released from jails or prisons into neighborhoods, or sanctuary gun cities or counties to protect guns from being confiscated, individual schools can declare themselves Christian sanctuary schools that would be protected by local laws from big government reforms. Non-Christians can choose to attend, but they would be required to participate in Christian prayers and activities. If atheists and Muslims refuse to participate in such things, they should just go to another school of their choice and stop forcing their ungodliness or their religion on Christians.

Dark Agenda by David Horowitz explains how the Left is trying to weaken, destroy, silence, and/or reform Christianity.

In April 2008, then senator Obama was caught on tape at a fundraiser in San Francisco stating that the blame for the loss of jobs in the last twenty-five years in the United States falls upon the Bush and Clinton administrations Obama claimed: "And it's not surprising then they get bitter, they cling to guns or religion or antipathy to people who aren't like them, or anti-immigrant sentiment, or anti-trade sentiment, as a way to explain their frustrations."[2]

In 2012, at the Democratic National Convention, Democrats actually removed God from the following statement: "We need a government that stands up for the hopes, values and interests of working people, and gives everyone willing to work hard the chance to make the most of their God-given potential."[3]

---

[2] Ben Smith, "Obama on Small-Town Pa.: Clinging to Religion, Guns, Xenophobia," *Politico*, April 11, 2008, https://www.politico.com/blogs/ben-smith/2008/04/obama-on-small-town-pa-clinging-to-religion-guns-xenophobia-007737.
[3] Ben Shapiro, "6 Times Democrats Demonstrated Their Hatred of the Bible," Breitbart, May 6, 2014, https://www.breitbart.com/politics/2014/05/06/6-times-democrats-demonstrated-their-hatred-of-the-bible/.

DNC Chairman Antonio Villaraigosa violated DNC rules by putting the name of God back in that platform phrase after having requested a voice vote on the issue.

Democrat Barney Frank's hatred of the Bible was exposed when he said that he was looking forward to his husband swearing him in on the Constitution rather than the Bible.

Ironically, sanctimonious Democratic politicians conveniently refer to the Bible for political gain. Rep. Charlie Rangel (D-NY) once stated that opposing increases to federal welfare would send a person to hell. How absurd.

Obama Became the Father of Same-Sex Marriage and a Hero of the LGBT Community

Not until several LGBT groups, several Hollywood celebrities, and the ACLU met with Valerie Jarrett, senior adviser to former president Obama, did Obama flip-flop on same-sex marriage, claiming he had "evolved" on the issue. On May 12, 2012, President Obama announced that he supported same-sex marriage. Former president Obama justified his flip-flop by citing the Bible's golden rule. The homosexual organizations praised Barack Obama for his "moral leadership" in changing his mind so they could proceed on the journey to homosexual marriages. On May 9, 2012, Obama said, "At a certain point, I've just concluded that for me personally, it is important for me to go ahead and affirm that I think same-sex couples should be able to get married."

Congressman Jerrold Nadler (D-NY) and Senator Dianne Feinstein (D-CA) reintroduced the Respect for Marriage Act, the bill that would fully repeal the Defense of Marriage Act (DOMA) passed during Bill Clinton's administration in 1996, particularly Sections 2 and 3, which Nadler and Feinstein claimed discriminated against same-sex couples. In June 26, 2013, the US Supreme Court struck down DOMA. On June 26, 2015, the Supreme Court approved same-sex marriage nationwide.[4]

---

[4] "Winning the Freedom to Marry Nationwide: The Inside Story of a Transformative Campaign," Freedom to Marry, http://www.freedomtomarry. org/pages/how-it-happened.

Democratic members of Congress such as Jerry Nadler support more privileges, which he falsely calls "rights," for homosexuals, transgender people, and cross-dressers.

The homosexual crowd now wants even more legislation to promote homosexuality and force it into public schools. Democrats began by redefining sex and sexual matters, which will result in the unacceptable practice of allowing transgender males to use women's showers and restrooms. Democrats support the practice of male transgenders competing with biologically born females in sports. In most cases, these transgender men win in sports such as track and field, weight lifting, and wrestling, along with other sports requiring strength, which is unfair. Male athletes should have no right to compete with females in any sport meant for females only.

My conclusions for this section are as follows:

- Democratic lawmakers in states such as California are already passing laws to introduce homosexuality to pre–high school youths in public schools to promote the advancement of homosexuality and pedophilia in public schools without the approval of parents.
- Democrats have gone mad redefining gender for men and women, seeking to replace the words *male* and *female*, which have been used since human beings were created.
- Democrats don't care about the rights of females, as they always falsely claim when running for office. If Democrats cared about the rights of women, then why do they approve of transgender men unfairly competing in women's sports?
- Democrats completely ignore the Bible in their redefinition of gender and their support for homosexuality, the transgender lifestyle, and cross-dressing.
- The Biden administration has already promised to reform places of worship to support same-sex marriages under the Equal Protection Clause used to protect homosexuality.

The Biden administration has already proposed reallowing gays and transgender people in the military, having transgender men use restrooms and gyms as females, and allowing transgender men to compete with females in sports.

Given the fact that most American adults do not want religion involved in politics, and given the fact that the Christian population has been significantly decreasing in the United States from 2009 to 2019, we can conclude that support for same-sex marriage, ignoring God and the Bible on the issue, trended upward while, simultaneously, Christianity in the United States trended downward. This is a statistical negative correlation indicating that issues such as homosexual marriage, specified in biblical scriptures as immoral, will be ignored and that God will not be a factor in passing and approving such laws. In other words, as the number of religious Americans decreases and most also choose to ignore religion in their political decisions, immoral decisions will likely be codified into law. Antibiblical laws passed on same-sex marriage were approved specifically under radical leftist president Barack Obama, by a majority of Democrats holding a majority in the House and Senate from 2008 to 2012, and by liberal members of the Supreme Court.[5]

The website Freedom to Marry claims that most Americans feel that religion is losing influence over social issues, but ironically, a majority of Americans want religion out of politics. That is conflicted thinking; the majority of Americans can't have it both ways. Example: If Democrats denigrate Amy Coney Barrett for her Catholic beliefs and oppose her nomination to the Supreme Court, that is destroying a nominee because of her religion, illegal under the Constitution. Yet, the majority want religion out of politics? Good luck with that.[6]

Public opinion on same-sex marriage appears in an article from the Pew Research Center entitled "Attitudes on Same-Sex Marriage." This survey indicates that support for same-sex marriage as of 2019 was 88 percent of self-avowed liberals and 64 percent of conservative

---

[5] "In U.S., Decline of Christianity Continues at Rapid Pace," Pew Research Center, October 17, 2019, https://www.pewforum.org/2019/10/17/in-u-s-decline-of-christianity-continues-at-rapid-pace/.

[6] "Americans Have Positive Views about Religion's Role in Society, but Want It Out of Politics. Most Say Religion Is Losing Influence in American Life," Pew Research Center, November 10, 2019, https://www.pewforum.org/2019/11/15/americans-have-positive-views-about-religions-role-in-society-but-want-it-out-of-politics/.

and moderate Democrats. Fewer than 36 percent of conservative Republicans support same-sex marriage, while 59 percent of moderate and liberal Republicans support same-sex marriage. Conclusion: US culture has changed in the first twenty years of the twenty-first century regarding the permitting of homosexual marriages, corresponding with a decline in religious beliefs. That is not a good culture change. Most Republicans are just as guilty as Democrats of this culture change, which conflicts with several verses in the Holy Bible. Worst of all, liberals make no mention of homosexuality conflicting with the Koran and the punishment that awaits homosexual men in Muslim countries.[7]

Culture Change and the Indoctrination of Millennials

So much has changed since the 1950s. Those of us who were children or teens back then had parents who disciplined us. Our schools honored our country; we prayed, thanking God for our food at lunchtime at school; we went to church on Sunday; and our country had courts that had no mercy on criminals.

Today, at least 50 percent of millennial adults are lost. They have abandoned God, they don't take discipline well at home or in school, they tend to hate cops, and they are not patriotic and hate many aspects of American life. Many are not taught love and respect; many are not ambitious to achieve goals and attain success; and some do not value life. Between 40 percent and 50 percent of millennials embrace socialism today, having no clue that it always leads to tyranny, destruction, and bloodshed; they are only concerned with the free stuff the socialist con artists offer.

In the first nine months of 2019, there were at least twenty-one deadly mass shootings across the United States, in which one hundred twenty-four people were killed. The perpetrators used guns; tomorrow, others may use cars or other vehicles, machetes, knives, poison, or bombs. School shootings and gang violence are committed by millennials. That is a culture change from the 1950s. Not all shootings are caused by

---

[7] "Attitudes on Same-Sex Marriage," Pew Research Center, May 14, 2019, https://www.pewforum.org/fact-sheet/changing-attitudes-on-gay-marriage/.

millennials, but the focus here is on the significant problem of millennial violence in the United States. But lying Democratic politicians blame guns as the root cause of mass shootings. These Democrats cannot do, and have not done, anything to solve millennial gang violence, school shootings, church shootings, or other public shootings in which multiple innocent victims are murdered. Ban guns and millennial psychos will find a way to kill people—and the problem of mass murder is not solved.[8]

As of December 31, 2020, Chicago had recorded 774 murders in 2020, 50 percent more than in 2019. Shootings increased to 3,237 as of December 27, 2020. This is a millennial problem.[9]

Only lying unscrupulous politicians blamed President Trump for the shootings and mass murders committed by psycho millennials, and only because they hated Trump. Ban guns, and psycho millennials will commit mass murder with some other weapon. Then, Democratic politicians still would have blamed Trump for it.

A Rising Number of Christians Are Abandoning Their Churches

Why do people abandon the church? Why do they leave organized religion? The following answers apply to some people:

- They have lost faith in their churches, whose leaders are unable to communicate morals and wisdom from biblical scripture.
- They disagree with church teaching on issues of morality, such as abortion, homosexuality, same-sex marriage, and chastity before marriage.

---

[8] Meghan Keneally, "There Have Been at least 21 Deadly Mass Shootings in the US so Far in 2019," ABC News, October 1, 2019, https://abcnews.go.com/US/deadly-mass-shootings-month-2019/story?id=63449799.

[9] Sam Charles, "After 3 Years of Progress, Chicago's Murder Tally Skyrockets in 2020," *Chicago Sun Times*, December 31, 2020, https://chicago.suntimes.com/crime/2020/12/31/22208002/chicago-murders-2020-skyrocket-crime-violence-cpd-homicides.

- They think religion is outdated and should be revised to keep up with the whims and desires of modern people.
- They think they can learn biblical scripture sufficiently on their own and thereby avoid going to church.
- They just don't like organized religion.
- They have lost interest in the church and choose to ignore it.
- They are holier-than-thou critics who judge churchgoers as hypocritical sinners driving them away.
- They have converted to a different religion.
- They have lost their faith in God.

The Results of a United States without Christian Moral Values

Without Christian moral values in life, young people tend to be drawn into socialism and big government as a way of life. They accept the liberal morality of abortion, homosexuality, transgender conversions, and getting free handouts from government paid for by the rich, who they think are evil and the cause of their misery and misfortunes, and they disrespect police and law and order. They are selfish, are unpatriotic, hate the United States' traditions, and can easily be influenced by the evil socialist fake news media. Members of the Democratic Party set examples of corruption for profit and greed for people without morals to enrich themselves. For these lost souls, biblical scripture or law and order mean nothing. However, unscrupulous Democratic politicians notoriously continue to use religion as a tool on TV to justify their corruption and sins, but they slam and stifle religion when it is convenient for them.

What Young People Are Not Being Told about Converting to Islam

Young people without values are also more apt to be influenced by Islam taught in US schools and in other countries as being the religion of peace. This could be no further from the truth. As pointed out in a previous section on Islam in *The Coming Tyranny*, Islam preaches peace among Muslims only. It defiles Western culture as immoral and populated with infidels who need to be converted under the threat of death. Islam never teaches that the jihad is an eventual takeover and domination of the world. Muslims never teach about the forced sterilization of Muslim women. They never teach converts about the oppressive control that Muslim men have over Muslim women. They never give potential converts instructions for how to properly beat one's wife or about Muslim child brides, or ever mention the horrors of what ISIS has done in the name of Islam. Muslims never teach potential converts the history of Islam, where Muslims have committed genocide and ethnic cleansing of Christians and Jews all over the Middle East at various times since the foundation of Islam in the early seventh century. The teachers of Islam do not teach the horrible acts committed by terrorists in the twentieth and twenty-first centuries, the conflicts the Muslim world was involved in, or the Christian churches Muslims have attacked or the parishioners they have murdered. Millennials embracing Muslims tend to be misled by the Muslim leaders who lie, mostly by omitting the truth.

Atheists Protest Christian Events and Crosses but Never Protest Mosques or Horrific Muslim-Committed Crimes

Atheists protest Christian events and Christian icons, but seldom do they protest mosques or horrific Muslim-committed crimes. Why is there no atheist activism against Islam, mosques, sharia law, Muslim terrorism, or ISIS? Why are atheists fearful of Muslims? It is interesting to note that atheists have not complained about sharia law being practiced in Detroit and other midwestern cities. Atheists have not complained about the loud calls to prayer coming from mosques. It is interesting that the evil fake news media fails to report the destruction and vandalism of Catholic churches in France and other European countries perpetrated by Muslims. It is interesting that the evil fake news media does not report that rape is the number one crime in all of Europe, including

Scandinavia, committed by Muslim refugees. It is interesting to note that the fake news media refuses to report anti-Semitism occurring and rising in Europe. It is interesting to note that the fake news media is not reporting how the old culture of Europe is slowly dying as a result of Muslim immigrants from the Middle East and Africa. And finally, it is interesting to note how LGBT people never hold protests against Muslims who customarily push queers to their death off tall buildings. I can see a scenario where liberals, atheists, and Muslims join forces to defeat conservatives. If they succeed, Muslims, to the surprise of atheists and liberals/socialists, there will be a religious cleansing of atheists and liberals/socialists once Muslims achieve power as they have done repeatedly in history.

Not a tear was shed by Crying Chuck Schumer about the religious cleansing carnage of Christians in Nigeria, nor was there a single word of protest uttered by Ilhan Omar or Rashida Tlaib about that genocide committed by Muslims. Why is that? Reason: Muslims don't consider the murder of infidel Christians as immoral, rather seeing it as being justified by the Koran.

7

THE FAKE NEWS MEDIA AS AN EXTENSION OF THE DEMOCRAT PARTY

Obama's Fake News Media

During the presidency of Barack Obama, the US news media covered his many appearances at prominent events and gave him favorable press. Obama appeared on the liberal-biased *The View*, whose hosts treated him like a cool celebrity and cuddled him as their favorite pet poodle. Michelle Obama, the former first lady, was pictured on the front page of several magazines. Obama was never treated with hate, whereas the biased liberal media reported defamatory garbage about President Trump and his family 24-7. Never before has there been such a vile, hateful liberal media that has broadcasted so much hate, negative propaganda, and fake news about a president in US history.

To win the media war against conservatives, Obama subsidized the liberal news media by giving them government contracts paid for with taxpayer money. In exchange, Obama and his cronies would get favorable news coverage. CNN, MSNBC, ABC, the *Washington Post*, *Time* magazine, *Newsweek*, and the *New York Times* typically gave Obama favorable press, giving the impression that he could do no wrong. If he did do something wrong, then the biased media would support his lies and excuses, which was the case with the Obama–Hillary Clinton mess in Benghazi, or would manufacture lies to place the blame for his messes elsewhere.

For example, in April 2012 the inspector general found many outlandish deficiencies within the General Service Agency (GSA), which became a scandal, but Obama blamed George W. Bush for the scandal and for the rising costs of the GSA. The media supported Obama and the executives responsible for the scandal. In Benghazi, Muslim terrorists linked to Hillary Clinton and Barack Obama killed four Americans who, twenty-four hours before being killed, had radioed for help, which was never provided by Obama or Hillary Clinton. The press sided with Obama, who placed the blame on an anti-Muslim video, saying that it was this that caused the attack, which later was proven false. Obama never was never questioned in a high-pressure, hostile way about these events. Instead, one reporter asked him how enchanting it felt to be president.

The liberal Obama-adoring media never complained about Obama's lavish trips. He and his wife, Michelle, flew to exotic vacation destinations on separate jets; he flew on Air Force One. And the media certainly did not give Obama bad press about his frequent flights to Hawaii and his frequent time out for golfing. The media was absolutely quiet when Obama gave himself a raise before leaving office.

The evil fake news media such as CNN, MSNBC, the *Washington Post*, the *New York Times*, and the *Huffington Post* worked 24-7 to defame President Trump with spin, conjecture, and manufactured tripe for more than four years. Members of the Washington, DC, "swamp" have been identified as criminals from the FBI, DOJ, CIA, NSA, and the White House. Our ambassador to the UN, the FISA Court, Fusion GPS, Hillary Clinton, members of the DNC, and other swamp agencies of the federal government that are primarily Obama-era leftovers are also criminals. The evil fake news media accepted *illegal leaks* from high-ranking officials from these swamp agencies without revealing their sources, but the reporters got no jail time for this. *They should be charged for accepting illegal leaks* and working with *leakers* for the purpose of overthrowing an elected president they didn't like. The fake news media is now just an extension of the Democratic Party that provides favorable press to Democrats, and spewed vile and slanderous comments against former president Trump and his family 24-7. Many of these Democrat-biased reporters collaborated/conspired with anti-Trump leakers, many of them being members of the swamp, to defame candidate Donald Trump with the fake DNC-paid-for Russian dossier in order to hand the win to Hillary Clinton. Some liberal reporters even reported that Trump was owned by Vladimir Putin.

The Fake News Propaganda Machine Pushes Lies and Slander to Defame Republicans 24-7

The fake news media, among which are CNN, MSNBC, the *Huffington Post*, Yahoo.com, AOL.com, the *New York Times*, the *Washington Post*, ABC, NBC, and Politico, are nothing more than low-level reporters paid to manufacture and dispense fake news. They defamed President Trump, his cabinet, and conservatives, and bamboozled low-IQ and mentally challenged individuals who will believe anything they hear in the news. Liberal politicians typically leak fake news to the media so these falsehoods can be broadcast so as to influence naive fools. Barack Obama, a pompous celebrity con artist, blamed his inabilities, failures, and incompetence on everyone else but himself by lying with his made-up excuses every time he was on TV. The arrogant con artist even took credit for Trump's economy, hoping to push that lie long enough so that fools would believe it. He used Saul Alinsky's eleventh rule (from the book *Rules for Radicals*): If you push a negative (or lie) hard and deep enough, it will break through to the opposing side (i.e., it will become a positive). Arrogant con artist Obama pushed a multitude of lies persistently enough so people would believe them.

Example 1: Obama pushed the constant lie that he had inherited a bad economy from the Bush administration, and Obama blamed Bush for his own inability to fix it.

Example 2: Obama pushed the constant lie that he started the Trump economy just before Trump got elected, and claimed credit for it. Over time, enough useful idiots came to believe it. Obama would never have cut regulations for businesses to grow the economy and would never have given corporations tax cuts to bring them back to the United States for economic growth, increased jobs, and record unemployment. Even Obama was quoted as saying Trump couldn't have created millions of jobs "unless he waved a magic wand."

Obama and the evil fake news media are cohort experts using this "eleventh rule" against millennials, their audience of naive fools, and blacks who have been repeatedly swindled and brainwashed with the history of race relations in the United States, and bashed as victims of slavery, racial oppression, and bigotry, which causes them to feel angry and resentful, making them insecure victims of today's Republicans, white people, and conservatives.

8

THE DEMOCRATIC PARTY OF TODAY

The Failures of Today's Far Left Democratic Party

The Democrats have never been so sick, demented, hypocritical, or in conflict with people who have common sense and good judgment as they are today. Their outrageous remarks are caused by their failures and desperation. They realized in the past four years that President Trump was successful, outdid each inexperienced Democratic fool, had tens of thousands of supporters attending his rallies, and had tens of millions of people watching him at his rallies on TV; **my wife** Patty and I were only two of them.

Never before in US history has there been such hate coming out of the mouths of Democratic politicians, including the Democratic presidential candidates, all twenty-five of whom were being hateful. The level of nastiness and hate is even worse among the nasty, perverted, violent Hollywood crowd. The fake news media, up until recently, lived 24-7 by ridiculing Trump and spreading hate and false propaganda about him and his family. The hate-Trump Democrats in Congress led by Nadler and Schiff spent three years trying to impeach the president. Finally, on December 18, 2019, the House Democrats voted to impeach him on two charges: abuse of power and obstruction of Congress. The charges were purely concocted from hearsay and rumors.

David A. Herrera

Why Radical Muslims Partner with Liberal and Socialist Politicians in the United States

Another thing to note about the Democratic Party is that socialists have partnered with radical Muslims with the intent of promoting socialism, destroying the status quo of a Trump America, and remaking the United States with illegal immigration through open borders.

In their greed for control and power, Democrats are blind to the spread of Islam throughout the world and its consequences, as they support, partner with, and promote the cancerous growth of Islam in the USA. Little do stupid and naive Democratic politicians know that if this cancer metastasizes, if conservatives are defeated and Christianity is weakened, then atheists, the leaders among queer Hollywood actors, and the leaders among the LGBT crowd will be on the chopping block. Feminists opposing Islam will be forced into sex slavery and/or beaten into compliance, or worse. Only those submitting to Allah will survive to live under sharia law, which will be brutal for women.

The first line of defense for our freedoms in the United States is law enforcement. Socialists like Julian Castro want to have complete political control of police agencies across the United States and to diminish the ability of police agencies to oppose tyranny from the federal government. Castro's policies would prevent law enforcement personnel from doing their jobs effectively by denying police agencies military-style equipment to use against mobs and rioters, which are mostly all Democrats.

The Democratic Party Is the Party of Illegal Aliens, Drugs, Open Borders, and Free Stuff for Illegals

Democrats who want open borders essentially lay out the red carpet for unchecked criminal illegal aliens entering the United States to commit crimes and kill Americans with their drugs and guns. The Democrats even protect former ex-convict illegal aliens in sanctuary cities; they don't inform ICE to deport them, so they go live in somebody's neighborhood, possibly becoming repeat offenders. A judge in New Mexico let a rapist out on bail who then committed more rapes in a week's time. How can the Democrats live with this insanity? Answer: Democratic politicians live in their expensive mansions and don't care about the safety of Americans, but Democrats like Speaker Nancy Pelosi pontificate about letting multiple caravans of illegal aliens traveling from Central and South America into Mexico and across our southern border. Democrats want illegal aliens to enter the country so these illegals can vote for Democrats—it's about power, money, and control, which the Democrats want regardless of who gets killed. Even clueless Alexandria Ocasio-Cortez and other clueless Democrats want ICE abolished. How was it possible that Democrats could run on a "sanctuary city" ticket in 2020? How could the Democrats run on an "open borders" ticket in 2020?

Reasons Liberal Democrats Want to Abolish the Electoral College

There's a good reason why sneaky Democrats want to abolish the Electoral College implemented by our founding fathers: They want the biggest populations located in blue states to vote in presidential elections so they can win simply by majority voting, when they know these are the most populous states. For example, California, New York, Oregon, Washington, and Massachusetts are blue states. If the government can attract millions of illegal aliens to those states and abolish the Electoral College, then the Democrats will forever win all presidential elections. Less-populated states won't matter then. The framers of the Constitution figured out that the most populous state would always determine who would win elections. New York was the most populous state in the colonies. Votes in the remaining states back then did not matter at all. So, our founders came up with the Electoral College to include equal votes for most populated and less populated states so as to be fair, which is the deciding criterion for presidential elections. Democrats are not about fairness or honesty.

Democratic Hypocrites Are the Most Intolerant People in the United States

Democratic politicians have worn out the race card, such as Cory Booker and Kamala Harris, who keep on playing it. The race card is used to place blame on people who are intolerant of people of specific races. But Democratic liberals are also offended by conservatives who oppose homosexuality, cross-dressers, transgender people, unchecked immigration, and radical Muslims who want to kill us or replace our culture. Liberal Democrats also don't tolerate or agree with Christians, Bibles, crosses, US flags, guns, Confederate statues, Confederate flags, conservative free speech, Christian relics, and rich white people.

Maxine Waters urged the constituents in her district to refuse service to Trump supporters in public places of business, such as malls and restaurants, by running them off and telling them they were not welcome—a civil rights violation like what white southerners used to do to black people in the South at lunch counters.

The videotape of a university student punching a conservative student shows the intolerance of liberal students on college campuses. Antifa holds protests and destroys Confederate statues of generals because they simply disagree with these persons from US history. Have I missed anything?

The Intolerant Hollywood Left

The Hollywood crowd, actors and actresses, are the vilest and most intolerant of all liberals who express their low-class mockery and hate of President Trump. For example, the Democratic Hollywood actor Peter Fonda (recently deceased) urged people publicly to kidnap Trump's youngest son, Baron, and throw him at pedophiles. Other Hollywood idiots suggested violence against Trump and the assassination of Trump. Madonna said she dreamed of blowing up the White House. Actress Kathy Griffin, who complained she couldn't get a job in Hollywood because of the old men preventing her from doing so, carried a mock severed head of Donald Trump shown on TV. Democratic candidate for president Cory Booker urged people to get in the faces of Republican members of Congress in protest.

Actor Robert De Niro said about President Trump on TV: "I'd like to punch him in the face." What a psycho loser. All these sick and shameless Hollywood Democrats and some Democratic politicians support violence and used to urge others to commit crimes against former president Trump and his family. Sick Hollywood idiots, desperate and useless Democratic politicians, and their gnashing, hate-Trump media all blamed Trump for the shootings committed by psycho millennials. The hate-Trump media should blame themselves for creating such an evil culture of hate with their propaganda. Then liberals like Peter Buttigieg, Nancy Pelosi, and Joe Biden act as holier-than-thou, morally superior people trying to apply "Christian morals" to support their political beliefs and lecture people on morality whom they disagree with.

Actor Alec Baldwin blasted Trump supporters, saying they caused "colossal destruction" to the United States. He had nothing of substance to offer to explain his remark, and no purpose other than to destroy morality in the United States and disenfranchise the poor. This does not make sense, as it's leftists like him from the Hollywood crowd who have brought down morals in this country. Since President Trump succeeded in growing the economy to a record level in fifty years, there should have been ample jobs and opportunities for the "disenfranchised" to get jobs and become prosperous. If Trump didn't exist, Alec Baldwin would be less rich. He was lucky to be given an acting job with SNL and earned some money posing as Donald Trump.

9

THE PROPONENTS OF ABORTION, THE GENOCIDE OF BABIES

Abortion: A Legal Method of Taxpayer-Funded Genocide of Infants

Some women make mistakes. Now they want to take someone else's life for the mistake they've made.

Don't be a fool and have irresponsible sex, as it will lead to having an unwanted kid, possibly getting dumped by your partner and being left as a single mother, and having to drop out of school before you're twenty years old because of it. Use common sense and *be all you can be* to achieve the American dream through education, seeking clever and available opportunities, and working hard. That's how Republicans think, not Democrats. President Trump increased opportunities for everyone. Just look at the number of jobs available when he was in office, many of which were good-paying jobs for people with the right qualifications. But blacks, Hispanics, or whites won't get to first base if they get pregnant or get someone pregnant and then have to drop out of school to support the child without a job or a good education. Guys, just tuck it in and get prepared for a good life after finishing your education without obstructions or regrets. Girls, just say no to prevent irresponsible accidents so you can obtain a good education and go on to have a good career for a better life without poverty.

Abortion: Shameful Genocide, and a Fraud to Kill Life

Women advocating abortion claim that it's their body and they can do whatever they want with it. The flaw in their thinking is that—while it is true that they have always had free will, given to them by God, to do anything they want with their bodies—they do not want to admit there are *two* bodies, not one, the baby's and the mother's. Pro-choice women want to get rid of the baby by having a doctor who performs abortions scrape the baby out of the womb and toss it in the trash as garbage. But now, in some states such as Virginia, Democratic state lawmakers and the governor want genocide abortionists to murder babies after they are born—and these dishonest women still claim it's their body. Fact: After the baby is born, the baby is no longer in the female body and no longer a health risk to the woman. I can only guess that if the baby is deformed, has Down syndrome, or is of a race the woman doesn't like, she can give a thumbs-down to have the doctor kill the baby. A question that pro-choice women seldom answer is: After a baby is born, does the baby have a soul?

Proponents of Legalized Baby Genocide

Senators Elizabeth Warren (D-MA), Cory Booker (D-NJ), Kirsten Gillibrand (D-NY), Kamala Harris (D-CA), Amy Klobuchar (D-MN), and Bernie Sanders (I-VT) all voted against the Born-Alive Abortion Survivors Protection Act, to let a born alive abortion survivor die. All these sick politicians are proponents of child genocide. More of this social engineering would have been in order had one of these pathetic socialists been elected as president. Booker, Gillibrand, and Harris quit the presidential race, and as of January 2020 Bernie Sanders was more supported than Elizabeth Warren. Bernie is not too far from lying restless with Alzheimer's disease in a rest home. I wonder if he'll request a doctor to perform a mercy killing on him in the event he becomes a useless old fart in a rest home dressed in a diaper?

Pro-Choice Women Who Advocate for Abortion Are Irresponsible, Callous, and Murderous

Liberal women have increasingly participated in the genocide of babies since the 1960s' sexual revolution. Loose, irresponsible women who got abortions because they had made a mistake, leading to unwanted pregnancy, should not punish taxpayers for their own stupid mistakes. These women never ask or care if the fetus in their womb will feel any pain at all during the cutting-up process. In some cases, callous women want their babies aborted even if the baby is born; they never ask or care if their baby will experience any pain or if the baby has a soul when it's murdered.

Do Women Who Support Abortion Care if the Baby Feels Pain or Has a Soul?

Have any pro-choice liberal politicians ever been asked if they believe a baby about to be aborted already has a soul or can feel pain? Let's pray that God may put an end to stop the genocide of babies (except in the case of incest or if a woman's life is in danger). I wonder if Democrats who believe in abortion know whether a baby in the womb or out of the womb feels pain during the abortion process. And at what point does a woman getting an abortion wonder if a baby has a God-given soul? Judging by how enthusiastic, godless, and enraged they are in favoring abortion, I don't think they care. Abortionists would likely respond, "What does God have to do with it?" Additionally, taxpayers should not reward irresponsible sexual behavior leading to unwanted pregnancies.

New York Politicians Cheered and Celebrated Laws They Passed to Take Away Life in the Womb

It is a sad day in the United States when politicians pass laws to sanction the murder of a baby living in the womb with a God-given soul, not because it will endanger the life of the mother to the point of death, but for any reason given with the simple request to a doctor. What's worse, liberal Democratic New York politicians cheered and celebrated the passing of this law on TV. Andrew Cuomo bragged that New York proudly enjoys the highest abortion rate in the United States.

Even worse, New York requires its taxpayers to pay for elective abortions through Medicaid, but these abortions are not supposed to be paid for by federal taxpayer dollars because of the Hyde Amendment. Still, audits have revealed that New York, and Planned Parenthood specifically, billed federal taxpayers for elective abortions.

Laws Passed in New York for Taxpayers to Fund the Taking of a Life in the Womb that Is the Result of Irresponsible Sex

Democrats in New York sanctioned laws for couples who have made irresponsible and regretful decisions in the bedroom; the mother may massacre her own kid at her whim and have you, the taxpayer, through Planned Parenthood, pay for it, or have the taxpayers of New York pay for it through Medicaid. This law, cheered by Democrats and Andrew Cuomo, was tailored specifically for the dumb, irresponsible, immoral, loose women who celebrated it.

In addition, corrupt Planned Parenthood has been funneling money into supporting Democratic candidates in congressional and presidential elections for decades. They recently announced they would be spending upward of $45 million to help flip some congressional seats and help a Democratic candidate win the White House.

It was reported in the *Daily Wire* by Matt Walsh that Planned Parenthood's economic support was "a money-laundering operation for the Democratic Party." This means Democrats give tens of millions in taxpayer money to Planned Parenthood, and Planned Parenthood then recycles millions of dollars back to the Democratic organizations as campaign donations to elect Democratic politicians—a criminal racketeering operation known as money laundering.

David A. Herrera

Mistakes Leading to Abortion

Some Democrats say that if female teens or adult women get pregnant and have an abortion, they should not listen to what other people say because it's none of their business. *Wrong!* It is our business when these baby killers use taxpayer money to pay for their abortions caused by their own *irresponsible* acts. If the mother's life is in danger, or if it's a case of rape or incest, I can see a good cause for an abortion. But if it was just a stupid mistake, these women and their partners must bear the costs on their own. Typically, the male skips out and lets the poor woman go it alone. Looking at it as a moral issue, if you are an atheist or want to ignore what God says in scripture, then know it's not people who should judge you; it's only God who will.

This is probably a good statistic from a reliable source: No one with common sense believes that a mother's life was in danger for the millions of abortions that happened in the last several decades. It's the pro-choice women who kill their kids, *not* because, in most cases, the women's lives are in danger, but because of their menagerie of poor excuses. If the woman pays for it, it's between the woman and God, and no one else's business. A mother and father of a young daughter might also be concerned, so it would justifiably be their business too. But for women who want taxpayers to pay for their dumb mistakes and listen to their poor excuses, pro-choice politicians should urge common sense and counseling for pregnancy prevention instead of allowing unconditional abortions at taxpayers' expense.

Parents should provide better counseling to their daughters and sons. Schools should also teach young girls and boys the many dangers of promiscuity that will take them to the road of poverty, stress, and other negative consequences. Many pro-choice nonreligious women have no conscience and don't care what other people think, but the ones who do and who care what their parents think will have the haunting memory of their abortion(s) for life.

Do Black Lives Really Matter? Ask Baby-Killing Supporters of Abortion

This is a human rights issue ignored by Democratic politicians who choose to promote the genocide of babies in or out of the womb. Democrats say black lives matter, but Democrats keep black people picking welfare and food stamps on Democratic plantations and promote the abortion of black babies. Democrats such as Jane Fonda falsely called our soldiers in Vietnam baby killers, yet Democrats have historically promoted abortions that kill born and unborn babies. Why have we not heard from the "quiet" UN about this genocide and about the human rights of born and unborn babies? Why is our country subsidizing the UN? Do any blacks remember Margaret Sanger? What were her views on abortion? She once said, "We don't want the word to go out that we want to exterminate the Negro population."

Perhaps not coincidently, nearly 80 percent of Planned Parenthoods today are located in black and Hispanic communities.[1]

White liberal women are the biggest supporters of aborting black babies; they are always protesting for abortion rights to choose what to do with their frumpy and flabby bodies. It's a form of black genocide, and they all know it (but it's legal).

Irresponsibility and Abortions

Videos showing a baby in the womb of a mother should be shown in junior high schools and high schools everywhere in the United States. The videos should be accompanied by a debate between a pro-choicer and a pro-lifer to be objective. Then show videos exposing the horrible consequences of abortions, girls who can't say no, guys who won't take no for an answer, the lack of parents in the family to advise kids in the

---

[1] Patrina Mosley, "Margaret Sanger: 'We Want to Exterminate the Negro Population.' Her Wish Is Coming True," Life News, March 10, 2020, https://www.lifenews.com/2020/03/10/margaret-sanger-we-want-to-exterminate-the-negro-population-her-wish-is-coming-true-2/.

home, the lack of morals not being taught at home, and the lack of common sense not taught in schools.

The rationale for abortion is not about a woman's rights to do whatever she wishes with her body; it's about what will be done to the body of an unborn living human being with a soul inside and outside the womb. It's about facing God someday about the choices one has made. It's about being responsible to prevent an accidental pregnancy that will lead to horrible memories for life. And in most cases, male partners just don't think about or care whether the female gets pregnant. Most of these irresponsible men will refuse to support a child, or don't have the financial means to do so, if it is born, which is also a reason a woman should say no. In the end, no matter what is argued, it's between the female and God. Atheists will do anything they want because they think God does not exist to hold them accountable. Rationale or not, some women may have no pangs of conscience after their own flesh and blood is scraped out of their womb and thrown in the trash.

Taxpayers should not pay for this horrible genocide of helpless born or unborn babies. Except in the case of rape or incest, the issue is not the choice of a woman to do as she wishes with her body; she always has that choice. The *real* issue is whether or not taxpayers should be forced to pay for baby genocide in this country committed by irresponsible men and women. Every woman has a choice to say *no* to sex in order to prevent unwanted pregnancies; abstaining from sex will never get a woman pregnant. The pro-choice issue should be to have or not to have irresponsible sex leading to an abortion.

The male partners are equally as irresponsible and stupid, if not more so, for their mistakes and their inability to perceive the risks of bringing their own flesh and blood into the world when they may not be able to support the child. Should males have a say in the decision to kill their own flesh and blood, or should they just let the woman go it alone?

It's also a moral issue, but today many people don't care about God; they only care about the free will God gave them without accepting any responsibility or consequences for their actions, then desiring that taxpayers pay for their stupid mistakes.

Women who decide to keep an unwanted child always have the choice to legally force the father to pay child support. Authorities should go after males who are delinquent in their child support payments or who evade providing child support.

Virginia Governor Ralph Northam's Approval of Born-Baby Abortions

Virginia governor Ralph Northam and Virginia lawmakers approved abortions performed on babies born alive. This is a Democratic state government's sanctioning of the outright murder of born infants. Police officers should arrest politicians who authorize the murder of born infants. I wonder why a governor who approved the unconditional murder of babies inside or outside the womb is a racist, as he appeared as a black-faced Michael Jackson imitator posing with someone in a hooded KKK costume in his yearbook. If he had posed in a picture masked as Obama with a noose around his neck or masked up like Obama next to his old KKK buddy dressing up as a mammy, or showing both picking cotton, would that be racist?

10

A COMPARISON OF PRESIDENT TRUMP AND BARACK OBAMA

The ego of arrogant con artist Barack Obama motivated him to slander President Trump. Trump outperformed schoolboy Obama on every presidential achievement, on all things that mattered to the American people. Serial liar Obama will be seen one of the most dishonest and corrupt presidents in US history, while President Trump will be seen one of the greatest presidents in US history. President Trump worked hard, showed positive results, and fulfilled his promises to Americans. Obama, on the other hand, could never stimulate the economy, reduce taxes to grow jobs, or reduce unemployment. He blamed George W. Bush for his failures, spent much time golfing and vacationing, and blatantly lied about almost anything to the American people on TV and in other media.

Arrogant Obama blamed Bush for the sluggish economy Obama could not improve for eight years, then after he left office, claimed credit for the success of the Trump economy two years after Trump enabled its tremendous growth and lowered unemployment to new record levels. Obama would *never* have reduced taxes for individuals and corporations, nor reduced crippling regulations on businesses. On the contrary, Obama sought to increase taxes to soak the rich and the middle class and to impose *more*, not fewer, regulations on businesses. Obama and his administration, full of corrupt agency heads and lawyers, failed with foreign policy for eight years and created messes with foreign nations they could not solve.

Barack Obama Claimed Credit for President Donald Trump's Successful Economy

On February 2020, Barack Obama claimed credit for the successful economy since the time Trump was in office. Democrats had a very slow-growth economy, which President Trump inherited. President Trump lowered taxes for corporations to jump-start the economy, and this developed into a great economy. Reducing any kind of taxes for corporations was something that Barack Obama would have never done. Corporations started coming back from foreign countries and setting up shop in the United States again, creating manufacturing jobs.

Obama was never smart enough to think that unfair trade deals were making China, Europe, Canada, and Mexico rich and putting the United States deeper in debt. President Trump solved all that by renegotiating new trade deals to prevent the United States from losing billions of dollars each year.

Obama was so weak-kneed with regard to foreign affairs that his brain never thought of NATO nations paying their fair share for their own defense. President Trump did.

Obama was against lowering taxes. He wanted to raise taxes even more and have people pay more than their fair share so he could redistribute the wealth. He would never have lowered corporate taxes so businesses would have to pay less in taxes as President Trump did to trigger job growth.

Obama stifled economic growth by overregulating businesses; President Trump got rid of Obama's business regulations to get the economy booming again.

Obama said that millions of jobs would not be possible unless Trump "waved a magic wand," and he said it would never happen. I guess President Trump schooled the arrogant con artist, who knows little or nothing about economics. We had record unemployment and more job opportunities than ever before, something Obama never accomplished in his eight years in office.

Donald Trump is one of the most successful presidents in US history. He continued to fulfill his campaign promises and continued to overachieve. That's why Democrats in the House wanted to remove him from office through impeachment. House Democrat Al Green of Houston, Texas, said, "If we don't impeach him, he'll get reelected." But isn't voting for a president the will of the people, not the will of a bunch of corrupt failed Democrats?

How Trump Made America Great in His First Term as President

President Trump made America great in less than two years. Here's why: In less than two years, he achieved a record low in unemployment, the lowest in fifty years; increased opportunities and jobs for blacks, Hispanics, and others to the highest level ever recorded in US history; saw the highest number of women working in decades; achieved more prosperity and higher wages; made our military great again; stepped up missile defense against Russian and Chinese hypersonic missile, which are threats to the United States; stopped the dictator of North Korea from shooting missiles over Japan and threatening to nuke the United States; got prisoners out of Korea without paying a fortune for them like Obama did from Iran; made much better trade deals with other countries; made NATO pay its fair share of the defense of NATO countries; tried to build a wall on the US border with Mexico for the safety of all Americans; backed H.R. 5682, a prison reform bill; tried to provide food aid to the starving masses in Venezuela; supported life of the unborn and born; enabled Israel to relocate its capital to Jerusalem; and assisted our veterans with VA reforms.

At the beginning of 2020, in his third year in office, Trump signed a new trade deal with China that finally promised to greatly benefit the United States, the US–Mexico–Canada (USMCA) Trade Agreement, which replaced NAFTA. The Dow reached over twenty-nine thousand in mid-January 2020 for the first time in US history. President Trump directed the United States military to assassinate Iraqi terrorist Abu Bakr al-Baghdadi in October 2019, and on January 3, 2020, the US government assassinated Iranian general Qasem Soleimani, a widely known terrorist who was responsible for killing hundreds of US troops in Iraq. The general, killed at the Baghdad International Airport, was planning to attack more US embassies in the Middle East. President Trump warned Iran not to retaliate or else they would be annihilated. Iran responded with missile strikes that intentionally killed no Americans. That's a lot of accomplishments for former president Trump.

PART 2

THE PROGRESSIVE DECAY OF US CITIES AND STATES RUN BY PROGRESSIVE DEMOCRATS

11

THE DEMOCRATS' MISMANAGEMENT OF CALIFORNIA

California used to be the best state to live in from the 1950s to the mid-1990s. Once RINO Arnold Schwarzenegger's term was over, Democrats took over and California went downhill, where it remains to this day. It's an overtaxed state with increased crime, illegal aliens flooding the state to receive free health care and other state government handouts, and people and businesses moving out of the state. It's a Democratic Party–run mess, a classic case of government mismanagement that will not end soon and that, when it ends, will end terribly.

It is shameful that one of the richest and most beautiful states of the union has had its legislature and state assembly taken over by Democratic politicians continuously since 1998 and has been under a Democratic governorship continuously since 2011. California has one of the highest poverty rates in the nation, and many of its cities have massive homelessness. Democratic politicians have morphed into an incompetent, struggling bunch of fools who cannot be trusted to lead this once great state. As we shall see, major factors that have changed California for the worse include corruption and extreme liberal policies. Under RINO Arnold Schwarzenegger, corrupt Democratic politicians guaranteed that the mob majority would always stay in office by passing election rules that allow only the top two candidates for governor to run against each other, instead of one Republican against a Democratic candidate.

The billionaires of California have mostly settled on the coast. They live in mansions and control the state with their money and influence; many are high-tech moguls. Rich moguls live in pricey neighborhoods in gated communities, many of them with community security. California politician elites keep illegal aliens away from their very expensive gated mansions. The homeless live in major cities, on beaches, in public parks, under bridges, in riverbeds, or in alleys in downtown areas. Since a significant part of the middle class, hammered with high taxes by California's Democratic politicians, is moving out of the state, who will be left? Answer: the very rich controlling the state, and the very poor taking unskilled jobs for cheap wages or relying on state and federal government for assistance with basic needs: welfare, food stamps, health care, and adequate housing. But the 151,278 homeless people in California are living proof that California lawmakers are doing a lousy job of providing basic needs for its homeless population, which is the largest in the United States.[1]

California Influx and Exodus

After living thirty-seven years in Southern California, my wife and I moved to Arizona for a new job in 1999. California has gotten much worse since Democrats have continued to ruin it for more than twenty years. A massive number of Californians have moved out of the state, particularly the middle class, to nearby states such as Oregon, Washington, Colorado, Arizona, Nevada, Idaho, and Utah. Some of my relatives don't want to move because their adult children and grandchildren live near them. Democratic politicians have figured ways so that a Republican will have almost zero chance of ever running for governor, thanks to RINO Arnold Schwarzenegger. Illegal aliens

---

[1] Patrina Mosley, "Margaret Sanger: 'We Want to Exterminate the Negro Population.' Her Wish is Coming True," Life News, March 10, 2020, https://www.lifenews.com/2020/03/10/margaret-sanger-we-want-to-exterminate-the-negro-population-her-wish-is-coming-true-2/.

will make it even harder to vote Democrats out of office. California politicians even tried to exclude President Trump from appearing on the 2020 ballot because he had not released his taxes for five years; that effort failed as the US Supreme Court overruled California. It is also a matter of civil rights if a voter is denied the opportunity to vote for a sitting president. But Democratic politicians seem to pass laws and file lawsuits to change elections based on corruption rather than the Constitution.

In 2018, a ballot-harvesting law was passed by the Democrat-controlled California State Legislature. Then, in the 2018 congressional election, four communist organizations mobilized thousands of their operatives to execute the Democratic ballot-harvesting program by collecting millions of absentee ballots from nonvoting Californians and illegally submitting them as votes cast by California voters in certain congressional districts at the Registrar of Voters on Election Day. That's voter fraud.

California is one of the most tolerant states that accepts illegal immigration into the state without opposition or deportations at the state level. Several California cities are "sanctuary cities" to protect ex-cons or illegal alien criminals released from jail from being deported by ICE. Illegal aliens have been overpopulating California since the 1980s and have been getting taxpayer-funded free health care. They also get welfare and food stamps. Bubonic plague, typhus, and other horrible diseases are likely to come from rat-and-flea-infested homeless shelters in alleys, under bridges, on beaches, in parks, along riverbeds, and in the downtown areas of major cities such as Los Angeles and San Francisco.

The Biden administration will allow a massive number of illegal aliens to enter states offering the most benefits; those states will mainly be California, New York, and Illinois. Note that as a massive number of illegal aliens enter these states, a massive number of state residents and businesses will be moving out. Illegal aliens seeking a better life will work for lower wages and apply for all the taxpayer benefits extreme liberals in Sacramento have to offer them, such as free medical care, welfare, food stamps, disability insurance, and unemployment insurance. Adult couples accept migrant children who are not theirs to live with them, then claim them as their own when applying for welfare. When the real parents enter the United States, they will catch up with their children and take them back. Only a DNA test will prove a blood-related parent–child relationship. Middle-class residents of California are also looking for a better life free from tax oppression—high income taxes, high sales taxes, high utility taxes, and any other oppressive taxes leftist lawmakers can create. California is too expensive a place to live anymore, and the standard of living in California is becoming too low. Many people owning small and large businesses are relocating outside California to avoid the massive taxes and regulations, which negatively impact them.

California Governor Newsom and Other Progressive State Politicians Are Ruining California

Gavin Newsom was elected and became governor of California in January 2019. Gavin is a staunch liberal and the nephew of Speaker Nancy Pelosi. Under his term, his policies have allowed more illegal aliens into California, causing an overpopulation of illegal alien students in public schools, leading to free health care and approved COVID-19 stimulus checks for illegal aliens, and causing businesses to replace millennials who hold higher-paying jobs with illegal aliens who will accept lower wages. Newsom approved higher levels of taxation on the residents of California. California State Legislature Democrats invented creative new ways to tax-oppress Californians. These taxes, which include increased sales taxes, utilities taxes, phone taxes, estate taxes levied on deceased people, property taxes, business taxes, and high gasoline taxes, are above and beyond what California residents pay in federal taxes and what they will pay under the Biden administration. In October 2019, Gavin Newsom signed fifteen new antigun bills into law.

According to an article by Chris Eger, "The bills include moves to make it easier to seize guns without a trial and place more regulations on firearm sales, ban gun shows at some state-owned facilities and outlaw direct sales of items such as '80 percent' lowers, among others."[2]

It appears politicians fear gun threats and violence against them. Socialist-trending Democrats fear that a revolution by California residents is coming, and they are preparing to disarm residents so they can't cause any damage.

California is well on its way to becoming a feudal state run by wealthy landlords who all live along the Pacific coast. The illegal aliens are peasants providing cheap labor for the land barons and the noble elites. These nobles and barons are the elite politicians and the billionaires living along the coast. The economic classes in California are the poor, whose numbers are increasing through immigration; the middle class, who are primarily employed homeowners; the wealthy; and the very wealthy.

Unfortunately, the trend in California is for Democrats to retain power using the majority of the population, which has morphed into liberal Democrats because of massive migration from Mexico, South America, and China, which immigrants all tend to vote Democrat. This means the loss of taxes from the middle class leaving California will have less of an effect because a massive number of immigrants will take on jobs for cheap wages. The foreign immigration population in California will continue to grow as long as businesses hire cheap labor for their own benefit, with the immigrant labor making up for the lost tax revenue. The rich will get richer and the poor will get poorer, always remaining poor. But what California's Democratic politicians don't realize is that inflation will rise and goods and services will cost more, which means an increasingly lower standard of living for poor people and immigrants, which means immigrants too will leave California for other states where the standard of living is good and that offer the same wages. The benefiting rich will still have to pay higher taxes, but as they retire, they will probably leave California for a better life and take their wealth with them.

---

[2] Chris Eger, "California Gov. Newsom Signs a Whopping 15 Anti-Gun Bills," Guns.com, October 14, 2019, https://www.guns.com/news/2019/10/14/california-gov-newsom-signs-a-whopping-15-anti-gun-bills.

The Biden administration, which promises to impose high taxes on the wealthy, on businesses, and on the middle class, will slow the California economy. Massive layoffs or bankruptcies will occur in an already declined economy because of businesses closing down or being locked down by Governor Newsom on account of COVID-19. If demand for products decreases, then businesses will fail, or move out of the state, or relocate overseas, causing massive loss of jobs. Democrat-mismanaged California will trend toward bankruptcy and beg for federal economic bailout.

The Biden administration will require wealthy California residents to pay considerably more in federal taxes, in addition to California's high state taxes and local taxes, leading to the ruination of California. Under socialism, the biggest hand reaching for your wallet will be that of the federal government, followed by the hands of state government, county government, and city government, all of which will take its own share of tax monies from residents.

How Democrats Run Their Cities: California Is a Good Example

Democratic politicians first bankrupt cities with high property taxes, the highest gasoline taxes in the country, and high local taxes. Stockton, California, has declared bankruptcy already. Now this is the way Democratic politicians fix the people's poverty: by giving free California taxpayer money to bail out cities that don't manage themselves well. California already gives free health care to illegal aliens, which is why illegals are flocking to the United States. The homelessness problem in California is getting worse. California politicians still can't fix poop city Los Angeles and poop city San Francisco's homelessness problem. These cities are also having difficulties cleaning the poop, trash, and urine left behind under bridges, in parks, in riverbeds, in downtown alleys, and on beaches. Now power outages are affecting millions of California residents. Democratic politicians are helpless and useless. California voters should vote out all Democrats to restore greatness to California.

Examples of Horrific Mismanagement by Democrats in California

Today, we are witnessing how badly Democratic politicians are managing states such as New York, New Jersey, ~~Maryland~~, California, Oregon, and Washington. We see how badly California politicians are mismanaging a capitalist state. We are seeing how California is losing its tax base as tens of thousands of wealthy and middle-class Americans are leaving the state each year to live in a different state where the cost of living is lower and they are no longer tax-oppressed. We are seeing how businesses in California are leaving the state because of the high taxes levied on businesses and expensive state government environmental regulations. We see how horribly California is managing its economy by giving illegal aliens free health care, prioritizing them over US citizens, while neglecting their infamous homelessness issue as a preview to socialism. If California politicians cannot manage their state with the higher and higher taxes they levy on residents under capitalism, then why do people think California will be better managed under socialism? If the present Democrats in California became socialists, their proven failed management practices and policies will ruin the state.

The state of California is giving its state money to illegal aliens, whom the state is urgently welcoming so these people will work for lower wages. Employers make more money with *cheap labor*, and the state gets more *tax* money from profit. But it's unskilled blacks and millennials who are victimized and displaced with their opportunities for jobs reduced or destroyed.

Democratic governor Newsom is giving illegal aliens Medicare; that will cost taxpayers money to support the massive number of illegal aliens waiting to get in, including approaching caravans. *More taxes will be needed from residents of every state where illegals settle.* In addition, instead of working, many illegals, especially women with their own children, mixed in with other children who are not theirs, will collect welfare and food stamps. Fraud is hard to detect. How much tax oppression can Californians take? Apparently not enough oppression yet to put on yellow jackets and take to the streets like in France.

In California, on June 6, 1978, nearly two-thirds of California's voters passed Proposition 13, reducing property taxes by about 57 percent. Proposition 13 is part of California's state constitution. Before Proposition 13 was passed, property taxes were out of control and could be raised by large percentages. Proposition 13 is the only law that prevents Democratic liberals in Sacramento from passing larger tax burdens on owners of personal property. But taxes on California homes still rise every year by 1 percent, although homes are assessed when sold, and then the tax rises 2 percent per year. Proposition 13 has a lock effect that restricts taxes levied by the state to low interest and benefits the very rich who live along coastal cities where property values increase the most, but the taxes are still mandated to be low. Those property owners who bought homes in the more distant past in coastal cities may pay extremely low taxes on property that has appreciated in the millions. Rent increases were also limited by Proposition 13.

The homeless are defecating and urinating all over main cities and rich neighborhoods and even inside grocery stores; still, Democrats *do not care about border security and say there is no crisis at the southern border.* Democrats do not have enough funding to care for the homeless. Democrats now fear a revolution from taxpaying citizens; watch as Democrats start to restrict the sale, purchase, and carrying of firearms in California, as they want more taxes from already overtaxed Californians.

The Results of the Incompetent Leadership of California Democrats

Illegal immigration and homelessness are overwhelming California, causing tax oppression of its residents, who are not getting anything for it, such as funding for infrastructure, road repairs, or bridge repairs. California Democrats are using taxpayer money for illegal aliens and to clean up the trash, poop, and urine left behind by homeless people on beaches, in parks, in forests, in downtown areas, and around some rich neighborhoods. This is causing the wealthy, the middle class, and businesses to leave the state, thus reducing the pool of tax money from which Democratic state politicians can draw to pay for state expenses. This can only lead to the following results:

1. Forcing California residents to pay higher state taxes.
2. Releasing more prisoners onto the streets of California because of lack of funding.
3. Cutting back on state services.
4. Declaring bankruptcy at some point because the state can't pay its debts to state pensioners and because legislators are unable to manage the state.
5. Begging the federal government for a bailout, that is, asking residents of all other states to throw their money at a bunch of incompetent buffoons who mismanaged the economy of California so said buffoons can continue to screw it up more.
6. Confiscating land in California and selling it to foreign countries who are our enemies, such as Iran, China, and Russia, who will use it for nefarious reasons.
7. Repossessing more homes whose owners are delinquent on taxes, and auctioning them off.
8. Thinking of more creative ways to levy more taxes against the people of California.
9. Welcoming more illegal aliens into the state to provide businesses with cheap labor and to fill in at jobs that used to be held people who have since left the state.

Lessons have been learned from a state that has gone from a golden age of greatness in the 1940s to the 1970s. Beginning in the 1980s, Democrats began managing California. Under Democratic rule, the following things occurred:

- Illegal aliens came in and voted for more Democrats to win a majority in the state legislature, the governorship, and the courts.
- A massive number of people entered California from other states between the 1960s and 1990s to get welfare and other

free stuff offered by Democratic politicians. California was a beautiful place then.

- Homelessness increased.
- Crime increased.
- From increases in population and businesses in the 1960s to the 1980s, blue- and white-collar jobs increased. Increased taxes from these sources gave rise to Democratic politicians enriching themselves at the city, county, and state levels with fat salaries, fat pensions, and fat travel perks.
- Democrats offered free health care to illegal aliens and urged open borders to welcome more in.
- Democrats passed sanctuary laws to protect illegal alien criminals from deportation.
- Democrats established a rule under RINO governor Arnold Schwarzenegger to allow only the top two candidates with the most votes to run for governor. That eliminates Republicans from *ever* winning because, with the massive mob of Democrats in the US population, Republican candidates will never make the top two spots.
- More illegal aliens mean higher taxes levied on businesses, goods, and services everywhere. And some people wonder why roads and bridges aren't being built. Hint: All taxpayer money is going to illegal aliens, toward cleaning up the poop and urine of the homeless, toward free health care for illegal aliens, toward the funding of fat pensions for retired state retirees, and toward fire and earthquake disasters.
- The hundreds of thousands of California residents who leave the state each year, as well as the businesses that leave, will reduce the state's tax base. But Democrats hope that letting in more illegal aliens will provide California with cheap labor and will allow the state to tax the employers of these immigrants for more money. The rich will be getting richer, and the poor will remain working for cheap wages as in Mexico.

In cities and counties where white flight is occurring, Hispanics and Asians will be filling in for anyone who is sick of being highly taxed in a variety of ways. Democratic politicians under Gavin Newsom and most of the Democrats in the California State Legislature have ruined California. Illegal aliens and the Chinese are populating the entire state, particularly in Los Angeles County, San Diego County, and the San Francisco area. Wherever Buddhist temples are built, you can expect a lot of Chinese migration.

White people, mainly from the middle class, are leaving the state because of taxation oppression, particularly rising property taxes, small business taxes, gasoline taxes, utility taxes, and state income taxes. The cost of living is rising, but ironically California politicians are offering free health care to illegal aliens, paid for by the very wealthy, the middle class, small businesses, and large corporations. Billionaires mainly live in mansions all along the coast, from San Diego to Northern California. California is becoming a state of the very rich and very poor, with a reduction of the middle class. Large corporations such as Google, and other tech giants and billionaires, are well connected with state politicians who donate to whom these corporations donate to, to receive significant tax breaks. The rich will be able to afford cheap labor from illegal aliens, who are legally permitted to vote in all state and local elections. Large high-tech corporations such as Google can hire computer programmer contractors from India at low-five-figure wages and then let them go when they no longer need them. In contrast, a senior-level software engineer who is a US citizen may require a salary of six figures. So, the American high-tech worker is replaced by a foreigner on contract.

Gavin Newsom and California Democrats Fear a Revolution, so They Will Restrict Guns

Newsom may become as despised in California as Emmanuel Macron is in France. How much tax oppression can Californians take? Apparently it is not yet enough for California residents to put on yellow jackets and take to the streets. California lawmakers are severely restricting the sale and purchase of guns, the carrying of guns, and the number of bullets civilians can carry in a magazine, as well as putting restrictions on gun manufacturers. Why? To prevent an armed revolution and protect themselves against one should it happen, just like the Mexican government elites are doing in Mexico. But Mexican citizens are not allowed to purchase, sell, or carry guns. So, who in Mexico has guns? The police, the Mexican military, and the drug cartels. Democratic lawmakers in California fear a revolution as they have many more tax laws to pass for Californians.

Illegal Immigration into California Exemplifies What Will Happen to the United States with Open Borders

California's Democratic politicians are giving free health care to illegal aliens, thus angering taxpayers.

Some states such as California and New York are giving illegal aliens free health care, not Medicare. Medicaid is funded by the state, whereas Medicare is funded by the federal government. However, Democratic socialists are proposing free Medicare for all citizens, including illegal aliens, and with open borders, any foreigner entering the USA would get free health care at US taxpayers' expense. Socialist politicians Bernie Sanders and Elizabeth Warren, who ran for president in 2020, support paying for Providing Medicare to all by taxing the wealthy, the middle class, and all businesses. Neither one of these two fools knows if there would be sufficient taxpayer money to sustain their Medicare proposals since they also believe in open borders, which will draw potentially hundreds of millions of foreigners into the USA to sign up for free everything, including free health care through Medicare.

Kamala Harris quit her run for the presidency in 2019. She also advocated free Medicare for every American, including for hundreds of millions of illegal foreigners entering the United States each year for free stuff and Medicare, since she believes in open borders. Kamala Harris never said *who* would pay for everyone's Medicare or how such a thing could be done, including providing Medicare to the millions of illegal aliens who could enter the country illegally through her open border policy. On August 11, 2020, Democratic candidate for president Joe Biden chose Kamala Harris as his vice presidential running mate because he wanted, and was urged to select, a black candidate to win the black vote.

House Democrat Alexandria Ocasio-Cortez (AOC) is a socialist who also advocates that free Medicare for all is a right, along with free housing and free tuition. She claims that since the United States is a rich country, a 70 percent tax should be levied on the wealthiest people in the United States to easily pay for all this, including Medicare for the hundreds of millions of foreigners who could potentially enter the United States each year through her proposed open border policy.

California Democrats Want Illegal Aliens for Votes and for Cheap Labor for Billionaires

Illegal aliens will work for less as teachers if they learn English. That's one reason why Governor Newson wants illegal immigrants in California—because he wants *cheap labor to replace teachers on strike.* Millennials, who tend to be Democrats and socialists, *will be replaced in the workforce by illegal aliens because the latter will work for less and work harder.* And the state of California doesn't have to fork out more money for malcontent US citizens indoctrinating schoolkids into becoming liberals. Ironically, millennials will vote for Democrats while illegal aliens take their jobs, putting them on welfare and food stamps.

In addition, most of the large high-tech companies in California are donating millions of dollars to Democrats' campaigns and are getting tax-deduction credits where they pay little or no taxes. California Democrats are receiving donations from the profits of high-tech companies such as Google and Amazon to fund their campaigns for reelection in exchange for tax breaks where these companies may pay little or no taxes.

Worse, California is becoming like the government of Mexico, full of millionaires and billionaires, and poor illegal alien peons who will work for practically nothing. Cheap high-tech labor from India will be used by high-tech companies such as Google and Amazon to save money.

While California loses its middle class, the very rich are living all along the coast from San Diego to Northern California. But Democrats don't understand that illegal aliens will take jobs from the large number of homeless people—a problem that Democrats cannot fix or control. Democratic neglect of the homeless will be publicized all over the world. Contagious diseases such as tuberculosis, typhus, dysentery, and the plague will affect poop city Los Angeles and poop city San Francisco in the near future. Governor Gavin Newsom and Eric Garcetti established very bad relationships with President Trump; all they wanted was federal money from Trump—and they wanted him out of the state. Was that going to work out for California? *No!*

Democrats complain about gun control and have passed more than a dozen gun control laws, yet California's crime rate has been increasing and will continue to increase as the cost of living gets higher, rents go higher, and joblessness increases because businesses are moving out of California. Does this make sense?

Poop city Los Angeles and poop city San Francisco cannot fix their homelessness problems because Democrats have prioritized giving illegal aliens funding to get free health care. Does this make sense?

It came out in October 2019 that Bill de Blasio, mayor of poop city New York, is secretly paying the homeless people of New York to move to other states without other states knowing his plan. I'll bet California's Democratic mayors and Governor Gavin Newsom will adopt that idea and will pay tax money to export their homeless populations to other states without letting those states know about this plan. Democratic fools like Bill de Blasio would say that he is fixing the homelessness problem by paying the homeless to move to other states and letting those poor sucker states worry about them.[3]

---

[3] Sara Dorn, "NYC Secretly Exports Homeless to Hawaii and Other States without Telling Receiving Pols," *New York Post*, October 26, 2019, https://nypost. com/2019/10/26/nyc-homeless-initiative-sends-people-across-us-without-telling-receiving-cities/.

12

THE HOMELESSNESS CRISIS IN CALIFORNIA AND ITS CONSEQUENCES

Homelessness and Democratic Mismanagement

Wishful thinking won't do a liberal troll any good. California has been taken over by leftist Democratic politicians whom voters adore. They are mismanaging a once great state, whose major cities are full of homeless people who leave feces, urine, and trash in alleys, in parks, along roads, on beaches, under bridges, around downtown businesses, and around the gated mansions of the very rich. Trash, urine, and feces in Los Angeles is breeding rats and fleas and causing people to get sick. Bubonic plague is spread by fleas biting infected rats around trash. Los Angeles and San Francisco can't manage the homelessness problem. Why? Because incompetent Democratic politicians are funneling money to give illegal aliens free health care and other state government handouts. California taxes are very high. California Democrats are advertising free stuff for illegal aliens for the sole purpose of maintaining their control of California; they expect the illegal alien vote and a larger representation in Congress because of the population of illegal aliens. That is why a massive number of people from the middle class are leaving California, because of taxation oppression. Therefore, California is becoming a state of the very rich and the very poor, as in Mexico. The rich live in mansions all along the coast from San Diego to Northern California. Why don't the liberal politicians in poop cities such as San Francisco and Los Angeles ban the things we are seeing in California and do something to fix the problem? Better yet, why don't the people of California take revenge on these incompetent Democratic politicians and recall them or vote them out?

High-tech companies will remain in California only if they are given significant tax breaks in exchange for the millions of dollars they use to bribe socialist left-wing politicians. That's the only reason high-tech companies stay in California—*corruption*. Mexico does the same; however, they have the backing of the drug cartels, which is yet to happen in California. State Democrats will make any deals with the Mexican cartels as long as they put money from their drug profits in the pockets of Californian politicians.

Politically corrupt Democrats will politicize and social engineer law enforcement in California, thereby making the public less safe, protecting criminals more, and restraining police departments across the state from arresting people. It's already begun in California. As in Mexico, even the police in major cities will eventually become corrupt.

After guns are confiscated from law-abiding citizens, only criminals will have guns that can't be traced, and California residents may likely become their easy victims. How else can tyranny work unless decent people don't have guns to fight with?

Some Democratic residents spoke out on TV saying that they want California to secede from the United States and become a separate country. That will never happen if Republicans are in power. Even if socialists were to gain power in the federal government, Democrats are anxious to rip off the wealth from every state, including California, to spend on their scams.

Los Angeles Is a Dangerous Poop City for Law Enforcement because of Homelessness

Los Angeles is now a dangerous city for police officers to work in. Patrolling the streets, any squad car may get calls to deal with problems with the homeless in trash-filled, rat-infested alleys and other areas of the city. No telling what the problem may be, but coming in contact with the homeless can result in transmission of contagious diseases such as typhus and tuberculosis. Bites from fleas from infected rats can spread the plague. The LAPD is already complaining about the lack of cleanup that exists in many parts of the city; some officers have already gotten sick. These cities can no longer be tourist attractions, as Mayor Garcetti is doing very little to solve the problem of trash, filth, and feces being left behind by the homeless. Governor Newsom is a helpless man from San Francisco who has difficulty solving California's problems despite his taxation oppression of Californians.

Legal Action that Can Be Taken against California for Its Homeless Problem

Without federal help, the homeless problem in California will not get better until Democrats are voted out of office and Republicans take over to manage the state. This means poop cities will spring up across California—and there's no amount of taxes high enough that can fix the stinky problems or prevent the spread of diseases caused in these filthy cities. Repeatedly throwing money at the homeless problem and expecting a different result won't fix it.

What the incompetent but power-hungry California Democrats should be worried about is getting sued by the following:

1. the homeless people in California, for their neglect and suffering
2. Residents of California may potentially face getting infected with horrible diseases, followed by death or disability, thanks to the negligence of Governor Gavin Newsom and the mayors of all poop cities such as Los Angeles, San Francisco, and others.
3. the residents of other states who may become affected by infected residents migrating to other states with diseases such as the bubonic plague, typhus, and tuberculosis, among other contagious diseases.

Lawyers in California and other states who sue the *poop state* of California for billions of dollars will get very rich. But in the recent past, when California politicians simply heard rumors of lawsuits, they desperately asked President Trump to help them with this crisis, as the Democrats are so inept but will make hundreds of excuses for why they cannot fix the problem. What the socialist Democrats of California will call for is a bailout from the federal government, which means using collected taxes from the rest of the country to bail out miserable California run by Democratic politicians who can't fix their stinky state despite bragging they are the sixth-largest economy in the world.

Worse, throwing money at Democratic politicians is like throwing money at idiots who will still fail. Democrats could never fix the problems with the taxes they have already collected. If they didn't have enough tax money, it was because they lost out from diverting a percentage of their allotment to the free stuff they hand out to illegal aliens. For these reasons, President Trump leveraged to dissolve the Democratic hold on California and replace all of California's Democratic politicians with elected Republicans and use any additional money to micromanage California in conjunction with the newly elected Republicans.

The Quarantine of California and the Danger of Mass Exodus of Its Population to Other States

The way California is trending with its increasing number of homeless people, who leave feces, trash, and urine—attracting rats—in several of its major cities, including along riverbeds, at beaches, under bridges and freeway overpasses, and in many downtown areas, causing plague, typhus, tuberculosis, and other horrible diseases, the end of California will come more likely in twelve years rather than the whole planet ending in twelve years caused by climate change as claimed by Alexandra Ocasio-Cortez.

In twelve years, watch out, Arizona, Nevada, Colorado, Utah, Oregon, Idaho, and Washington, because a mass exodus of sick and dying people will be making a panicked exit from California and flooding your states. *The homeless and the sick will overwhelm the economies of these states.* Health inspectors from the CDC should be at the borders of these states to check for stricken dying people so as to prevent the spread of these horrible contagious diseases. California politicians should be quarantined and not be allowed to leave their state.

How to Solve the Homeless Problem in Los Angeles and Other Poop Cities

How should the Democratic politicians of California handle the massive homeless problem in the state? They should take note of how Europeans have handled the massive migration of Muslim immigrants from the Middle East and North Africa for the last few decades. Homeless people could be prevented from defecating in the streets, near businesses, in parks, next to the high-gated fence around Nancy Pelosi's mansion, on beaches, and at other places so as to prevent dangerous, unsanitary conditions that may cause deaths among the homeless, and Californian politicians could prevent contagious diseases from spreading in their poop cities if only Mayor Garcetti of Los Angeles, Mayor London Breed of San Francisco, and Governor Gavin Newsom of California were to divert tax money from funds allocated for illegal aliens to the following causes:

1. Directing all homeless people to homeless camps built by workers hired by city administrators.
2. Providing homeless camps with tents, portable toilets, showers, blankets, and cots.
3. Providing free transportation services to homeless camps for all homeless people.
4. Providing security for the homeless living in camps, tents, or temporary housing.
5. Cleaning the poop, urine, and trash from the city.
6. Exterminating to get rid of the city's rat infestation.
7. Working with hospitals to diagnose the homeless population for contagious diseases, and treating them as necessary.
8. Dividing homeless camps into quarters—for dope addicts, the mentally ill, disease-ridden people, and the disabled—thereby keeping the healthy, able-bodied people separate.

9. Working with community businesses and charitable organizations to find shelter and work opportunities for the homeless who can work to transition themselves out of homeless camps.

The same applies to growing poop cities such as Seattle, Washington; Portland, Oregon; and Las Vegas, Nevada. Note that the mayors and governors of all these poop cities and states are Democrats.

My prayer is, "Lord, give us the wisdom and guidance to unite and support leaders whom you assign to protect us and to save our country. Amen."

California's Spending Priority Isn't the Homeless or Infrastructure; It's Illegal Aliens

Each state, not the federal government, is responsible for building and repairing its own roads. But Congress can assist states by funding infrastructure building and repair from their yearly budget. For example, Democratic politicians in California have taxed the living daylights out of the citizens of their state in order to pay for free health care for illegal aliens; welfare and food stamps for illegal aliens; an expanded number of schools, more teachers, and higher salaries because of the massive increase in the number of illegal immigrant children attending those schools; cleaning up the poop and urine of the growing homeless population across California cities, from riverbeds, under bridges, on beaches, in rich neighborhoods, and so on; and personnel to arrest, convict, and incarcerate illegal aliens committing crimes. In addition, Governor Newsom and California lawmakers enjoy fat wages and fat pensions, vote themselves fat raises, and receive a number of fat travel perks, all at the taxpayers' expense.

What are taxpayers getting in return for paying high taxes? Little or nothing. Certainly not repaired roads and highways or a solution to the homeless problem. That's why, over the past ten years, approximately five million people have moved away from California. This rate of this mass exodus appears to be accelerating. This means the left-behinds will have to pay more in taxes, or else Democrats will let in more illegal aliens to tax them if they can. New York has lost 3.4 million people in the last ten years because of high taxes. More are expected to leave California and New York in the next three years because of taxation oppression.

13

HIGH TAXES CANNOT FIX DEMOCRAT-CREATED MESSES IN CALIFORNIA

California Taxes Are Killing Everyone, and Democrats Still Can't Fix the Problems

Teachers in California are all useful idiots who supported Democrats—still do—and have no clue why they are in the mess they're in. They hate Trump and love leftist politicians. Now they can't make a living because their leaders are taxing the living daylights out of them and giving their tax money to illegal aliens in the form of welfare, food stamps, free schools, free health care, and other government handouts. A percentage of destitute illegal aliens join US citizens as homeless people. Recently, California has continued to clean all the caca and urine from the beaches, parks, riverbeds, bridges, downtown areas, alleys, and some rich neighborhoods.

California will need more taxpayer money from people who own homes, own rental properties, and pay sales taxes, car registration taxes, and taxes on utilities, gasoline, and phones. And don't forget to obey traffic laws or you will pay some very hefty fines, unless you are an illegal alien, who then goes to another state, gets a license there, and returns to California. Californian taxpayers can't say no to higher taxes; it's not their call. Democrats can't take care of the homeless, much less of veterans. Even California water is being taxed.

Teachers brought this mess upon themselves and even indoctrinated their students to believe that the leftist Democratic policies are wonderful and that Republicans are bad. Even adults with a minimal education are being bamboozled, snookered, and swindled by what they hear from the evil fake news liberal media, and even from their dumber relatives, who spread nothing but gossip and fake news to them as facts. These fools only learn, not by looking at facts or logic, but by taking the word of their dumb relatives or what CNN or MSNBC says as gospel.

Misconceptions about Voter Fraud and Why People Are Leaving California

Here's why people are leaving California:

1. Illegal aliens can vote in federal elections once provided with a driver's license in several (mostly blue) states with no questions asked. All they do is show the license and vote; that's election fraud. They keep voting for Democrats who are ruining the state because they are addicted to their free handouts from the state.

2. Corrupt Democratic leaders do not want voter ID cards for everyone so as to ensure that only citizens can vote. Dishonest Democrats call voter IDs "election interference." However, Democrats know better; they just want to win elections with the assistance of voter fraud.

Two ways voter fraud can be eliminated are as follows:

a. Fingerprint everyone who registers to vote. This way, when a voter shows up to vote, one machine with a restricted database of fingerprints can match the fingerprint pictured on the voter registration card and verify the person's identity.

b. Voters can elect to donate a DNA specimen that will be recorded on a voter registration card. When the voter shows up to vote, his or her DNA can be tested at the polling location so as to match the DNA type recorded on the voter registration card.

Democratic politicians will likely reject these voter registration verification methods, saying they are an invasion of privacy. Democrats support corruption and voter fraud to win elections.

3. Clueless leaders in Congress, for example, "Crying" Schumer and insane Nancy Pelosi, want open borders in order to remake the US population so as to weaken the tens of millions of Trump voters so these congressional leaders can win elections. Schumer and Pelosi opposed Trump's building of the wall and don't care about the safety of US citizens. They don't care about criminals entering the United States to commit crimes or illegal aliens smuggling dangerous drugs into the United States that kill thousands of Americans each year. Pelosi chided Trump on his immoral border policies, but she never mentioned the human trafficking and sexual assaults on women as they trek to the southern border of the United States through Mexico.

4. The *middle class* of each blue state, for example, Illinois, New York, and California, is leaving the state in droves. Why? *Taxation oppression.* Clueless Democratic leaders should be concerned about the loss of tax revenue, but they think illegal aliens will fill the tax gap and, at the same time, work for cheap wages.

5. California politicians also fail to see that illegal aliens are poor and destitute; they will need a place to live. How will Democratic politicians accommodate housing for poor and destitute illegal aliens? If immigrants have no friend or relative to connect with who will allow them to live with them, then these illegal aliens will be homeless and on the streets. One may see homes in some communities with multiple families with children living in one house until each family can afford to live in their own home. That's why most illegal aliens are young men entering the United States. They room together with friends in homes set up for them while they work from

the home and pay their share of rent. Most homes are owned by Hispanic citizens who, for a fee, accept someone else's children and care for them until the parents enter the United States and reunite with their children; these homeowners may operate like a day-care center and draw welfare and food stamps by listing these children as theirs and getting away with it. This practice has been going on for a long time.

6. Members of MS-13 and other illegal aliens who are members of gangs do not settle in middle-class or wealthy neighborhoods; they settle in barrios or poor Mexican American neighborhoods. Most are accepted by or initiated into existing US gangs in their neighborhoods, or they retain their own gang if a number of them settle in the same neighborhood. They likely continue to live a life of horrible crime, including murder, mayhem, robbery, illegal drug sales, burglary, and sexual assault, here in the United States.

California Democrats Prioritize Benefits to Illegal Aliens over Benefits to Millennials, Veterans, and Homeowners

Most schools in ghettos and barrio neighborhoods are inferior and plagued by troubled students, one-parent students, undisciplined students, and students who don't care about learning or becoming productive citizens. In Chicago, gang members contribute to the high murder rate, killing each other, fighting for turf, and killing innocent bystanders. In New York, young people dump water on uniformed police and will kick and punch a police officer trying to arrest a suspect. In Los Angeles, young people readily riot and burn buildings if police officers beat or kill a black man, even if it's in self-defense. These youth have no morals and no respect for law and order. They brand themselves as oppressed victims of white people. And schools have done nothing to change their criminal minds. Instead, many schools reinforce black victimization and make students insecure and angry by exposing them to the parts of US history dealing only black oppression perpetrated by white people.

Many schools in California need to be revamped with new teachers and new school administrators. Teachers in the public schools of Los Angeles, California, are a bunch of liberal malcontents indoctrinating naive kids; they are not teaching kids anything useful about US history, civics, or patriotism, or any details about the US Constitution. To make things worse, the state of California is giving its state money to illegal aliens, whom California is welcoming into the state to work for low wages for employers. Employers then make more profit from this cheap labor, and the state therefore gets more tax revenue from this profit. But it's US-born millennials who are victimized and displaced, with their opportunities for jobs reduced or destroyed.

Democratic Governor Newsom is giving illegal aliens free health care, which will cost taxpayers a great deal of money. In addition, instead of working, many illegals, especially women with their own children, mixed in with other children from countries south of the border who are not theirs, collect welfare and food stamps. Fraud is hard to detect. How much tax oppression can California's taxpayers take? Apparently not enough oppression yet for them to put on yellow jackets and take to the streets in protest like in France.

The homeless are defecating and urinating all over main cities, inside businesses, and around rich neighborhoods; either Democrats do not have enough funding to care for the homeless, or they have the money and haven't a clue how to fix the problem. California Democrats now fear a revolution. Watch as Democrats start to extremely restrict the sale, purchase, and carrying of firearms in California as they have more taxes in store for already overtaxed Californians.

Obamacare Brought Back by Crazy Democratic Politicians in California

Obamacare was brought back in California by unscrupulous Californians. Passage of SB 78 created the "individual mandate" to require Californians to purchase health insurance, or else have a fine imposed for failure to do so, on January 1, 2020. This is just another way to tax the people of California, just like Obamacare was doing. It's a "shame on you" punishment for a resident of California refusing to buy health insurance. Democratic politicians continue to make it miserable for middle-class residents and would rather funnel tax money to give illegal aliens free health care and welfare than help the homeless with the horrible trash they leave everywhere, and would prefer free health care for illegal aliens rather than free health care for US veterans, or pay for infrastructure or street repairs for residents who pay taxes.

California Issues Driver's Licenses to Illegal Aliens to Make It Easier for Them to Fraudulently Vote in State and Federal Elections

Although California has not implemented a law authorizing noncitizens to vote in federal elections, California has implemented a law providing for the automatic voter registration of motorists who obtain or renew driver's licenses. Critics contend that the law will make it easier for noncitizens to vote unlawfully.

According to a *California Political Review* article published on June 3, 2015, written by Stephen Frank, a poll conducted in 2013 by John McLaughlin found from a sample size of eight hundred Hispanics from California; of those who were foreign-born and were registered voters, 13 percent admitted they were not US citizens. The article also indicated that 80 percent of noncitizens vote Democrat in elections. The conclusion is that granting driver's licenses to illegal aliens enables a percentage of these people to obtain documents indicating they are US citizens so they may collect welfare and food stamps and gain the ability to vote fraudulently. For example, if a noncitizen resembles a Hispanic who is a US citizen—approximately the same age, weight, and height—then the noncitizen who has moved to a different address could apply for a new license and use it to draw benefits and register to vote. Another way is to obtain a new license in another state, stealing a US citizen's identity and thereby obtaining benefits and registering to vote.

However, the low percentage of illegal aliens registered to vote would only make a difference when election results were close. However, if Democrats had their way, they would give at least two million illegal aliens amnesty to become US citizens and remake the political landscape of the United States.[1]

As it turned out, the Trump administration challenged the election results showing a win for Joe Biden. Evidence was gathered to submit to the Supreme Court. There is much evidence that election fraud occurred and that the Democrats conspired to steal the election in many ways.

Traffic Fines Are Another Form of Taxation in California

Traffic fines are another form of taxation oppression instituted by California Democrats, which is unfair to most Californians who are already being overtaxed by the state, county, and city. These huge fines don't make any sense, because more than 50 percent of the traffic violators are illegal aliens—and Democrats want more of them to enter California. How can illegal aliens being paid low wages afford any of these fines? Teenagers and young adults statistically violate more traffic laws than older folks and also have lower-paying jobs. How are they going to afford these high fines?

Tax Oppression in California, which Benefits Illegal Aliens More than California's Citizens, Is Driving the Middle Class Out of California

Taxes collected from California taxpayers that benefit illegal aliens more than they benefit the state's citizens are driving the middle class out of California. All California residents: before you vote for a-Democrats

---

[1] Stephen Frank, "Poll: 13% of Illegal Aliens *Admit* They Vote," *Capitol Political Review*, June 3, 2015, http://www.capoliticalreview.com/capoliticalnewsandviews/poll-13-of-illegal-aliens-admit-they-vote/.

should think about the foregoing comments next time they vote. If you vote Democrat, expect to pay higher taxes on the following:

1. utilities (water, trash, electricity, phone, and iPhone) and any other environmental taxes that California officials create;
2. gasoline, for infrastructure and road repairs, although these taxes are really going to fund illegal alien health care and other handouts;
3. the sale and purchase of guns—socialists in California don't want a law-abiding person to buy or own guns so as to prevent rebellions against their future tyrannical laws and oppression;
4. sales (i.e., purchases);
5. one's California state tax franchise board, based on one's annual income;
6. property as defined by Proposition 13, passed in 1978 (the more your home value goes up, the more money California's Democratic politicians collect, at a rate of 1 percent or 2 percent per year);
7. business; and
8. business property.

Californians can also expect to pay higher vehicle registration rates and also heavy traffic fines, which are merely a form of tax revenue imposed on traffic violators.

All this tax oppression by the state of California is driving residents out of the state *in droves*. What do you think will happen as a result? Answer: California will experience a major loss of tax revenue, forcing even higher taxes on the remaining California residents *and* welcoming more illegal aliens into the state to provide cheap labor to businesses so as to prevent these businesses from leaving the state, as many have done already. Californians already know the *incentives* (freebies) the state of California is offering to illegal aliens, prioritizing them above its own citizens, including homeless people, people without medical insurance, and veterans, to get them into California—*at the expense of taxpayers.*

David A. Herrera

Why California Residents Are Leaving the State

No one can ignore the reasons why the middle class is leaving the state of California, why California is losing its tax base, why illegal aliens are moving into the state, why California has the highest poverty rate, why California has the highest homeless population, and why roads and bridges and other infrastructure has been ignored for years. Governor Gavin Newsom should know that California was beautiful before a liberal incompetent such as he took control of the state and ruined it. California cities are stink-holes and are being ignored. Gavin should note that California, once a beautiful state to live in, might be the death of a large portion of the US population with bubonic plague, which is spread by rats and fleas, which congregate around trash, feces, urine, and other debris homeless people leave in alleys, in streets, in riverbeds, in parks, under bridges, and near Nancy Pelosi's gated mansion. The state is having trouble cleaning it all up. California is becoming known as a Third World country and the stink-hole of the USA. It's liberal Democrats who caused this mess and continue to make it worse.

Life is not good for many in California. Liberal Democratic leaders have oppressed the residents of California with high taxes, which continue to rise—and taxpayers have little or nothing to show for their hard-earned taxes. It's taxation without representation. All tax money is going into the pockets of liberal Democrats running the state, to welfare and free health care for illegal aliens, toward cleaning up the feces, urine, and trash the homeless leave behind, and to provide shelter for the homeless population.

California still has beautiful oceans, but only the very rich—that is, billionaires—own and live in mansions along the coast from San Diego to Northern California. California is composed of the very rich and the poor to very poor. And I think that's the way Governor Newsom and the other California state legislators like it. You have to be rich to live in California. If you're not, you're either homeless, leaving the state, stuck in California struggling with high taxes to make ends meet, or relying on the very rich who control California for low-paying jobs. Governor Newsom and the very rich should be informed about the

French Revolution and what happened to the rich elites living like kings and queens, and to what is happening with the yellow vests in France today.

According to Stephen Frank, there are thirty-five reasons to leave California. Frank mentions one survey showing that 47 percent of all Californians are thinking about moving out of California within the next five years, and another survey showing that 53 percent living in the state would like to leave. A factor that should be added as another reason to leave the state is the smog. See the full article to learn of additional problems with California living.[2]

New York, California, and Illinois Will Become States of Indentured Servants and Feudalism, and of the Poor and Very Rich

New York City is implementing "creeping socialism," which, after it becomes full-blown socialism, will prompt a revolution of the city's residents. Why: *taxation oppression* and *taxation without representation*. New York City, Illinois, and California are overtaxing their citizens and are losing the middle class and businesses, which are moving out of these states.

For instance, Gavin Newsom of California is a nutcase who will become as hated in California as Emmanuel Macron is hated in France. How much tax oppression can Californians take? Apparently not enough to put on yellow vests and take to the streets. I foresee upcoming California laws severely restricting the sale and purchase of guns, the carrying of any firearms, and the number of bullets civilians may carry in a magazine; promoting the confiscation of firearms in light of any negative allegations; collecting high taxes on the sale and purchase of firearms; and placing restrictions on gun manufacturers. Why? To protect themselves, just as the Mexican government elites have been doing in Mexico for many decades. In Mexico, citizens are not allowed

---

[2] Stephen Frank, "35 Reasons Why You Should Move away from California," *Citizens Journal*, November 18, 2019, https://www.citizensjournal.us/35-reasons-why-you-should-move-away-from-california/.

to purchase, sell, or carry firearms. Democrats fear a revolution because they have more taxes in store for citizens of California, New York, and Illinois—also throw in Connecticut and New Jersey. What is occurring in blue states is called taxation oppression.

What Needs to Be Done for the United States in 2021, Especially in California

It's time to take care of all Americans, not the rich liberals living along the coast or the high-tech corporations that get tax kickbacks for their donations to Democratic politicians. It's time to take care of American citizens instead of illegal aliens. It's time for the country to grow the economy and to increase jobs and opportunities for all so they can work hard to achieve the American dream.

Democrats don't want the United States to succeed as it had been doing under President Trump. Since Democrats were rejected in 2016, they want to remake the United States with open borders to "seed" US states with illegal aliens for future votes and cheap labor. In California, all who will be left will be the very rich and the very poor, just like the case in Mexico now. That's why there is massive emigration by the middle class and businesses in California. The same thing is happening in the state of New York. California politicians can't fix their poop cities, which will grow even larger under the Biden administration and become a crisis. The already high crime rate is increasing in California, especially property crimes now that Proposition 47 was passed. Democrats passed fifteen antigun laws, but gun violence has been increasing. Explain that.

California Politicians Begging President Trump to Help Their Deteriorating Economy

Under Nancy Pelosi, the COVID-19 bills had been in the works because House Democrats wanted to bail out states with irresponsible policies, seeking to give them billions of dollars. Republicans and President Trump opposed the House's COVID-19 relief bill for months.

In December 2020, Democrats in the House voted for a $900 billion pork bill that they never even read, expecting Republicans in the Senate to pass it. It was rejected because of too much spending unrelated to COVID-19 and because it promised to help Americans with only $600 per person, including illegal aliens. President Trump said he would reject it and suggested $2,000 COVID-19 assistance checks to people who qualified for them based on their income.

But a smart Trump could not have been expected to throw money at Governor Newsom or the incompetent California lawmakers because of their bad financial handling of the state and their inability to fix an economy they'd destroyed. California politicians cannot be trusted to fix anything.

More likely, President Trump would have assigned an agency of the federal government to provide a get-well plan for the California economy. Soup lines would have been established in the mostly poor areas to feed the poor and the homeless. Things would have been done to provide shelter for the homeless, provide jobs for the able-bodied, provide mental health for the mentally ill on the streets, have the DOJ coordinate with local law enforcement to attack the rising crime rate, fund local law enforcement, allow ICE to deport criminal aliens, and force lawmakers to pass laws that would stimulate the California economy and reduce business regulations. Trump likely would have canceled free health care for illegal aliens and reduced welfare fraud and food stamp fraud. All these policies would have embarrassed Governor Newsom and California lawmakers.

14

THE CALIFORNIA HOMOSEXUAL LOBBY

The homosexual mafia is a chimera with multiple ugly heads. Homosexual organizations show their ugly heads: the head of the pedophile monster, of the corrupt homosexual, of the irate homosexual, of the sanctimonious homosexual, of the homosexual deviant and pervert, of the transgender oddball, of the cross-dressing homosexual, and of the arrogant homosexual. The homosexual mafia has many faces that lobby every kind of influential entity, such as schools, churches, political offices, psychiatrists, government leaders, and lawyers, to promote their homosexual agenda.

How the Homosexual Lobby Plans to Promote and Protect Homosexuality and Social Engineer It into US Culture

California Assembly Bill 2943 was introduced by Evan Low. At Factcheck.org, it says this bill does not ban the Bible; it is only designed to prevent anyone from seeking professional help to find a cure for "sexual orientation" in exchange for money.

So, for example, if you "turn queer" and try to find a cure for your same-sex feelings, you find that it is illegal to pay a doctor to cure you of your homosexual feelings. This bill is designed to preserve/protect anyone's homosexual feelings and to make it against the law for parents to hire professional help to find a cure for their children in exchange for money. A church or individual may still practice conversion therapy to return to normality and sanity, if they do so without charging for this "fraudulent service," Low says. Again, the bill does not ban Bibles, nor does it ban the basic sales of books, because to do so would violate the First Amendment of the Constitution.

Out-of-the-closet homosexual California State assemblyman Evan Low, who introduced Bill 2943, announced in August 31, 2018, that he would shelve the legislation and work on crafting a new law. "Despite the support the bill received in the Assembly and Senate, I will not be sending AB 2943 to the Governor this year," he said in a statement. "I am committed to continuing to work towards creating a policy that best protects and celebrates the identities of LGBT Californians and a model for the nation to look towards." The reason he shelved his bill was that the bill was unconstitutional; he could not legally stifle business and free enterprise to satisfy his own unhealthy homosexual desires or those of the homosexual lobby. Homosexual lobbyists cannot silence free speech or prohibit Christian ministers from teaching or preaching that homosexuality is wrong and immoral based on several passages in the Bible, because to do so would violate the First Amendment of the Constitution. This homosexual lobby cannot ban the Bible, but they would like to.

California may eventually ban Bibles, or at least restrict Bibles to only churches and private homes, within the next thirty to fifty years, or sooner if Democrats take control of the House, the Senate, and the presidency. Bible control is, pure and simple, social engineering of the youth of California by the LGBTQ crowd. It might be time to plan to move out of California, a state that not only mismanages its poop cities, contributes to homelessness, and tax-oppresses its residents and businesses but also appears to be full of homosexual legislators who promote homosexuality—and they want to start with kids in schools. California is already teaching about the safe practice of teenage homosexuality in public schools under the guise of health education. The LGBTQ crowd loves it, but many parents don't. The homosexual crowd hopes and anticipates that LGBTQ education will lead to acceptance of, and better yet conversion to, homosexuality, unless stopped. California also approved its first LGBT textbooks for K–8 classrooms in 2017. The teaching of homosexual history is now required in four states— Colorado, California, New Jersey, and Illinois—to teach the roles and contributions of lesbian, gay, bisexual, and transgender people in US history under the guise of tolerance and civil rights. These states are being ruined by depraved Democrats and perverts. I personally think there will be *no* peaceful solution to getting California back to how we knew it before the mid-1960s.

Former socialist presidential candidates Beto O'Rourke, Cory Booker, and Peter Buttigieg had declared war on Christian churches and institutions by claiming that if any religious institutions discriminate against socialist policies, such as same-sex marriages or hiring of homosexuals in the Catholic Church, then they should be punished by eliminating their tax-exempt status and denying them federal grants for religious colleges. It matters absolutely nothing to these tyrants whether an individual will refuse to do something because it goes against Christian beliefs, or interferes with individual religious rights, or directly goes against passages in the Bible. It matters nothing to these Democratic politicians that there are serious risks and potential harm to children supervised by homosexual employees who serve in youth group events and Bible study, gaining the trust of naive children. Look at what happened to the once great Boy Scouts of America: In 2013, under the Obama administration, the Boy Scouts decided to admit openly gay scouts, and in 2015 the ban on gay scoutmasters was lifted. Just five years later, in February 2020, the Boy Scouts of America declared bankruptcy because of the sexual abuse lawsuits filed against homosexual scoutmasters who were once banned to protect children. We cannot trust gays hired by religious institutions to protect our children. We cannot afford to have gays infiltrate Christian churches and then go on to promote homosexuality or sexually abuse boys in order to bankrupt these religious institutions. If religious institutions cannot be reformed by leftists, they eventually will be destroyed, to the pleasure of George Soros, his operatives, and past and present US Democratic political leaders who are loyal to him.

This is tyranny from the Left, waging an economic war against religious freedom and religious institutions. It's intrusive. Socialists are imposing big government mandates on the private lives of individuals and violating their First Amendment religious rights. As a result of socialist politicians passing these tyrannical mandates, many charity organizations, churches, synagogues, mosques, and religious-affiliated organizations could have to shut down. President Joe Biden has promised to "reform" religious institutions in his first one hundred days in office to "protect" homosexuals from discriminatory practices. At his advanced age, Joe Biden should know the perils and risks his promised religious reforms would cause to besiege religious institutions.

In June 2019, California assemblyman Evan Low, a man of Asian descent who is a self-avowed homosexual, and three dozen other lawmakers passed a resolution in the California State Assembly Judiciary Committee urging religious leaders in California to preach certain things from their pulpits. The California Family Council reports that Assembly Concurrent Resolution 99 (ACR 99) calls on "counselors, pastors, religious workers, educators" and institutions with "great moral influence" to stop perpetuating the idea that something is wrong with LGBT identities or sexual behavior. ACR 99 also condemns attempts to change unwanted same-sex attraction or gender confusion as "unethical," "harmful," and leading to high rates of suicide. This is the homosexual mafia in California dictating to all Christian religions what they should preach about homosexuality in their sermons, ignoring religious doctrine and ignoring homosexuality as a sin in the Bible. According to the article, professionals and Christian ministers can help individuals who are attracted to people of the same sex to live a healthy lifestyle with the opposite sex; it cites examples.[1]

---

[1] Andrea Morris, "CA Lawmakers Trying to Force Pastors to Embrace Pro-LGBT Ideology," CBN News, June 18, 2019, https://www1.cbn.com/cbnnews/us/2019/june/ca-lawmakers-trying-to-force-pastors-to-preach-pro-lgbt-sermons.

David A. Herrera

California Pro-Homosexual Politicians Pass Laws to Introduce and Protect Homosexuality in Public Schools, Trampling on the Rights of Parents

California Assembly Bill 2943 was introduced by California State assemblyman Evan Low, a psychologically deviant homosexual. Factcheck.org indicates his bill does not ban the Bible; it only seeks to prevent anyone from hiring professional help to find a cure for sexual orientation in exchange for money.

So, for example, if a child becomes sexually attracted to someone of the same sex and tries to find a cure for these same-sex feelings, the bill makes it illegal for a doctor to provide a remedy in exchange for money. The bill is designed to preserve/protect anyone's feeling of homosexuality and make it against the law for parents to hire professional help to find a cure for their child in exchange for money. A church or individual may still practice conversion therapy, attempting to return the child to normality and sanity, if this is done without charging a fee for the "fraudulent service." The bill does not ban Bibles, nor does it ban the basic sale of books, because to do so would violate the First Amendment of the Constitution.

California State assemblyman Evan Low, a self-avowed homosexual who introduced Bill 2943, announced in August 31, 2018, that he would scrap the legislation and craft a new law. "Despite the support the bill received in the Assembly and Senate, I will not be sending AB 2943 to the Governor this year," he said in a statement. "I am committed to continuing to work towards creating a policy that best protects and celebrates the identities of LGBT Californians and a model for the nation to look towards." The reason he shelved his bill is that he cannot stifle businesses and free commerce to satisfy his own unhealthy homosexual desires or the desires of the homosexual mafia. This pro-LGBT California lawmaker also cannot prevent parents from seeking a remedy for their child's psychological maladies or prevent parents from raising their children in the way they want. This homosexual lawmaker cannot silence free speech or prohibit Christian ministers from teaching or preaching that homosexuality is wrong and immoral based on several passages in the Bible, because to do so would violate the

First Amendment of the Constitution. This homosexual mafia cannot ban the Bible, but they would like to.

California may eventually ban the Bible, or at least restrict Bibles to only churches and private homes, within the next thirty to fifty years, or sooner, if Democrats take control of the House, the Senate, and the presidency. Keeping the Bible away from youths, or "Bible control," or revising biblical history and redefining new morality in the Bible, are all pure and simple social engineering practices put upon the youth of California and the young people of other states by the homosexual mafia. It might be time to move out of California, a state that not only mismanages its poop cities, has a homelessness problem, and tax-oppresses its residents and businesses, but also appears to have a significant number of homosexual legislators who overwhelmingly promote homosexuality as a sick social reform. California is already teaching the safe practices of teenage homosexuality in public schools under the guise of health education. The LGBTQ crowd loves it, but many parents don't. The homosexual mafia hopes this education leads to pedophilia, unless prevented or stopped. California also approved its first LGBT textbooks for K–8 classrooms in 2017. The teaching of homosexual history is now required in four states, Colorado, California, New Jersey, and Illinois, to teach the roles and contributions of lesbian, gay, bisexual, and transgender people in US history under the guise of tolerance and civil rights. These states are being ruined by sick Democrats and perverts. I personally think there will be *no* peaceful solution to getting California back to how we knew it in the early 1960s.

Socialist presidential candidates Beto O'Rourke, Cory Booker, and Peter Buttigieg declared war on Christian churches and institutions, claiming that if any religious church or institution discriminates against socialist policies such as same-sex marriage, the hiring of homosexuals in the Catholic Church, or serving wedding cakes to homosexuals, or condemns or refuses to support those among its employees who perform or have had abortions, they will be punished by the elimination of their tax-exempt status and by denying Christian colleges federal money grants. Joe Biden planned to do the same thing once he was inaugurated as president on January 20, 2021. It matters absolutely nothing to these tyrants whether an individual will refuse to do something because it goes against Christian beliefs, or interferes with his or her religious rights, or directly goes against passages in the Bible. This is tyranny from the Left, waging a war against God and religious freedom, and an economic war against religious institutions. It's intrusive. Socialists are imposing big socialist government mandates onto the private lives of individuals, thus violating their First Amendment religious rights. As a result of socialist politicians passing their tyrannical mandates, many charity organizations, churches, synagogues, mosques, and religious-affiliated organizations might have to shut down.

Homosexual Indoctrination of Young Kids in Public Schools

Indoctrinating kids with homosexuality, the history of homosexuality, and the adoration of homosexuality should never be done in public schools. It's sick and perverted. Sane parents just don't want sex taught to little kids, even in high schools as California is trying to do. The goals of the perverted politicians of California are to introduce young teens to homosexuality and indoctrinate kids to believe that homosexual behavior is "normal" behavior. What is really the goal behind these laws from Sacramento, California? Answer: Enthusiastic promoters of homosexuality from Sacramento want culture change in public schools in order to convert young teens into homosexuals and increase the homosexual population. Another goal is to satisfy sick pedophiles, who prey on children. Queer lawmakers are sick creeps who promote homosexuality to children in public schools without the consent of parents. Teachers who teach this crap in classrooms are also promoting it and *are not worthy* to teach in public schools.

The Holocaust is taught only as part of the history of World War II. Black history is never taught in public high schools. Neither are Chicano studies. Those are all electives taught only in certain colleges and universities that offer them. Why should fifth grade through eighth grade kids be taught same-sex perversion? They are not mature enough to know much of anything about sex.

The 2011 FAIR Education Act made California the first state to require the teaching of LGBT history. Liberal Democratic LGBT-inclusive bills are all promoted under the guise of equality, diverse inclusion, and tolerance. In Illinois, Governor J. B. Pritzker signed House Bill 246 on August 9, 2019, sponsored by Rep. Anna Moeller (D-Elgin), to go into effect in July 2020. It makes Illinois the fourth state to mandate the teaching of LGBT history, after California, New Jersey, and Colorado. The legislation reads: "In public schools only, the teaching of history shall include a study of the roles and contributions of lesbian, gay, bisexual, and transgender people in the history of this country and this state." The bill requires that textbooks authorized for purchase must contain roles and contributions of all people protected under the Illinois Human Rights Act.

It is indeed a dark day for the state of Illinois, whose governor has imposed immoral pedophile law mandates in public schools to promote the introduction of homosexual behavior and perversion to young kids via the history of homosexuals, cross-dressers, and lesbians. This is another step to introduce kids to the notion of being the victims of pedophiles and child molesters and to please the pedophile lobbyists. The New Jersey Family Policy Council, similarly, believes that "teaching about a person's contribution to history is one thing, but their sexual feelings are irrelevant and should not be a part of the discussion. Sexual orientation, desires, and feelings of historical figures are not appropriate or relevant to the teaching of the social contributions of historical giants of the past," as it said in a blog post on the matter.

This extreme leftist social engineering began under the Obama administration and was promoted as "hope and change." Do parents have a say about what their kids should be taught in schools? Do parents have a voice in courses taught to arouse their children's curiosity about homosexuality? Do parents have a say in what the governor of Illinois is mandating for kids in the eighth grade, that they must become familiar with the accomplishments of homosexuals in order to graduate?[2]

As long as liberal progressive Democrats with no common sense allow men wearing bloomers or knickers to compete as women, it is a rigged contest.

Liberal Democratic Social Engineering: Use of Nongender Bathrooms, and Conflicts

On June 6, 2016, a Michigan school district stopped the practice of allowing members of one biological sex to use the restrooms of the opposite sex after parents pulled their two sons out of elementary school because of this issue.

A week prior, Matt Stewart's nine-year-old son told him, "There was a girl in the boys' bathroom," that is, with him and other male elementary kids. When Stewart called the school, the principal told him the Obama administration's federal guidance on transgender students had forced them to allow transgender students in the bathrooms, locker rooms, and showers of the gender of their choice, and not their biological sex. Violating the policy meant losing federal funding. Stewart talked it over with his wife, and they decided to take their sons out of Southwest Elementary School in Howell, Michigan.

These gender policies started under Obama's "Hope and Change" social engineering policies. A child of any gender was allowed to use "genderless" restrooms, showers, and locker rooms as a prerequisite for receiving federal funding. The possibility for criminal abuse of this policy in high schools is enormous.

---

[2] Heather Clark, "Ill. Governor Signs Bill into Law Requiring Students to Be Taught about Historical Contributions of Homosexuals," Christian News Network, August 14, 2019, https://christiannews.net/2019/08/14/ill-governor-signs-bill-into-law-requiring-students-to-be-taught-about-historical-contributions-of-homosexuals/;

Alana Mastrangelo, "Illinois Governor Mandates LGBT History Curriculum for Public Schools," Breitbart, August 11, 2019, https://www.breitbart.com/education/2019/08/11/illinois-governor-mandates-lgbt-history-curriculum-for-public-schools/.

This nonsense has to stop across the country. Obama supported liberal homosexual activists who promoted these federal regulations. To enforce the awful regulations regarding genderless bathrooms, pressure tactics were used to deny federal funding to those who failed to comply. Noncompliance means the state and local taxpaying communities become the sole funding source for the school, putting the school at risk in that it might be abandoned because of lack of funding for student resources and teacher wages. That's economic warfare.

15

OTHER US CITIES AND STATES MISMANAGED BY PROGRESSIVE DEMOCRATS

Democratic Management Style: If You Live in Oregon, California, Washington, New York, or Nevada, Wake Up and Smell the Poop

Wake up and smell the roses: The US economy is doing well, and our country had a brilliant president with several outstanding accomplishments he made and promises he kept. However, if you live in San Francisco, Los Angeles, Portland, Seattle, New York City, or Las Vegas, you may wake up and smell the poop, because it's cities like these that are being run by incompetent liberal Democrats. They didn't promise their city residents trash, stink, and diseases from the homeless when they ran for office, but that's what they delivered. These states each have at least one poop city with a massive homelessness problem that is causing a variety of horrible diseases and pestilence to spread in the state. In these states' major cities, diseases such as tuberculosis, typhus, and measles occur among homeless people. The bubonic plague comes from fleas from infected rats thriving on the trash, feces, and urine on streets, on beaches, in riverbeds, in parks, in alleys, and under bridges left behind by the homeless. Most of the homeless population is made up of the very poor, the mentally ill, dope addicts, and some illegal aliens. The Centers for Disease Control and Prevention (CDC) should investigate these filthy feces- and trash-infested poop cities in California and other states before a nationwide epidemic occurs. For example, bubonic plague, typhus, and tuberculosis are all contagious. Have California's Democratic mayors, Governor Newsom, and California's state lawmakers contacted the CDC yet to prepare in case of an emergency?

How did Democratic politicians bamboozle naive useful idiots, low-IQ millennials, freeloaders, drug users, and uneducated fools to get votes? Now such leftist politicians are ruining California—but these pompous Democratic politicians living in gated mansions and mismanaging their poop cities say that Trump is bad? Just give control of the federal government to Democratic politicians such as those who are ruining California, and in a few years, socialist fools will *try* to turn the United States into a cesspool and/or Venezuela.

Seven of the Worst Cities Are Managed by Incompetent Democrats

Seven of the worst cities in the United States are run by incompetent or corrupt Democrats. Los Angeles, San Francisco, New York City, Baltimore, Portland, Oakland, and Seattle are known as "poop cities" and are getting worse. Democratic politicians are good at ruining the cities in their states, making the middle class leave the state, and overtaxing the middle class. Above all, they mismanage every city they control.

In Detroit, massive white flight occurred many decades ago, leaving the city managed and controlled by corrupt liberal Democratic administrators. The city is now significantly in shambles and looks like a war zone. Many houses and businesses have been abandoned. Detroit's tax base has significantly diminished. Incompetent politicians from liberal cities such as Detroit asked President Obama for a quid pro quo in exchange for their having voted for him, the con artist.

It's a matter of time before the other cities mentioned will become like Detroit. Governor Newsom of California is giving free health care to illegal aliens with taxpayer funds collected from people who own homes. Illegal aliens will be the ones to move into the abandoned houses that will be left for them. The billionaires will all live along the coast, from San Diego to Northern California. The economy will be similar to the feudal system of that of the Middle Ages in Europe. Illegal aliens will be cheap labor peons working for the baron-like billionaires living in mansions along the coast of California.

Democrats Have Mismanaged Major US States for Many Decades

Democrats have been mismanaging blue states such as California, Illinois, Michigan, New Jersey, New York, and Washington, and other major cities across the country. During the Democratic presidential debate, no one heard any of the candidates asked by news media hosts to give the American people a response to the following questions:

- Given the magnitude of the homelessness problem in major California cities and the potential for bubonic plague, typhus, tuberculosis, and measles epidemics caused by the trash, feces, and urine that the homeless are leaving all over California and in other states run by Democrats, how do you propose to fix the homeless problem?
- What is the burden on taxpayers giving a massive number of illegal aliens, free health care, tuition, welfare, and food stamps? Additionally, what do you estimate the cost will be for additional judges, court trials, police officers, and prisons for those illegal aliens who commit crimes?
- By offering free stuff to illegal aliens to draw them into the United States under Democratic immigration reform, and subsequently giving them amnesty to enable them to vote and apply for more government handouts and assistance, don't you

think these are good political policies for Democrats to maintain power and riches forever?

- Who is for open borders? Raise your hands. If President Trump completes a wall along the southern border of the United States, who will tear that wall down? Raise your hands.

- Who wants waves of caravans of illegal aliens to enter the United States illegally to get their free stuff paid for hardworking Americans, which may cause US taxpayers economic hardship? Raise your hands.

- Other than giving DACA migrants amnesty, who is for giving millions of incoming illegal aliens amnesty?

- Do any of you see that taxation without representation and that tax oppression of the wealthy, middle-class homeowners, and business owners may lead to an armed civil war?

- Will illegal aliens take jobs away from average workers in the United States? Does giving amnesty to illegal aliens take away jobs from US citizens?

- Why are Democrats hell-bent on confiscating guns or banning them altogether? Is it to prevent a revolution by oppressed Americans against the tyrannical Democratic ruling elites, who will continue to oppress US citizens, destroy the Constitution, eliminate the Electoral College, and pack the US Supreme Court with more liberal socialist or communist judges?

- Will Democrats weaponize every agency in the federal government to go after conservatives, tax evaders, right-wing terrorists, white supremacists, and conservative militias, and will they confiscate any wealth that conservatives have in IRAs, bank accounts, retirement funds, annuities, and their homes?

- Who will terminate social security for seniors? Give your reasons.

- Who will terminate government compensation for US veterans afflicted with service-connected injuries or illnesses? Give your reasons.

- Why hasn't one Democrat presented simple arithmetic to show the total taxpayer cost for all spending items?

- Why hasn't one Democrat done any arithmetic to figure out the costs of reparations for blacks and reparations for homosexuals as advocated by most Democratic presidential candidates? None have mentioned if reparations are a onetime deal or for every generation of blacks. If this program is approved by socialists, still none of them have mentioned when payments will stop. None have indicated who specifically are victims today and who will pay for all this mess.

- How would you fund the military if most of the federal funding goes toward health care for illegal aliens, black and homosexual reparations, the Green New Deal, the rejoining of the Paris climate accord, college loan debt relief, welfare and food stamps for a large percentage of amnesty migrants, increased homelessness, the rising crime rate, and free college tuition? How can defense corporations be funded to provide the military the required weaponry to defend the United States from nuclear attacks and terrorism?

- Should the United States grant US sovereignty to the UN to be included as a member under a global one world government?

- About inflation. Most of today's Democrats know little about capitalism, but Democratic socialists are clueless about it. If insufficient taxes are collected from US taxpayers, would any of you propose to seize the bank accounts, social security, or pensions, and/or confiscate the homes, of US citizens? Or would you, at any time, print more money to fund your pet spending programs? Do any of you know that printing more money devalues the US dollar, causing inflation and putting the country on a path to economic collapse? If the economy collapses in the United States because of socialist policies, will the United States see bloodbaths much worse than those that happened to rich French ruling aristocrats during the French Revolution in the storming of the Bastille (where heads rolled)?

- Who said about unemployed Americans in poverty and the homeless peasants who had no bread to eat after the US economy collapsed, "Let them eat ice cream"? Answer: Nancy Marie Antoinette Pelosi (joke).

The wealthiest Californians appear to be workers in high-tech corporations and Democrats who donate to the campaigns of Democratic politicians in exchange for favors (pay-to-play or quid pro quo schemes). Billionaire Democrats tend to live in mansions all along the southern coast and the northern coast of California. Democrats support income inequality but think that this applies to other people only, not to them, as they will be enjoying their high salaries, raises, and pensions, along with the best health care and other perks. Democrats love to spend other people's money. To maintain power and riches, they rely on foreigners, instead of Americans, to gain reelection. California's high-tech companies will be heavily taxed by the repeal of the corporate tax President Trump had put in place. But corporations will be subsidized by their tax write-offs, given to them by California politicians whose campaigns high-tech corporations will donate to. This is crony capitalism as in Obama's administration; corporations that donated to Barack Obama got massive tax breaks, and some paid very little taxes. On top of tax-deduction favors, California corporations will be able to replace high-paid US workers making between $100,000 and $200,000 per year with foreign contractors from India and pay them between $20,000 and $40,000 per year. That's a significant savings when subcontractors will not be paid retirement pension benefits or medical benefits after their contracts expire.

TABLE 1. The worst-run cities in the United States, 2019

City	Mayor	Political party
Cleveland, Ohio	Frank George Jackson	Democrat
Hartford, Connecticut	Luke Bronin	Democrat
Flint, Michigan	Karen Weaver	Democrat
Oakland, California	Elizabeth Beckman Schaaf	Democrat
Detroit, Michigan	Michal Edward Duggan	Democrat
New York, New York	Bill de Blasio	Democrat
Chattanooga, Tennessee	Andy Berke	Democrat
San Francisco, California	London Breed	Democrat
Gulfport, Mississippi	William Gardner Hewes	Republican
Washington, DC	Muriel Bowser	Democrat

Statistics for 2019 showed that the most dangerous cities in the United States were cities managed by liberal Democrats with high black populations.

TABLE 2. The most dangerous cities in the United States, 2019

Rank	City	Percent of population that is black	City managed by
1	St. Louis, Missouri	47.61%	Democrat Lynda Krewson
2	Detroit, Michigan	79.12%	Democrat Michael Edward Duggan
3	Baltimore, Maryland	63.30%	Democrat Bernard Young
4	Memphis, Tennessee	63.91%	Democrat Jim Strickland
5	Little Rock, Arkansas	41.40%	Democrat Frank Scott Jr.
6	Milwaukee, Wisconsin	69.00%	Democrat Tom Barrett
7	Rockford, Illinois	21.21%	Democrat Tom McNamara
8	Cleveland, Ohio	50.41%	Democrat Frank G. Jackson

- As of November 6, 2019.
- St. Louis overtook Detroit as the nation's most dangerous city.
- According to the American Community Survey of August 28, 2019, the racial composition of Memphis included a population of 63.91 percent black or African American people.

TABLE 3. Homeless populations of cities or counties managed by Democratic or Republican politicians, 2019

City or county	Estimated homeless population	City managed by
Los Angeles County	50,000 to 60,000	Democrats
San Diego County	8,201	Republicans
Chicago, Illinois	80,000	Democrats
New York, New York	61,674	Democrats
Portland, Oregon	38,000	Democrats
Seattle, Washington	11,199	Democrats
San Francisco, California	9,784	Democrats
Washington, DC	6,521 to 9,794	Democrats
Honolulu, Hawaii	6,530	Democrats
Las Vegas, Nevada	5,286	Democrats

Milwaukee, Wisconsin	4,907	Democrats
St. Louis, Missouri	2,170	Democrat s
Detroit, Michigan	1,769	Democrats
Baltimore, Maryland	7,689	Democrats

TABLE 4. US cities with the largest homeless populations, 2019

Rank	City	Homeless population	City population	Percent homeless
1	New York, New York (includes 3,711 unsheltered)	78,676	8,560,072	0.92%
2	Los Angeles, California Estimate includes the City of Los Angeles and Los Angeles County (includes 37,570 unsheltered)	49,955	3,949,776	0.04%
3	Seattle, Washington Estimate includes King County (includes 6,320 unsheltered)	12,112	688,245	0.25%
4	San Diego, California Estimate includes the City of San Diego and San Diego County (includes 4,990 unsheltered)	8,576	1,390,966	0.12%
5	San Jose, California Estimate includes Santa Clara City and Santa Clara County (includes 5,448 unsheltered)	7,254	1,023,031	0.17%
6	District of Columbia (DC) (includes 600 unsheltered)	6,904	672,391	0.26%
7	San Francisco, California (includes 4,353 unsheltered)	6,857	864,263	0.79%
8	Phoenix, Arizona Estimate includes Mesa and Maricopa Counties	6,298	1,574,421	0.40%
9	Boston, Massachusetts (includes 163 unsheltered)	6,188	669,158	0.92%
10	Las Vegas, Nevada Estimate includes Clark County (includes 3,884 unsheltered)	6083	621,662	0.28%
11	Philadelphia, Pennsylvania (includes 1,083 unsheltered)	5,788	1,569,657	0.11%

Rank	City	Homeless population	City population	Percent homeless
12	Oakland and Berkeley, California Estimate includes Alameda County (includes 404 unsheltered)	5,496	417,442	1.32%
13	Chicago, Illinois (includes 1,357 unsheltered)	5,450	2,722,586	0.20%
14	Denver, Colorado Estimate includes Denver metropolitan area (includes 1,308 unsheltered)	5,317	678,467	0.25%
15	Houston, Pasadena, and Conroe, Texas Estimate includes Harris, Fort Bend, and Montgomery Counties (includes 1,614 unsheltered)	4,143	2,267,336	0.08%
16	Dallas, Texas Estimate includes Dallas County (includes 1,341 unsheltered)	4,121	1,300,122	0.32%
17	Portland and Gresham, Oregon Estimate includes Multnomah County (includes 1,668 unsheltered)	4,019	630,331	0.27%
18	Sacramento, California Estimate includes Sacramento County (includes 2,052 unsheltered)	3,621	489,650	0.74%
19	Miami, Florida Estimate includes Dade County	3,516	443,007	0.39%
20	Atlanta, Georgia (includes 740 unsheltered)	3,076	465,230	0.66%
21	San Antonio, Texas Estimate includes Bexar County (includes 1,353 unsheltered)	3,066	1,461,623	0.21%
22	Minneapolis, Minnesota Estimate includes Hennepin County (includes 404 unsheltered)	3,013	411,452	0.42%
23	Baltimore, Maryland (includes 546 unsheltered)	2,508	619,796	0.40%
24	Nashville, Tennessee Estimate includes Davidson County (includes 616 unsheltered)	2,298	654,187	0.35%

Rank	City	Homeless population	City population	Percent homeless
25	Austin, Texas Estimate includes Travis County (includes 1,014 unsheltered)	2,147	916,906	0.23%
26	Fresno, California Estimate includes Fresno and Madera Counties (includes 1,681 unsheltered)	2,144	519,037	0.33%
27	Fort Worth and Arlington, Texas Estimate includes Tarrant County (includes 678 unsheltered)	2,015	835,129	0.21%
28	Long Beach, California (includes 1,208 unsheltered)	1,873	470,489	0.37%
29	Columbus, Ohio Estimate includes Franklin County (includes 288 unsheltered)	1,807	852,144	0.21%
30	Kansas City, Missouri (includes 324 unsheltered)	1,798	151,042	1.14%
31	Jacksonville and Duval, Florida Estimate includes Clay County (includes 429 unsheltered)	1,794	867,313	0.20%
32	Detroit, Michigan (includes 1,308 unsheltered)	1769	679,865	0.26%
33	Indianapolis, Indiana (includes 136 unsheltered)	1,682	853,431	0.20%
34	Charlotte, North Carolina Estimate includes Mecklenburg County (includes 209 unsheltered)	1,668	826,060	0.20%
35	Colorado Springs, Colorado Estimate includes El Paso County (includes 513 unsheltered)	1,551	450,000	0.38%
36	Omaha, Nebraska Estimate includes the Omaha– Council Bluffs metropolitan area	1,411	463,081	0.37%
37	Tucson, Arizona Estimate includes Pima County (includes 363 unsheltered)	1,380	530,905	0.26%
38	Albuquerque, New Mexico (includes 384 unsheltered)	1,340	556,718	0.31%

Rank	City	Homeless population	City population	Percent homeless
39	Memphis, Tennessee Estimate includes Shelby County (includes 102 unsheltered)	1,226	654,723	0.26%
40	New Orleans, Louisiana Estimate includes Jefferson Parish (includes 594 unsheltered)	1,188	388,182	0.31%
41	Oklahoma City, Oklahoma (includes 394 unsheltered)	1,183	629,191	0.19%
42	Tulsa, Oklahoma Estimate includes the City of Tulsa and Tulsa County (includes 226 unsheltered)	1,083	401,352	0.27%
43	Raleigh, North Carolina Estimate includes Wake County (includes 1,030 unsheltered)	983	449,477	0.22%
44	Louisville, Kentucky Estimate includes Jefferson County (includes 153 unsheltered)	926	615,478	0.28%
45	El Paso, Texas Estimate includes El Paso County	892	678,266	0.13%
46	Milwaukee, Wisconsin Estimate includes the City of Milwaukee and Milwaukee County (includes 161 unsheltered)	871	599,086	0.15%
47	Wichita, Kansas Estimate includes Sedgwick County (includes 58 unsheltered)	573	389,054	0.44%
48	Virginia Beach, Virginia (includes 72 unsheltered)	243	450,057	0.05%

- Statistics taken from _24/7 Wall Street_, a *USA Today* content partner offering financial news and commentary. Its content is produced independently of *USA Today*.

There Is a Statue of Vladimir Lenin in Seattle, Washington? Support for Communism in the United States

Vladimir Lenin and Karl Marx were known as the "Fathers of Communism." Why is Lenin honored with a statue here in the United States? What is wrong with liberals in Seattle? Joseph Stalin, a follower of Lenin and Marx, was a notorious mass murderer of millions of human beings in Russia and in the Ukraine. In the United States, Robert E. Lee was one of the greatest generals in US history, although he reluctantly joined the Confederacy. Many young liberals in Seattle are violent activists and psychos, ignorant of world and US history, and very insecure. A lot of them are leftists who escaped from Northern California, particularly from gay and hedonist San Francisco. Most are millennial freeloaders and dope addicts raised by people of the 1960s hippie generation. Seattle is another city mismanaged by liberal fools. It appears people from California are infecting other states with their insane diseases: liberalism, socialism, and communism. That statue of Lenin ought to be roped, broken with sledgehammers, and dumped in the city sewers. That's what I think about the evil mass murderer.

All Tax-and-Spend Blue States Are in High Debt and Have Budget Troubles

Tax-and-spend policies are not just a problem in Los Angeles; they're a *blue state* problem. Teachers in public schools will go on strike. This happened in European countries such as Greece, France, and Italy, caused by unions. Germany has already bailed out these overspending European countries once. I don't think they will do it a second time. *Pensions for all union jobs in California are now and will be increasingly in peril* as Gavin Newsom and the California State Legislature, which is infested with Democrats, will run out of tax money because people and businesses are leaving the state. New York, New Jersey, Connecticut, and Illinois will come across the same problems with unions, only to be disappointed when illegal aliens replace union workers.

David A. Herrera

On March 11, 2021, Joe Biden signed the $1.9 trillion COVID1-19 Tax Relief Bill into law. When it passed the Senate by 50 to 49 vote, Republican Senator Pat Toomey of Pennsylvania tweeted, *"This isn't about COVID relief. It's about using a health crisis as an excuse to ram through a left wing wish list"*. Among the non-related COVID relief, was for bailing out pensions for mismanaged Democratic blue states, for Endowment of the Arts and Humanities, environmental grants, reparations for black farmers, massive expansion of Obamacare. Source: An article in Fox Business News by Morgan Phillips entitled, *"Democrats' COVID relief by-the-numbers breakdown is jaw-dropping "*, dated 03/06/2021. Refer to website: https://www.foxbusiness.com/politics/senate-covid-relief-bill-heres-what-republicans-dont-approve-of.

PART 3

HOW PROGRESSIVES WILL REMAKE THE UNITED STATES WITH ILLEGAL IMMIGRATION

16

THE EFFECTS OF OPEN BORDERS AND MASSIVE ILLEGAL IMMIGRATION INTO THE UNITED STATES

House Democrats Want Open Borders, No Wall, and No ICE Raids

Speaker of the House Nancy Pelosi and House Democrats support providing free government handouts to illegal aliens and want additional judges to process illegal aliens entering the United States. She and the House Democrats don't want border security; she wants a welcoming party of ICE agents with goodies waiting for the caravans of people striving to enter the United States and be cared for by ICE agents at the border. Democrats do not want border security; they want to exploit illegal aliens for power and cheap labor. House Democrats want open borders, no walls, and no ICE raids. They want the ICE agency eliminated or reassigned to another task, or just purposed to house, care, and feed illegal aliens at the border while court judges process them into the United States.

Eliminate ICE and DHS, and Allow Open Borders

The 2019 strategy of Democratic politicians was a coordinated effort between state and federal Democratic politicians to offer illegal aliens free government handouts, offer millennials taxpayer-funded college loan debt relief and free tuition, and offer all Americans Medicare. Some Democrats are advocating amnesty for all foreigners, open borders, the elimination of ICE, the elimination of the Department of Homeland Security. One socialist former candidate, Andrew Yang, is proposing to give every US citizen over eighteen $1,000 a month free and wants a pathway for illegal aliens to citizenship; once they become citizens, they too will get $1,000 a month for years. Yang did not say how long $1,000 per month would be given out. That promised to attract hundreds of millions of foreigners from all over the world to come to the United States and claim their benefits. It could have attracted between 25 percent and 35 percent of the population of China and Africa and 30 percent to 50 percent of the population from south of the border, from Mexico to South America. The government handouts in the "Alice in Wonderland" utopia the Democrats are proposing are not free as they claim. They will be paid for by the wealthy, the hardworking middle class, small businesses, and large corporations by up to 90 percent taxation oppression imposed by socialist tyrants.

The fall of Rome was in part the result of the immigration of barbarians—the Huns in Europe, the Visigoths, the Vandals, and the Berbers from North Africa, all lawless uncontrolled immigration. It has been common knowledge for millennia that invaders and uncontrolled illegal immigration has negative economic, safety, and security effects on each individual country. Foreigners joined the Roman military, and because they were improperly trained, the Roman military ceased to be powerful. Barbarian looting, along with mismanagement of the economy and the military, brought Rome down. To preserve its sovereignty, security, and safety, each country has immigration laws to control both legal and illegal immigration. That's why immigration laws are important to the political sovereignty of the state and the safety of citizens. The following addresses the consequences of uncontrolled illegal immigration:

The Undesirable Effects of Massive Immigration into the United States

Reasons why Democrats want open borders in the United States is not because Democrat politicians are illogical or ignorant, or have ignored or not learned the ill-effects of massive illegal immigration from history, but rather, reasons are:

1. to benefit from the cheap labor of immigrants,
2. to remake the United States, consolidate power, and win elections forever

Biden has already halted border wall construction and plans to give amnesty to eleven million immigrants. Democratic politicians understand that a massive number of illegal immigrants entering the United States through open borders will change our culture, our politics, our economy, our safety and security, and our moral values. Democrat politicians simply don't care about the safety and security of this country. By allowing millions of illegal aliens per year into our country through open borders, Democrats will make America last and Democrat perpetual power first.

Muslim immigration is our worst nightmare. We are letting in hundreds of thousands of unvetted Muslims from all over the world, including refugees from the Middle East and Somalia, who *refuse* to assimilate into our culture because they hate our culture, they think our culture is immoral and find it foreign to them, and their religious leaders urge a jihad against the United States to Islamize the United States. In Europe, massive immigration from the Middle East and Africa is leading to the overpopulation of several European Union countries with the immigrants demanding sharia law, destroying Christian statues, and causing an increase in crime. Muslims consider Islam as the supreme religion of the world.

Immigration through our open southern border has become an economic burden with over 18,000 unaccompanied children stuck in squalor camps along the states of Texas, Arizona, and New Mexico. States such as California and New York welcome illegal aliens and attract them like a magnet by *advertising* free health care or free tuition for them. In March 2021, Biden has allocated $86 million to house illegal crossers into the US.

Democrats don't want ICE putting any illegal aliens in their sanctuary cities or states. How ironic. In reality, Democratic politicians don't care about illegal aliens; they only want them to settle in *red* border states such as Texas so as to flip red states blue, when illegal aliens vote in the future. Democratic politicians are truly racist, but they play a good con game.

The Effects of Increasing Illegal Immigration in the United States

What are the effects of immigration on the United States? More immigration into the United States means the following:

- more homelessness, because some immigrants won't have friends or relatives to stay with, or won't be able to afford to rent or own a home in the United States;
- more taxes for school resources and for hiring more teachers to educate immigrants;
- more police officers to enforce laws for the increased population in areas where immigrants settle;
- more taxes for welfare in places where immigrants can get it;
- more welfare fraud with families claiming they are caring for multiple nonrelated children;
- more welfare fraud committed by Muslim men who may have multiple wives and numerous children in different locations;
- more prisons and prison guards because of increased criminal activity by the illegal alien population;
- more judges and lawyers to hold trials for those contributing to the increase in crime;
- increased taxes paid by residents of states where free tuition is given to illegal aliens;
- increased taxes to pay for border enforcement;

- increased costs to clean the trash, feces, and urine left by the homeless off city streets;
- increased costs to treat citizens for contagious diseases that may spread from the homeless;
- more fraudulent votes cast by illegal aliens in all state elections, particularly in blue states (Democrats benefit by picking up more seats in the House);
- a percentage of unscreened illegal aliens who will commit crimes, affecting the safety and security of Americans;
- a percentage of Muslim migrants who will refuse to assimilate into US culture, which they hate;
- a percentage of radical Muslims who are setting up terrorist militia training camps inside the United States to plan acts of terror against the United States;
- more illegal aliens joining liberal social engineering organizations or groups to participate in liberal protests, especially if paid.

Consequences of No Immigration Vetting

Democratic politicians are indirectly killing US citizens by allowing unvetted immigrants, illegal aliens, and refugees from the Middle East, South and Central America, and Africa to enter the United States. Safety and security are *not* a concern of the Democrats in power; their goals are all about money, power, and control over the lives of Americans. House Speaker Nancy Pelosi said on TV that the murder of Americans by illegal alien criminals is "collateral damage," but Democrats still refused to provide any funds for security because Trump was in the way of obtaining their goals.

Democratic politicians like Nancy Pelosi and Chuck Schumer want open borders so as to let in hundreds of thousands of immigrants each year to exploit them for cheap labor, to win votes in future elections, and to get their support for future Democratic tyrannical legislation.

Note that high-tech companies in the Silicon Valley favor open borders because they hire close to 50 percent of their computer experts from India to do contract work. Companies like Google, Amazon, and

Apple would prefer to exploit workers from India, who will work for cheap wages, rather than hire US citizens for high wages. They lobby Democratic politicians for guest worker visas to hire foreigners and then pay them cheap wages for higher profits. This prevents American citizens from getting certain high-tech jobs.

Some Catholic Leaders Support Sanctuary Cities, Ignoring Criminals Who Endanger the Safety of Americans

The Catholic Church should not support sanctuary cities for the following reasons:

1. Illegal aliens who have served time in jail or prison should be handed over to ICE to be deported because they are in the country illegally and are a risk to the communities they otherwise would be released to.
2. Illegal alien criminals who are released back into communities are often repeat offenders of serious crimes.
3. It is a myth and an outright lie told by Democratic liberals that ICE will arrest people who turn in illegal alien criminals for any crime for fear of deportation.

Who in their right mind, except for insane politicians, would want a convicted pedophile, murderer, or sex offender released from prison moving next door to families with several children?

The Catholic Church does not permit admitted homosexuals as part of the clergy, as leaders of youth groups, teaching catechism, involved in Catholic schools as teachers, or holding in any position involving activities with children. There are very good reasons for this: gays are a risk to male children, and to the reputation of the church and the Catholic faith. Risks come in the form of victimization of children, psychological damage to children, grief to Catholic parents, defamation of the Catholic Church, multimillion-dollar lawsuits against the church, and the slandering of Catholics for being members of a church that tends to cover up child molestation, with the perpetrators often not being punished.

The Knights of Columbus, a Catholic charity organization, does not allow homosexuals as members because homosexuals are a risk to the youth in the parish. They also open up the organization to being slandered by the media, which are hungry to broadcast sexual offenses committed by members of the Catholic Church and affiliated groups, and the church's involvement with youth group charities. A convicted sex offender who has a history of sex crimes is prohibited from joining the Knights of Columbus because of the risks stated. The reputation and honor of the Knights of Columbus must be preserved, and we Catholics must do everything in our power to prevent the victimization of children in any of the organizations of the Catholic Church. Nothing is stopping homosexuals, particularly gay men, and sex offenders from joining other private charities or being part of activities involving children in other religious organizations that allow it.

So why are we allowing sanctuary cities to release convicted criminals who have committed murder, rape, pedophilia, home invasion, burglary, or physical assault to be released into communities without notifying ICE? Statistics show that many criminals released from prison are repeat offenders. The choice is clear: Do we want to take the *risk* of allowing criminals to continue victimizing our citizens, or do we want to have zero risk of repeat offenses and have ICE deport illegal aliens with a history of serious crimes? We know what the choice of liberal Democrats is: protect every one of them to get their votes at the expense of the safety of Americans in every neighborhood in every state that illegal alien convicts move to.

The irony of the fake news media, which support the failed policies of liberal Democrats, is that they slander the Catholic Church for not preventing pedophile priests from victimizing children while, at the same time, slandering the Catholic Church for being biased against and intolerant of gays when it is trying to prevent the victimization of children.

David A. Herrera

Chuck Schumer Cries on TV for Separated Kids at the Border but Never When Illegal Aliens Murder, Rape, or Savagely Beat American Citizens

Chuck Schumer was seen crying on TV about children separated from their families; that's why President Trump rightfully called him "Crying Schumer." Chuck Schumer cries about illegal aliens, but why doesn't he cry about the following things?

1. American citizens murdered by illegal aliens.
2. Wives or husbands who will never again see their spouses because their spouses were murdered by an illegal alien.
3. Children who will no longer see a parent, brother, or sister who was murdered by an illegal alien.
4. The number of American children killed by MS-13 members from Central and South America.
5. Families who have lost a family member working as a border patrol agent killed in the line of duty by an illegal alien.
6. Family members who have lost a father, son, mother, or daughter who worked as a police officer and was killed in the line of duty by an illegal alien.

In March 2021, there were more than 5000 children separated from their families at the border held in large storage containers. This is an ongoing major US crisis that is owned by Joe Biden and the Democrats. Why isn't Chuck Schumer crying now? In reality, Chuck Schumer couldn't care less about illegal alien children; he was only grandstanding on a liberal media network as a dramatic fool with alligator tears and phony compassion. Schumer and Nancy Pelosi consider the murder of a police officer, a border patrol agent, a mother, a father, a brother, a sister, or a child as "collateral damage" of allowing as many illegal aliens into the United States as possible without regard for the taking of a human life by an illegal alien.

Victims and Their Families Should Seek Remedies from Sanctuary Cities and the State

Victims and their families should seek remedies from sanctuary cities and the state because Democratic politicians are aiding and abetting illegal alien criminals to go free in sanctuary cities. These people repeatedly commit serious crimes after they are released, and certain cities and states refuse to hand them over to ICE for deportation. If someone gets murdered or raped by an illegal alien who had a record of murder or a sex offense and was released by sanctuary city politicians, the victim's survivors or relatives should sue the city and state for hundreds of millions of dollars for each occurrence in a *civil* lawsuit. Federal funds to the city and state should also be withheld to sanctuary cities whose duty should have been to deport offenders of horrible crimes who were released but, instead, who allowed the criminal to be released to commit the same crime again.

Economic Predictions after the 2020 Elections

Democrats stole the 2020 election. Now that there are an equal number of Democratic and Republican senators, with Vice President Kamala Harris's vote being the tiebreaking vote in the Senate, the US economy will collapse within a matter of years. No investor under this socialist government will invest in any business listed on the stock market because socialists in federal government will impose heavy taxes on their profits, impose a variety of costly regulations on businesses they must comply with, or nationalize businesses. The stock market will cease to exist under socialism, and the following will occur:

1. The federal socialist government will confiscate the wealth of the very rich, the rich, the middle class, and small and large corporations through tax oppression, thus driving hardworking middle-class Americans into poverty.
2. Socialists will levy high taxes on industry and businesses; layoffs and bankruptcies will occur.

3. Industry, businesses, and college students will be unable to pay their loan debts; therefore, some banks will fail.

4. Interest rate hikes will follow the high risks involved in lending money, causing inflation to rise.

5. Socialists will just make things worse by printing more money, increasing inflation even more.

6. Industry may be nationalized by socialist elites; socialists will run industries like they run poop cities.

7. Socialists will repossess homes from taxpayers who are in tax arrears, and some citizens will have their bank accounts and retirement accounts seized; these punitive actions may drive many Americans out of the country, into poverty, or into homelessness.

8. Fearing a revolution, socialists will confiscate guns and ban firearms; a revolution will occur in the United States in reaction to this tyrannical effort.

9. The socialist government will eventually run out of other people's money (taxes). There will not be enough money collected from the high taxes imposed on people and businesses to fund costly socialist plans and simultaneously run the rest of the country, such as paying workers, paying for the Green New Deal, offering free health care for all, giving free handouts to the massive numbers of illegal aliens entering the United States, providing free college tuition, instituting college loan forgiveness, making donations to the Paris climate accord, paying out worker retirement funds, paying for federal, state, and local pension plans, funding the US military and its operations, and building defense weapons. Socialists will probably eliminate social security for seniors and federal compensations to all veterans with a service-connected injury or disease. No socialist has ever responded to any items listed here out of fear.

10. Bread and soup lines will spring up everywhere; homelessness and poverty will significantly increase.

11. Poop cities will continue to pop up across the United States, cities like Los Angeles and San Francisco today, and socialists

will be helpless to fix homelessness everywhere because of economic stagnation.

12. Crimes against persons and property will increase across the United States because of economic stagnation.

13. Military spending and the building of defense weapons will be significantly reduced, leaving the United States vulnerable to enemy aggression, terrorism, and nuclear attacks.

14. Socialists will have an open border policy, thus endangering the safety and security of Americans.

15. Socialists will allow massive immigration in the United States with immigrants seeking to claim their free handouts, which will make the economy much worse.

16. Owing to the socialist open border policy, more drugs will be smuggled into the United States by Mexican cartels, and more Americans will die from illegal drugs.

17. If most of the aforementioned dire predictions occur as a result of a US economic collapse, the results will be significant homelessness, high crime rates, poverty, and misery.

18. History repeatedly shows that significant confiscation of wealth must occur by passing tyrannical laws, which must be enforced to succeed. Armed rebellion against the federal socialist government then becomes inevitable.

19. The Biden administration may likely reverse China-US trade policy, which will monetarily favor China.

These are very likely scenarios predicted to occur under a leftist United Sates. Worse, no socialist in the Democratic Party has any clue that all these things will very likely occur.

Migrants and Citizens, Using Mexican Children, Are Committing Welfare and Tax Fraud

There are a lot of tax scams used by illegal aliens, and some of these make use of children. The scams involve using many illegal alien children belonging to parents inside or outside the United States, with the scammer taking large tax credits for each child. This amounts to using these children as cash cows for tax refund checks. In many cases, the children don't even belong to the scammers; they are children brought in from Mexico, Latin America, South America, and other places, awaiting their parents to come into the United States at a later date and reunite with them. In other cases, these kids are orphans who will be claimed by nonparent families for tax credits and welfare checks. These scams are hard to detect and are probably going undetected today.

17

DEMOCRAT POLITICIANS' GOALS FOR MASSIVE IMMIGRATION INTO THE UNITED STATES

Reasons Liberal Democrats Want Open Borders

There are two major reasons why Democratic politicians at the state and federal levels want open borders, as follows:

1. They want the illegal alien vote in state and federal elections to increase their political power base.
2. They want illegal aliens to fill jobs in blue states for low wages, and then they want to tax these illegals to make up for the lost tax revenue from businesses and the middle class moving out of the tax-oppressive states.

President Trump was fighting for the safety of Americans to end *illegal* immigration into the United States by doing the following:

- building a wall and implementing other security measures to prevent illegal immigration;
- offering the option of closing the southern border;
- sending US troops to assist ICE in securing the border;

- declaring a national emergency to secure funding for the wall without an obstructing Congress;
- taking the issue to the American people by appearing on the media and making his case on border security; and
- increasing his leverage to win concessions from the Democrats— but not to the point that Nancy Pelosi and Crying Schumer became willing to concede.

Keep Illegal Aliens in Red States. Don't Send Them to Blue States

The practice of keeping illegal aliens in red states is unfair for the following reasons:

- Only states sharing a border with Mexico will take in all illegal immigrants.
- Hypocritical sanctuary cities will reject taking immigrants into their communities since they welcome illegal immigrants and protect the criminals among them from deportation.
- Red states such as Texas and Florida will be allowed to take in illegal aliens in order to flip these states blue in the future, with illegal aliens voting in federal elections.
- Border states, especially if a red state such as Texas, will have to accept illegal aliens, which is the equivalent of *gerrymandering*, which produces the same effect.

It is also hypocritical to keep illegal aliens in red states for the following reasons:

- It is contradictory and hypocritical that Democratic politicians want illegal aliens to enter the United States with an open border policy to win votes and to use the illegals for cheap labor, offering them government handouts in blue states but refusing to allow ICE to take them into blue states.

- It is ironic that New York boasts of giving illegal aliens free college tuition but now doesn't want illegals in their state.
- It is hypocritical that California draws illegal aliens by advertising free health care for its residents, but now the state is refusing to take them into its sanctuary cities.

President Trump proposed having ICE transport all the tattooed MS-13 gang members, whom Pelosi defended on May 17, 2018, as human beings, not animals, to San Francisco, California, and to send all homosexual deviant illegal aliens to Oakland, California. The remaining ones would be sent to Hawaii, New York, New Jersey, Illinois, and Maine. Every Democratic politician needs to have these illegal aliens in their cities to live as a result of their own open border policy. Needless to say, the hypocritical illegal-alien-loving liberals rejected President Trump's suggestion, and Trump received a lot of hate rhetoric from Democratic politicians.

Democrats Enrich Themselves with Drug Profits by Having Open Borders like Mexico

A former Democrat and current Trump supporter, Jeffrey Peterson, says the reason the Democrats would never support the border wall was because they were being paid off by the Mexican cartels. Jeffrey Peterson states in his profile on Twitter that he is a former Democrat who "walked away." He claims that the Democrats will never give in on a wall because they are being funded by the Mexican mafia. He says he has connections with Arizona politics and says Mexico is the main reason the wall is not supported by the Democratic Party![1]

It's been previously stated that the reason Democratic politicians want open borders is to remake the United States to win votes and

---

[1] Joe Hoft, "Former Democrat: The Truth Is Democrats Won't Build Wall Because They're Under Influence of Mexican Mafia," the Gateway Pundit, January 22, 2019, https://www.thegatewaypundit.com/2019/01/former-democrat-the-truth-is-democrats-wont-build-wall-because-theyre-under-influence-of-mexican-mafia/.

to exploit illegal aliens for cheap labor. But if what WikiLeaks put out is true, then another reason Democrats fight for open borders and welcome immigrants into the United States is because they have a quid pro quo scheme with the Mexican cartels. California governor Gavin Newsom and New York City mayor Bill de Blasio both advertise free health care for illegal aliens. Bill de Blasio is also allowing illegal aliens to receive free housing in New York City, as applicants for free housing will no longer need a Social Security number or tax ID number for each adult member of the household to be considered for the lottery to get housing. Governor Andrew Cuomo of New York State is offering free college tuition for everyone, including illegal aliens, but with the stipulation that they remain in the state for four years. The state of New Jersey will allocate $3.8 million in state funds to pay college tuition for illegal immigrants, authorized by a bill signed by Democratic New Jersey governor Phil Murphy in 2018. It is hard to say whether these Democratic mayors and governors from New York, California, or New Jersey are being bribed by the Mexican cartels or whether they are all a bunch of incompetent fools ruining their states. Each of these states is presently undergoing a massive exodus of its population because of illogical overspending by its lawmakers, governors, and mayors.[2]

Free housing, free health care, and free college tuition are not free; the funding for these spending items comes from significantly taxing wealthy individuals and businesses that are trying to make a profit. By tax-oppressing the very rich, the wealthy, and the middle class, the Democrats reduce their power and influence. Tax oppression by Democrats and socialists is a tool to diminish the wealth of the powerful Right, thereby diminishing their power to contribute money to their favorite conservative pro-capitalist candidates and conservative organizations. In the end, taxes diminish the influence of the Right. Tax oppression is a Democratic/socialist tool or strategy that reduces the power and influence of right-wing Republicans.

---

[2] M. Dowling, "NY & NJ Give Housing & College to People Here Illegally before Americans," *Independent Sentinel*, November 23, 2019, https://www.independentsentinel.com/ny-nj-give-housing-college-to-people-here-illegally-before-americans/.

Additionally, if Democrats are in power and control the government, they will distribute wealth to their liberal crony friends to support the social engineering of US institutions and culture toward the left. Former president Obama was notorious for funding his pet liberal organizations and cronies to empower them and increase their influence. He also provided taxpayer money to Iran and Palestine. Obama looked the other way when his top aides participated in corruption to enrich themselves in pay-to-play and quid pro quo schemes with other countries. Refer to *Profiles in Corruption: Abuse of Power by America's Progressive Elite* by Peter Schweizer, published in 2020, for details on the corruption of the Left.

Corruption of Democrats and the Mexican Government in View of Horrible Murders

If the Mexican government were really serious about eliminating its drug cartels, then it would obliterate the homes of every drug cartel member in Mexico with bombs and a military invasion, but the Mexican government doesn't do this because the politicians and police at almost every level receive part of the profits from the sale of drugs in the United States and other countries, thus enriching them every year. Mexican politicians, judges, and police protect or ignore the horrific killings, executions, assassinations, intercartel drug wars, torture, and other negative impacts to the Mexican people. It is mutually understood between the Mexican federal government that federalist politicians in Mexico City will look the other way while drug cartels feud between each other or kill each other. Drug cartels typically do not assassinate or attack high-ranking politicians in the federal government or state leaders. If cartels cross that redline and assassinate Mexican police, mayors, or federal officials, then the Mexican federal government will send the Mexican marines to destroy whatever cartel is responsible for crossing that redline. As long as cartels can bribe Mexican politicians, they will exist and continue their drug trafficking into the United States and other countries. If they don't pay their bribes, then Mexican politicians will go after the cartel. Since corruption is almost at every level, any low-level politician who campaigns to rid Mexico of cartels is assassinated. Mexican police officers who enforce the law and resist lawlessness by cartels are frequently assassinated. Journalists who print the horrific criminal activities of cartels in the media or in newspapers are also assassinated.

Mexico's murder rate hit a record of 33,000 in 2018. At the time, this was the highest number since the government began keeping records more than twenty years ago. Figures released by the Interior Ministry show 50,341 homicides in 2018, including 33,341 murders and 17,000 culpable or negligent homicides.[3]

> The number of homicides in Mexico rose to 35,588 in 2019, the highest number on record, but the rate of annual increase in murders has slowed according to government figures. President Andrés Manuel López Obrador has acknowledged that crime and violence are the toughest challenges he faces. But on Tuesday, he said corruption is the country's main problem. López Obrador said white-collar criminals have done more damage to Mexico than the drug cartels responsible for many of the killings. "We are giving the almost the same weight to (fighting) white-collar crime as we do to drug cartels," López Obrador said.[4]

Mexican president Andrés Manuel López Obrador is not serious about fighting the drug cartels. He fears for his life, which is why he resisted President Trump's offer to use the US military to go after the drug cartels to destroy their homes, arrest them, or kill them. He merely explains the problem away as a lower priority than white-collar crimes of kidnapping and extortion, and corruption. Nothing will be done to bring anyone to justice on the killing of six American children

---

[3] "Mexico's Murder Rate Hits Record 33,000 in 2018," BNO News, January 21, 2019, www.bnonews.com/index.php/2019/01/mexicos-murder-rate-hits-record-33000-in-2018/.

[4] "Mexico Homicide Rate Edges Up in 2019; Rate of Rise Slows," ABC News, January 21, 2020, https://abcnews.go.com/International/wireStory/mexico-homicide-rate-edges-2019-rate-rise-slows-68428038.

and three adults in what is known as the LeBarón and Langford family massacre, which happened in November 2019. One baby girl survived the massacre.

The Mexican president might even be taking bribes from cartels in exchange for looking the other way on the increasing level of crime. If he were serious about destroying the cartels, he would order the Mexican military to attack every cartel location and mansion in Mexico.

President Trump's border security plan A was to do the following:

- Secure the border by building a wall to prevent illegal immigration into the United States.
- Have ICE keep dangerous drugs and pushers out of our country.
- Apprehend drug pushers and confiscate illegal drugs smuggled into the country.
- Deport any known criminals and undesirable illegal aliens from the United States.
- Apprehend illegal aliens and hold them until judges determine their refugee status. Deport nonrefugees.

After the murder on November 5, 2019, in which nine members of a family, including six children, with dual citizenship in the United States and Mexico, were killed in an ambush attack by suspected drug cartel gunmen in northern Mexico, President Trump offered to assist the Mexican president in using US military forces to go after the Mexican cartels to destroy them. Mexican president Andrés Manuel López Obrador refused to accept the offer.

If the United States were serious about winning the drug war, plan B is a better alternative to achieve that end. This plan involves invading cartels in Mexico with US warplanes *only* to carpet-bomb every known location and every mansion of every drug cartel in Mexico. Wipe them off the map with extreme prejudice and diligence. Mexico should celebrate us and thank us for ridding them of a cancer that has even affected their political machine in Mexico City, their justice system, their law enforcement agencies, and their local and state politicians for many decades. Plan B would prevent deaths from dangerous drugs imported from Mexico into the United States. It would be a win-win for the United States and Mexico.

The Exploitation of Illegal Aliens to Gain Power and Control

One of the reasons Democrats are attracting a massive number of illegal aliens into the United States is to exploit them. The United States simply cannot afford to take care of the vast number of illegal aliens who are mostly illiterate, unskilled, and destitute. Democrats do not want immigrants to settle in their communities, but rather they want them to settle in red states to "seed" red states in order to flip them blue. It's a political power-grab scam, and it is unfair and unethical to use illegal aliens for their votes to remake the United States into a socialist country, resulting in Americans' loss of freedom. In a nutshell, we must not allow illegal immigration into the United States if we wish for our nation to survive, or if we desire unbiased elections that do not completely favor only one party, or if we want to ensure a strong economy and national security. Democrats such as the "morally superior" Nancy Pelosi would have you believe that those who prevent illegal aliens from entering the country are racists and morally wrong. Democrats exploit illegal aliens to gain power and control.

Mexico's population consists of the very rich and very poor, with the very rich exploiting the very poor. Socialists want to do the exact same thing in the United States by exploiting illegal aliens as a source of cheap labor. California is a good example of a state with a population consisting of the very rich and the very poor. The middle class is migrating out of California because of the oppression of high taxes, leaving only the very rich and the very poor. We do not want this kind of scenario, but Democratic politicians are driving this socioeconomic class structure in California. Billionaires live in mansions all along the coast of California, from San Diego to Northern California. These people can afford to live well. Some are even California politicians who enrich themselves from the high taxes they collect. The very poor are seen competing with well-paid California citizens to take their non-white-collar jobs because small businesses prefer to hire cheap labor to stay in business. Large corporations such as high-tech companies benefit from cheap labor when they hire software developers from India for temporary contract work and pay them 20 percent of what they pay American engineers and software developers. The high-tech companies also donate large sums of money to keep Democrats installed in power in exchange for lucrative tax breaks where they end up paying little or no taxes. Blue states such as California and New York were cheating the federal government by claiming inflated deductions taken by corporations and small businesses. In turn, blue states would file those business deductions as lost tax revenue with the federal government to get compensation. That tax scam stopped under President Trump's tax reduction plan as all states were restricted to claiming limited losses. Blue states could no longer inflate their losses from the inflated tax deductions corporations take to avoid paying much in state taxes. The limit on state losses allows the government to reimburse states less money from the federal tax pool, a tax law for which blue state politicians hated President Trump.

By using the cheap labor of illegal aliens, corporations would increase their profits and could better afford to pay blue states and the federal government taxes and stay in business. But some corporations are still relocating to states that have no state taxes such as Texas, Nevada, and Florida. To prevent businesses from leaving, say, California, thereby reducing a blue state's tax revenue, Democrats seek cheap labor from illegal aliens, certain this will keep businesses inside California, as these illegals replace California residents who once were paid high wages.

If Americans are to become prosperous by way of hard work at good-paying jobs, then we must prevent socialists from destroying capitalism in the United States. We must not let socialists reverse President Trump's tax breaks to wage earners and to corporations, because these tax breaks help grow our economy, grow jobs, and create wealth for those who want it and are willing to work for it. We must not allow tax oppression by a socialist government to force businesses to lay off millions of American workers from their good-paying jobs, which would cause massive unemployment. We must not allow socialists in power to cause businesses to go bankrupt or to relocate outside the

United States. We must not allow socialist elites in power destroy the US economy because they want to confiscate corporate wealth, which may well affect our jobs, our wages, and our standard of living and may drive us into increased debt, poverty, or homelessness.

If socialists ever gain power and the economy fails, there will be millions of angry Americans out of work. The cost of goods will become high as the production of goods decreases and fewer goods become available. As demand for food and other health necessities goes up and food products become scarce, the cost of food and other health necessities will go up again, causing inflation and more anger. As inflation of prices continues to occur, civil unrest and lawlessness will follow. The stock market will fall to record low levels as lack of investments will take capital from businesses, preventing them from continuing to operate or manufacture goods. Worse, retirement pensions will be significantly reduced; banks, with debt less likely to be repaid, will fail; the stock market will fall; and retirement checks might be reduced. There will be a massive number of applications for unemployment insurance and welfare, a massive number of bank withdrawals, and possible reductions in social security, military pensions, and veterans' benefits.

But socialists in power will have already anticipated a possible rebellion by angry Americans should this economic mess occur, for example, loss of wages, loss of jobs, illegal aliens replacing US citizens in the workforce, high taxes levied on homes and businesses, and the driving of the middle-class base out of blue states. Socialists will resort to plan B and plan C before this ugly economic scenario occurs. Plan B will be the voluntary or forced confiscation of firearms to prevent a potential armed revolution against the socialist regime. Plan C will be for the regime to print more dollars and put limits on prices of goods and services to pacify angry citizens so they can afford food and other necessities. The socialist government will likely nationalize and run all manufacturing (production) as needed, along with sales and distribution of goods. That's what socialists typically do.

One might ask, "Why hasn't the same thing occurred in Russia or Europe, or in other socialist or communist countries?" Answer: It has several times in history in several countries. Study how Nicolás Maduro of Venezuela confiscated the wealth of all wealthy citizens, nationalized the oil industry and all other companies, and turned the Venezuelan government into a vicious tyrannical dictatorship by controlling the citizenry, confiscating all weapons of law-abiding citizens, and torturing, oppressing, imprisoning, and starving citizens who opposed the regime and were unable to flee to other countries. Other examples of oppressive tyrannical actions or governments in world history that controlled the wealth of those nations are the Russian Revolution; Europe ruled by monarchies; China ruled by emperors, then by communists; Fascist Nazi Germany; and Latin America ruled by dictators; these can all be studied and their economies can be compared to the capitalist economy of the USA. Which is better?

To answer the question of why Americans will likely rebel against a tyrannical government is the following: Americans are freedom-loving people compared to Europeans, who are traditionally used to longtime socialism. Americans love their freedom, their constitutional rights, their God, and their country. See how the freedom-loving people of Hong Kong are being oppressed and attacked by police with the Chinese communist military on standby to control dissent and put down protests as necessary. The citizens of Hong Kong are used to freedom, not tyranny. We patriotic Americans are used to freedom, not tyranny. Many of our ancestors, friends, and relatives fought and died in wars for the freedoms that we have today in the United States, and we will not surrender our freedoms to socialist elites to control our lives. My thesis: Socialism will never work in the United States.

Democrats didn't expect President Trump to threaten Mexico with tariffs on their goods exported to the United States if Mexico failed to prevent caravans of migrants from Central and South America from entering the United States. Mexico successfully stopped caravans of migrants from entering the United States, to the disappointment of sanctimonious Pelosi and crying Schumer.

David A. Herrera

Other than Rigging or Stealing Elections, Immigrants Are What Democrats Need to Win All Future Elections

The Biden administration will likely grant amnesty to at least six hundred fifty thousand DACA members, who will vote Democrat in exchange for the favor. Additionally, by allowing a massive number of illegal aliens into the country, Democrats will replace the insidious corrupt practice of trying to rig or steal elections, along with eliminating the Electoral College.

Democrats will take the rich for all they can get to support their addictive spending programs and will reach into the pockets of middle-class Americans when not enough taxes are collected. Democrats need amnesty migrants to vote Democrat and to support Democratic social engineering of US institutions. Giving amnesty to DACA members will not be enough to win all future elections, hence the open borders and advertised free stuff for illegal aliens, to draw them into the United States in numbers of more than a million per year. Democrats need a buffer of more than one million new illegal aliens, and to give them amnesty, so most of them will vote Democrat. Democrats will then always win future elections, and no constitutional checks and balances in our government will exist.

Democrats cannot offer the United States economic prosperity and opportunities to achieve the American dream because they cannot match the proven capitalist policies of President Trump, who provided the United States with unparalleled economic growth and opportunities for attaining wealth and prosperity. So, Democrats are painting Trump voters as racists, homophobes, Islamophobes, xenophobes, sexists, and so on. The Democrats embrace socialism as a way to solve their manufactured income inequality and racial injustice. Socialist Democrats embrace a policy of a massive distribution of wealth for all Americans, which wealth they will share with the massive number of immigrants from all over the world who are destitute, unskilled, and looking to share in the United States' redistributed wealth.

The shocking realization of the Democratic Party is that they know they can't win future elections without "seeding" the United States with immigrants, because most US citizens abandoned the Democrats and elected to support Trump and his successful economic policies for better opportunities and prosperity. Even a significant percentage of blacks supported President Trump over the Democratic Party leaders. Blacks discovered that Democratic leaders playing the race card won't put food on their tables.

As a result of this apparent lack of votes for Democrats, Democratic politicians have to rely on immigrants to enter the country legally or illegally in order to get votes. To attract immigrants, Democratic leaders such as California's Governor Newsom and New York's Governor Cuomo have been offering government handouts such as free tuition, free health care, and free housing. Democrats are also urging passage of gun laws to destroy the Second Amendment so as to turn law-abiding Americans into helpless, defenseless citizens as in Venezuela. Their goals are to prevent a future armed revolution against a tyrannical socialist government in Washington, DC, that will be confiscating the wealth of most prosperous Americans via tax oppression, and then to redistribute these trillions of dollars to illegal aliens and the Democrats' crony socialist supporters. These plans by Democratic losers who are desperate for power and self-enrichment will destroy the United States if we don't stop them.

Illegal Aliens Are Merely Useful Sheep to Socialists for Exploitation

Under the Obama administration, taxpayers were paying taxes to fund political corruption and didn't know it. Extremist Democrats insidiously invested to enrich their leftist power base and their crony supporters. In the 2020 election, Democrats planned to invest in illegal aliens through their open border policy as the new "capital" supply of voters that will allow them to attain power in the future and will support their future tyrannical laws.

Their scandalous tax gigs will result in gross taxation without representation. They will create new tyrannical tax laws that will rob the wealth of the rich and significantly reduce the wealth of the middle class in order to redistribute the wealth to, as they say, achieve income equality. Several socialist Democratic candidates were seen on TV kissing "Pope" Al Sharpton's ring and promising reparations for blacks. Costs associated with massive Democratic spending can only be met by passing tyrannical laws, and these laws will be hard to enforce as they will be met by much anger and resistance from freedom-loving Americans. But socialists will have anticipated opposition to their scheme of confiscating wealth from Americans. To prevent any opposition, any hostility, or a potential armed rebellion against these horrible, oppressive, tyrannical tax policies, socialists will find it necessary to ban and confiscate the firearms of law-abiding citizens if they wish to maintain power and implement their future tyrannical laws that will destroy more of our freedoms.

Another way Democrats planned to win the 2020 election, besides rigging or stealing it, was to impeach President Trump so that he could not run for president in 2024. Since the Robert Mueller witch-hunt had failed to indict President Trump for Russian collusion, Democrats tried a second way to remove the president from office. Democratic members of Congress submitted articles of impeachment to the Senate to impeach President Trump for threatening to withhold funds from Ukraine if they didn't investigate Joe Biden and his son Hunter for corruption. House Democrats, on a purely partisan basis, alleged President Trump withheld funds from the Ukraine to defend against Russian aggression to interfere with the election of a Democrat running for president in 2020—Joe Biden. House Democrats also claimed that Trump obstructed Congress. These were two farcical, unimpeachable allegations made by desperate House Democrats. The Democratic fake news media supported the impeachment and added slander and defamation of the president. That impeachment attempt died in the Senate, and Trump was exonerated as he had committed no crime. Little did Americans know that during the House's second impeachment attempt, Joe Biden and his son were deeply involved in corrupt deals with China and the Ukraine, possibly involving money laundering. Nancy Pelosi's son, Mitt Romney's son, John Kerry's stepson, and the Biden family were all involved in these corrupt deals. This was the real reason Pelosi and House Democrats did not want President Trump fishing for crimes that may have been committed by Joe Biden and his son.

"Seeding" the United States with Illegal Aliens for Future Votes and Cheap Labor and to Flip Red States Blue

On June 4, 2019, Speaker Pelosi and House Democrats passed H.R. 6, the American Dream and Promise Act of 2019, with a vote of 237–187, to grant amnesty to more than two or three million illegal aliens. Arizona congressman Andy Biggs voted against this legislation and issued the following statement:

> Our border is being overrun. Our nation is being invaded. Our Border Patrol agents are outnumbered. And yet Democrats just passed an amnesty bill to reward and incentivize the lawlessness besieging our country— without any measures to address the humanitarian and security emergency at the border.
>
> If enacted into law, this bill would permanently exacerbate the crisis at our southern border. This legislation legalizes millions of illegal aliens, incentivizes fraudulent applications, provides green cards to criminals and gang members, gives taxpayer-funded dollars for green card assistance, and adds tens of billions of dollars to our national debt. This is irresponsible governance. The American people should be outraged at the Democrats' partisan maneuvers around the rule of law. I call on my colleagues to stop their attempts to reward illegal aliens with amnesty and access to taxpayer dollars. Let's secure the border and address the humanitarian crisis first and foremost. Let's protect the American people.[5]

---

[5] Andy Biggs, "House Democrats Pass Massive Amnesty Bill for Illegal Aliens," June 4, 2019, Congressman Andy Biggs's website, https://biggs.house.gov/media/press-releases/house-democrats-pass-massive-amnesty-bill-illegal-aliens.

This bill was not considered in the Senate for a vote and went nowhere. President Trump threatened to veto it.

The Biden administration delayed its policy of immigration reform until the summer of 2021 because of COVID-19 fears, massive caravans accumulating at the border, chaotic problems at the border, and the economic effects of massive migration. However, US citizens will be faced with Democratic policies of open borders and unvetted mass immigration into the United States in 2021 or 2022. It is only a matter of time before Democratic politicians grant amnesty to the millions of legal aliens in the United States, who will be eligible for welfare, food stamps, unemployment insurance, free health care, and free tuition. US taxpayers will be *forced* to pay for it all in a massive distribution-of-wealth scheme.

Why Illegal Aliens Are in High Demand in Liberal States such as New York and California

Foreigners don't know about, don't care about, or hate the US Constitution, and California's Democratic politicians are allowing them to invade the state? As I said before, this is the beginning of establishing a tyrannical socialist government where foreigners are allowed into California and hired as police officers to enforce tyrannical laws. California's Democratic politicians are now proposing legislation, led by state senator Scott Wiener of San Francisco, to allow illegal aliens to hold Democratic Party offices in the state (SB 288). This will add additional support for the Democratic Party in California. But if illegal aliens are given amnesty, they will be eligible to vote or be elected in state, local, and federal elections to support, propose, or enact tyrannical laws such as taxation oppression, the banning of weapons, the confiscation of guns, and the silencing, restricting, or banning of free speech. The Democrats will enact laws that stifle the Christian religion and conservative organizations, and propose that new foreigners entering the United States be permitted to vote in state and local elections. Democrats will methodically take away our freedoms and constitutional rights. One way of doing this is to hire amnesty migrants in order to replace conservatives elected to state offices. The goal is to cause an imbalance of power between Democrats and Republicans.[6]

---

[6] J. D. Heyes, "California Dems Now Proposing to Allow Illegal Aliens to Hold Party Offices in the State in Direct Rebuke of POTUS Trump's Enforcement Policies," Libtards.News, December 1, 2019, https://www.libtards.news/2019-12-01-california-dems-proposing-illegal-aliens-in-party-offices.html.

18

BORDER SECURITY AND IMMIGRATION REFORM

Immigration Reform

The Democrats in the House found that immigration reform as they wished it to be was impossible under President Trump. Immigration reform is badly needed in the United States, but the House Democrats refused to meet with the Senate to discuss it and instead spent all their time feverishly trying to impeach President Trump since the 2016 election. President Trump's immigration reform consisted of the following:

1. Secure the border to make the United States safe. For example, complete the building of the border wall.
2. Extreme-vet all immigrants for qualification to enter the United States and become citizens.
3. End the policy of lottery selection of immigrants.
4. Eliminate the catch-and-release loophole in immigration policy because more than 80 percent of the illegal aliens who have been caught at the border promise to show up in court to prove their refugee status but never show up.
5. Eliminate the policy that border states only have to absorb illegal aliens and care for them. Immigration policy should

include sharing that responsibility; therefore, there should be a fair distribution of accepted illegal aliens based on agreed-upon documented criteria.

6. ICE should be designated to transport illegal aliens caught at the border to agreed-upon states.

7. Close the border if Mexico allows waves of migrants in caravans to reach the US border to enter the country.

8. If Central and South American countries refuse to cooperate with US immigration policies, stop all foreign aid to Mexico and to all Central and South American countries.

9. Place tariffs on all Mexican goods entering the United States if Mexico does not prevent the caravans of migrants from reaching the southern US border.

10. Stop all travel to and from Cuba, and stop all trade between Cuba and the United States.

11. Deport all MS-13 gang members immediately, sending them back to their countries.

12. Extreme-vet illegal aliens from Middle Eastern countries and Africa. For instance, if Muslims refuse to assimilate into US culture or if Muslims hate our culture and morality, then our immigration policy must refuse them citizenship and deport them to their respective countries.

13. The United States must not allow any illegal aliens into the country with contagious diseases, particularly COVID-19. Pull the costs of diagnosing illegals at the borders from the foreign aid meant for Mexico or other countries if it doesn't stop.

We Need to Pass Legislation to Extreme-Vet All US Immigrants for US Loyalty

We must allow only people who will accept the culture of the United States and contribute to our nation's greatness to immigrate here. We must *not* allow immigrants who do not like our culture or want to impose their culture on us to immigrate to the United States. We must not allow people who hate the United States and refuse to assimilate into our culture to enter the United States. We must not allow immigrant criminals or gang members into our country. Illegal aliens should not be given priority for benefits over our citizens who are homeless, poor, or veterans. We should require loyalty from immigrants entering our country, and we should require adult immigrants to have job skills and be physically able to work.

In Part 6 of *The Coming Tyranny*, a likely scenario is presented in which the US government strategizes to enforce the coming tyranny. An economic collapse, tyrannical laws, our loss of freedoms, Democratic corruption, and nonstop oppression of freedom-loving people will lead the United States into another civil war. To prevent bloodshed from a potential civil war against socialist tyrants, the United States needed Donald Trump. Now that the election was stolen and Joe Biden is president, the chances for a future civil war in the United States are high. Note that Biden's call for unity of Americans is a lone voice, not echoed by Democratic politicians in his administration or in Congress, or by the corrupt fake news media, or by any high-tech corporation. Contrary to what Biden's lone voice says, more division was generated by Nancy Pelosi's impeachment of a president already out of office and by the corrupt fake news media's calls for "reprogramming" Trump voters and setting up "retraining camps" for them. Democrats want no input on legislation in the House, and the cancel culture continues attacking conservative voices.

Process and Quality Control Are Needed on Immigration

Most members of Congress unfortunately are not motivated to develop robust immigration laws that will have but a minimal effect on taxpayers of the United States. What the Biden administration will have is out-of-control spending, funded by soaking the rich and, subsequently, the middle class. Quality control must oversee and audit good law practices to ensure they benefit the American taxpayer. But the US government does not do that. Democrats are notorious for passing bills that contain excessive pork and unbeneficial junk that does not benefit the American people. Worse, Democrats do not even read the bill to see what's in it, but they pass it to the Senate to be signed in a few hours, before senators have a chance to read it. The first COVID-19 compensation bill and Obamacare are two major examples.

Conservatives must fight for immigration reform to filter out people who do not want to conform to our *present customs and traditions and who wish to maintain theirs.* We want only legal immigrants who can assimilate into our culture and be productive, not come here to freeload. We need to weed out every criminal and prevent them all from entering the United States, and we must put *all* immigrants *on probation* as a quality control requirement to ensure that they are assimilating, conforming to our culture, supporting themselves, and refraining from committing serious crimes. *This will prevent freeloaders who are attracted by socialists* from the Democratic Party from getting government freebies in exchange for their votes. *Extreme vetting of all immigrants* is a solution that will *prevent socialism* in this country, keep our valued customs and traditions, ensure our safety, preserve our economic stability, and preserve our culture. Those who want to social engineer our country with socialism or sharia law should be deported very quickly for violating extreme-vetted immigration laws.

For example, if Subject A is a citizen of Somalia who applies for US citizenship, is extremely vetted, and agrees to abide by US local, state, and federal laws, then Subject A will be on probation his entire life in the United States as a naturalized citizen. If Subject A violates his probation agreement for citizenship by committing a horrific crime, usually a felony, then that person should serve prison time and be subject to deportation after release from prison.

If Subject B is a Muslim and demands sharia law, then Subject B is subject to deportation. Subject B will be happier living under sharia law in his own country.

A law should be passed that prohibits the establishment of all sanctuary cities and states. All law enforcement should hand over to ICE, for deportation, any illegal aliens who have committed felonies and been released from prison. If any illegal alien with a criminal record of felonious behavior is caught by ICE, then that illegal alien should be deported. The safety of Americans trumps the protection of illegal aliens released back into our communities.

The Purpose of Building the Wall along Our Southern Border

President Trump built the wall for border security and safety reasons, as follows:

1. To prevent illegal aliens from crossing the southern border, because it's a crime. They should come in legally.
2. To protect all Americans from criminal illegal aliens, many of whom have committed serious crimes such as rape, robbery, and murder, who were previously deported and who recrossed the border numerous times.
3. To prevent an economic disaster in the United States with many living on government handouts, as already mentioned. With open borders, it is easy math to compute the trillions of dollars that will be required to give "free stuff" to illegal aliens. Democrat-run states such as California, New York, and Illinois may go bankrupt.
4. To prevent terrorists from entering the country carrying weapons of mass destruction or committing acts of terror.
5. To prevent illegal aliens from fraudulently voting in federal elections, thereby becoming useful idiots for Democratic politicians. Democrats will get the votes of illegal aliens, and their support on socialist legislation, should they take control of all three branches of government. Should Democrats ever get control, they will give amnesty to *all* illegal aliens and draw millions more illegal aliens to the United States with their open border policy. This means even higher taxes for the very rich, property owners, and businesses, and any other taxes the Democrats can levy on US citizens so they can give foreigners government handouts—a policy that will draw many more

millions of foreign immigrants into the United States, who will say, "Where do I go to get my free stuff?"

No wall means Mexican cartels will push more drugs into the United States and thousands more young Americans will die from illegal drug overdoses every year. No wall means that violent gangs such as MS-13 will enter the United States a lot more easily and infiltrate many US cities and neighborhoods, where they will viciously attack and kill US citizens; MS-13 gangs are famous for brutal murders. Illegal aliens crossing the southern border are not screened for any diseases they may carry, such as tuberculosis, hepatitis, skin diseases, venereal diseases, smallpox, measles, the Ebola virus, or the coronavirus. And some of these people, if stricken with disease, tend to work in restaurants, in fast-food places, in the fields picking tomatoes and other vegetables, and in hospitals. Especially alarming is that Muslims who want to kill us have been caught sneaking across the southern border, originally having come from Muslim countries. Muslims do not want to assimilate into US culture or contribute to the greatness of the United States; they want to convert everyone to Islam by way of Muslim overpopulation or terrorism, with the goal of taking control of government in the United States and establishing sharia law.

6.   To prevent multiple caravans of illegal aliens, mostly boys and men, from entering the United States illegally.

These are major reasons to prioritize building the wall over enacting some other legislation Congress may have. More importantly, if we don't build border security, our country will eventually become a socialist country because of the future amnesty for illegal aliens who will support and vote for socialists in the Democratic Party. A tyrannical agenda will follow that will deprive Americans of freedom. The United States will end up like Venezuela unless socialists are defeated in a bloody second US civil war. The building of border security is a national security issue. Our safety, our economic well-being, our culture, our constitutional freedoms, and our sovereignty are all at stake if we don't have effective border security.

Drugs have been transported across the border for decades, having killed Americans. Illegal alien drug-runners are killing Americans, and sanctuary states such as California are protecting these people from deportation. Where do these illegal alien criminals go when released from prison or jail? Right back into US neighborhoods. We don't have enough ICE agents to prevent illegal aliens from crossing the border. The border wall was projected to reach 450 miles by the end of 2020. Democrats want illegal aliens to cross the border to do the following:

- Provide cheap labor and thereby displace young people, as employers and restaurants can pay illegals less and illegals will work longer hours.
- Make up for lost tax revenue. Democrats need to make up for the thousands of people leaving California on account of high taxes; the people of California are being overtaxed, and that is taxation oppression. Businesses are leaving California because of the high taxes as well. Democrats want illegal aliens to get jobs, want to tax them for their fair share of taxes, and want to tax their employers, who will make higher profits thanks to the cheap labor.
- Upset the political balance of power in their favor. Democrats want to build a strong Democratic voter base in all blue states. Many illegals will vote fraudulently in federal elections. Democrats hope one day to give them amnesty so they can outnumber conservative voters and vote Democrat for the next one hundred to two-hundred-plus years.

Governor Newsom and the Democratic lawmakers are already giving illegal aliens free health care, welfare, and food stamps, and providing free schooling for their kids, along with welcoming more illegal aliens into the state. And who's paying for all these freebies for illegal aliens in California? The taxpayer is, with increased property taxes, utility taxes (gas, electric, water/trash), telephone taxes, dog license fees, clean water taxes, gasoline taxes, higher fines for traffic violations (same as taxes), higher vehicle excise taxes, and every other creative tax Democrats can think of.

Yet Democrats don't have enough money to clean up the feces and urine left by the homeless around bridges, on beaches, in parks, in riverbeds, in lakes, in the downtown areas, in rich neighborhoods where they beg, and in alleys. Democrats can't take care of the homeless for lack of funds. Higher taxes are expected from Democrats to make a dent in the massive homeless problem in California. But, oh wait … California tax money is being siphoned to pay for free handouts to illegal aliens, *and more caravans are on the way.*

In Denver, Colorado, there were 289 cases of public urination or defecation in 2018, where police merely gave citations or multiple warnings to the homeless who committed these misdemeanors.[1]

San Francisco has one of the largest homeless populations in the United States and is one of the main poop cities in California, along with Los Angeles. "Mohammed Nuru, the Director of the Public Works Department, estimates that $30 million of the street cleaning budget, about half of it, goes toward cleaning up the mess left by the homeless encampments. The entire Democrat-operated West Coast has been experiencing a troubling homeless problem. Since 2015, the homeless population in West Coast cities has seen such an explosion that 10 city and county governments have declared states of emergency."[2]

Democratic politicians are greedy for power, control, and wealth, and above all, they are opposed to border security—even though they were for it in previous administrations. They changed their minds because they hated President Trump and didn't want to give him a win on border security, fearing he would be reelected in 2020. A vote for Democrats in 2020 was a vote to make the United States socialist, shred the Constitution, and tax the hell out of the rich and the middle class all across the United States to benefit illegal aliens more than American citizens, so that *taxation oppression* would drive businesses out of the USA

---

[1] Jason Gruenauer, "Poop in Denver: How Bad the Problem Is and What's Being Done about It," Denver Channel, November 29, 2018, https://www.thedenverchannel.com/lifestyle/health/poop-in-denver-how-bad-the-problem-is-and-what-s-being-done-about-it.
[2] Paul Bois, "San Francisco Spends $30 Million Cleaning Feces, Drug Needles," *Daily Wire*, February 20, 2018, https://www.dailywire.com/news/san-francisco-spends-30-million-cleaning-feces-paul-bois.

and businesses would lay off *millions* of people. This will destroy the great economy we had under Trump.

Muslim Immigration and the Need for Immigration Reform in the United States

The red flags indicating that Islam is a threat to the Western world are as follows:

- Imams, Muslim religious leaders, are encouraging the takeover of Europe and other Western countries by way of massive migration, hoping to overpopulate these countries and intimidate and terrorize their non-Muslim population. Muslims refuse to assimilate in any country; change the country's culture and replace it with sharia law; forbid personal freedom rights and promote submission to Allah; destroy Jewish synagogues and Christian religious statues; and eventually further the jihad to establish an Islamic caliphate.

- Assimilation means becoming a productive part and a law-abiding member of the community within the country, to add to its success and enjoy its prosperity. Refusing to assimilate means making demands to change the existing culture to enable a foreign culture to replace it. It means a refusal to respect or abide by the existing laws of the country. For Muslims, it means promoting a jihad, a fight to change a disliked, undesirable culture that is immoral and incompatible with Islamic law. It means that instead of becoming part of an organ that adds to the vitality and functionality of the body, enabling it to grow healthy, Muslim immigrants become a cancer that will take over an organ and spread until the organ ceases to function and dies. We must not have nonsensical laws that permit foreigners to migrate to our country, hate our country, and fight to metastasize their culture in order to replace our culture. For all migrants, the criterion for citizenship should be a willingness to conform to our culture, respect our laws, and respect our culture—or else not be allowed into the country. Further, if you lie on your application after agreeing to this criterion, or if you disrespect our laws and demand changes to our culture, then you will be deported, or imprisoned if you commit a crime at any time during your citizenship probation of ten years. We cannot have the cancer of radical Islam spread, causing Muslims to engage in a jihad to destroy our culture; those who do so must be kicked out of the country with their families. It is better to prevent immigrants who hate our culture from becoming citizens and to deport them rather than dealing with them for violating their oaths of citizenship after they become probationary citizens or naturalized citizens.

Progressive politicians are opposed to vetting criteria. Good examples are California politicians who protect illegal aliens who have committed crimes of rape, murder, mayhem, or pedophilia and were released back into the community instead of being handed over to ICE for deportation. This goes against good common sense, morality, the safety of American citizens, and good logic. Worse, once these criminal illegal aliens are released, they can move to other states and cause problems there.

- Muslim members of Congress make anti-Semitic speeches in public.
- Muslim wars of religious cleansing in the Middle East, Africa, South Asia, and Malaysia are ongoing. Do a statistical count of the religious wars started by radical Islamists all over the world compared to those started by people of other religions.
- Genocide of non-Muslims by Muslim extremists continues in several places around the world. Count the number of historical genocides caused by Islamists compared to those caused by people of other religions.
- The rate of crimes committed by Muslims has increased significantly. Monitor crimes committed by Muslims as a percentage of the migrant population in any Western country.

Note that rapes committed by Muslims are the most widespread crimes in European countries (including Scandinavia).

- Muslim religious leaders preach hate against Jews, whom they call infidels. Note which religious organizations are preaching hate in the sermons at their places of worship. It's time to bulldoze those places.
- Muslims in Western countries demand death for blasphemers of Islam and of Prophet Muhammad.
- Muslim migration and overpopulation have begun making an undesirable economic impact on Western economies because of Muslims' refusal to work, their inability to work, their low skills to get work, and/or their inability to speak the language to get work.
- Suicide bombers and terrorists have begun to intimidate the citizens of the Western countries they immigrate to in order to make demands on Western governments. People of no other world religion represented in Western countries commit suicide bombings and other horrifying acts of terror, such as beheading men and children, throwing homosexuals off high buildings, plowing into crowds with trucks, and holding women as sex slaves, as do Muslims.
- Muslim terrorists have begun using mosques as places to hide weapons of terror and receive funds from foreign radical Muslim countries meant for charity. Instead, the mosques distribute those funds to jihadist Muslims for terrorist activities. It's time to bulldoze their mosques.

Migration Policy Institute Findings on Immigration

The Migration Policy Institute, which keeps statistics on immigration history in the United States, provides a chart showing the number of immigrants in the United States and the percentage of the US population they account for from 1840 to 2018. It appears on their chart that the increase in significant immigration into the United States began in 1970 and thereafter increased exponentially. As of 2017, more than forty-four and a half million immigrants (legal and illegal) resided in the United States, the historical high since census records have been kept. One in seven US residents is foreign born according to 2017 American Community Survey (ACS) data.[3]

Immigration Population and Percentage of the US Population from 1850 to 2019

An article posted by the Migration Policy Institute (MPI) entitled "U.S. Immigrant Population and Share over Time, 1850–Present"[4] refers to immigrants as noncitizens at birth who are residing in the United States legally or illegally. The chart is derived from data obtained by the MPI from the US Census Bureau, 2010–2019 American Community Surveys, and the 1970, 1990, and 2000 Decennial Census.

MPI's website shows a graph that depicts the increase in immigration into the United States as a percentage of the population. The graph shows a sharp increase in the immigration population from 1970 to 2018, which continued to increase into 2019. A chart on the website shows there are about forty-five million immigrants in the United States, which makes up about 14 percent of the total US population. In 2020, the US southern border wall was being built to prevent illegal immigration into the United States. It should have a declining effect on immigration as more of the wall is completed.

---

[3] Jeanne Batalova, Mary Hanna, and Christopher Levesque, "Frequently Requested Statistics on Immigrants and Immigration in the United States," Migration Policy Institute, February 11, 2021, https://www.migrationpolicy. org/article/frequently-requested-statistics-immigrants-and-immigration-united-states#Unauthorized.

[4] "U.S. Immigrant Population and Share over Time, 1850–Present," Migration Policy Institute, https://www.migrationpolicy.org/programs/data-hub/charts/immigrant-population-over-time.

David A. Herrera

Pew Research Center Findings on the Racial Makeup of the United States from Immigration

According to the Pew Research Center (PRC), immigrants today account for 13.6 percent of the US population, nearly triple the share (4.7 percent) of 1970. Most immigrants (77 percent) are in the country legally, while almost a quarter are illegal aliens, according to new Pew Research Center estimates based on census data adjusted for undercount.

"From 1990 to 2007, the illegal alien population more than tripled in size—from 3.5 million to a record high of 12.2 million in 2007. By 2017, that number had declined by 1.7 million, or 14%. There were 10.5 million illegal aliens in the US in 2017, accounting for 3.2% of the nation's population. More than 1 million immigrants arrived in the US each year. In 2017, the top country of origin for new immigrants coming into the U.S. was China (149,000), India (129,000) people, followed by Mexico (120,000), and the Philippines (46,000)."[5]

The PRC projects Asians will become the largest immigrant group in the United States by 2055, surpassing Hispanics. The Pew Research Center estimates that in 2065, Asians will make up about 38 percent of all immigrants; Hispanics, 31 percent; whites, 20 percent; and blacks, 9 percent. Immigrants and their descendants are projected to account for 88 percent of US population growth through 2065, assuming current immigration trends continue.

The PRC estimates that about 45 percent of the nation's 44.4 million immigrants live in the following three states: California (24 percent), Texas (11 percent), and New York (10 percent). California had the largest immigrant population of any state in 2018, at 10.6 million. Texas, Florida, and New York had more than four million immigrants each.

About 68 percent of immigrants lived in the western (34 percent) and southern (34 percent) regions of the United States. Roughly 21 percent lived in the Northeast, and 11 percent were in the Midwest.

---

[5] Abby Budiman, "Key Findings about U.S. Immigrants," Pew Research Center, August 20, 2020, https://www.pewresearch.org/fact-tank/2020/08/20/key-findings-about-u-s-immigrants/.

According to a map on the Pew Research Center's website, in 2018, most immigrants lived in twenty major cities, with the largest populations in New York, Los Angeles, and Miami. About twenty-eight million seven hundred thousand immigrants lived in these top twenty cities, or 64 percent of the nation's total foreign-born population. Most of the nation's illegal alien population lived in these top twenty cities as well.

The twenty metropolitan areas with the highest number of immigrants in 2017 were mostly Democrat-run cities.

"With large number of people are moving out of riot-torn and high-crime cities such as Seattle, Los Angeles, Chicago, New York, Minneapolis, Washington, DC, some of these states are offering illegal immigrants free health care and free tuition to make up for massive job losses in those cities and states. People are also moving out of the Democrat-run states because of high state taxes, especially in New York and California."[6]

According to the Pew website, an estimated half million illegal aliens enter the United States each year. Illegal border crossings have declined substantially from 2000, when 71,000–220,000 migrants were apprehended each month, to 2018, when 20,000–40,000 migrants were apprehended.

Noncriminal (NC) and criminal convictions (CC)

Year	NC	CC	Total deported
2001	116	73	189
2002	92	73	165
2003	127	84	211
2004	148	92	240
2005	154	92	246
2006	182	98	280
2007	217	102	319
2008	255	105	360

---

[6] Ibid.

Year	NC	CC	Total deported
2009	260	132	392
2010	212	170	382
2011	197	189	386
2012	217	200	417
2013	237	199	436
2014	247	168	415
2015	193	140	333
2016	204	136	340
2017	174	121	295
Total	3,232	2,174	5,406

TABLE 5. US deportations from 2001 to 2018 (in thousands)

Source: Abby Budiman, "Key Findings about U.S. Immigrants," Pew Research Center, August 20, 2020, https://www.pewresearch.org/fact-tank/2020/08/20/key-findings-about-u-s-immigrants/.

The Pew Research Center website contains a vertical histogram listing deportation of immigrants in the thousands each year from 2001 to 2017. An MS Excel representation of that data is represented here in tabular form, showing criminal convictions (CC) and noncriminal convictions (NC) for deported immigrants each year. Data for 2017 indicates 174,000 deported immigrants were noncriminal and 121,000 deported migrants were convicted criminals. That's 41 percent convicted and 59 percent not convicted.

From 2001 to 2017, a majority (60 percent) of immigrants deported have not been convicted of a crime:

$$\frac{3232}{5406} = 0.597854 \approx 0.60 \approx 60\% \text{ noncriminal convictions}$$

40% criminal convictions

Note that in 2017, about 121,000 immigrants (41 percent of 295,000 = 120,950 ~ 121,000) had criminal convictions; this number of convicted criminals is not good for the United States. Worse, a total of 2,174,000 immigrants were convicted of crimes in the United States from 2001 to 2017; that is unacceptable. This kind of study should be done in every country in Europe and presented to the pope to show that his well-intended open border policy, integration policy, and policy of peaceful coexistence with immigrants may not work as expected. In the United States, this statistical data should be shown to Democrats in the House to justify building the wall and instituting immigrant reform to properly vet those who are seeking to come into the United States. The type of crimes matter, and the US federal government has a responsibility to ensure the safety of its citizens. Above all, the United States doesn't welcome or want immigrants who commit crimes.

According to the Pew Research Center, politically, Democrats and Democratic-leaning Independents think that 88 percent of immigrants strengthen the country with their hard work and talents, and just 8 percent say they are a burden. In contrast, Republicans and Republican-leaning Independents say 41 percent of immigrants strengthen the country, while nearly half, 44 percent, say they burden it. Americans were divided on future levels of immigration. The sentiment of approximately 30 percent of Americans was that legal immigration into the United States should be decreased by 24 percent, while 38 percent said immigration should be kept at the present level, and 32 percent said immigration should be increased.[7]

Kamala Harris wanted to reexamine ICE and called for changes to the agency's function.[8]

In 2018, the immigrant share of the population was 13.7 percent. Let's assume that the immigrant population increased to 14 percent in 2020. As of December 6, 2020, the US population was 330,676,544. How many illegal immigrants are in the United States? Answer: 14 percent × 330,676,544 = 46,294,716 immigrants ~ 46 million.

In a future election, Democrats may take control of all three branches of the federal government and grant amnesty to all illegal immigrants. In such a case, assume that 75 percent of immigrants are

---

[7] Ibid.

[8] Daniella Diaz, "These Democrats Want to Abolish ICE," CNN, July 3, 2018, https://www.cnn.com/2018/07/02/politics/abolish-ice-democrats-list/index.html.

adults. Then 75 percent of 46 million = 34,500,000 or 34.5 million. Then assume only 80 percent of immigrants vote for Democrats. Then 80 percent × 34.5 million = 27,200,000 or 27.2 million. Now we have 27.2 million new amnesty immigrants who are eligible voters for the Democratic Party.

Joe Biden supposedly won the 2020 election with a recorded 81,009,468 Democratic votes, compared to 74,111,419 votes for President Trump, if you can believe it. The difference was ~ 81.0 million − 74.1 million, meaning Biden received 6.9 million more votes than Trump. Add 81 million to 27.2 million to get 108.2 million, the total number of Democratic voters in the United States if illegal aliens are given amnesty.

Conclusions

If approximately 27.2 million voters had been given amnesty prior to the 2020 election and had been able to vote, then illegal immigrants, 27.2 million more voters, would be added to the number of people who voted for Joe Biden (81 million), which would be 108.2 million, against President Trump's 74 million. Then 108.2 million − 74.1 million = 34.1 million more than Trump voters. Democrats would win every future US election with the aid of amnesty given to existing immigrants in the United States alone, and that doesn't count packing the Supreme Court and abolishing the Electoral College so as always to retain power in future four-year elections.

If we now consider one million illegal aliens entering the United States every year for the next four years after Biden has stolen the election, then we will have 27.2 million + 4 million × 75 percent × 80 percent = 27.2 million + 2.4 million = 29.6 million more Democratic voters in 2024. No checks and balances will ever be in place, and Democrats will always win future elections. The scales are already tipped, and the United States is gone.

With open borders, peasants will work for low wages for the rich elite socialist politicians and their rich friends. The confiscation of wealth and guns will proceed, and gradual erosion and elimination of our freedoms will begin. A new dark age in US history will emerge with a new tyrannical United States leading to a great civil war. Now that Joe Biden has been fraudulently elected, the chances of the coming tyranny leading to a second civil war in the United States are very high. Trump's wall was working, but a stolen election that could not be reversed changed the course of US history for the worse.

If the population of immigrants has a higher birthrate than that of US citizens, and if millennials are continuously bamboozled into thinking they will be given free health care, a free college education, and free housing, then immigrants will join socialists to remake the United States into a socialist country, causing it in time to end up as another Venezuela.

It is absurd to pay taxes so that reparations may be made to African American citizens of the United States for their slave ancestors and because of Jim Crow laws. Blacks demand reparations from whites and all other nonblack races who had nothing to do with owning, buying, or selling slaves. A Conference of Mayors in mid-July 2020 concluded that reparations for the forty-one million black Americans will cost $6.2 *quadrillion*.[9]

We are a divided country, roughly 50 percent liberal and 50 percent conservative. Any weight gain from immigration to either side will tip the scale of voters (see figure 2). Immigration, legal or illegal, must be either stopped or significantly curtailed if we want to preserve our country. In doing so, we will preserve individual freedom and our constitutional rights, achieve prosperity, and reduce homelessness. This means preventing or fighting tyranny and taxation oppression. Do the math and ask yourself, how many immigrants does it take before the United States is remade and socialist tyrants will begin their corrupt politics and oppressive agenda? The Democratic politicians have already done the math, figuring that by allowing millions of immigrants to enter the United States, by attracting them with free stuff, Democrats will achieve a majority both for the popular vote and in the Electoral College to win elections forever and control all three branches of

---

[9] Morgan Phillips, "US Conference of Mayors Supports Commission to Study Giving Reparations to African-Americans," Fox News, July 13, 2020, https://www.foxnews.com/politics/conference-of-mayors-supports-study-reparations-african-americans.

government. Then the systematic encroachment of socialism will begin in the United States. The win by the Biden administration, including the win to control the Senate, marked the beginning of the tyranny to come to the United States. Democrats already control the House, so there will be no checks and balances between branches.

Open Borders and Destruction of European Culture Is Already Happening in Europe

Note that, similarly, a massive flux of immigration is occurring in European countries with people coming from the Middle East and Africa, all designed by the policies of the ruling European Union in Brussels, Belgium. Look at all the European problems with immigration:

- The cultures of European countries are being destroyed.
- Christian artifacts are being destroyed.
- Immigrant-perpetrated crime is increasing.
- Muslim leaders are encouraging Muslims settling in Europe to partake in a jihad to overpopulate Europe with Muslims and have Muslims enter politics so as to eventually take over a country and establish a caliphate in Europe without having to fire a shot.
- Most immigrants are uneducated, unskilled, and destitute and can't speak the language in the country they reside in; they will have to live off free handouts, paid for by taxpayers in the country they reside in.

Uncontrolled and unvetted immigration can radically change the political, religious, economic, and cultural makeup of any country. The mathematical analysis of using immigrants to tip the scales to remake the United States and win elections has already been carried out by Democratic politicians. Uncontrolled immigration is one of the pathways to achieving creeping socialism in the United States. Brave Americans must prevent the United States from becoming a haven for immigrants who are preferred to freedom-loving American citizens by standing against tyranny. We must also prepare to fight an armed revolution against tyranny and oppression. We must stop Democrats from achieving their goals of gaining power, seizing control, and engaging in corruption and self-enrichment, and we must prevent them from winning elections by way of fraud or by remaking the United States with open borders and thereby risking the lives of US citizens.

Why Do Massive Caravans of Hopeful Immigrants Travel to the US Border?

Neither Congress nor the UN has been interested in looking for the root causes for why massive waves of immigrant travel in caravans from South America and Central America into Mexico and to our southern border.

Politicians and think tanks should identify *factors* that cause massive amounts of people to leave their countries. It's the UN's job as well; what are we funding them for? Instead, the UN urges countries like the United States to accept more immigrants as a remedy for immigrant poverty, regardless of the consequences. The UN should be studying why these mass migrations lead to human trafficking, narcotic trafficking, health emergencies, crime, poverty, and starvation during the migration journey and to problems originating in the countries they came from. Significant factors that cause these crises should be identified and analyzed, such as form of government, economic activity, government corruption, crime, religion, public health and disease containment, police corruption, military corruption, and economic corruption. Some countries could be advised to follow a get-well plan, a solution to help them, and even receive funds to implement a solid solution, but leaders who control these countries may be so corrupt that no get-well plan will work to assist them, especially in countries where socialist politicians oppress their own people. But corrupt government leaders from these countries will accept millions of dollars in economic assistance and will promise to create jobs for the emigrants they oppress.

Pope Francis and His Morality Steps into the Political World

Pope Francis joined civil representatives in Rome on March 26, 2019, to commemorate the city's history of welcoming immigrants, as Italian politics trend toward populism. During his speech in Rome on March 26, the pope stated: "Rome has a universal vocation. It carries a mission and an ideal aimed at overcoming mountains and seas and to be shared with everyone, near and far, regardless of which people they belong to, whichever language they speak and whatever color is their skin."

The pope indicates Rome has been a multifaith and multicultural city, able to integrate diverse cultures without offensive prejudices of human character, and urges the Italian population, including welcomed migrants, to integrate with respect for one another and move toward a common destiny.

Pope Francis offers to work together with private institutions and government to help refugees and the poor rebuild a secure and dignified life.[10]

Contrary to President Trump in the United States, who was building a wall to keep illegal immigration under control and provide security for the American people in the face of immigrant lawlessness in the United States, the mayor of Rome supports the pope in welcoming immigrants from the Middle East and Africa with open arms and in making Rome a multilateral and multicultural city, that is, an open city to the world. Pope Francis addressed a Roman crowd, asking them to care for one another and to respect each other for a united community that lives in harmony and works for justice.

The pope's message signifies tolerance, welcoming foreigners to share wealth and resources, respect and dignity, and compassion for

---

[10] Claire Giangrave, "Pope Francis Calls on City of Rome to Be Welcoming to Immigrants," Crux Now, March 26, 2019, https://cruxnow.com/church-in-europe/2019/03/pope-francis-calls-on-city-of-rome-to-be-welcoming-to-immigrants/.

the poor and disabled. But there are issues that the pope doesn't realize must be handled by the government if these norms are to be followed:

1. Some immigrants are heinous criminals and should neither be tolerated nor allowed in any country because of the potential harm they cause and the crimes they commit.

2. Every government in the world has quotas or criteria for accepting immigrants into the country. But every country in the world, including the wealthy ones, cannot allow unlimited immigration. Excessive immigration affects taxation and wealth, takes jobs from citizens, and requires free hospitalization at times, stressing hospitals and public assistance.

3. Most immigrants are poor and need food, water, shelter, medical care, and shower facilities.

4. Most workers have little or no skills and would require public assistance.

5. There are many Muslim immigrants who do not want to integrate to make a better life in European countries. Rather, jihadist Muslims would like to make those European countries Muslim.

6. Some immigrants are terrorists who would like to plant bombs to kill Americans.

7. Democratic politicians in the United States are exploiting immigrants, legal or not, allowing them to enter the country for votes and for cheap labor.

8. Criminal enterprises such as Mexican cartels are trafficking women and children to the borders of wealthy countries.

9. There is a homelessness problem in many countries of the world, including the United States. Allowing open borders in the United States to welcome all immigrants would add to the homelessness problem, which the federal socialist government may not be able to resolve. Homelessness is causing filth, trash, feces, and urine in parks, on beaches, in downtown alleys, in riverbeds, and under bridges. This filth is causing an increase in rodents and fleas, which could give rise to serious contagious

diseases such as the bubonic plague, typhus, COVID-19, and tuberculosis.

10. Countries of the world can only tax their citizens so much before the citizens themselves are driven into poverty or homelessness. In hard economic times, rich governments can no longer help immigrants or their own citizens. In tax-oppressed countries, even violent rebellions may happen.

11. Socialist countries are the worst-affected countries if they allow immigration. They have limited wealth and limited industrial resources. Wealth cannot be created in these countries; they will likely go bankrupt. It is more possible these countries will go bankrupt if more taxes are drawn to assist immigrants.

George Soros has been funding millions of dollars to liberal progressive Catholic organizations that are not truly Catholic but are political operatives whose intent is to influence American Catholics to accept abortion and same-sex marriage and view them as moral. Nancy Pelosi's and Joe Biden's attempts to convince Pope Francis and the Vatican to change Catholic doctrine failed. Hillary Clinton, who hates Catholicism, chose Tim Kaine, a lifelong progressive Catholic who advocates abortion and homosexuality. Had Catholic doctrine been changed during the Obama administration, and had Hillary Clinton been elected president, then she would be justifying abortion and homosexuality today as "moral values" sanctified by the Catholic Church and bragging about the morality of the leftist Democratic Party, saying it is 100 percent aligned with the Catholic Church. This would have divided conservative traditional Catholics and progressive Catholics in the United States and eventually may have destroyed the Catholic Church as George Soros had hoped.

Divine intervention enabled Donald Trump to be elected president of the United States in 2016, and that put an end to Hillary's vice presidential candidate's preaching the new morality from the political pulpit about funding abortion and advocating same-sex marriage in the Catholic Church. Overlooked by Hillary and those who wanted to see changes to Catholic doctrine is that abortion is the genocide of the unborn and the just born, an execution order from the mother bearing the child for her actions. Additionally, there are several passages in the Bible that conflict with homosexuality, an immoral issue that leftists can never change.

Pope Francis has the right to reach out to Catholics in China, or wherever they may be, despite liberal or conservative opposition. The Catholic Church's business should not be to get into politics, or preach politics, or tell corrupt governments to shape up or resign. The Catholic Church should be concerned with the salvation of men and women and what they can do solely with the power of God and his Word. It is the free will of human beings that allows people to choose to be corrupt. The pope's job should be to lead the Catholic Church to save human souls, according the Bible, and to resist the advice of politicians, lobbyists, and heretics who want to change his views in favor of their own self-interests.

Pope Francis on Immigration

Pope Francis means well when he suggests that countries accept immigrants in a mixed culture where all citizens and immigrants ideally peacefully coexist and get along. Pope Francis assumes or hopes immigrants will get along as part of a multicultural society and that government leaders will urge Muslims to get along with Jews, whom they've hated for more than fourteen hundred years. Governments cannot force Muslims to coexist with Christians or people of any other religion. This pope doesn't understand that the Muslim culture doesn't want to get along or coexist with western European culture, our US culture, non-Muslim African cultures, Scandinavian culture, or Australian culture. The pope does not understand that Muslims want to change every non-Muslim culture they immigrate to into an entirely Islamic culture. This pope does not understand that Islam is incompatible with Western culture—and world history for the last fourteen hundred years has proven it: Today, Muslims are involved in multiple conflicts and terrorist efforts around the world, and their Muslim leaders seek to make Islam the "master religion" of the world, rather than coexisting with other religions.

Pope Francis does not understand that public safety, a nation's economy, and the preservation of its culture are extremely important for the survival of any country, or that every country is limited in terms of the number of immigrants it can accept based on its economics, laws, and culture. In addition, the safety of a nation's citizens must not be compromised, so extreme vetting and immigration laws should always be required to accept *legal* immigrants into the United States. The United States has sought to vet immigrants in terms of the criteria to enter the United States, but House Democrats obstructed President Trump in that effort. We must not accept criminals into the United States from any country. All immigrants should promise and agree, at the risk of deportation at any time, to assimilate into our country in good faith as a condition of entry and as a condition of remaining in the country. All immigrants should promise they will join US citizens in adding to the greatness of the United States, domestic peace, and the prosperity of all Americans, not just Muslims.

Pope Francis should not meddle into the politics of a country or criticize its leaders, or tell them how to run their country, as he does not know the reasons for their policies or the agenda that best benefits the country in question. Catholics pray that God will give the pope the wisdom to lead the Catholic Church righteously and confer this religious wisdom upon leaders of countries to contain and confound the evildoers of the world.

PART 4

THE GOALS, CORRUPTION, AND TYRANNY OF THE DEMOCRAT PARTY

19

THE SOCIALIST AGENDA OF THE DEMOCRATIC PARTY

Democratic candidates were deficient at every level running against Donald Trump, basing their campaigns on perceived hatred of Trump and advocating economically disastrous socialist policies. The fake news media such as the *Washington Post*, the *New York Times*, CNN, and MSNBC manufactured vile and slanderous remarks against President Trump to help the failing, do-nothing Democrats get elected. Democrats lost reason and common sense and were blinded by hate. Democrats and their liberal hate-Trump media manufactured vile falsehoods against President Trump and broadcasted them 24-7.

The few socialist Democrats who remained viable candidates who were offering socialism as a way to govern the United States showed that they don't care about the United States, because they are in the political game for the power and in order to satisfy their greed, not because they wish to serve the interests of the American people. Additionally, these socialist candidates ignored the fact that socialism won't work in the United States and were clueless about the disastrous results to the economy, our culture, and our values that their policies would bring if these socialists ever were to get control of our government. Hang on to your fat wallets, because tax oppression and more homelessness is coming if socialists are elected. But be assured that socialists advocating open borders will use your tax money to give free stuff to a massive number of illegal aliens.

What Democrats Stand For

Democrats today are

1. the party of illegal aliens;
2. the party of open borders;
3. the party that advertises giving away free government stuff to attract illegal aliens into the United States;
4. the party that takes money from its citizens to give illegal aliens free stuff;
5. the party that never vets illegal aliens entering the United States for criminal records or according to other criteria;
6. the party that wants to radically change the culture of the United States;
7. the party that draws illegal aliens into the United States for Democratic votes;
8. the party that will confiscate wealth from the rich, the hardworking middle class, and businesses to pay for their federal spending plans that cost several trillion dollars;
9. the party that will appease foreign governments that sponsor terrorism;
10. the party that will weaken the US military;
11. the party that will indoctrinate students to celebrate homosexual history and hate the United States;
12. the party of hypocrisy and intolerance;
13. the party of corruption, whose leaders look the other way at corruption in their own party;
14. the party that wants to stifle, weaken, or take away the constitutional freedoms of Americans by
    - confiscating weapons, eliminating the Second Amendment, or imposing tyrannical gun laws;
    - committing violence against or stifling the free speech of anyone they disagree with on college campuses;

- stifling, weakening, or eliminating religious freedom; and
- obtaining illegal warrants from liberal judges to surveil, gather illegal data on, and arrest people who disagree or resist their tyrannical laws;

15. the party of socialism that must pass tyrannical laws to confiscate wealth and must use stricter law enforcement to enforce their oppressive tyrannical laws;

16. the party that uses their government offices to enrich themselves through bribes, quid pro quo deals, pay-to-play "donations," and lobbying;

17. the party of crony capitalism that distributes millions of dollars to fund their crony friends and pet organizations;

18. the party that partners with radical Islamists to target our US military, our law enforcement, our culture, and conservatives;

19. the party that will give millions of dollars to racial groups or gender groups who pose as victims of historic US oppression;

20. the party of evil and corruption claiming to be self-sanctimonious and holier-than-thou;

21. the party that is currently trying to destroy the Catholic Church by bribing Vatican officials and ill-counseling the pope to change biblical history and morality to coincide with US political liberalism;

22. the party that is legalizing dangerous drugs and wants to legalize even more dangerous drugs;

23. the party that wants to steal elections, rig elections, or change election laws so that socialists and Democrats will win every election;

24. the party of big government whose leaders think they know better than individuals what is good for them;

25. the party that will ruin the economy of the United States should they come to control all three branches of government;

26. the party that allows massive homelessness in blue states and can't fix the problem;

27. the party that will incite a major civil war in the United States by way of creeping socialism, encroachment upon individual liberties, corruption, gross incompetence, and their eventual

use of gestapo tactics or the hiring of UN Peacekeepers to enter US soil to kill Americans who are opposed to tyranny.

Democrats know they have absolutely nothing to give American citizens, as President Trump was already very successful in meeting Americans' needs, so Democrats *abandoned* US citizens and resorted to drawing in foreigners who, coming into the United States illegally, *will* vote for Democrats in exchange for free stuff paid for by US citizens.

In reference to number 16 in the foregoing bullet list, people with little or no knowledge of government should know that the only way to rip off hardworking taxpayers and businesses is through *tyranny*. Little do they know that taxpayers will start a revolution the likes of which have never been seen in US history. Conservatives and US patriots, keep your guns; we're going to fight tyranny again.

The Platform of Democratic Socialists That Ran for President in 2020

Democratic socialist politicians who ran for president in 2020 were consistent with many socialist policies:

1. Reparations for blacks and homosexuals
2. Amnesty for the twelve million to thirty million illegal aliens in the United States
3. Government handouts to all new amnesty migrants, costing American taxpayers trillions of dollars
4. Allowing prisoners to vote
5. Allowing sixteen- and seventeen-year-olds to vote
6. Allowing open borders to let massive numbers of illegal aliens into the United States for free handouts, amnesty, and cheap labor
7. Abolishing the Electoral College so mob rule wins elections (the majority of the US population is concentrated in blue states)
8. Legalizing prostitution and marijuana to keep young drug users on the Democratic plantation

9. Increasing the size of the Supreme Court and appointing leftist justices so as always to get the majority vote for leftists

10. Advertising free handouts to attract freeloaders, millennials, and illegal aliens in exchange for votes regardless that this adversely affects the safety and economic well-being of Americans

11. Tax-oppressing the rich and hardworking Americans who have good-paying jobs in order to redistribute the billions of dollars to the Democrats' friends, Democrats' pet organizations, and illegal aliens for their support

12. Giving free tuition to every freeloader and all foreign immigrants in the United States in exchange for votes

13. Forgiving college loan debt owed by students, which is about $1.5 trillion of taxpayer money

14. Allowing tax-funded on-demand abortions of babies in or outside the womb for any reason, and eventually neglecting or denying health care for senior citizens deemed too old

15. Confiscating weapons from law-abiding patriotic Americans by passing tyrannical laws and using force if necessary

16. Reform law enforcement agencies to enforce socialist tyrannical laws

17. Social engineering the military to defend tyranny and put down rebellions from freedom-fighting conservative patriots.

Climate Change Tax Oppression

Bernie Sanders adopted the Green New Deal as suggested by Alexandria Ocasio-Cortez (AOC), which had the largest price tag of any policy of all the presidential candidates in 2020: $16.3 trillion. Bernie and AOC, who are avid socialists, think tax revenue would easily be collected from rich and middle-class Americans, and from the income taxes of new workers in the twenty million new jobs Sanders predicts will be created. Still more taxes would be collected by placing costly regulations on the petroleum industry, and tax monies would be saved and diverted to the New Green Deal by cutting the defense budget.

Money collected from oppressive taxation on the petroleum industry would then be spent on maintaining and inflating climate change slush funds, deploying renewable energy, building a high-voltage direct current network, and giving US taxpayer money to the United Nations Green Climate Fund and to the Paris climate accord, to which Joe Biden has been reinstated.

Bernie's plan also called for zeroing out emissions from transportation and power generation by 2030. In addition to raising taxes on the carbon fuel industry and pursuing civil litigation, Sanders wanted criminal prosecution of greenhouse gas emitters such as oil companies.

Bernie Sanders proposed the United States fund genocide by way of baby-killing abortions in poor countries across the world to curb the world population and to prevent climate change, although he didn't present scientific facts to back up his assertions. God or morality was not an issue in Bernie's proposal. Bernie's proposal of committing genocide by way of aborting babies prompted a woman at an Ocasio-Cortez meeting in New York to say, "We're not going to be here for much longer because of the climate crisis! We only have a few months left! I love that you support the Green Deal, but getting rid of fossil fuel is not going to solve the problem fast enough. I think your next campaign slogan has to be this: 'We've got to start eating babies.'"[1]

She either was mocking AOC or Bernie Sanders or was serious about urging everyone to promote Bernie Sanders's proposal for a worldwide genocide of babies by some means before the world, as AOC claims, ends around 2030.

Joe Biden won the Democratic vote as a presidential candidate, beating out the numerous socialist candidates, in 2020. Under pressure to get the black vote, Biden chose socialist Kamala Harris as his vice presidential running mate. Kamala Harris, who is Jamaican and Asian Indian, is a self-avowed black person who may have little or no black ancestry.

---

[1] Ryan Saavedra, "Woman Snaps at AOC Over Climate: 'Start Eating Babies! We Only Have a Few Months Left!,'" *Daily Wire*, October 3, 2020, https://www.dailywire.com/news/woman-snaps-at-aoc-over-climate-start-eating-babies-we-only-have-a-few-months-left?%3Futm_source=twitter.

Joe Biden proposes a climate change policy costing upward of $5 trillion that he claims would lead the United States to net-zero carbon emissions by 2050. Additionally, he calls for $1.7 trillion in federal spending over ten years, with the rest of the investments coming from the private sector. Biden proposes covering the taxpayer costs by repealing the corporate tax cuts that President Donald Trump signed into law in 2017, while eliminating existing subsidies to the fossil fuel industry. That's $0.167 trillion + $0.17 trillion = $0.337 trillion added to the federal budget each year for the next ten years, continuing with $0.167 trillion each year until 2050. In billions, this is $337 billion per year for ten years, and $167 billion from 2030 to 2050.

The main question not asked by socialists who support costly climate change legislation is, Will there be any significant effect on climate change if the United States and a few other small European nations eliminate pollution and carbon emissions, when China and India are among the world's largest polluters?

Joe Biden's Corruption with His Son Hunter Biden in China and the Ukraine

Joe Biden was heard by millions of Americans in a video on TV saying he had coerced the Ukraine to stop an investigation of his son Hunter Biden, who was hired by Burisma, a Ukrainian contract oil and gas company, and was paid about $1 million a year without having any experience. Then–vice president Joe Biden threatened to cut off US aid unless a Ukrainian official stopped investigating his son; so, the Ukrainian prosecuting official was fired. Joe Biden was guilty of a quid pro quo or pay-to-play scheme, enabling his son to enrich himself. Tony Bobulinski, a former business partner of Hunter Biden, is a whistleblower who claimed he had emails on a laptop computer about Hunter Biden's corrupt deals in the Ukraine that he submitted as evidence to the FBI. Bobulinski said one of the emails on Hunter's laptop indicated that Joe Biden was the "big guy" who allegedly got 10 percent of an unknown but significant amount of money from a Chinese communist–run energy company. Joe Biden is corrupt. This was a crime Barack Obama allowed that went unchecked, until recently discovered. The FBI is currently investigating Hunter Biden for money laundering and other serious accusations.[2]

How the Left Wants to Remake the United States

The objectives of the Left in the United States are to acquire power and control by whatever means they can get it, corrupt or not, and pass laws to keep them in power forever. The first set of examples are the corrupt and criminal means Democrats will use to gain power. The second set of examples indicate how a corrupt Democratic Party will have the means, the opportunity, and the will to remake the United States.

Democrats have experience in corruption in trying to rig elections, trying to remove a president multiple times by impeachment, stealing elections by election fraud, and using the fake news propaganda machine to declare a propaganda war on a president. President Trump is a good example of a Republican president, whom Democrats tried to remove from office before and after the 2016 election, for four years. To win elections, Democrats did the following things:

- They used the corrupt fake news media to deliver false propaganda against the Republican president in office and to slander, excoriate, vilify, condemn, denounce, and denigrate him and his family throughout his term in office. They omitted from the press any major accomplishments/achievements of the president that benefited the United States; omitted or played down Trump's awards for major accomplishments in foreign policy and his Nobel Peace Prize nominations; refrained from reporting any discovered alleged pay-to-play scandal instigated by a Democratic candidate; blamed the president for insufficient

---

[2] Matt Vespa, "Joe Biden Is the 'Big Guy' Referenced in Hunter's Massive China Business Deal," Townhall.com, October 17, 2020, https://townhall.com/tipsheet/mattvespa/2020/10/17/fox-news-source-says-joe-biden-is-the-big-guy-referenced-in-hunters-massive-c-n2578275.

handling of all crises; blamed all psychos who commit mass murder on the Republican president in office for being pro-gun; blamed the president for having massive campaign rallies, thereby causing people to spread COVID-19; distorted all presidential policies as being racist, sexist, homophobic, xenophobic, Islamophobic, and/or criminal; and pushed a false label on a Republican president like Donald Trump, calling him a Nazi or a white supremacist enough times so that some among the public eventually came to believe it. As an arm of the Democratic Party, the corrupt media's goal was to destroy the president with fake news 24-7.

- They used a former president (Barack Obama) to campaign for a weak and senile old Democratic candidate (Joe Biden) who mostly hid in his basement. The former president stooped low enough to attack, criticize, and demean the president in office, and then claimed credit for the success and tremendous growth of the economy brought on by that same Republican president, whom Obama criticizes.

- They made Hollywood videos about a woman carrying the severed head of then president Trump; suggested his youngest son be kidnapped by pedophiles; showed a Hollywood play of then president Trump being beaten; showed a Hollywood actor dreaming of blowing up the White House; showed actors talking about assassinating then president Trump; showed an actor threatening to punch then president Trump in the face; and advertised in the media that many Hollywood actors and actresses were threatening to move out of the United States if Trump was reelected.

- They used the press to show that the liberal Hollywood crowd hated President Trump.

- In 2020, Democratic supporters used fraudulent election software in computers to secretly flip votes from a Republican candidate to Joe Biden, so Joe Biden won the presidency. Democrats claim there is no trace of fraud and, therefore, no probable cause for investigation. Nancy Pelosi and Dianne Feinstein both have ties to Dominion election computers. Is that a coincidence?[3]

The *first moment* Democratic liberals gain control of the majority in both houses of Congress and of the presidency, they will do the following things:

- Allow caravans of illegal aliens to enter the United States through their open border policy to reach an increased population level and give them amnesty. This way, amnesty migrants, when put in the pool with liberal US citizens, will always significantly outnumber conservative voters in future elections. This means from that point on, socialists can change the Constitution, change election laws, and forever hold power. This includes appointing socialist and communist justices to the Supreme Court and socialist and communist judges to lower courts without opposition. Democrats in Democrat-run cities will either defund police or hire amnesty migrants as police officers, as a preference, to enforce their tyrannical laws. Democrats will introduce laws requiring the military to induct amnesty aliens into the military over natural-born US citizens. The next complete takeover of the federal government will give socialists unopposed opportunities to remake the United States.
- Politicize the Supreme Court by packing it with additional liberal or socialist justices to outnumber the number of conservative judges so as always to have the desired political majority vote to approve their legislation. This means a leftist president will always win all appeals. This means the SCOTUS will approve amending the Constitution as desired by leftists, or will vote to approve the restriction or elimination of the constitutional rights and freedoms we have now. It means approving tyrannical, oppressive tax laws to redistribute wealth, approving costly

[3] Dean Garrison, "Nancy Pelosi, Dianne Feinstein Both Financially Tied to Dominion Voting Systems," SGT Report, November 24, 2020, https://www.sgtreport.com/2020/11/nancy-pelosi-dianne-feinstein-both-financially-tied-to-dominion-voting-systems/.

reparations for today's black victims whose ancestors were historically oppressed, approving gun confiscations, approving antireligious legislation, allowing transgender people and homosexuals into the military, and much more.

- Target conservatives for hate speech, and monitor churches and other religious organizations for politically conservative voices and political activism that opposes the government.
- Politicize and weaponize all agencies of the US government so as to form a "Deep State II" that can spy on US citizens through the approval of FISA with warrants issued by leftist judges to dig up dirt or manufacture dirt on conservative politicians Democrats don't like (a repetition of what was done to candidate and president Trump).
- Win future elections by mob rule. Eliminate the Electoral College to change the United States from a republic to a democracy, meaning that only the most populated states, such as liberal New York, Illinois, and California, will always dictate the winner of federal elections.
- Politicize police department leaders to draw down police during leftist rioting, urging them to retreat when rioters are attacking police precincts or police stations, and allowing rioters to burn and destroy them, all of which have been done by Democratic leaders in Democrat-run cities, counties, and states. Democrats will hold back the National Guard and the US military so they do not stop leftist rioters who endanger public safety, and reduce the number of police or defund the police as necessary to allow crime to rise in cities. Socialists are aware that a breakdown in law enforcement and the military is a way for them to increase their power and tyranny. We have already seen rioters in Portland, Seattle, New York City, Chicago, and Los Angeles whose city leaders failed to achieve law and order with their police officers. We have already seen examples of tyranny in New York, California, and Michigan by governors who mandated people to stay indoors during the rise in COVID-19 cases but who allowed protests and rioting to occur—or else the elite Democratic governors themselves

violate their own rules. Tyrannical laws will not just come from a socialist federal government; they will come from tyrannical Democratic leaders of cities, counties, and states.

- Politicize the military. Under orders from President Joe Biden, Secretary of Defense General Lloyd Austin has begun to politicize the military by indoctrinating the US military personnel to leftist propaganda. One allegation for indoctrination equates white racist extremists to Donald Trump. General Austin is also screening all military personnel for extremism and their removal.

The following are examples of typical socialists who want to invade our privacy and take away our freedoms:

Democrat **Beto O'Rourke**, former House representative, campaigned on a platform to buy back semiautomatic weapons from all law-abiding Americans; if they refused, he was in favor of police confiscating those weapons. How would he know where to look? That's the reason socialists, as a first step, are proposing laws to require federal registration of guns, so they know who has them and where they are.

On October 10, 2019, Beto O'Rourke responded to a CNN reporter in an LGBTQ town hall meeting that he would eliminate the tax-exempt status of churches that do not allow same-sex marriages. He also said, "There can be no reward, no benefit, no tax break for anyone—or any institution, any organization in America—that denies the full human rights and the full civil rights of every single one of us. So, as president, we're going to make that a priority and we are going to stop those who are infringing on the rights of our fellow Americans." This means all churches that stand in favor of biblical doctrine and against homosexuality and that do not perform same-sex marriages— Christian churches such as the Baptist Church, the Church of Jesus Christ of Latter-day Saints, and the Catholic Church—will lose their tax-exempt status if their clergy choose not to marry homosexuals in their churches. This is pure tyranny from an anti-God socialist. Now that he is in office as president, Joe Biden plans to do the same thing—impose another tyrannical policy to reform Christian churches by applying economic pressure to change their belief in the Holy Bible.

Democratic vice president **Kamala Harris** wants to create and issue an executive order to confiscate semiautomatic assault weapons in the United States. How she plans to enforce this law is not clear. Joe Biden picked her as his vice president. Many predict Joe Biden will either resign or be removed as president on account of his failing faculties and senility. Kamala Harris will become president, and tyranny will accelerate.

Democratic senator **Cory Booker** wanted to create an anti–white supremacist federal agency that goes strictly after white people suspected of right-wing terrorism or white supremacy. Cory Booker also advocated investigating Democrat-defined "hate speech" crimes and monitoring hate speech on social media websites such as on Facebook and Twitter. The problem with socialists like Cory Booker, whose buddy is racist Louis Farrakhan, is that these Washington, DC, elites will silence, monitor, or arrest any individual for expressing hate speech as defined by Democrats. The definition will be used as a socialist tool to stifle or ban conservative free speech, thought, or opinion. Cory Booker's gestapo agency would be a war on conservative white people who would voice their opposition to a tyrannical-style government.

Democratic congressman **Eric Swalwell** of California, who promptly dropped out of the presidential race for 2020, said he would propose a gun buyback law using $15 billion in taxpayer money to buy back semiautomatic assault rifles from law-abiding Americans; if they refused to participate in the plan, he would have them jailed. This is tyranny.

All four of these socialist Democratic presidential candidates of 2020 wanted to severely restrict the freedoms afforded by the Second Amendment, or ban the amendment altogether, because they all predict an armed revolution against a socialist-style government whose goal would be, as in Venezuela, to disarm the citizenry so they no longer have the weapons to oppose big government. The major goal of socialists who seek to disarm the citizenry is to prevent a full-scale revolution when they assume dictatorial power and control and pass more tyrannical laws oppressive to the citizenry, which include the following:

1. Confiscating wealth
2. Seizing the personal property of those who evade taxes or are in tax arrears
3. Seizing bank accounts and/or retirement funds, investments, and annuities
4. Usurping social security and VA benefits to divert these funds into a single-payer health care system for all (no one will be allowed to keep their present private insurance)
5. Nationalizing businesses and their properties
6. Controlling the means of production and distribution of goods
7. Stifling free speech and opposition protests
8. Stifling religious rights and declaring economic war on churches if they don't marry homosexuals
9. Weaponizing federal agencies to spy on conservative citizens by invading the privacy of individuals, using personnel and surveillance equipment and by monitoring social media and the internet for hate speech, antisocialist dissent, and suspected right-wing militia speech and activity, as China is currently doing to its citizens using Google's artificial intelligence software
10. Putting down rebellions by groups of freedom-loving Americans composed of conservatives, veterans, former conservative law enforcement personnel, and people from Christian and Jewish groups
11. Partnering with radical Muslims to hire more Muslims to law enforcement agencies by increasing Muslim immigration

Alexandria Ocasio-Cortez, Kamala Harris, Bernie Sanders, and Elizabeth Warren are at the extreme left of the Democratic Party and are hard socialists. None have a clue about the repercussions of their free stuff for all or even if such a thing could be done at all. Ocasio-Cortez, a utopian socialist, is completely clueless and uneducated about the US economy. Bernie Sanders, Elizabeth Warren, and Kamala Harris also fail to understand the repercussions of tax oppression, that the wealthy will escape paying taxes, or how their massive spending plans will destroy the US economy. *None* of these four socialists realize that tax-oppressing hardworking people with government mandates can only be enforced by a tyrannical government, which enforcement would result in a major revolution and civil war in the United States. This is exactly why Kamala Harris and other socialists adamantly want to ban weapons, abolish the right to bear arms (Second Amendment), and remove an American citizen's right not to submit to an illegal search and seizure (Fourth Amendment). The result of taxation oppression, confiscation of wealth, and destruction of US constitutional freedoms would very likely be a major civil war in the United States. That civil war would be a fight between traditional conservative Americans and the socialist tyrannical elites, along with the foreigners and freeloaders who support the socialists.

This is who the Democratic Party is in 2021, and who they will be, a party with socialists who have infiltrated it, along with liberal Democrats, to make it a party of hate, lies, deceit, corruption, scandals, socialism, incompetence, self-enrichment, and greed.

Taxpayers will be robbed and not represented. If socialists enact Medicare for All, then people who are not working, including illegal aliens, would be provided with free health care. One socialist, Democratic representative Ilhan Omar of Minnesota, introduced legislation in the House that would socialize US housing and give COVID-19 benefits to illegal aliens. She was joined in agreement by her fellow Democratic "squad" members Rep. Alexandria Ocasio-Cortez of New York, Rep. Rashida Tlaib of Michigan, and Rep. Ayanna Pressley of Massachusetts.

Democrats expect amnesty migrants to vote them into office so they can change the Constitution and change election laws to forever hold power. This includes appointing socialist and communist judges to the Supreme Court and the lower courts; hiring illegal aliens, not US citizens, as police officers to enforce their tyrannical laws; inducting amnesty migrants into the military, preferring them to natural-born US citizens; and eliminating the Electoral College. Look at how Democrats have mismanaged Detroit, Baltimore, Chicago, Los Angeles, San Francisco, Seattle, and New York City; they have helped create many poop cities full of homeless people that they cannot fix. Look at how Democrats fear a revolution in the near future from people with guns; that's why they want to severely restrict gun sales or ban guns altogether.

The Democratic Party of Today Has Become a Party of Agents of Cultural and Institutional Change

The Democratic Party has become a party of institutional and social change; even Democratic supporters or Trump haters do not brag about this on social media. Those who support Democrats only spew vile hate and negative propaganda about Donald Trump and his family on the news and social media. Public schools are targets of institutional change as youths and millennials are indoctrinated by liberal teachers. The Democratic propaganda machine known as the fake news media has already been molded by rich donors to be agents of social change to destroy conservatism and glorify socialist reforms. They also omit corruption and failures of the socialist government to win the war against conservatives who want to maintain traditions and our freedom. On Facebook, AOL, and other social media, not one of these Democrats brags about Democratic policies that have benefited or will benefit Americans. These poor, misinformed Trump haters only express their hate and poke fun at the former president and his family, never mentioning his successes or accomplishments. Democratic politicians who ran for president are a bunch of socialists and Trump haters who are incompetent and full of malfeasance, ill will, and buffoonery. The socialist Democratic Party is the party of tax oppression, extremely high spending, illegal aliens, open borders, government handouts for all, and lawlessness. The Democratic Party is antipolice, antiwhite, anti-Semite, antimilitary, and anti-Constitution.

Since Democratic candidates can't win the hearts and minds of Americans, they have to resort to cheating, lying, and committing the crime of election rigging to win.

This is the socialist solution to acquire power and keep it—five ways to remove a Republican president and shoo-in the Democratic opponent:

1. Rig an election for the Democratic candidate by weaponizing the agencies as former president Barack Obama did in concert with the Democratic president running for office (Hillary Clinton), using manufactured foreign documents to defame, slander, and shame the Republican candidate and expose any wrongdoing on his part by spying on him and his staff. Ensure all investigations into and spying on the Republican candidate are leaked to the pro-Democrat news media to wage a propaganda war against the conservative candidate.

2. If the Republican candidate gets reelected, continue with the Deep State and New World Order conglomerations so the federal government will continue to spy on the Republican president throughout his term, using fake documents as probable cause to get a "legal" warrant to spy on him. If evidence is found, the House will impeach the president. If no evidence of wrongdoing is found, then they will find other areas of possible wrongdoing to impeach the president.

3. If impeachment fails, seek out Deep State whistleblowers who may be witnesses or may have evidence and ask them to come forward and testify against the president of the United States for any impeachable crime that can be dug up. Manufacture evidence and collect whistleblowers to impeach Trump. Note that if Democrats have a majority in both houses of Congress, it is much more likely that a conservative president will be impeached and removed from office because of false charges and hearsay evidence.

4. If that fails, House Democrats may subpoena the president's tax returns from the last eight to ten years to dig up dirt on him to impeach him. Democrats will illegally leak the returns to the Democratic propaganda news machine so as possibly to expose him as a crook.

5. Rig the elections by coordinating the purchase and use of fraudulent election computers with software written to flip thousands of votes in many states from Republican to Democrat, by persons controlling and accessing computers so their Democratic candidates will win. For example, the Dominion election computer is well-known by some military top brass, Democratic politicians, the CIA, and the Deep State.

So, for example, with regard to item 5, corrupt Democrats from key corrupt Democrat-run cities, districts, counties, and states would all, in concert, use election computers purchased from Dominion Systems with fraudulent election software so some unknown election manipulators could suddenly flip votes from Trump to Biden at will. That's criminal. The 2020 election was the biggest election scandal in US history, sullied by a Democratic Party that has been corrupt for decades. More than one hundred investigators were investigating computer fraud, fraudulent ballot counting, stuffing ballots by mail, destroying ballots, harvesting mail-in ballots and filling them out for seniors, voting in multiple states, voting more than once, accepting late or incomplete ballots, and so on. Sidney Powell and Rudy Giuliani were heading the investigations.

Now that Democrats are in power, socialists plan to change the institution of the federal government by eliminating the Electoral College, eliminating the filibuster in the Senate, eliminating ICE, admitting Washington, DC and Puerto Rico as states, and packing the Supreme Court with socialist and communist justices. After establishing a "reformed" federal government designed with no checks and balances, the socialist big government will be ready to function as a socialist machine. The social engineering of the United States will begin step by step, methodically, by eliminating the political opposition. The social engineering of the United States has already been planned and promised by President Joe Biden.

Democratic socialists will continue to indoctrinate students in public schools, redefine sex and gender, reform local, state, and federal law enforcement, reject old Christian beliefs by claiming that their newly defined moral views conform with the Bible, target conservatives with new tax laws, reform labor practices, offer free tuition to students in colleges and universities, eliminate college student loan debt, reform the US military, increase spending on climate change, phase out fossil fuel energy, manipulate the food supply, and put heavy environmental restrictions on small businesses, large corporations, and manufacturing. The goal of social engineering is to shape government and US culture to support socialist values and ideals, and to garner votes and support from foreigners. This is the Democrats' vision to control all aspects of American life, including domestic wealth, the economy, the justice system, law enforcement, and liberty. Creating another "Deep State" is essential to destroying the opposition. Socialists plan to ban guns to prevent resistance to their tyrannical laws and to prevent a potential revolution by people they will label as white supremacists, who will be accused of hate speech, as defined strictly by socialists. Democrats will control all news media and hire only socialists who spread nothing but pro-socialist, antiracist, and anti-capitalist propaganda. Democratic politicians will control social media to clamp down on dissenters and conservatives opposed to socialism. All white people who oppose the socialist government will be called racists, instigators, and white supremacists, and their names will be on a target list. Examples:

Beto O'Rourke planned to define hate speech and ban all social media websites that he thought were hostile to socialism and tyranny. This would have meant socialists at the federal level would have controlled social media such as Twitter, Google, and Facebook and censor all conservative comments and remarks—a violation of the First Amendment of the US Constitution.

Muslims such as Ilhan Omar and Rashida Tlaib will partner with socialist liberal Democrats to fight rich white people in the United States and implement their own culture wars to remake the United States into a Muslim nation. Non-Muslim secular Democrats in power don't know they are being played for fools, especially homosexuals. By allowing more Muslims into the United States from all over Africa, Asia, and the Middle East, the United States will become overpopulated with Muslims, as is happening in Europe, where Muslim immigrants are changing European culture. China, which is currently holding millions of Chinese Muslims in concentration camps, will ship, get rid of, and release these Muslims into the United States as a form of culture warfare to destroy the US economy and drastically change the culture. This will bring about enormous culture wars and bloody conflicts. Muslims will deal with the LGBTQ crowd very harshly.

Now that Joe Biden has been elected president and Democrats have the majority in the House, with Kamala Harris having the tiebreaking vote in the Senate, which is currently 50 percent Democrat and 50 percent Republican, how do socialists plan to seize the wealth from all wealthy Americans, small businesses, and corporations to pay for free government handouts? Socialists think Americans want income equality and think they will save the planet from destructive climate change. Socialist spending plans include spending for the following:

- Free health care.
- Free college tuition.
- About $1.5 trillion in college loan debt relief.
- Trillions or quadrillions of dollars in reparations for blacks.
- Welfare, food stamps, and unemployment insurance for all.
- The hiring of law enforcement officers who will obey orders to confiscate guns.
- Inducting foreigners and illegal aliens into the military and paying them to prevent or stop white supremacy and conservative rebellions.
- Hiring people into an anti–white supremacist federal agency to go after white people using hate speech that liberals don't like.
- Implementing the Green New Deal to transition into green energy and thereby eliminate energy dependence on fossil fuels, and replacing all forms of gasoline- and diesel-powered transportation with vehicles that run on electric energy. Replacing nuclear energy; reducing or eliminating meat, milk, cheese, and butter from diets across the United States; and funding abortion all over the world to reduce the progress of climate change.

How will socialists pay for their spending? Answer: by tax-oppressing every small business, every large corporation, every homeowner, and every worker so as to collect money to pay for all the government handouts and spending items and to increase the amount of money in the slush funds Democrats want to use. In order to gather more tax revenue, Democrats will tax utilities, phone lines, personal property (including real estate), and business property; reimplement the death tax; increase taxes on gasoline when used; restrict or prevent gun purchases; confiscate guns from law-abiding Americans; and rescind the Trump tax reductions that made the economy grow.

What happens if corporations leave the United States and relocate to another country to avoid taxes? Socialist politicians will likely impose new taxes or nationalize any corporation that leaves the United States to make better profits or to avoid high taxes. Such an act by the socialist government is illegal and will cause much conflict. But Democrats will say it is a matter of national security. Corporations fleeing to avoid paying previously incurred taxes will have their assets seized.

Rich people will hide their money in offshore accounts; the US government will never know about it. Rich people will shelter their money from taxes in charity foundation gimmicks. Rich people will sell their mansions and purchase other mansions in Europe or South America. The rich may acquire a reverse mortgage to collect as much money as they can from their mansions, then flee the United States at some future time. Some Americans are smart enough to renounce their US citizenship to avoid paying taxes.

Many American homeowners will be unable to pay the high taxes and make ends meet. Many Americans may become in arrears on their taxes. Some Americans will refuse to pay taxes and may be arrested on account of their debt to the IRS. Homes may be repossessed and wages garnished for people in tax arrears, people who have evaded paying their taxes, or people who have refused to pay taxes. All of this will undoubtedly create much conflict and even a rebellion.

What happens if the socialist government cannot get enough tax money to pay for its spending plans? Answer: Socialists will significantly reduce or seize Social Security funds and perhaps eliminate Social Security altogether. Socialists may resort to reducing or eliminating VA benefits for veterans with service-connected disabilities. Socialists may even seize a percentage of private bank accounts, pension retirement funds, 401(k)'s, investment funds, gold and silver coins and bullion, or insurance annuities. If banks fail, bank customers may not be able to withdraw all or part of their money. Banks have contracts with customers to disallow withdrawals from customers to cover their losses. Unless the customers' money is insured by the FDIC, it may be lost forever.

What happens if the socialist government runs out of the people's tax money? Answer: They will have to cut back on spending and print more dollars. But printing more dollars will devalue the dollar, and then the dollar may no longer be the standard world currency according to the World Bank. It will cause inflation, requiring people to pay ever-higher prices for goods and services. What is the result of socialism on the economy of the United States? Answer:

1. businesses leaving the United States
2. a collapsed economy
3. massive unemployment
4. massive poverty
5. massive homelessness
6. cities stricken with trash, feces, urine, rats, fleas, and makeshift homeless shelters
7. outbreaks of the bubonic plague, COVID-19, typhus, leprosy, dysentery, pneumonia, tuberculosis, and other communicable diseases in cities across the nation
8. high increases in crime, such as burglaries, homicides, rapes, assaults, home invasions, robberies, and car-jackings; mob violence; rioting; and looting and shoplifting—along with the inability of law enforcement to enforce laws
9. a massive number of patients to care for or treat in hospitals
10. people leaving the United States for other countries
11. massive chaos, hoarding, and corruption
12. massive soup kitchen lines for the homeless and the unemployed
13. in the end, a civil war.

In the end, socialists will run out of taxpayer money and begin confiscating a percentage of private wealth—assets from social security, private bank accounts, pensions, investment accounts, and 401(k)'s—and will force the IRS to seize the property of those who are in arrears on taxes. If that doesn't work, socialists will print more dollars, thereby devaluing the dollar and causing inflation to rise.

Cities in the United States run by Democrats currently have a homelessness crisis. Cities such as Los Angeles, New York, Seattle, San Francisco, and Sacramento are experiencing massive homelessness issues, and they are all run by incompetent Democratic city administrators who are blaming the rich in their respective states for the problem, not themselves, even though they were elected to solve these problems.

California is a good example. Its major cities have major nests of homeless people living in alleys, under bridges, in parks, on beaches, and around downtown businesses. The homeless leave trash, feces, and urine all over where they reside, which breeds rats and fleas, which can cause a variety of diseases, including bubonic plague. California's multimillionaires and multibillionaires live in luxurious mansions along the coast, from San Diego to Northern California; they ignore the homeless while living inside their high-gated communities. The middle class are leaving California in a massive "Cal-exit" because of taxation oppression caused by the state government and Governor Gavin Newsom. The combination of federal, state, and local taxes is overwhelming to the middle class—the taxes are unaffordable. The high cost of living, including high property taxes, utility taxes, income taxes, gasoline taxes, capital gains taxes, the cost of rent, the cost of medical care for US citizens, and the cost of education, is killing the middle class, while the rich are living comfortably in their coastal mansions.

A large portion of California taxpayer money is going to pay for free health care for all illegal aliens, which many California taxpayers oppose. As the middle class "Cal-exits," California will be a state of the very rich and the very poor, just like Mexico, except that in Mexico, citizens are not allowed to possess guns, which is also the case for Venezuelans in Venezuela. But California is gearing up to repeal the Second Amendment if socialists get into power in Washington, DC. The ultimate goal for socialists is to gain power by turning the United States into a Venezuela through tyranny.

What do you think freedom-loving patriotic Americans will do about all this? Answer: fight like hell.

Democrats Will Pass Laws to Attain Perpetual Power

If the Convention of States (Article V of the Constitution) were to be abolished, then liberals/socialists could also abolish the constitutional right for states for two-thirds of them to meet to propose laws and approve amendments to the Constitution. Article V would be the last chance to save our republic from a forever one-party tyranny. At least two-thirds of all states (34) would be required to meet. A Convention of States could vote to enact term limits for members of Congress, and amend or propose other amendments. At least a three-quarters majority of states (i.e., thirty-eight states) is needed to ratify the proposed amendments. However, amendments would be restricted to do the following:

1. Limit the size, scope, and jurisdiction of the federal government.
2. Impose fiscal restraints on the federal government.
3. Create term limits for government officials.

Unfortunately, as of 2020, the United States was deeply divided, so it appears there will not be thirty-four states to have a Convention of States, much less thirty-eight states to ratify any amendments to change items 1–3, above.

By eliminating the Electoral College, people from the most populous states, where Democrats live, would vote to win all presidential elections using only the popular vote or majority vote; that's governing by mob rule. Mob rule will always win to reinforce the Democrats' power for all time. In addition, other corrupt methods will be used, such as packing the United States with immigrants and granting them amnesty for votes, and by rigging elections, no matter what the vote counts are, to win them.

To win future elections, Democrats would reinforce their power by passing immigration reform laws to allow open borders and allow a huge population of foreigners into the United States each year. After millions of illegal migrants are given amnesty, Democrats will destroy the chances of Republicans, or any other political party, from ever winning the presidency. Democrats would initially attract multiple caravans of immigrants to the United States by offering them free government handouts in order to significantly increase their population. The wealthy 1 percent to 5 percent would be taxed to pay for this Democrat-benefiting corruption. The main benefit would be that leftist US citizens, along with amnesty immigrants, would vote for Democrats so they win all future elections. Democrats would most likely win the majority in both houses of Congress. By easily packing the Supreme Court, Democrats would win all Supreme Court cases related to all bills passed and all court appeals. This would essentially destroy all future checks and balances in our government, which the founders of the Constitution intended to prevent a tyrannical government from taking over. Packing the United States with illegal immigrants and granting them amnesty would have ugly consequences for the economy, our culture, our moral values, and most importantly our freedoms. Tens of millions of amnesty migrants would be eligible for welfare, food stamps, free health care, and in some states, tuition. They would become part of the socialist mob who would vote Democrat. Socialists would remake the United States to be much different from what it is now with their social engineering laws and policies.

Socialist politicians would remake morality in the United States by redefining traditional Christianity and replacing it with their own brand of progressive Christianity, which would be heresy, in conflict with biblical scripture. But socialists would claim that the morality of progressive Christianity supports socialist political philosophy, socialist policies, human rights, and human dignity. In short, leftists would claim progressive Christianity coincides with traditional Christianity. The fact is, progressive Christianity is politicized morality that coincides with socialist ideology; it is fake Christianity, a reinterpretation of traditional Christianity designed to stifle or replace traditional Christianity and used to justify socialist policies and court practices. Under progressive Christianity, abortion and homosexuality would be moral human rights that socialists would promote and protect as civil rights.

It is my thought that the "Deep State" is guilty of the highest miscarriage of justice ever by trying to rig an election with Democrats weaponizing all agencies of the federal government and colluding with Russia to create a fake dossier leaked to the media to destroy Donald Trump and use it as an excuse to spy on him without probable cause. The Russian dossier Hillary Clinton paid for was not probable cause, but Obama's weaponized agencies used it as such. If Democrats, now that they are in power, destroy the Electoral College, they will social-engineer the US justice system, that is, the DOJ, FBI, CIA, NSA, ATF, DHS, IRS, GSA, DoD, Supreme Court, and State Department. ICE may be dissolved. Only the elites in power will enrich themselves with the socialist policies and laws they pass. They will again weaponize all agencies of the federal government for control, including the IRS and the Federal Reserve.

In addition, socialists may create new federal agencies, such as the one Cory Booker wants, that will enforce all their laws, particularly social engineered laws and culture, which will be controversial. An anti–white supremacy federal agency, such as the one Cory Booker's proposed, would have been designed to micromanage and politicize all police departments in the United States. In a future socialist government, it is likely that such a federal police agency will focus on targeting white people, to track, arrest, and prosecute any involved with hate speech who are suspected of being white supremacists. The expanded role of this police force would include micromanaging all local police departments in the United States to enforce all socialist laws that take away our freedoms. Unconstitutional laws passed would be considered as tyrannical laws, opposed by freedom-loving Americans, and will result in dissent, protests, and secession, and foment a revolution.

How Else Can Democrats Win, other than by Corruption and Fraud?

As stated before, the Democrats conspired to commit the biggest election fraud in US history in order to steal the 2020 election, but they failed. President Trump should have easily won the 2020 election because of the following:

- American citizens overwhelmingly voted for Donald Trump as president, defeating Joe Biden.
- President Trump made promises that he kept, gaining immense support.
- President Trump was successful in creating jobs and strengthening our economy and military.
- President Trump had tens of thousands of supporters present at each of his rallies, compared to a few supporters at Biden's sparse number of rallies.
- Democratic House members feared that if Trump could not be impeached and removed from office, he would be reelected.
- President Trump was nominated for at least three Nobel Prizes for negotiating peace in the Middle East.
- Thousands of Democratic voters are suspected of voting illegally.
- Democrats at the state, federal, and local levels criminally conspired with corrupt election officials, ballot counters, and computer experts who manipulated election voting data to commit election fraud.

Democrats Attempted to Rig Another Presidential Election in 2020

In the 2020 election, Democrats could not rely on having enough Democratic voters since they did not have millions of additional illegal immigrants in the country and could not give them amnesty for votes, thanks to Trump's wall. Therefore, Democrats resorted to rigging the presidential election again; Democrats are still as corrupt and evil as ever. Dominion computer experts partnering with the Deep State, state politicians, election officials, ballot counters, and China used computer software that could easily be hacked and then abused by corrupt key state election officials to manipulate recorded votes and flip them from Trump to Biden. This means Democrats ignored the will of US citizens and showcased themselves as corrupt election frauds. Evidence mounted that Democrats attempted to steal the election. The election is not over, no matter what the corrupt states say or what the corrupt propaganda news media says. At least seventy-four million US voters no longer trust the election results of 2020. Senator Ted Cruz challenged the electoral vote count and demanded a vote audit. Given that Joe Biden won the election, by the next presidential election, Democrats will no longer need to rig or steal elections. Democrats will rely on giving amnesty to tens of millions of illegal aliens for votes, rely on changing election rules, and rely on receiving secret campaign funds indirectly from nefarious Democratic organizations, who will likely receive laundered money from China, Iran, high-tech companies, and US Democratic billionaires, for the reelection of Biden.

The Biden administration will favor open borders to draw caravans of illegal aliens into the United States and give them amnesty to vote. This process is a form of foreign interference in our elections.

Democrats Plan to Pack the US Supreme Court

On August 2019, House Democrats threatened the Supreme Court of the United States (SCOTUS): "Shape up … or we'll fundamentally restructure you."

The following is from a Fox News article by Ronn Blitzer:

"Several high-profile Senate Democrats listed in the above website warned the Supreme Court in pointed terms this week that it could face a fundamental restructuring if justices do not take steps to 'heal' the court in the near future. … Democratic candidates, including former representative Beto O'Rourke of Texas, and Sens. Cory Booker of New Jersey, Elizabeth Warren of Massachusetts, Kamala Harris of California, and Gillibrand, all have signaled an openness to expanding the number of judges on the court should they reach the White House."[4]

---

[4] Ronn Blitzer, "Senate Dems Deliver Stunning Warning to Supreme Court: 'Heal' or Face Restructuring," Fox News, August 13, 2019, https://www.foxnews.com/politics/senate-dems-deliver-stunning-warning-to-supreme-court-heal-or-face-restructuring.

This means that Democrats, particularly the socialists in the party, have threatened to increase the size of the Supreme Court from nine to fifteen justices, that is, to pack the Supreme Court to some number greater than nine. Doing so would allow a president in office who appointed the justices to approve practically any legislation with an easy victory for the president and Congress, thus eliminating the systems of checks and balances. This is a bad idea because it politicizes the Supreme Court and polarizes its approval of legislation so it is favorable to only one party. Since President Trump appointed three justices to the Supreme Court, Democrats have been extremely displeased with the constitutional conservative decisions made in the Supreme Court, so they want to bias the SCOTUS by adding more liberal, socialist, and/or communist justices.

A packed, one-party-polarized Supreme Court may reject any calls for investigations into crimes committed by Democrats and corruption schemes embarked upon by Democrats, approve or let stand all tyrannical laws proposed by a Democrat-controlled Congress, reject all appeals or lawsuits submitted by Republicans, or approve changes to, or the elimination of, any amendment to the Constitution.

How Much Will a Socialist Spending Plan Cost?

Democratic candidates never gave a detailed estimated cost of for all the items they proposed to implement with their policies in the Democratic debates. Joe Biden promised that immigration reform would occur within his first hundred days in office. He never told Americans how much tens of millions of immigrants will cost taxpayers when all are given amnesty. Biden did say his administration would tax all Americans with an income of $400,000 or more per year. How much will Joe Biden tax-oppress these taxpayers so he can pay for all the government entitlements to illegal aliens? Neither any of the socialist candidates nor Joe Biden has done the following:

1. shown the math that estimates the total cost of caring for indigent immigrants after they enter the United States;

2. stated the percentage of taxes on an income of $400,000 or more;

3. stated how taxpayers with incomes of $400,000 or more paying these taxes will be represented;

4. stated what the response of taxpayers with incomes of $400,000 or more will be to the prospect of paying these taxes;

5. indicated what will happen to taxpayers if Democratic politicians don't collect enough taxes;

6. spoken word about what Democrats will do to oppose a revolt of taxpayers who would refuse to pay for any of it;

7. said a word about what will happen to our economy if the Democratic Party oppresses businesses and taxpayers with high taxes;

8. said whether Democrats would go after taxpayer bank accounts, take away their social security, seize their pensions or annuities, or confiscate their homes for nonpayment of taxes.

Further questions the leftist Biden administration needs to answer are as follows:

*   What is the total sum of the Biden–Harris administration spending plan, including everything?
*   Will Democratic spending plans bankrupt the United States? If not, what is your plan to prevent this from happening?
*   What do taxpayers think about being forcefully ripped off so Democratic socialists can spend their tax money on immigrants?
*   How will you change the high taxes you impose on Americans if the top 10 percent to 50 percent of all rich Americans shelter their money from taxes or move their millions and billions overseas?
*   Do you fear that a civil war could come because of Democratic taxation oppression, which will anger taxpayers?
*   How will Democrats enforce the taxing of citizens and businesses if there is massive opposition and avoidance? What if nobody were to pay taxes as a form of protest?

- How will taxpayers who pay high taxes be represented and benefited, and still meet expensive socialist spending plans with their taxes? What will the middle class get out of it?
- How exactly will Democrats restrict the sale of, confiscate, or ban guns or assault rifles?
- What will Democrats do if rebellions occur because of their oppressive tyranny?
- How many millions of illegal aliens will Democrats allow under the open border policy from all over the world, running to the United States to claim their free government handouts from a Democrat-controlled government?
- What will the Biden administration do about unvetted immigration, which will likely increase crime and terrorism in the United States? And what will Biden himself do about it?
- What will Democrats do if the economy collapses? For example, will they seize bank accounts, investment accounts, our social security funds, organized labor pensions, or local and state pension funds, or seize/repossess personal property for resale?
- Will Joe Biden allow the FBI or DOJ to investigate him and his son Hunter for corruption in China and Ukraine?
- Will the House plan to appoint its own investigative committee to impeach Joe Biden for his and his son's criminal corruption in their alleged dealings with Ukraine and China?
- Will Democrats drop all of Special Counsel John Durham's investigation results of Barack Obama, Hillary Clinton, James Comey, John Brennan, and the many other Democratic criminals involved in spying on Donald Trump? Will they ignore the John Durham report?
- Will the Biden administration allow China to have the old preferred trading advantages it had before Trump became president?
- A Biden and Nancy Pelosi question: Does a baby in a mother's womb have a soul? If so, then why kill it? If the answer is no, then does the baby have a soul when it is born? If yes, then why kill it after it is born? (If the answer is no, then neither Nancy Pelosi nor Joe Biden has a soul.)

- Does the support and promotion of civil unions, same-sex marriages, and abortions go against not only Catholic doctrine but also biblical scripture? (This question should be asked to Joe Biden, Nancy Pelosi, and John Kerry, and all three should be demanded to respond.)
- Will Joe Biden or Kamala Harris ever answer any of these questions instead of hiding from reporters?

None of these questions were asked of Democratic presidential candidates because they were all afraid of providing answers about their "Alice in Wonderland" utopia spending plans. Worse, none of them added up all their own projected *accumulated total* cost. Elizabeth Warren during the first debate chided the host for asking for the cost of anything, saying that it was a Republican talking point that should not be asked of any of the candidates.

Socialists are too squeamish to tell the American people they will take American taxpayers to the cleaners, taking them for all they've got, bleeding them dry like turnips, and expecting every wealthy taxpayer to gleefully comply with tax oppression, especially when a lot of their tax money will be going to illegal aliens under an open border policy. Estimating that one million to two million immigrants will be entering the United States under an open border Biden policy, the costs for Medicare for All or revived Obamacare for all, including illegal aliens; implementing the Green New Deal; rejoining the Paris climate accord; paying reparations to blacks; providing welfare and other government entitlements for all amnesty immigrants; providing government assistance for disabled, indigent, and unskilled illegal aliens, along with free college tuition for illegal aliens in some states such as New York; paying the costs to run the country each year; funding the military; paying for government housing for illegal aliens; and providing the funding to address the growing homelessness crises in major cities across the United States were not totaled or stated.

Spending predictions aforementioned are already coming true. On top of Biden's $1.9 trillion COVID Bill and printing more US dollars, Joe Biden's next spending initiative could cost as much as $4 trillion and would include a tax increase in both the corporate tax rate and the individual rate for high-income earners. According to Fox News, planned tax hikes would include: raising the corporate tax rate to 28% from 21%, raising the income tax rate on individuals earning more than $400,000, expanding the estate tax, creating a higher capital-gains tax rate for individuals earning at least $1 million annually.

Source: An article in Fox News by Megan Henney entitled, *"Biden reportedly planning first major tax hike since 1993 in next economic package"*, dated 03/15/21 at: https://www.foxbusiness.com/economy/biden-reportedly-planning-first-major-tax-hike-in-next-economic-package.

Biden's tax plan would replace Trump's tax plan that had reduced many Americans' tax burdens with one that would raise everyone's taxes while slowing the economy. Five independent agencies determined that his tax policy would raise taxes across all income levels, bring back the Obamacare individual mandate tax penalty, repeal Trump's tax cuts, and impose a carbon tax. Thus, a Biden presidency would oversee tax increases for just about every working American.

Source: An article in The Federalist by Paulina Enck, dated 08/25/2020 at website: https://thefederalist.com/2020/08/25/bidens-plan-will-raise-taxes-on-americans-who-earn-less-than-400000-a-year/

Income Inequality in a Socialist United States

Socialist elites in power will enrich themselves with the immense amount of taxes they will collect from taxpayers to increase their already high salaries and to further fatten their pensions, accumulating wealth that no common peon in the United States will ever have in a lifetime. But these are the same rich elitist politicians who complain about and pay lip service to the income inequalities between victimized blacks and the white rich capitalists who oppress them. Ironically, wealthy socialist elites never mention income inequalities between blacks in the ghetto and socialist elites living in multimillion-dollar mansions, eating fancy ice cream from their refrigerators. Socialists Joe Biden, Nancy Pelosi, John Kerry, Barack Obama, Elizabeth Warren, and Bernie Sanders are all multimillionaires with fat pensions who own multiple mansions. These rich leftist elitists have made their fortunes from working in a capitalist United States. They buy and sell property, and they tax-shelter their money using charity foundations to avoid their own oppressive taxes.

The form of socialism in the United States would be one-party rule without checks and balances, consisting of three branches of government in control of a capitalist system of government that redistributes economic wealth from the richest individuals, the middle class, and from business profits to an enriched ruling class, low wage earners, and a class of migrants exploited for cheap labor. The goal of socialist politicians in the United States is to reduce the concentration of wealth from oppressive capitalists and redistribute it to make the ruling class wealthy and simultaneously give workers the ability to negotiate higher wages for workers. However, capitalists exploit immigrants by hiring them for cheap labor at the expense of the working class. A small number of unions have formed in businesses the working class work for, to negotiate better wages and to prevent businesses from hiring immigrants for cheap wages. The purpose of unions is to get a fair share of profits the businesses make from the hard work of their workforce.

In the United States, businesses slow down when they must pay higher taxes to federal, state, and local governments, and when they must pay to meet the costly regulations imposed on them by the federal government. Businesses will therefore spend less on capital for their operations and be less able to expand. As long as cheap labor is available, businesses can reduce labor costs and may survive, but not expand. The exceptions are multimillion-dollar high-tech businesses like Microsoft, Google, Facebook, and Amazon, which make immense profits and have plenty of capital to expand their businesses. These business giants can even create new businesses or purchase competitor businesses to earn even more profit. By hiring high-tech employees for cheaper wages on a contract basis from, say, India, who are skilled software developers, US high-tech companies will make higher profits by not having to pay these foreign contractors lifetime pensions, retirement, or insurance once the work contract expires. However, relatively low skilled and uneducated immigrants are always kept at the lowest wages.

Reducing corporate taxes and reducing income tax for workers stimulates and grows the economy. This is what President Donald Trump did in his first three years in office. Businesses expanded and hired more workers at higher wages. Job opportunities increased to new record levels, business profits increased, unemployment reached its lowest point ever recorded in US history, and the stock market rallied to new high levels because investors also profit when businesses grow and increase their profits. Workers take home more pay and can afford to buy more goods and services from businesses. Unemployment drops to record low levels. It's a win-win economy. This economy is the legacy of Ronald Reagan and Donald Trump. Former president Ronald Reagan also cut regulations and cut taxes, and believed government is best when it is small and lets wealth trickle down from businesses to the workers without government interference. Redistributing wealth by big government through high taxes and imposing costly regulations on businesses under the Obama administration caused little or no economic growth but, rather, caused businesses to relocate outside the United States and caused high unemployment. The Biden administration wants to do the same, which will likely tank the economy over time and reduce employment.

High taxes will slow the economy in places where businesses and industry dish out more taxes to the federal, state, and local governments. Having to comply with high-cost environmental regulations will slow the economy down.

Many US businesses prefer to hire illegal aliens over US citizens because illegals provide cheap labor. Ironically, in the socialist elites' "Alice in Wonderland" utopia, such elites denounce income inequality between US citizens and oppressive capitalists. Why is there income inequality between cheap labor immigrants and workers who are US citizens? What about the income inequalities between the socialist ruling class, their working-class citizens, and their cheap labor migrants? These are income inequalities that socialist elites should be asked to explain. It's income inequality in the making when cheap labor immigrants are preferred over higher-paid US citizens. Why should the Biden administration have open borders to allow businesses to replace millions of US citizens with immigrants, who would be paid significantly lower wages? Laid-off workers will then be forced to seek the types of jobs they held previously, or take lower-wage jobs, or go on government assistance. It appears the oppression of the American worker will be the result of immigrants replacing US workers in the workforce. The socialist ruling class believes it should earn much more than the oppressed American workers and cheap labor migrants. Income inequalities, which socialist elites always complain about, are merely transformed from one group to another. Income equality among the new socialist economic classes is never truly resolved or achieved in the "Alice in Wonderland" socialist utopia as claimed. Whether the form of government is right-wing fascism, dictator-run banana republic, Muslim theocracy, or communism, income equality has never been achieved historically.

It's a remake of the United States when illegal aliens are exploited for cheap labor to make businesses more profitable at the expense of workers who are US citizens. The very socialist elites who blame rich capitalists for oppressing the poor are the ones who open the floodgates at the southern border for cheap labor immigrants to enter so they may take US jobs and enrich the same capitalists the socialists demonize. Then the socialist ruling class in the United States tax-oppresses rich people and profitable businesses to move themselves into a higher income class. Who's the oppressor in a leftist United States?

Socialists should understand that income inequality can be a good sign of a healthy economy where people with different abilities and areas of expertise can work hard and be rewarded for their work.

Another part of the Democratic strategy is to increase taxes on goods and services. This will cause price increases and the cost of living to go up, thus forcing illegal aliens to move to other states. For example, illegal aliens working for minimum wage in California will not be able to afford higher taxes for gasoline, housing, or utilities; higher car registration fees; higher car insurance rates; higher fees to receive a driver's license; increased traffic fines; and so on. The rise in the cost of food will also cause illegal aliens to move to other states where taxes are not high and the cost of living is much lower. This means that a steady migration of illegal aliens from a blue state such as New York or California to a red state may at some point change the red state to a blue state. The Electoral College in red states into which illegals move may also change the political landscape of those states. It also could mean flipping a red state to a blue state because of immigrants moving to red states. Blue states will intentionally raise taxes to increase the cost of living in their states and drive out illegal aliens, forcing them to go to other, red states, which they will overpopulate and flip to blue states in order to increase the number of Senate and House votes for Democrats, who thereby will win elections.

Democratic politicians in states such as California are even letting illegal aliens run for elected state government positions and for positions in local city and county government. This strategy will allow Democrats to remain in control forever in California. Once Democrats attain forever power and control of states and all three branches of federal government, they will then try to change or destroy the Constitution to fit with their socialist tyrannical-style government. That will complete their strategy.

But the Democratic strategy is flawed. It is a strategy that will be opposed by patriotic and powerful Americans. A second US revolution will very likely occur if all the aforementioned Democratic government handout policies are implemented, putting illegal aliens first, ahead of taxpaying US citizens. American citizens:

- will not accept taxation without representation;
- will not be bullied by tyrants into pay high taxes;
- will not give up their guns to tyrants or to police agencies consisting of foreigners acting like gestapos, or who enforce laws to destroy our rights and freedoms;
- will not give up guns to UN Peacekeeping troops called by a president's executive order to confiscate weapons from armed law-abiding citizens;
- will refuse to give this country away to illegal aliens;
- will refuse to pay for free stuff Democrats are handing to illegal immigrants or foreigners, even if such immigrants are given amnesty in exchange for votes, which goes against taxpayer interests;

- will take up arms against federal government tyrants and against blue states such as California if necessary;
- will take up arms against UN Peacekeeping troops made up of foreigners if they kill Americans on US soil.

To prevent a red state from flipping to blue, laws in red states should propose that if states such as New York and California funnel a massive number of illegal aliens into red states, the red states should sue California, New York, and other blue states for the costs of care and other expenses incurred by illegal aliens sent from those blue states. All Democratic lawmakers in California should be sued as well. California and New York bear costs when they allow or pay illegal immigrants to migrate into red states. Blue states should be responsible for caring for these illegals when their high cost of living causes the illegals to leave the state and move to red states. All illegal aliens coming from California or other blue states into red states should not be allowed to collect welfare and food stamps, unless California, New York, or the other blue state from which they came foots the bill. A wise plan in red states is to stop illegal aliens from crossing into California and deporting them when they do, or for the federal government to charge California a large tax for each migrant. Why should taxpayers from the rest of the country foot the bill for illegal aliens flooding out of California and New York? California caused the problem, so it should be held accountable for the massive migration coming out of California into other states, which cannot handle the migrants either.

What Do Democrats Offer the American People?

Today's Democrats offer big government control over the lives of the American people to build and reinforce their power. Democrats have little or nothing to offer to benefit Americans. Since Democrats cannot win the hearts and minds of Americans or transform the United States into a prosperous, great country, they have to resort to corruption schemes to rig or steal elections to attain power, for example, impeaching Donald Trump, packing the United States with illegal aliens, packing the Supreme Court of the United States, and eliminating the Electoral

College. Democrats draw hundreds of thousands of illegal aliens each year to the United States by offering them free government handouts, for example, free health care, free housing, and free college tuition. After they are given amnesty, illegal aliens become US citizens who can apply for welfare, unemployment insurance, free public school, and food stamps. From 2016 to 2020, the only accomplishment the obstructive and irresponsible Democrats were notorious for was trying to remove President Trump from office and drawing paychecks they did not deserve.

On June 3, 2019, Joe Bidden said at the annual Human Rights Campaign that passing the pro-LGBT and pro-abortion Equality Act would be the first thing he would try to get done if elected president.[5] Joe Biden claims to be a Catholic yet has been a shameless and unrepentant longtime supporter of abortion and homosexuality, going against Catholic doctrine and biblical morality.

[5] Martin M. Barillas, "Biden Names Pro-LGBT 'Equality Act' as Top Priority if Elected," Life Site News, June 23, 2019, https://www.lifesitenews.com/news/biden-names-pro-lgbt-equality-act-as-top-priority-if-elected.

20

SOCIALIST CANDIDATES ON REPARATIONS FOR BLACKS AND SAME-SEX COUPLES

Democratic socialists are offering free money for blacks to get their votes. Some black politicians have been campaigning on this reparations scam for decades, and all have failed. But these are race-baiters such as Al Sharpton, Jesse Jackson, John Conyers, and Cory Booker, along with other blacks, who have played the race card in every election year to use US history and slavery to anger and rile up blacks and turn them into victims today. It's all a scam for House Democrats to get votes from black districts they represent, offering their African American constituents the lure of free money, but at the same time neglecting the poverty, crime, gangs, abandoned homes, and run-down businesses and neighborhoods in their districts. The black reparations never came; it was all empty campaign rhetoric.

Has anyone read US history? About 330,000 white Union soldiers lost their lives fighting the Confederacy at the end of the Civil War so that blacks could be free. Reparations have already been paid by whites in blood. Where are reparations from the pockets of blacks today to pay the white descendants of Union soldiers who died in battle against the Confederacy to set their black ancestors free?

But out of desperation, and because of their low support, the most recent batch of Democratic presidential candidates had nothing useful to offer Americans to get elected other than government giveaways, which are mainly advertised for illegal aliens. Democrats are the party of the KKK. Socialists exploit US history to shame whites for bringing slaves into the United States from Africa. Beto O'Rourke and several other socialists call the United States racist and were asking for a "free money" black reparations solution for the present-day victimized black culture, falsely claiming blacks are victims today because of a three-hundred-year-old culture no one today had anything to do with. The reason that Democrats appear desperate to enact black reparations is simply to get the black vote. Unfortunately, socialists from the Democratic Party never say which racial groups in the United States should be exempt from paying trillions of dollars in reparations to blacks, such as the following:

1. Latinos
2. Asians
3. Native Americans
4. people of mixed races
5. Caucasian immigrants to the United States
6. Caucasians who claim their ancestors fought in the Union Army against the Confederacy
7. today's illegal immigrants
8. whites with low or moderate incomes
9. veterans
10. active military personnel
11. African immigrants whose ancestors came from countries known to have sold slaves to white Americans
12. people from religious groups
13. whites incarcerated in prison.

Another problem for Democratic socialists is that they have no clue what reparations will cost. Estimates proposed have ranged from trillions of dollars to $6.2 quadrillion. Any estimate proposed in Congress will be challenged because it will arouse anger in the majority of whites and nonblack and nonwhite races in the United States. Some Democratic politicians have submitted black reparations bills to Congress, but these never got approved in the Senate or by the president. If black reparations don't come as promised, race-baiting politicians will blame white supremacists for rejecting the bill.

Another problem with black reparations is that blacks may demand reparations for every future black generation in the United States. This is because blacks and their politicians will claim that reparations cannot be made with only one generation. Reparations for blacks of all future generations is a Pandora's box that will lead to many bad potential consequences, such as the bankruptcy of the United States, the decline of the US economy, civil war against any federal administration passing reparations, and an increase in white hatred and violence and discrimination against blacks. Whites will argue that none of them ever owned blacks as slaves, that they do not oppress blacks today, that today's blacks are not victims, and that nothing should be owed to blacks by the whites of today. A majority of whites will also argue that the blacks of today have a higher standard of living than the people in most Third World African countries where their ancestors came from (assuming their ancestors did not come from the West Indies). Most American blacks are wealthier than most African blacks. Blacks should be grateful to be Americans today; it is a blessing, not a curse.

Hypocrite Leftists Play the Race Card When They Have Nothing Beneficial to Offer

Hypocrite leftists play the race card when they have nothing beneficial to offer. Besides blaming Barack Obama for dividing the races during his administration, people should cast blame upon race agitator Al Sharpton, racist Louis Farrakhan, and race whiner Jesse Jackson for racial division, agitation, self-victimization, racial anger, and unrest. Playing the race card repeatedly by black politicians, activists, and white politicians, such as Hillary Clinton and all Democrats running for president in 2020, does nothing to provide blacks with jobs, opportunities for prosperity, or ways to put food on the table. These politicians exploit blacks for self-enrichment and power.

Self-victimized blacks want people to think they are victims because their ancestors were historically oppressed in the US, and therefore demand a lot of money from the Federal government. Liberals have worn out the race card. People do not feel pity for those insecure, phony victims. It's a money-making scam for victims and a vote-getting scam for leftist Democrat politicians when they can't win arguments and they have nothing else to lay on the table.

Hypocrite leftist politicians in California contradict themselves when talking about illegal aliens. Democratic California politicians such as Governor Newsom, Nancy Pelosi, Eric Swalwell, Dianne Feinstein, and Kamala Harris, and the fake news media, play a good con game of welcoming illegal aliens to their state, providing them free health care, and protecting any criminals among them from deportation, but then they hypocritically refuse to take any illegal aliens from ICE into their communities. How does that make any sense?

21

THE DEMOCRAT PARTY SOCIALISTS' MASSIVE SPENDING AND TAXATION OPPRESSION

The American Revolution was about taxation without representation and about tyranny. Who would refuse to pay taxes and fight the revenuers? Who refuses to bow to tyrants and give them money? Founders of this country fought against taxation without representation and for freedom. Today, freedom-loving Americans would rather fight to be free and die with dignity rather than lose their freedoms to tyrants.

What Democratic Presidential Candidates Never Revealed in Any of Their Debates

Of the twenty-five Democrats who ran for president in 2019, about 95 percent of them were socialists. Socialist Bill de Blasio said we need to tax the hell out of the wealthy; none of the other candidates opposed him. Socialist Democrats have nothing beneficial to offer Americans other than pain, misery, and taking other people's money to spend on their own whimsical schemes and give illegal aliens free government handouts, give blacks and homosexuals reparations, forgive college loan debts for irresponsible millennials, provide costly Medicare for All, pay for programs to slow climate change before we all die in eleven years, and pay for the Green New Deal scam. Did any Democratic candidate mention the following?

- how to pay for all their spending, who would pay for it, and what the total cost was estimated to be;
- whether the spending plans would bankrupt the United States or ruin the economy;
- what taxpayers thought about being forcefully ripped off so Democratic socialists could spend their money;
- the coming civil war, caused by Democratic taxation oppression, which has angered taxpayers;
- how Democrats would enforce taxation oppression;
- the idea that illegals under open borders would benefit from free stuff, and what taxpayers would get out of it;
- how Democrats would confiscate guns or ban them before rebellions could occur nationwide;
- how many millions of illegal aliens would be allowed into the United States from all over the world, running to claim their free stuff; or
- how the costs related to increased crime and homelessness would be paid.

Spending Proposed by Democratic Socialists

Democratic politicians are akin to thieves who collect our money with the laws they make by raising our taxes. Then they give our money as free handouts to illegal aliens, who mostly have no skills, are poverty-stricken, and cannot speak English. Taxpayers do not want to give free money to blacks or homosexuals for historical oppression; today's people did not oppress them and are not responsible for compensating any of them.

It is still unknown how many trillions per year the Biden administration plans to spend on the Green New Deal, on climate change, on reparations, on health care, on their own costly salaries and pensions, on donations to the Paris peace accord, on foreign aid, on UN contributions, on caring for the homeless, on COVID-19 health care, and on indoctrination of our youth in public schools. While Democrats enrich themselves with no accountability, socialists will only throw taxpayer money at Democrat-run city administrators who have been incompetent in solving the homeless problem in every major city in the United States. Democrat-run cities in the United States have neglected the filth, crime, and poverty in their cities.

Democratic Presidential Candidates Refuse to Total Their Spending

Democratic presidential candidates in presidential debates have dared to claim that other Democratic candidates were proposing spending that is unaffordable, such as the following:

- trillions of dollars on the New Green Deal
- trillions of dollars on government-provided health care
- trillions or quadrillions of dollars on reparations for blacks (is it a onetime deal or continued black reparations for every future black generation?)
- $1 trillion each year for government handouts to about one million illegal aliens who will cross the border each year (for how long?)
- trillions of dollars in taxes to redistribute the wealth Democrats want for income inequality
- trillions of dollars desperately needed for the climate change or global warming scams so the world won't end in eleven years
- $1.6 trillion for student loan forgiveness to lazy, irresponsible millennial freeloaders
- billions of dollars to Planned Parenthood and other abortion clinics for the purpose of funding the genocide of babies in and out of the womb and providing an illegal kickback of taxpayer money donated to liberal Democrats' campaigns, which is a money-laundering scam.

Why don't Schumer and Pelosi list the goals and explain how the Democrats will meet the goals set by Democrats every year? How much will they steal from hardworking taxpayers?

Democrats who dream of living in a utopia of zero discrimination and equal distribution of wealth, of a life free from tyranny and oppression, and of a perfect world are living in an "Alice in Wonderland" fantasy. Historically, that utopia has never been achieved. The world today is not ready for that kind of imagination because of the lust for power and greed, and the class struggles, that exist in the world today. Only pragmatic economic systems that are well-known to have worked in the past, though imperfect, are the systems that governments should use to create and implement policies that are successful as promised, beneficial, and tested. President Trump proved that such a government style was effective in our republic.

House Democrat from the Bronx Alexandria Ocasio-Cortez (AOC) wants open borders and free stuff for illegal aliens too, and extra money for reparations for blacks today because their ancestors in the United States were slaves. AOC has little or no knowledge of the real world. Her "Alice in Wonderland" Green New Deal project will cost $100 trillion, but she thinks the rich should be taxed to pay that sum. She doesn't cite what levels of taxation will be imposed on the rich and the middle class to provide all this free stuff in her fantasy utopia world. It's as if AOC thinks money grows trees. Then taxpayers can pick money from their tax trees to pay local and sales taxes, county taxes, city taxes, state taxes, and federal taxes, in addition to any monies for climate change programs, her Green New Deal, and surmounting costs to assist illegal immigrants from all over the world.

Alternatively, Ocasio-Cortez wants the federal government to guarantee jobs for everyone so they can all get decent wages, free health care, and a pension. How to pay for it? Employers, of course, will come up with the magic money, and the federal government will have to subsidize private industry to guarantee jobs by collecting taxes from the rich and middle-class Americans.

David A. Herrera

What Liberal Democratic Politicians Want
to Take Away from American Citizens

Democratic liberal politicians want to take away rights to remake the United States so that socialists will remain in power. They seek to do the following things:

- Take away your guns.
- Take away your wealth.
- Reform or remove your right to free speech and expression.
- Take away your religious rights.
- Reform your churches.
- Eliminate the Electoral College to reduce power to a handful of the most populated states.
- Neglect your safety (with threats coming from drugs, diseases, criminals, undesirable immigrants, and pedophiles).
- Take away your medical insurance that you want to keep.
- Invade your privacy by monitoring your posts on social media they consider to be hate speech.
- Diminish or make insignificant your voting power by allowing immigrants to make your votes insignificant or by rigging/stealing elections.

Higher and Higher Taxes

Democrats are always afraid to answer the question of who will pay for their "Alice in Wonderland" socialist utopia. Will it be only the very wealthy? or every homeowner in the United States? or every hardworking wage earner who makes good wages? or every small business owner? or every large corporation in the United States? Not one Democratic presidential candidate ever said how he or she would enforce taxes on the rich if they were to oppose Democratic socialist spending, other than Bernie Sanders, who said, "We can afford it." One needs to look at California for the answer.

Federal, state, and local taxes would come from the death taxes (revived again), personal property taxes, business taxes, corporate taxes, utility taxes, internet taxes, capital gains taxes, medical expense taxes, sales taxes, tourism taxes, gasoline taxes, real estate taxes, driver's license fees, car excise taxes, phone taxes, and any other kind of creative new ways they can come up with to grab other people's money. Joe Biden has said he would reverse the Trump tax reductions that created jobs and economic growth in the United States.

In August 2020, Biden proposed a $7 trillion tax plan over ten years based on the rationale of former president Barack Obama's legacy to "unite a fractured nation." The Biden administration plans to spend the money primarily on health care, housing, and climate change programs. Biden plans to spend the tax money to improve blighted and riot-torn cities run by Democrats; this means Democrats want to throw more money at cities mismanaged by corrupt, lazy, incompetent Democrats, expecting a different result. In reality, Democrats will likely continue to mismanage their cities and lose accounting of the billions of dollars in federal money. In January 2021, Biden wanted to spend $1.9 trillion to provide economic relief to businesses affected by COVID-19. The US national debt will rise to new heights.

Biden plans to pay for his spending items by imposing $4 trillion in new taxes on corporations, investments, and wealthy Americans. That will include reversing President Trump's massive $1.5 trillion Tax Cuts and Jobs Act, which reduced the corporate tax rate from 35 percent to 21 percent and temporarily reduced individual income taxes.[1]

The Fox Business website links to another article that lists Biden's point-by-point tax rate plans and changes: "Joe Biden's 2020 Tax Plan: The Key Points."[2] Joe Biden's income tax rate would revert to 39.6 percent from 37 percent for individuals making more than four hundred thousand dollars per year.

---

[1] Megan Henney, "Joe Biden's $7 Trillion Spending Proposal: What's in It?," Fox Business, August 18, 2020, https://www.foxbusiness.com/politics/joe-biden-proposes-7-trillion-in-spending.
[2] Brittaney De Lea, "Joe Biden's 2020 Tax Plan: The Key Points," Fox Business, November 7, 2020, https://www.foxbusiness.com/politics/joe-bidens-tax-plan.

How does it make sense for Joe Biden to charge businesses higher taxes and for Democrat-run states to mandate COVID-19 shutdowns on businesses to prevent them from making any income? How can businesses such as restaurants and bars afford to pay taxes? If businesses go bankrupt and never come back, taxes from these businesses will be permanently lost in many cities. What about the Biden administration reimposing costly environmental regulations on businesses while Democratic governors and mayors lock those same businesses down with COVID-19 rules? That adds costs to locked-down businesses that they cannot pay. Businesses will be negatively impacted, causing the biggest depression in the United States since 1929. The federal government's raising of already high taxes and imposing costly government regulations on businesses, while state officials lock down businesses or restrict them from doing business on account of COVID-19, is a nasty and incompetent process that will destroy businesses.

In the event elected Democratic socialists start running out of other people's money, they will try a variety of ways to get money to pay for their spending plan, possibly by doing the following:

- manufacturing/printing more paper dollars;
- borrowing money from Social Security to fund their costly spending plans;
- increasing taxes on Americans' personal bank and investment accounts, pension funds, insurance annuities, or social security received, and increasing income taxes;
- reverting to a favorable trade practice with China in order to buy cheaper products from China and import them, rather than buying the same products from US companies. This will make China prosperous.

In addition, states will increase taxes on property, personal income, vehicle registration and sales, and so on. City and county officials will increase taxes on utilities, phone service, and every conceivable service they provide local citizens.

Democrats have no clue what any of these policies will do to the United States if implemented. These are increases in taxes at every government level, eating away at the pocketbook of every American. In summary, Democratic economic policies will cause massive unemployment, force companies to relocate out of the United States, reduce the United States' tax base, and cause massive inflation. The very rich will hide their wealth out of the country in a second home, move out of the country, and/or renounce their citizenship before they are ever taxed. Social security checks will be reduced or eliminated, crime will increase, and cities will go bankrupt. City, county, and state pension checks paid out will be reduced or lost, or worse, a major collapse of the US economy could occur, with major cities in the United States looking like Los Angeles, San Francisco, New York City, or Baltimore.

Further repercussions will develop. Our military will be weakened; our enemies will be emboldened; our enemies will develop nuclear weapons and threaten us with them; our military weapons will be weak; and our borders will be open to terrorists, indigenous people from all over the world, criminals, and undesirables, and radical Muslims will be attracted to the United States. Democrats will have state control of the media and social websites and will distribute false propaganda 24-7.

Americans are not stupid; most are wise and love their freedom and prosperity. To patriotic Americans, God, family, and country come first. Before the worsening of economic conditions and before American might is weakened under socialist rule, Americans will revolt. Americans, seeing the dangers of tyranny on the horizon, will take action at some point to prevent further decay of the United States caused by Democratic socialist rule. Increasing armed rebellions will cause the federal socialist government to declare martial law, that is, if the military and police agencies across the United States fail to stop rebellions.

In the extreme event that socialists are persistent in retaining power as in Venezuela, a second US civil war will occur between patriotic freedom-loving people and federalist socialist tyrants who want to control the wealth and retain power. Tyrannical Democrats may do the following:

• Pay amnesty migrants or foreigners to join the military or police agencies to enforce tyrannical laws.

- Reduce the food supply going to seceded states and to pockets of rebellion in the United States.
- Launch a massive campaign of confiscating registered weapons.
- Fail to contain the COVID-19 epidemic, which may worsen.
- Request assistance from UN Peacekeeping troops to put down rebellions using Chinese or Muslim soldiers.
- Perhaps create assassination squads to go after leaders of militias and revolutionaries.

Registering guns, imposing taxes on existing guns, and taxing guns purchased at the federal level, as Joe Biden proposes, is the first sign of preparation for future tyranny, followed by a step-by-step confiscation of guns or banning them.

Mathematical Analysis of Greenland Data Shows No Problems Caused by Climate Change

Very little data on global warming is found on the internet. The only data I found was temperature data collected over several centuries in Greenland. Scientists estimated temperatures for thousands of years of earth history from layers of rocks and soil composition indicating hot temperatures. I did a regression analysis (curve-fitted) on the temperature data presented and got the best polynomial fit equation (temperature vs. time in years). It appears there were outliers in the earth's history when temperatures spiked, but this was probably caused by volcanic activity, because centuries after such an occurrence, the temperatures went back to their previous low levels for thousands of years. There was no indication from the curve plotted against the data showing a constant upward trend in the data. In other words, this was no proof of global warning. Predictions using the polynomial fit to the data did not indicate a rising earth temperature, but rather, a stable level temperature. Granted, if there is volcanic activity, the temperatures may be higher for many years. If a large meteor hits the earth, there may be heat initially, but a cloud covering the earth would cool temperatures as the clouds blocked out more of the sun.

Joe Biden promised to rejoin the Paris climate accord and submit to UN requests for US taxpayers to pay for problems related to global warming. The fact is, if only the United States and a few European countries eliminate their pollution, the remaining pollution in the world will still be high, so there will be little reduction in global warming and carbon emissions, as China, India, and parts of Africa are major polluters. So-called liberal experts cannot explain why the earth is hit with major blizzards like never before when they argue the earth is getting warmer.

No one can explain why liberal billionaires live in mansions all along the coast of California, from San Diego to Northern California, but are not afraid of rising oceans, a result of global warming. Socialist politicians don't care if scientists are right or wrong on global warming, as long as they can usurp the wealth from rich people, put that money in a climate change slush fund, and spend it on anything they want. Democrats make up "global warming" excuses to collect, spend, and redistribute money for control and political purposes. Global warming and climate change are used as excuses for socialists to confiscate money and redistribute it to their cronies for the purpose of obtaining and maintaining political power.

22

THE CORRUPTION OF THE DEMOCRAT PARTY

The Corrupt and Immoral Nature of Liberal Democrats

Liberal/progressive Democrats, including Democratic politicians, have the following traits in common:

1. They are corrupt and are serial liars.
2. They are dishonest elites who rig or steal presidential elections in a concerted effort. This includes Democratic state politicians, ballot counters, election officials, users of corrupt election computers to flip votes, and corrupt billionaires and foreign countries who have links to the computers used for election fraud. China is suspected of manufacturing thousands of election ballots and sending them to US cities to be completed in the United States for election fraud.

The fake news media and leftist teachers in public schools indoctrinate young students to become socialist activists and to hate the United States. Low-educated Americans are influenced by the propaganda and twisted lies of the fake news media. The Democratic news media is an arm of the Democratic Party.

318

Most lazy Democratic freeloaders think they deserve free government handouts paid for by taxpayers.

Socialist leaders will enrich themselves and their cronies from the redistribution of wealth. Democrats have proposed to raise taxes on businesses while, at the same time, preventing them from producing income with tyrannical COVID-19 restrictions. Democrats also impose costly environmental regulations, which only adds to the cost of doing business.

Racist hypocrite elites play the race card, paying lip service to minorities for purposes of political expedience. Elites will say or promise anything for votes and to keep power, even if it's detrimental to Americans. Democrats will support the censorship of the media and social websites because corrupt Democrats received a lot of money from high-tech corporations for their campaigns and for their legislative votes. In addition, Joe Biden has appointed some leftist executives from high-tech corporations to serve as White House staffers.

Democrats plan to give amnesty to millions of illegal aliens to vote Democrat. They also plan to change election laws so that they may win all future elections.

Democratic politicians and judges apply two standards of justice, one for themselves, and another for peons and conservatives. Many Democrats think the Constitution is antiquated and racist, and want it revised or replaced.

Muslim Congress members hate US culture and want to make the United States a Muslim nation.

Democrats stifle Christianity, the Bible, free speech, and the conservative news media. They are antipolice and want to defund police in Democrat-run cities. The Biden administration wants to social engineer US culture and institutions as part of "Hope and Change Part II." Democratic politicians want to legalize pedophilia and controlled substances, charge high fees for gun registration for law-abiding citizens, and **to** expand same-sex marriage ceremonies in all religious temples. Elites want to eliminate or heavily restrict the Second Amendment to confiscate and ban semiautomatic rifles and large-capacity magazines, and impose higher taxes on gun ownership and purchase of guns and rifles.

Socialists want to ban ICE, thereby allowing open borders for potential criminals, terrorists, and heavy narcotic trafficking. Democrats want to ICE to babysit, shelter, and care for thousands of illegal alien children amassed in border states.

Democrats weaponize their computers to illegally monitor conservative news broadcasters, private citizens, and politicians so they may influence elections, steal elections, blackmail politicians, and destroy anyone they don't like.

What do the wealthy gain by paying oppressively high taxes to the socialist government, other than a significant loss of their wealth to be redistributed to illegal aliens, reparations for blacks, and other Democratic pet projects? Answer: nothing.

Joe Biden Performs a Same-Sex Marriage

Joe Biden, like Nancy Pelosi, uses religion for political gain only and to grandstand as a religious enthusiast. Both Biden and Pelosi are unrepentant Catholics who promote homosexuality and abortion. Creepy Joe Biden says he wants to make the United States moral again so fools can vote for homosexuality education in public schools and support California legislators in legalizing pedophilia. "Progressive" Catholic Biden wants you to support the genocide of babies through abortion. On August 1, 2016, Joe Biden officiated a same-sex wedding, marrying two White House male staffers who worked in the Obama administration, Joe Mahshie and Brian Mosteller, at Joe Biden's residence in Washington, DC.

"Progressive" Catholic Biden visited the Vatican and the pope during his years in the Obama administration to try to influence the pope to change Catholic doctrine to accept LGBT behavior and abortion as moral human rights issues in line with Obama's "hope and change" crap. Seeing that Joe Biden is so sanctimonious, does he have a clue that marrying two men is contrary to several verses in the Bible?

Corrupt Democrats Stole the 2020 Election

Democrats stole the 2020 election and gifted Joe Biden the presidency. Joe Biden was inaugurated on January 20, 2021; he is living a lie as president. Responsible for the biggest election fraud in US history were fraudulent state leaders, election officials, ballot counters, the corrupt US courts, and corrupt makers and users of fraudulent election computers. From the electoral votes counted, Joe Biden won the presidency despite his low energy and frail mental character, his corruption in foreign dealings in China and Ukraine, his lack of campaign activities, his creepy habit of touching women and little girls at public events, his frequent inability to articulate, and his resistance to answering important questions.

Biden's brain has degraded to the point of mischaracterizing women and children, thinking they like to be touched, kissed, or hugged without their permission, and then thinking he did nothing wrong. He jokes about little kids rubbing his hairy legs on TV. He can't articulate because his brain is forgetting words of the English language and how to put two sentences together. He can't remember his email, and his Alzheimer's disease is taking a toll on his ability to recall. During his campaign, he refused to take questions from the media whenever he occasionally crawled out of his basement to give a speech. The rare times when Biden took questions, the questions were prefabricated and passed to the audience so when asked, he could have ready-made responses that he read from a teleprompter. Biden is easily intimidated and will be easily manipulated. His anger could easily be piqued by foreign leaders.

He can't see well, hear well, or talk well, and he only perks up when he's kissing or touching women or children without their permission. His past experience was of being a gaff jester comedian in King Obama's court. Biden is ready for a quiet retirement in a rest home. He crawled out of his basement at times with his mask stuck to his face and always blamed President Trump for mishandling the coronavirus pandemic. He mistook a city where he was campaigning for another in a speech he gave on TV. During the first presidential debate on TV on September 29, 2020, he was unprofessional in calling President Trump a clown and told him to shut up. Worst of all he refused to answer specific questions asked by Chris Wallace, the moderator, and when he did respond to questions, he lied more than 90 percent of the time.

Yet the vote counts indicated he won the 2020 election. Many people think there was a concerted effort by nefarious corrupt Democrats in key states to count illegal votes. That is, illegal ballots from different sources were illegally stuffed. This was done by ballot counters and election officials working in concert. Dominion computers, which were used in thirty states, were suspected of flipping votes from Donald Trump to Joe Biden. An unknown number of ballots were transported elsewhere, lost, or destroyed by US postal workers. The US Supreme Court tragically refused to hear lawsuits by Texas and seventeen other states that wanted to present evidence of the biggest election fraud in US history. Since when does a justice court refuse to hear evidence of election fraud? Since when can a few key states engage in election fraud and the Supreme Court refuses to hear any arguments, so as to allow the rest of the US states to be affected by the corrupt ruling?

Texas is already proposing secession from the Union. On December 12, 2020, the US Supreme Court became dysfunctional and corrupt, with no further legitimacy or credibility to operate as the highest court in the land. A secession of law-abiding states to form a union has already been considered in Texas as suggested by former US Army colonel and House Republican Alan West of Texas.

Joe Biden and his son Hunter Biden were suspected of illegal quid pro quo deals with the Ukraine and China. Hunter Biden's law firm received nearly six million dollars from a Chinese oligarch who sought power and influence in Washington, DC.[1]

---

[1] Alana Mastrangelo, "Fact-Check: Joe Biden Claims 'My Son Has Not Made Money' from China," Breitbart, October 22, 2020, https://www.breitbart.com/2020-election/2020/10/22/fact-check-joe-biden-claims-my-son-has-not-made-money-from-china/.

A *Washington Times* source says that Hunter Biden was receiving a $10 million annual fee from a Chinese billionaire who has been accused of corruption.[2]

On TV, Joe Biden bragged that he threatened Ukraine leaders with denial of more than one billion dollars in loans to Ukraine if a Ukrainian prosecutor was not fired for investigating his son. As a quid pro quo deal, the Ukrainian investigator was fired and Ukraine got the assistance from the United States. Hunter Biden, with no experience in energy, as an attorney was paid $83,333 a month by Ukraine.[3]

The FBI was conducting an investigation into Hunter Biden for money laundering prior to the 2020 election. A laptop that Hunter Biden turned into a shop for repair was never picked up, so the shop owner, hearing about Hunter Biden's corruption, turned it in over to the FBI.

According to the Townhall website, former Hunter Biden business partner Tony Bobulinski held a press conference to present a collection of information to reporters about the Biden family's dealings with China and directly implicated Joe Biden.[4]

Tony Bobulinski, a former naval officer, reported, "I'm making this statement to set the record straight about the involvement of the Biden family—Vice President Biden, his brother Jim Biden, and his son Hunter Biden—in dealings with the Chinese."

As is the case with Joe Biden, Nancy Pelosi's eighty-year-old brain struggles to articulate and can't come up with the right words to express herself at times. Her words all come out illogical, nonsensical, confusing,

---

[2] Rowan Scarborough, "Hunter Biden Demanded Chinese Billionaire Pay $10 Million for 'Introductions' Alone, Emails Show," Breitbart, October 15, 2020, https://www.breitbart.com/2020-election/2020/10/22/fact-check-joe-biden-claims-my-son-has-not-made-money-from-china/.

[3] Brie Stimson, "Hunter Biden Got $83G per Month for Ukraine 'Ceremonial' Gig: Report," Fox News, October 19, 2020, https://www.foxnews.com/politics/hunter-biden-paid-80g-per-month-while-on-board-of-ukranian-gas-company-report.

[4] Katie Pavllch, "'Here Are the Facts': Bobulinski Brings Trove of Receipts on Biden Family Foreign Deals," Townhall.com, October 22, 2020, https://townhall.com/tipsheet/katiepavlich/2020/10/22/bobulinski-brings-trove-of-receipts-on-biden-foreign-deals-n2578635.

and fake. She appears to be lying and making up stuff that really doesn't describe the situation well. Pelosi and Joe Biden should each retire; they're both losing it and getting too old for jobs they can't handle.

Biden Wants to Make the United States Moral? Note the Following:

Democratic politicians continue to set bad examples of morality as Biden never criticizes the behavior of Maxine Waters, who wants people to run Trump supporters from public places, or the anti-Semitism of Congresswoman Ilhan Omar, or Black Lives Matter people rioting, destroying statues, and attacking police. Nor does Biden condemn the attacks on conservatives on college campuses, or the stifling of conservative free speech on college campuses. He fails to call for morality when a Hollywood actor who is a Democrat suggests kidnapping Donald Trump's young son and throwing him at pedophiles, or when Robert De Niro expresses his desire to punch Trump in the face, or when a Hollywood bimbo working for the hate-Trump media holds a mock bloody head of Donald Trump. You call that morality? Joe Biden is on the wrong side of morality.

Sanctimonious Joe Biden Will Not Make the United States Moral Again

Joe Biden said he wants to make the United States moral again. The corrupt propaganda media portrays Biden as a moral decent guy. Here are some facts:

- Joe Biden secured a billion-dollar deal with China just after he visited China in 2013 for his son Hunter Biden, who had no experience working with China.
- Joe has a reputation for being a longtime sniffer and a touchy-feely guy with several women; he has offered no true apology for his creepiness.

- On August 1, 2016, Joe Biden officiated a same-sex wedding, marrying two male White House staffers who worked in the Obama administration, Joe Mahshie and Brian Mosteller, at Creepy Joe's residence in Washington.

- Biden, a Catholic, visited the Vatican and the pope during the years of the Obama administration to try to influence Pope Francis to change Catholic doctrine to accept LGBT behavior and abortion as moral human rights in line with Obama's "Hope and Change" reforms.

- Democrats continue to set bad examples of morality as they never criticize the behavior of Maxine Waters, who wants people to run Trump supporters from public places, or the anti-Semitic speeches of Congresswoman Ilhan Omar, or Black Lives Matter members when they riot, destroy statues, or attack police. Democrats never condemn the attacks on conservatives or the stifling of conservative free speech on social media, and they never call for morality when Hollywood actors who are Democrats say they want to kidnap Trump's youngest son or punch Trump in the face.

- Biden thinks "dignity" for homosexuals is the new morality, which merely means Biden wants to prevent discrimination against homosexual perverts in religious institutions.

- Catholic Biden thinks abortion is moral. He needs to be asked.

- While Democrat Bill Clinton was a groper and a rapist, Joe Biden settles for being a creepy sniffer and a touchy-feely old guy.

Joe Biden is as corrupt as Hillary Clinton. His quid pro quo deals are similar to Hillary Clinton's pay-to-play schemes where she provided government support, uranium, and/or favorable US policies to a country in return for donations to the Clinton Foundation. In Joe Biden's case, he provided technology to China as a US policy in return for $1 billion in business deals for his **inexperienced** son, and millions of dollars in deals with the Ukraine.

David A. Herrera

Peter Buttigieg and Andrew Cuomo Claim
that the United States Was Never Great

Peter Buttigieg and Governor Andrew Cuomo of New York gave speeches in which they claimed the United States was never great. Homosexual Buttigieg's main allegation as to why the United States is not great is that the United States has a history of intolerance toward blacks and homosexual groups. In April 2019, Buttigieg called for abolishing the death penalty and for reparations for the descendants of slaves. Buttigieg regards the death penalty as discriminatory. Buttigieg claims the United States is segregated by race and dissimilar allocation of resources and that the United States has always been a systemically racist nation that has excluded racial groups and still excludes them presently. He plays the race card and includes intolerance of homosexuals as a reason why the United States has never been great.

Neither one of these two Democrats can explain why the United States is the greatest country in the world. We have won two world wars, were first to develop nuclear power, are the only country to put a person on the moon and the only country to explore planets beyond Mars, have the most advanced technology on the planet, and are the greatest country in the world today. Both of these fools should answer the question: if the United States has never been as great as advertised, why are there caravans of migrants from other countries wanting—dying—to enter the United States illegally? If the United States is not great, then why don't Buttigieg and Cuomo get the hell out of the country?

Buttigieg wants a greater tolerance of homosexuality, wants same-sex marriages performed in every church, wants to modify religion to align with political correctness and liberal political morality, and wants to turn the United States into a socialist country. With increased homosexuality in the United States and the world, Bernie Sanders would flatter Peter Buttigieg by saying he was contributing to the effort to reduce the negative effects of climate change by not having babies with his male marriage partner and thereby would avoid going through the horrors of a baby-killing abortion.

Governor Andrew Cuomo said that the United States was never a great country because, historically, Americans never achieved equality. Cuomo completely ignored the economic success of the Trump administration and the fact that there is no slavery today and that discrimination based on race, color, or creed is outlawed. Women have never had more opportunities for advancement and wealth than they do now. Cuomo ignores that the United States has evolved into a nation that urges opportunities for and advancement of all people. The reason Andrew Cuomo alleges the United States is not great is that he is a socialist who thinks the United States will be great if it becomes a socialist country. He falsely believes equality for all will be achieved only through socialism.

There is ample evidence to prove the United States has always been a great nation, accomplishing many things that most nations of the world have not accomplished. Both Buttigieg and Governor Cuomo are misguided socialists who think people will change their character under a socialist regime.

Bernie Sanders and World Population Reduction with Abortion

Socialist Bernie Sanders advocated raising taxes on Americans so that billions of dollars would be used to pay for abortions across the world, which means he would fund the genocide of potentially hundreds of millions of unborn babies throughout the world in order to reduce the effects of climate change. This would greatly help China, India, and Pakistan; parts of South America, Central America, and Mexico; and the entire continent of Africa. The sum total of the population from these countries is, respectively: $1,439,323,776 + 1,373,603,573 + 220,892,340 + 432,425,572 + 180,662,677 + 128,932,753 + 1,340,598,147 = > 5.116$ billion people. Only a percentage of the total populations from these countries are women who would get abortions. How much is this world baby holocaust going to cost American taxpayers? Bernie forgot to say.

To fund abortions for countries and regions that need it the most— China, India, Bangladesh, all of Africa, parts of the Middle East, and all freeloading countries who would jump for joy over this Bernie giveaway—Bernie would have to tax every American citizen into poverty, unemployment, debt, and homelessness *and* would have to heavily tax all corporations and small businesses, forcing them to dismiss millions of American workers and forcing some of them to relocate overseas or go bankrupt. This is Bernie's socialist utopia.

Had socialist Bernie been elected president, he would have requested the Treasury print more money since he would have run out of other people's money to pay for additional spending items such as climate change programs, the Green New Deal, reparations for the historically oppressed, and free stuff for illegal aliens. Note that most of the countries that will need abortions are South America, Asia, and Africa, numbering in the hundreds of millions of abortions for these people of color. Would race-baiting liberals or socialists accuse Bernie of being a racist for funding the genocide of unborn people of color? Bernie never estimated the cost for the abortions across the world.

According to the World Health Organization (WHO), there is an estimated 40 million to 50 million abortions per year in the world (including the United States), corresponding to 125,000 abortions per day.[5] Let's do the math. Since Bernie did not say how much he would propose paying for world abortions, let's assume an average of $400 for each abortion. Then, $400 × 125,000 a day × 365 = $18,250,000,000 per year, or approximately $18.25 billion per year of taxpayer dollars spent on abortions worldwide. How much of it will be fraud? Bernie never discussed or computed figures on abortion costs.

Elizabeth Warren, Another Socialist Who Hid the Total Costs of Her Spending Tax Plan

Failed Democratic presidential candidate Elizabeth Warren refused to provide estimates for the grand total of her spending plans, or say how much she was going to tax billionaires, millionaires, and the middle

---

[5] "Abortions This Year," Worldometer, accessed February 22, 2021, https://www.worldometers.info/abortions/.

class, or mention how would she would force taxpayers to pay for the following:

1. health care for illegal aliens (approximately one million entering the United States per year through open borders)
2. Medicare for all US citizens
3. college debt relief for lazy, irresponsible millennial freeloaders
4. reparations for present-day victimized blacks for the slavery of their ancestors, which happened more than one hundred fifty years ago
5. reparations for historically oppressed homosexuals in the United States
6. free taxpayer-paid college tuition
7. the Green New Deal
8. climate change, before it kills us in eleven years or less
9. the disbanding of ICE, to allow millions of foreigners into the United States, running to get their free stuff
10. costs for the care and rehabilitation of drug addicts, made possible by illegal drugs crossing our southern border
11. the cost in American lives of illegal drug deaths.

Elizabeth Warren claimed she would tax the top 2 percent richest Americans, the middle class, small businesses, and large corporations in order to pay for her spending spree. Warren would pass laws to repeal the Second Amendment and have law enforcement confiscate guns from law-abiding Americans. Worse, she would have caused a revolution in the United States with her tyrannical tax oppression and taxation without representation. On October 1, 2019, Elizabeth Warren endorsed an Alexandria Ocasio Cortez–supported proposal that included taxpayer-funded welfare benefits for illegal immigrants.

Socialists typically never address how they plan to enforce their unattainable high-cost spending plans if the majority of Americans refuse to pay oppressively high taxes to a socialist government with excessive spending. Socialists will have to reduce government spending or find creative ways to enforce taxation oppression; seizure of property and businesses will be the norm. But if they fear a revolution of people opposed to their high taxes, socialists may pass laws, in anticipation, to confiscate guns. If the wealthy tax-shelter their wealth or move their millions or billions of dollars overseas, socialists will be unable to collect enough money from them. In reality, there may not be enough tax wealth to steal and satisfy a socialist's spending plan.

Tyranny with a Vengeance

Kamala Harris said: "Like Cheeto. He's [Trump's] just bad, and we will impeach! There is so much evidence against this guy, the mind boggles. And once he's gone and we have regained our rightful place in the White House, look out if you supported him and endorsed his actions, because we'll be coming for you next. You will feel the vengeance of a nation. No stone will be left unturned as we seek you out in every corner of this great nation. For it is you who have betrayed us."[6]

Kamala Harris, Beto O'Rourke, and Alexandria Ocasio-Cortez all served as naive and clueless members of Congress, socialists who never knew much about economics or about the value of capitalism. When Kamala Harris ran as a Democratic presidential candidate, she promoted her socialist agenda of taxation and redistribution of wealth to pay for her fantasy of free tuition, free health care, free housing, and so on, with no indication of how she would collect the money needed. Alexandria Ocasio-Cortez (AOC) is another socialist who is clueless about any horrific effects that her socialist spending plan would have on the US economy. It's as if AOC thinks money grows on trees or cavalierly thinks the rich will gleefully pay for her plan—and then everyone will be happy.

How many socialists will keep offering free government handouts to continue to corral blacks back onto the Democratic plantation? Why can't socialists see that blacks need jobs and opportunities to become prosperous and successful?

---

[6] "Kamala Harris: 'After We Impeach, We Round Up the Trump Supporters,'" CBNC News, May 1, 2020, https://www.cnbc-news.com/kamala-harrisafter-we-impeach-we-round-up-the-trump-supporters/.

Before Joe Biden selected her as his Vice President, socialist Kamala Harris wanted to give $100 billion in housing assistance to blacks only. She also advocated reparations for blacks and free health care for illegal aliens. Harris, when running for president, said she would take executive action on gun control if Congress failed to act within one hundred days of her taking office as president—a tyrannical attack on the Second Amendment. Warning: Joe Biden chose Kamala Harris as her vice president. Harris proposed an executive order to require background checks across the United States to ban assault weapons, which is a violation of the Second Amendment. Like Beto O'Rourke's plan, this would be just another step to confiscate weapons from law-abiding citizens. Why would socialists confiscate weapons? Answer: to defend themselves against an armed revolution of Americans fed up with oppressive taxes that are driving them into poverty and causing them to lose their homes. Banning guns is a "Paul Revere" signal that must be heard across the United States—socialist tyranny is coming, and socialists will be banning semiautomatic weapons and other firearms to prevent an armed revolution against the coming tyranny. The socialist policies of these vengeful tyrant leaders, which are against capitalism and freedom-loving people, would cause another bloody civil war in the United States. When guns are taken away from tax-oppressed people, no one will have the ability to oppose the government.

It was a curse to have Joe Biden select Kamala Harris as his VP running mate. If Joe Biden goes senile, becomes unable to perform his job as president, and consequently is removed, or is impeached and removed from office for his corruption in the Ukraine and China with his son Hunter, then Kamala Harris will become president. She is a socialist who will destroy democracy and freedom.

Socialists Are a Danger to Our Republic Who Will Cause a Civil War

Never in US history has the Democratic Party run on a platform of socialism. Usually, socialists run as part of the Socialist Party, as Bernie Sanders did in 2016, against Republicans, Independents, and

Democrats. But in 2020, socialists, including Bernie Sanders, infiltrated the Democratic Party and ran as Democrats to stand a better chance of getting a socialist elected.

Socialists such as Kamala Harris, Rashida Tlaib, Ilhan Omar, Alexandria Ocasio-Cortez, Kirsten Gillibrand, Cory Booker, Bernie Sanders, and Elizabeth Warren would all undermine the US Constitution. If Vice President Kamala Harris were to become president because of Joe Biden's failing mental faculties, she would likely cause a second US civil war, and she would be one of the main targets of an armed revolution. Kamala Harris wants to stifle the influence of Christianity, repeal the Second Amendment, destroy free speech, and tax-oppress the wealthy and middle class to support an unaffordable socialist spending agenda. This is a Stalinist strategy, implemented to benefit only those who support her socialist agenda—and she'll destroy or oppress the rest. She would allow open borders to *massively* increase the population of socialist supporters and voters, who seek to receive free government handouts, which they receive in exchange for the socialists' gaining amnesty migrant votes in all future US elections, which will transform the United States into a socialist nation if borders are not protected. Joe Biden put VP Kamala Harris to handle the border crisis. God help us.

But because of the corruption of Democrat-run districts, cities, and states, corrupt ballot counters, corrupt mail carriers, and the Dominion computers and software used to commit election fraud, President Trump lost the election, and no federal agency wanted to hear any evidence gathered by the many witnesses who observed instances of election fraud, or hear about the investigations done by Rudy Giuliani and Sidney Powell. The FBI and DOJ were total failures in investigating election fraud. Evil succeeded and good failed; that is how to characterize this election. Now the goal of socialist politicians will be the socialist transformation and takeover of the United States by way of open borders, suppressing resistance, changing election laws, packing the Supreme Court, and forcing the wealthy to pay for the transformation. That evil plan can only lead to conflict and revolution.

We owe a debt of gratitude to our military personnel, our veterans, and police officers across the United States, all of whom defend the

United States from enemies, prevent or respond to terrorism inside the United States, support our Constitution, enforce our state and local laws, and protect our lives. We rely heavily on this group of Americans for the survival of the United States, both inside and outside the United States.

If Conservatives Do Not Unite, They Will Be Ruled like Sheep by Democrats

Recall that not all Americans love their country. Many millennials are taught that the United States was never great and that it bears responsibility for the sin of slavery since its founding. They claim that systemic racism remains with rich white people oppressing blacks and people of other races. Patriotic Americans need to unite as one body and never surrender their firearms to a creeping socialist government. Instead, our military, veterans, and police should unite and organize to resist and obstruct the banana republic leaders of Democrat-run cities who refuse to enforce laws to protect lives and our freedoms. Since the faux election of Joe Biden, and since Democrats took the majority in both houses of Congress, a system of checks and balances no longer exists in our branches of government. Watch for signs of the coming tyranny from a united, unopposed socialist government.

If we fail to unite to fight terrorism within our country from socialist activists such as the "brownshirts" of Antifa, Black Lives Matter, or the New Black Panther Party, and from white supremacists, then we will become sheep, allowing big government to control our lives. Socialist politicians will make laws to enhance their power and maintain it. Passing more tyrannical laws will take away more of our constitutional freedoms, and socialists will keep robbing us with taxes to fund their socialist agenda and to enrich themselves and their supporters.

If we don't change our schools and stop the indoctrination of our youth with hate-America history, with textbooks written expressing hatred of the United States for slavery, for having taken land from the Natives, for having taken land from Mexico, and for damning the Constitution, then we are in for more damage. Indoctrination-focused public schools will become a form of reeducation camps that, it could be said, are diluted versions of the retraining camps in China that enslave prisoners opposing the Communist Party of China. These camps indoctrinate people to love Chinese communism, China's "wonderful" government, and its benefits. In the same way, public schools in the United States will become centers of retraining for our youth, teaching them to hate the United States, uphold socialist government reforms to our culture and institutions, and live in an "Alice in Wonderland" utopia with total equality, free education, work provided by the state, and an absence of racism.

If US citizens or Congress fails to prevent illegal aliens from entering the United States, someday in the future, our police departments may be transformed into liberal politicized police departments packed with amnesty migrants who will enforce tyrannical laws in Democrat-run cities and states. Police will also be faced with the defunding of police departments and heavy restrictions on what they are allowed to do during riots, looting, and destruction of businesses and cities. Socialists at either the federal level or in Democrat-run cities will have a "don't shoot or don't choke blacks" policy despite increased crime. Socialists may fire generals who are conservatives or those who refuse to allow cross-dressers, transvestites, transgender men or women, or homosexuals in the military. The military will have no Bibles and no chaplains. The military, the police, and our veterans should organize patriotic Americans for the purposes of waging an armed revolution against a new, transformed United States filled with massive numbers of foreigners who will allow socialists to rule every aspect of American life. At this rate, the United States will become another Venezuela in less than *five* years.

"Paul Revere" Yells That the Socialists Are Coming

The socialist plan of every Democrat running for president in 2020 was very insidious, deceptive, and dishonest. Their plan was a step-by-step methodical plan that, as time continued, would have collected more taxpayer funds and allocated these to their socialist spending scams with no total estimated cost for each spending item. Then laws would have been passed to confiscate weapons to prevent a revolution against tax oppression, and guns would have been banned for law-abiding Americans. Socialists know ahead of time that there will be opposition to tax oppression, increased immigration, weakening of our economy, soup kitchen lines, much more homelessness, tax debt driving property owners into poverty or homelessness, and homeowners and/or businesses losing their properties to the IRS for nonpayment of taxes or arrears in tax payments demanded by the socialist government. Who will enforce confiscation of guns of those who refuse to hand over their weapons and collection of taxes from those who refuse to pay taxes? Answer: those who support socialism; those who are unfamiliar with or don't care about the Constitution; those who are destitute and who need a job and will do anything to keep one; and lastly, leftist presidents who may use an executive order to seek the assistance of UN Peacekeeping troops, asking them to arrive on US soil to enforce taxation, put down rebellions, and enforce gun confiscation laws.

Illegal aliens will likely be given amnesty, and some subsequently may be hired as law enforcement officers with good pay. This means socialists at the federal level will demand local police agencies across the United States to comply with their laws or else lose any funding for their state, including money for distribution of food and other essential needs. In other words, socialists at the federal level will ignore all states' rights and use federal tax assistance to states, along with the means of production and distribution of food and other goods, as leverage or punishment to force city administrators to politicize police agencies to comply with federal socialist demands. This means patriotic law enforcement officers must comply or get fired. To fill in the gaps of those who are fired or quit, socialists will hire amnesty migrants to replace law enforcement personnel needed to enforce the coming tyrannical laws that will take away the constitutional freedoms of Americans.

Socialist elites will seize control and nationalize large corporations that refuse to pay taxes. An economic war will be declared on the rich 1 percent or 2 percent, most of whom will renounce their citizenship and take their wealth out of the country long before socialists are elected into office. The only people left to pay taxes after the rich abandon the United States with their immense wealth are the middle class and union workers.

In another methodical step, unions will no longer be necessary as the federal government will confiscate or nationalize the manufacturing industry. In such a case, workers will not be allowed to bargain for increased wages. Unions don't yet understand that open borders under socialism mean that all union workers will be replaced by lower-paid illegal aliens hired by any remaining private businesses or by industries nationalized by the socialist federal government. Unions will be dissolved in all socialized businesses. Has anyone ever heard of labor union disputes in China, Russia, Iran, or Venezuela?

Socialist Greece, a member of the European Union (EU), was going bankrupt because its leaders had run out of other people's money to pay for the cushy early retirement of Greece's union workers; Germany had to bail Greece out with an infusion of money. The same will happen to retired union workers already in a state deep in debt, like Illinois. A socialist regime in the United States would have to bail out Illinois to spare the state from bankruptcy.

Manufacturing industries may be nationalized, or they may be kept under private ownership as long as they pay their proper taxes to the socialist government. Extremely high taxes on corporations will reduce profits and reduce competition between businesses operating in similar industries. Corporate executives and managers will no longer have the exorbitant salaries they were accustomed to in the capitalist system of government. Individual prosperity is not the goal of socialism; all corporate profit goes toward the common good, to be shared equally, in conformance with socialist distribution and allocation plans. Supply and demand may still exist under socialism, but corporate profits will be highly taxed based on the level of corporate income. This system of high taxes has the effect of lowering corporate production to meet lower demand, account for inflation, and account for the lowered income of the middle class. Much of the profits will be skimmed by the socialist government. In some socialist countries, demand is replaced by socialist government planning that allocates products according to a predetermined plan. Prosperity from any sales becomes practically nonexistent because producing individual wealth for profit, as in capitalism, is not a goal of socialism.

Once manufacturing industries such as the oil industry, steelmakers, and the food and agriculture industry are nationalized, the socialist government will control the manufacture, production, and distribution of goods, shipping them to favored states that support the government. This is something that Joseph Stalin did. History shows that the communist tyrant only allowed distribution of food to areas in Russia that supported his communist-style government, thereby starving the millions of poor souls who didn't support him.

Corruption will increase with a socialist federal government. Socialists will pack the Supreme Court with socialists and communists to support every law Congress is tasked with passing. There will be no checks and balances between branches of government. Socialists with amend the Constitution or thrash it step by step, to strengthen socialism, until socialism as a form of government can no longer be stopped. People uninterested in politics will be led like sheep because they are silent as lambs. Freeloaders will get their free stuff in exchange for votes but will never become wealthy. To survive, Americans will find that they have to comply with socialist laws and support socialism or else starve. All one has to do is search for socialist countries to see why their government elites are all immensely rich, such as in Iran, Saudi Arabia, Russia, China, Venezuela, Britain, Syria, and Cuba, compared to their peons.

A hybrid of socialism and capitalism in different forms may work in Europe (including Scandinavia), Mexico, or South America, but it won't work in the United States. The American people love their freedom like the people of no other country in the world and will not succumb to socialist tyranny. Law enforcement officers and freedom-loving Americans will oppose a socialist government (as in Venezuela) made up of people who, as Obama correctly pointed out in a speech in California, will stick to their guns and Bibles. A massive united American rebellion will absolutely occur at some point in time, while socialist elites, amassing great power and control, will use law enforcement, the US military, or UN Peacekeeping soldiers on US soil to enforce their socialist laws and go after those who rebel against the socialist government. If necessary at some point, the socialist government will use the military or, in case of a national security argument, use UN Peacekeeping mercenary forces to defend the socialist elites, put down rebellions by freedom-loving patriotic conservatives, and punish rebels by entering their private homes to confiscate their registered guns. They may also confiscate their homes and wealth, which will drive Americans in the end to defeat the socialist federal government and attack every police agency, attack every military installation mainly composed of foreigners given amnesty, and attack UN foreign mercenaries and drive them out of the United States. Food will be distributed to useful idiots loyal to the social elites and not to states with large pockets of resistance. This is a prelude to tyranny, the coming of the second US civil war between those who stand for freedom and those who stand for tyranny.

How can Americans prevent the coming tyranny? Answer: Since Joe Biden stole the 2020 election, and since President Trump, law enforcement, the state courts of key states, and the US federal court system failed to resolve the greatest election fraud in history, Joe Biden was certified as the winner of the 2020 presidential race.

Corrupt Socialists Want to Redistribute the Wealth and Power in America to Leftist Democrats

Kamala Harris and other socialists want to move the United States away from religion with legalized prostitution, same-sex marriages, and abortion, killing babies in or out of the womb. Kamala Harris is an atheist who has disrespect and disdain for Catholics and the Knights of Columbus (a Catholic charity organization), has disregard for the life of an unborn baby, and thinks, much like Alexandria Ocasio-Cortez, that if she were president, she would tax the rich, taking 70 percent to 90 percent of all their wealth, giving them absolutely nothing in return, and giving their tax money to illegal aliens and freeloaders. By way of her policy of oppression by taxation, she will cause a major economic collapse in the United States. In July 2020 in Minnesota, Kamala Harris bailed out a man accused of sexually assaulting an eight-year-old girl. She also donated money to bail out rioters and other felons.[7]

The goal of Democrats in the Biden Administration is to shift wealth and power from conservatives to leftist Democrats by nefarious means.

Now that Democrats have control of the federal government, Democrats will pass laws allowing them to stay in power permanently, such as packing the US with illegal immigrants, giving them amnesty to aid US voters in winning all future elections. Insidious Democrats will change election laws so they can always win elections by packing the Supreme Court with leftist judges, reestablishing another "Deep State", eliminating the Electoral College, and eliminating the Convention of States. Socialists will radically change the US Constitution step by step as they gain more power in government.

The "disarming of conservative America" is only part of the continuing plan by socialists to take away power from capitalist entities and wealthy Americans, that is, *disarm conservatives them*, then *take away their wealth and power*, then *take away more of their constitutional freedoms*. This is essentially waging an undeclared war of destruction by leftists against freedom-loving Americans through presidential executive orders and leftist Congressional legislation designed to shift the wealth and power away from conservatives until the war is won. Severely restricting gun rights, stifling free speech and religious liberty, changing election laws so Democrats always win votes, oppressive taxation without representation, and making Americans defenseless against a tyrannical government, are precisely actions currently being taken and planned by the Biden Administration.

One might study the history of Venezuela as a classic example of the socialist agenda. In the United States, one might consider the following:

- Banning firearms destroys the due process of law-abiding citizens who are falsely accused of shootings committed by

---

[7] Andrew Kerr and Ryle Hootten, "Bail Fund Promoted by Kamala Harris Helped Man Accused of Sexually Penetrating a Child," *Daily Caller*, September 16, 2020, https://dailycaller.com/2020/09/16/kamala-harris-minnesota-bail-fund-accused-sexual-assault-child/.

criminals and psychos who obey no laws. Law-abiding people should never be forced to give up their Second Amendment rights.

- Drug cartels run opioids, cocaine, marijuana, heroin, and methamphetamines across the border, which drugs kill hundreds of thousands of Americans each year. Open borders will enable cartels to kill more Americans with their illegal drugs. How will Democratic leaders stop a rise in murders in major cities across the United States as a result of gang violence, with gangs competing to sell drugs in their own territories? Note how horrific the drug war in Mexico has been for decades and the heinous torture and murder of people from rival cartels competing to sell drugs. How about the displaying of the heads of beheaded members of drug gangs in several major cities in the United States to serve as warnings of crossing "marked" drug trafficking territories?
- When have Democrats complained about illegal aliens committing murders, rapes, burglaries, robberies, and assaults on Americans after coming across the southern border? How about MS-13 gang members who brutally killed high school students using machetes?
- How will open border Democrats prevent terrorists from crossing our southern border carrying dirty bombs to nuke one or more of our cities if left unprotected?
- How will the Biden Administration stop the spread of COVID-19 from the massive surge of illegal aliens that are not being tested for COVID-19 and are being transported by buses to communities in the US?
- Does any Democratic immigration policy address the sexual abuse and human trafficking that occurs with caravans of illegal aliens traveling to the United States?
- Joe Biden will repeal the civil protection of manufacturers of guns; ban the manufacture and sale of semiautomatic assault weapons and high-capacity magazines; seek to regulate possession of existing assault weapons; end online sales of firearms and ammunition; and extend the background check for

purchasing a firearm to ten days. States will require citizens to get a license prior to purchasing a gun and will require owners of firearms to report stolen or lost weapons.[8]

- Without effective assault weapons, how can Americans protect themselves against hardened and experienced criminals, terrorists, gangs, and a tyrannical socialist government?

- Even if the Biden administration passes tyrannical laws to repeal the Second Amendment, *no* law-abiding American is going to give up his or her weapons. Even police departments say everyone should defend themselves against threats to human life as police can't be everywhere to prevent a defenseless person (i.e., a person without a gun) from being killed.

The lessons from US history should have taught us that the cause of the American Revolutionary War was socialism and tyranny, fought against a socialist government that confiscated the wealth of American colonists to enrich the English Crown, leaving American colonists poor without any political representation or benefits from their taxes. The British treated American colonists like a colonial nation, extracting their wealth for the benefit of the British elites in power. History is repeating itself in the United States. That is why defenders of freedom must never give up their guns.

Democratic Plans to Confront Hate Crimes and White Supremacist Violence

In an article entitled, "Cory Booker Proposes Office to Fight White Supremacy,"[9] we learn that failed presidential candidate Cory Booker addressed his plan to confront hate crimes and combat white supremacy if elected. Booker's proposal would have brought anti–gun

---

[8] Joe Biden, "The Biden Plan to End Our Gun Violence Epidemic," JoeBiden.com, https://joebiden.com/gunsafety/.
[9] "Cory Booker Proposes Office to Fight White Supremacy," Newsmax, August 15, 2019, https://www.newsmax.com/newsfront/russia-police-attack/2020/01/02/id/928636/.

violence legislation that would have, among other things, established a national licensing program for gun ownership. Joe Biden is planning precisely that, including a $200 registration fee for every gun registered or purchased. Biden will set the stage for federal agents to infringe on a law-abiding citizen's right to bear arms. Knowing locations of registered firearms, federal agents can confiscate them from law-abiding citizens. Joe Biden will task the FBI to focus on white supremacy threats and hate crimes but avoid focus on Black Lives Matter and Antifa donors to his campaign.

The Biden–Harris administration will define hate speech, in concert with high-tech giants behind social media, to allow the FBI to surveil users and establish probable cause to investigate Americans suspected of using hate speech, who would be labeled as white supremacists. Biden will use the FBI to spy on Trump supporters for revolutionary activity on all social media websites. The socialist propaganda news media is pursuing a reprogramming or reeducation of all Trump supporters, along with censorship between the FCC, Wall Street, and high-tech corporations, which are all in bed together, to ban, block, or censor all conservative thought. The rationale this three-headed snake is using is that conservative violent speech threatens democracy and the Biden administration. The corrupt Democratic propaganda media is pushing for government to partner with big businesses to regulate free speech. That is, socialists and big businesses will become fact-checkers of free speech.

Biden–Harris Spending Plan List

The cost of government spending plans, such as funding abortion, climate change programs, salaries of government employees, our military, pensions, welfare, food assistance, disaster relief efforts, health care, and education, is not unsustainable. The Biden–Harris spending plan is an "Alice in Wonderland" fairy tale. After adding free health care for illegal aliens, costs for the New Green Deal, reparations for blacks, reparations for homosexuals, government subsidies to states for cleaning up feces, urine, and trash left behind by the homeless, and coronavirus spending, there will be little or no money left for the military, police departments, fire departments, or government workers and their retirement funds. Social security and VA benefits will likely be robbed, canceled, or reduced.

If a scenario occurs where the Biden administration ever runs out of US taxpayers' money and cannot collect enough of it, the IRS will confiscate US homes and use them as subsidized rentals for low-income people or sell them to collect tax revenue. Businesses unable to pay taxes or that abandon their factories will be confiscated by the IRS, sold, or nationalized as in a socialist country. Unable to confiscate wealth from the top 20 percent rich, and given the administration's inability to collect sufficient taxes from the middle class, the Biden White House will likely issue emergency presidential executive orders that will cut a percentage of everyone's retirement funds, union funds, IRAs, 401(k)'s, bank accounts, savings accounts, and insurance annuities so that his administration may run the country with its spending scams. The United States will be turned into Venezuela and will be much worse off than California is now. The Biden administration spending plan will add significantly to the US national debt, which, as of November 22, 2020, was more than $27.28 trillion. See the Real-Time US National Debt Clock at: https://usdebtclock.org/

How are overtaxed Americans going to pay trillions of dollars in taxes per year, not counting the costs of the new influx of immigration projected because of Biden's new open border policies? Joe Biden has already pledged to give amnesty to between eleven million and twenty-two million DACA immigrants living in the United States, which means they will be given citizenship and the right to vote and will become eligible to receive welfare, unemployment insurance, social security, Medicare, and food stamps. This would cost American taxpayers billions of dollars more.[10]

It appears that spenders in the Biden administration are not interested in using arithmetic to estimate the *grand total* for their dubious spending

---

[10] John Binder, "Joe Biden's Immigration Plan: Amnesty for Illegal Aliens, Free All Border Crossers into U.S.," Breitbart, December 11, 2019, https://www.breitbart.com/politics/2019/12/11/joe-bidens-immigration-plan-amnesty-for-illegal-aliens-free-all-border-crossers-into-u-s/.

plan; all they want is to give free government handouts to amnesty migrants paid for by American taxpayers—some rich, but most of them middle class—in exchange for votes. For a review of Joe Biden's tax plan, see the article "Details and Analysis of President-Elect Joe Biden's Tax Plan."[11]

Biden's spending items are not listed on the Breitbart website, which is where the aforementioned article appears. Note that the death estate tax will be reactivated; that is, if you die, your heir(s) will owe the federal government a tax on your estate, ranch, or farm. Far worse, no *grand total* is found for all the spending items in the Biden–Harris spending plan listed on the Tax Foundation's website. Why is that? Answer: fear of what the American public might think. Plus, this is a prelude to the many trillions of dollars in taxes that must be collected to pay for all Biden's monstrous spending, which could stir up a revolution.

Taxation oppression alone will **likely** bring the US economy to a major recession and send Wall Street into a quick nosedive under socialism. This means corporations will no longer sell their products as demand goes down and people earn less money to spend. Reduced demand for products slows down manufacturing. As a result, businesses have to lay off workers because of a slow economy and reduced profits. There will be massive unemployment in the United States. Worse, as the economy and manufacturing slow down, the demand for food and basic necessities will be higher and prices for food and other products will go up. Unemployment will lead to poverty, and poverty will lead to crime. Long soup lines will reappear, and homelessness like that in San Francisco and Los Angeles will multiply across the United States. Homeowners, unable to pay property taxes on their homes, may lose their homes; the IRS may repossess homes whose owners are in significant tax arrears, and may even go after the owners' bank accounts, savings, social security, and so on, or send them to prison for tax evasion.

If the Federal Reserve prints more dollars, this will only devalue the dollar, causing massive inflation. Prices will increase on food and

---

[11] Garret Watson, Huaqun Li, and Taylor LaJoie, "Details and Analysis of President-Elect Joe Biden's Tax Plan," October 22, 2020, https://taxfoundation. org/joe-biden-tax-plan-2020/.

other basic necessities. The World Bank will remove the dollar as the standard world currency and may switch to the gold standard, because gold can't be reproduced as can the currency of any nation.

Could this horror scenario happen? Answer: Yes, it can, but it's not likely. Partial solution and a hint to end this madness: *Don't give up your guns.*

At no other time in US history have Democrats been so dishonest, obstructive, hateful, sinister, or insidious, offering little or nothing to improve the lives of Americans without advocating tyrannical socialist power and control, aiming to destroy several of our constitutional freedoms.

The Biden Administration's Changes in Less Than One Hundred Days

In the first one hundred days of the presidency, the Biden administration has signed at least 37 executive orders (only some are included below):

1. Call for reparations for blacks because their ancestors were slaves more than one hundred fifty-seven years ago.
2. Allow prisoners to vote in federal elections.
3. Allow sixteen- and seventeen-year-olds to vote.
4. Allow open borders to let tens of thousands of foreigners **to** caravan into the United States to obtain free government handouts and seek jobs as cheap labor. On January 18, 2021, a massive caravan was headed toward the US border from Honduras, demanding Joe Biden keep his promises of open borders and amnesty. More caravans will be coming.
5. Cease the building of Trump's border wall and pass immigration reform laws to give amnesty to all DACA members in the United States. Open borders and free government handouts will attract more illegal aliens into the United States, regardless how it affects the safety and economic well-being of Americans.
6. Abolish the Electoral College; keep only the popular vote to win presidential elections.

7. Kamala Harris favors legalizing prostitution and illegal drugs.
8. Increase the size of the Supreme Court to more than nine justices with more liberals, socialists, or communists so as always to win court decisions.
9. Reverse Trump's reduction of taxes for income earners and for businesses. Raise taxes on businesses and on hardworking middle-class Americans who own homes and have good-paying jobs. Businesses and the wealthy will pay more in taxes in order to give trillions of dollars in government handouts to illegal aliens and for COVID-19 relief.
10. Pay for the college tuition of US students and the massive numbers of immigrants entering the United States illegally.
11. Forgive college tuition loan debt students already owe, which is about $1.6 trillion in taxpayer money.
12. Allow abortions on demand, paid for by taxpayers, of babies in or outside the womb for any reason.
13. Spend trillions of dollars on Medicare for All, which neglects or denies health care.
14. Confiscate weapons from law-abiding Americans. Democratic politicians, and particularly the corrupt fake news media, are fearful of a conservative revolution and will therefore seek to repeal the Second Amendment.
15. Reform law enforcement agencies to tightly control use of deadly force. These agencies then will hire amnesty migrants who will not hesitate to enforce tyrannical laws on US soil.
16. Social engineer the military to fire conservative patriotic American soldiers, and then remake the military into something that is more socialist-friendly, its soldiers willing to fight right-wing "terrorists," put down right-wing white-supremacist hate groups and protesters, assist police agencies to put down free-speech protests by Trump supporters, defend and protect socialist elite tyrants, and enforce tyrannical laws.

As proven when history repeats itself, once socialists become powerful, they enrich themselves and embolden themselves to use corrupt methodical strategies and propaganda, and offer a false vision of utopia to the citizenry. Socialism often leads to the following:

- bloody revolutions between freedom-loving people and tyrannical governments;
- persistent oppression, imprisonment, and/or genocide of a huge class of people opposing tyrannical government;
- punishment, censorship, and oppression of those who oppose a powerful autocratic government, with violators of tyrannical laws being imprisoned, fined, or executed;
- an ultimate decline and eradication of customs, traditions, morals, and freedoms. Moral values will be replaced by a new politically derived false morality that is nonbiblical.

When Has America Been Great?

Eric Holder and Andrew Cuomo have expressed publicly that America has never been great. How unpatriotic, and a slam to the men and women who fought and died to defend the home they loved—the United States. These two repugnant politicians are liberal Democrats who have political careers because the United States is great. The United States doesn't deserve such a thing said about it by these two characters.

To answer Eric Holder's question "When has America been great?" consider the following points and questions:

- We are and continue to be the most powerful country in the world, both militarily and economically.
- We won two world wars together with our allies and saved the world from tyranny.
- We live in a freedom-loving nation under God where brave people died so we could be free.
- We have the highest number of Nobel Prizes in the world, 388.
- We are the only country that has put a person on the moon.
- We invented the atomic and hydrogen bombs and actually used the A-bomb to end a world war.

- We paid in blood, losing 330,000 white US soldiers in order to free the slaves during the Civil War.
- If the United States isn't so great, then why are millions of immigrants trying to get into our country?
- Our country has been the most charitable country in the world.
- If the United States is not a great country, then why don't Eric Holder, Barack Obama, Cher, Rosie O'Donnell, and a bunch of other malcontents leave the USA forever?
- Our country has the most advanced technology in the world.

The American people have made America great because they elected Donald Trump as president of the United States. In less than two years, we had the lowest unemployment ever on record, the most women working in decades, more prosperity, and higher wages for workers. We made our military great again, stopped the dictator of North Korea from shooting missiles over Japan and threatening to nuke the United States, made much better trade deals with other countries, made NATO pay their fair share of their European defense, began building a wall for the safety of all Americans, and more.

Democrats, on the other hand, have offered nothing beneficial for Americans other than trying to impeach Donald Trump without finding a crime. Their dislike for former president Trump led them to obstruct him in his attempts to benefit the American people. Trump addressed the lack of congressional laws to prevent caravans of tens of thousands of migrants from crossing our southern border, assisted Israel to relocate its capital to Jerusalem, enacted successful prison reforms, and assisted our veterans with VA reforms. Democrats spent three years trying to impeach Trump, and failed miserably.

23

WHO ARE THE BAMBOOZLED AND BRAINWASHED VICTIMS OF THE DEMOCRATIC PARTY?

The "free stuff" being advertised by socialists to draw foreigners from all over the world is not free. It would be paid for by the system of high government taxes imposed on the very rich, the middle class, and businesses across the United States to promote income equality, which is blamed on capitalist oppression. Socialists propagandize capitalists as highly paid, greedy corporate executives who exploit workers. Under socialism, no one is allowed to be prosperous over anyone else unless a person works longer hours for more pay. Socialists portray capitalists as getting rich on the backs of workers and living in mansions with ample food and exceptional medical care. Rich white capitalists, they say, hire cheap labor to increase their profits.

The exploited minds of our youth are taught that oppressed workers are neglected poor victims of capitalist greed, living in squalor and filth and without health care on the poor side of town. These exploited victims are called to rise as revolutionaries against the capitalist oppressors to resist and fight the latter's agenda.

Socialists omit the fact that socialist countries often seize the wealth of their nations—industry, agriculture, banking, natural resources, and so on—for their own enrichment. Thus, the socialist ruling class becomes wealthy themselves on the backs of those of the working class. The socialist elites now exploit the working class as capitalists once did. The government of Venezuela is a perfect example of a once prosperous capitalist country with a constitution that was taken over by a socialist dictator, who took control of the economy and the military, rewrote the Constitution, and confiscated his nation's wealth and natural resources for the benefit of his dictatorial regime. The once prosperous people are the new poor who are starving or moving out of the country.

Democrats, big businesses, high-tech giants, and the fake news media are now calling for war against Trump supporters, after Democrats stole the election. Fear of exposure of their corruption is the reason Democrats are hell-bent on changing the hearts and minds of the seventy-five million Trump supporters by planning oppressively high taxes on wealthy Americans, the middle class, and corporations, passing gun control laws, silencing free speech, violating religious rights, stopping wall construction at the border and creating an immigration crisis at the border, causing economic chaos with the massive illegal aliens and Biden's spending plans, issuing bailouts for mismanaged states disguised as a COVID relief bill, and more. President Trump exposed the corruption of the Left that began with the Obama administration and continued during Trump's administration. The vile and hateful Democrats in the House, the Deep State, the Supreme Court, the corrupt fake news media, high-tech corporations, the FBI, and the DOJ tried to remove Trump from office. Nancy Pelosi filed impeachment charges to impeach President Trump so he could never run for president again; that's how vile and vindictive House Democrats have become. Democrats accused President Trump of orchestrating the violence at the Capitol during the massive Trump rally held in Washington, DC. Ten Republican traitors voted to impeach President Trump just a week before he left office.

Of Millennials, People Ages Eighteen to Twenty-Four, 56 Percent Favor a Mostly Socialist System of Government

The following is from the article "64 Percent Say Democratic Party Supports Socialism, Says Poll"[1]:

> Nearly two-thirds of registered voters in a Harvard CAPS/Harris Poll survey released exclusively to The Hill believe that the Democratic Party supports capitalism. Sixty-four percent of respondents said that they believe the Democratic Party backs such an economic system, while 36 percent believe the party is opposed to socialism, the poll found.
>
> Most registered voters in the Harvard CAPS/Harris Poll survey—65 percent—said that they believe that the U.S. economy should be built around a "mostly capitalist" system, compared to 35 percent who want a "mostly socialist" system.
>
> Fifty-six percent of registered voters polled who are between the ages of 18 and 24 favored a "mostly socialist" economic model; 48 percent of respondents between the ages of 25 and 34 said the same.
>
> Respondents between the ages of 55 and 64, only 27 percent said they prefer a "mostly socialist" system. But voters 65 and older, only 22 percent said the same.

The youngest voters, between the ages of eighteen and twenty-four, were the most likely to say that the Democratic Party backs socialism,

---

[1] Max Greenwood, "64 Percent Say Democratic Party Supports Socialism, Says Poll," the Hill, January 26, 2019, https://thehill.com/homenews/campaign/431641-64-percent-say-democratic-party-supports-socialism-says-poll.

at 71 percent, according to the Harvard CAPS/Harris Poll survey. Conversely, 29 percent said they see the Democratic Party "opposed to socialism." What groups are likely to support a socialist style form of government? The answer includes the following:

- millennials
- drug users
- college students with college loan debt
- illegal aliens
- Muslim immigrants
- self-victimized blacks
- homosexuals
- the hate-Trump liberal Hollywood crowd
- the fake news media
- most convicts if allowed to vote
- freeloaders
- criminals
- Antifa, Black Lives Matter, the New Black Panthers, and other liberal protest groups.

Antifa and Black Lives Matter (BLM) accused President Trump of being a racist and a fascist. They also claimed Trump supporters, who are primarily conservative Americans, were racists and fascists. These allegations have been proven false, as the president whom conservatives elected lowered the African American unemployment rate to its lowest point ever, approved prison reform, and empowered Ben Carson to implement a ghetto neighborhood redevelopment plan; these are accomplishments Barack Obama never attempted. Conservatives support these policies. But because former president Trump is white and a Christian, BLM accused him of being a racist.

Antifa stands for "Antifascist." People who align themselves with Antifa falsely accuse conservatives, the Trump administration, Trump supporters, and white people in general of being fascists. In the 2020 Minneapolis riots, Antifa brought death and destruction to the United States, funded by New World Order elites such as billionaire George Soros, who wants to destroy law and order in the United States. Antifa's objectives are chaos and lawlessness. Antifa members are violent liberal thugs hiding behind masks by day and being cowardly nerds by night, living in their mommies' garages. These masked criminal thugs block traffic and intimidate innocent bystanders. Multiple thugs at a time beat up old men, storekeepers, and whomever else they dislike during protests. Some throw trash and urine at police, and stifle conservative free speech.

About 20,000 Trump supporters attended a Trump rally in Minneapolis, Minnesota, that was opposed by Mayor Jacob Frey. The rally went on quite well. But as Trump supporters left the rally, about a thousand members of BLM and Antifa, protesting outside, set fires, attacked Trump supporters, and tossed urine and bottles at police. How many liberal Democrats have condemned Antifa violence at protests? Answer: Only one. Nancy Pelosi criticized Antifa violence in Berkeley, California. This is the ugly character of all House Democrats.

Antipolice Liberals

Liberal mayors in liberal cities supported the actions of Antifa and BLM. Mayors from Berkeley, California, Portland, Oregon, and Raleigh, North Carolina ordered their police to stand down during Antifa and BLM events.

Liberal mayor Ted Wheeler condemned conservative free speech as hateful and bigoted. But when Antifa and BLM beat up conservative journalist Andy Ngo, Mayor Wheeler ignored the incident. Conservative speech was absolutely not hateful or racist, but rather was meant to express conservative values and support for smaller government, Christian values, and freedom. Unfortunately, during the event, Antifa and BLM blocked intersections and tried to direct traffic while officers on motorcycles watched from a block away, doing nothing. Activists chased down a seventy-four-year-old man after he made a right turn, ignoring Antifa, who were pounding on his car and causing damage. Antifa thugs also attacked a man in a wheelchair. Ted Wheeler, Portland mayor, stands by his decision to allow Antifa to block traffic and hassle motorists.[2]

We Have a Duty to Defend Our Values, Our Morals, and Our Culture—We Must Not Stay Silent

Every generation is put to the test to defend freedom and the values we represent in the United States. Shirking this responsibility and getting out of the way means victory for the enemy, with dire consequences for all freedom-loving people, and dire regrets for the sheared sheep who did nothing.

---

[2] "Mayors and Antifa: The Deliberate Replacement of the Rule of Law with Anarchy," Conservative Insight, https://conservativeinsight.net/wp-content/uploads/2019/07/MAYORS-AND-ANTIFA-THE-DELIBERATE-REPLACEMENT-OF-THE-RULE-OF-LAW-WITH-ANARCHY.pdf.

PART 5

A SOCIALIST GOVERNMENT IN THE FREEDOM-LOVING UNITED STATES IS A PRELUDE TO TYRANNY

24

WHAT IS SOCIALISM?

Socialism is a political and economic theory of government in which the organized citizenry collectively owns, controls, and regulates the means of production, the means of distribution, and prices. Under socialism, workers are, in theory, no longer exploited because they own the means of production. Profits are spread equitably among all workers according to their individual contributions, not to capitalist CEOs who make ludicrous salaries. The cooperative system also provides for those who can't work. It meets their basic needs for the good of the whole society. Through graduated taxation, socialism, in theory, eliminates poverty and provides equal access to health care and education. Also in theory, no one is discriminated against. Everyone works at what they do best and what they enjoy. If society needs jobs to be done that no one wants, it may offer higher compensation to make the work worthwhile.

However, socialism relies on collective cooperation. It assumes humans are willing to work cooperatively and will not compete to gain an economic advantage. Under socialism, industry may compete for business, but the government takes a significant portion of taxes for its spending plans. As a result, socialism doesn't reward people for being entrepreneurial or inventive in their efforts to "build a better mousetrap." Socialism takes away the incentives to be innovative and/ or creative as in a capitalistic society. Socialists in government maintain power as long as they represent the will of the people. But government leaders, as history shows, often become corrupt. Powerful elites or tyrants find ways to destroy their opponents to maintain rigid power and continued on their path of self-enrichment.

A socialist government controls planning for all industry and manufacturing, works with manufacturing bosses to meet milestones related to production and quotas, and decides what products are to be built, how much products will cost, and where to distribute them. Demands for products are *not* considered as a basis for planning.

In a socialist country, all property is state-owned, and individuals are lifetime renters in their homes. Socialists will begin transitioning the United States from a capitalist economy to a socialist economy; they may gradually and eventually confiscate private property of the wealthy. In the end, all property is owned by the people but controlled by the state, and there will be no private ownership. All property will be included in the socialists' product plan to achieve wealth equality for all, including for disabled people who cannot work. The state will assign a citizen to a "residence living quarters," which the citizen will never own but, rather, will just use until he or she moves out or dies. Then the property reverts back to the state for reallocation to another citizen. However, a lazy person who refuses to work may keep his or her living quarters but may not be able to eat or enjoy other necessities that others "earn" by working collectively as the state expects; this may be a shock to freeloaders.

A worker receives benefits, for example, wages, according to his or her ability and according to his or her contribution. Everyone in society receives a share of benefits from the production based on how much each has contributed. This system motivates citizens to work long hours if they want to receive more. Workers receive their earned share of production profits after a percentage has been deducted by the government for use toward the common good.

There are many forms or hybrids of socialism in which the economy is a mixture of capitalism and socialism, as is the case with Scandinavian countries. Some socialist countries have democratic socialism or hybrid socialism, which is governmental ownership and management of the means of production and distribution, with government determining the price of goods. The socialist government hires workers to regulate and manage industry, production, distribution, and price of goods.

Some European countries allow private ownership of homes and some businesses. Socialist countries in Scandinavia are democratic socialist countries that allow forms of capitalism. But all forms of socialism rely heavily on taxation of the rich with a percentage levied on the working class to pay for socialist health care and retirement.

Socialism can only sustain itself if there is enough of other people's money to do so. As long as money can still be collected from the labor of workers in industry, and as long as there are enough workers contributing to the planned production of goods, socialism survives. Should a socialist government run out of other people's money—for example, if the socialist government fails to collect enough taxes to provide for the common good, that is, to give its citizens what they need—then socialism will fail.

In contrast, in a capitalist country such as the United States, individual liberty is granted to us by the Constitution. The United States is a republic consisting of fifty states united under the Constitution with three equal branches of government: the executive branch, the judicial branch, and the legislative branch. The government allows free enterprise and the ability for a private individual to create and own a business for profit in a competitive business environment. Federal government laws are enacted to regulate commerce to ensure fair business practices. Courts in capitalist countries allow civil lawsuits to resolve business disputes. The American dream is achieved when each individual obtains training or an education, seeks opportunities for employment in a job, works hard for good wages, and is able to accumulate wealth to have a family and purchase a home he or she can own. As corporations succeed, wealth is trickled down to workers who serve the business well. For businesses to succeed, business executives are hired and are paid well to enable the company to compete well with other businesses and be rewarded with a substantial profit. As businesses succeed and grow, many become part of Wall Street, where investors invest in stocks issued by companies that the investors are confident will succeed. With investments, a small start-up business or a well-known corporation will use investment funds to allocate within its industry the capital and resources it needs to grow, prosper, and succeed. The investor receives return on investment or a loss based on economic factors that drive the markets. Prices are set by supply and demand, not by government interference, or planning and control.

Every citizen has the opportunity to achieve the American dream in capitalist America. The proof is in the pudding. Contrary to what socialist and Trump-hating fanatics say about how unfair or racist capitalism is, or that rich white people are oppressing the poor, such socialist and hateful propaganda is false. Private enterprise is not about oppressing workers in a capitalist United States but, rather, is about establishing a win-win situation where a rugged individual can achieve his or her full potential, be rewarded for it, and become prosperous. Under the Trump economy, all races were urged to be all they could be, to seek and learn a profession, to work hard, and to achieve the American dream. No one is excluded from accomplishing that dream. Why do you think millions of immigrants of every color and creed are migrating to the United States, legally and illegally, to find a better life? Why aren't people from South or Central America traveling in waves of caravans to seek economic opportunities in Cuba or other Latin American countries? Answer: because of our powerful capitalist economy, our wealth, and our high standard of living, which anyone with talent, desire, and energy can work to achieve.

The Goal of Socialism in the United States

Communism is a form of socialism. It's a political form of government derived from Karl Marx that advocates a revolution leading to a society where all property is publicly owned and each person works and is paid according to his or her abilities and needs. All profits made from the sale of goods are funneled to the state for further production planning. Again, the government owns all industry, and controls production and distribution of goods.

In communism, central planners replace the forces of competition and the laws of supply and demand that operate in a capitalist market economy. They also replace the customs that guide a traditional economy. The state owns businesses on behalf of the workers. The government monopolizes businesses and rewards company managers for meeting the targets, details, and deadlines of its plan.

In his *Communist Manifesto*, Karl Marx proposes the following:

1. Abolition of property in land and application of all rents of land to public purposes.
2. A heavy progressive or graduated income tax.
3. Abolition of all rights of inheritance.
4. Confiscation of the property of all emigrants and rebels.
5. Centralization of credit in the hands of the state, by means of a national bank with state capital and an exclusive monopoly.
6. Centralization of communication and transport in the hands of the state.
7. Extension of factories and instruments of production owned by the state, the cultivation of wastelands, and the improvement of the soil generally in accordance with a common plan.
8. Equal liability of all to labor. Establishment of industrial armies, especially for agriculture.
9. A combination of agriculture and manufacturing industries; gradual abolition of the distinction between town and country, by a more equitable distribution of population across the country.
10. Free education for all children in public schools. Abolition of children's factory labor in its present form. Combination of education and industrial production, and so on.

A communist state controls the distribution of produced goods. We see from history that Joseph Stalin starved millions of people in his country by refusing to distribute food to parts of Russia and neighboring countries where he had no communist support—that is, his opposition. Stalin distributed food only to his cronies and to geographical areas that supported him—his crony communist supporters. As a result, millions of human beings died of starvation. This only proves that insidious evil tyrants who control the distribution of goods can funnel life-necessary goods only to their supporters, to maintain and reinforce their power, while starving the opposition, which may be millions of human beings.

Socialism and communism may or may not work in other countries. Studying world history shows the repeated follies of socialism. Countries still under socialism or communism have never achieved the greatness that the regulated capitalist republic under our Constitution has achieved. There are many instances in world history that expose the horrors of socialism, communism, fascism, and fascist theocracies. We have seen many examples of atrocities and genocides committed by tyrannical Muslim theocracies, and we have the example of Fascist Germany waging war in Europe, Africa, and Asia and gaining notoriety for perpetrating the Holocaust in Europe. Muslim theocracies and fascist governments are a form of despotic socialism controlling nearly all lives of the citizenry with tyrannical laws. And they have the tyrannical authority to enforce those laws.

Socialists Underestimate the Cost of Socialism in the United States

Kamala Harris, Bernie Sanders, Elizabeth Warren, and former barmaid Alexandria Ocasio-Cortez (AOC) don't know of the positive achievements of capitalism. Above all, they never did have a good estimate of what their spending plans would cost the American taxpayers. All these clueless socialists don't realize that green energy has to slowly evolve and won't be entirely implemented before the world ends in twelve years, as AOC predicts. Eliminating fossil fuels eliminates a huge tax revenue, which will be economically catastrophic to the car industry, the airline industry, the railroad industry, and the trucking industry. And, petroleum products would no longer exist. Eliminating farting cows would put high-scale restaurants out of business, would put fast-food places out of business, would be catastrophic to food stores and meat markets, and would eliminate milk, cheese, and other dairy products from the American diet.

Worse, the United States would be the only country spending money on green energy, climate change programs, and global warming programs, which would cost taxpayers hundreds of trillions of dollars more. Countries such as China and India that are major polluters would not spend much compared to the United States to reduce pollution or reverse global warming. As a result, global warming would *not* be significantly reduced and climate change would basically remain the same. Additionally, China and India will not listen to a clueless bimbo, a crazy old communist, or a senile old man from the United States lecturing them on how to spend their money.

In November 2017, President Donald Trump announced that the United States would withdraw from the Paris climate agreement. This agreement, which committed the United States to drastically reducing greenhouse gas emissions, was a truly bad deal—bad for American taxpayers, American energy companies, and every single American who depends on affordable, reliable energy. It was also bad for the countries that remain in the agreement. Here are four reasons Trump was right to withdraw:

1. The Paris Agreement was costly and ineffective. The energy regulations agreed to in Paris by the Obama administration would have destroyed hundreds of thousands of jobs, harmed American manufacturing, and destroyed $2.5 trillion in gross domestic product by the year 2035.
2. The agreement wasted taxpayer money. Participants in the Paris conference called for a Green Climate Fund that would collect $100 billion per year by 2020. The goal would be to subsidize green energy and pay for other climate adaptation and mitigation programs in poorer nations, and to get buy-in (literally) from those poorer nations for the final Paris Agreement. The Obama administration ended up shipping $1 billion in taxpayer dollars to this fund without authorization from Congress. Some of the top recipients of these government-funded climate programs have in the past been some of the most corrupt governments, which means corrupt governments collect the funds, not those who actually need it.
3. Withdrawal was a demonstration of leadership. China, a main polluter country, corruptly falsifies its pollution data, which cannot be trusted. Why subsidize countries like Iran and North Korea, which are some of the fund recipients?

4. Withdrawal was good for American energy competitiveness. US companies continued to invest in new energy technologies and to work with other countries on green energy on their own. Third World countries will still need their own petroleum energy resources to survive. American energy companies have become energy-independent, no longer relying on foreign oil.

The article entitled "4 Reasons Trump Was Right to Pull Out of the Paris Agreement," by Nicholas Loris and Katie Tubb (June 1, 2017), can be found at https://www.heritage.org/environment/commentary/4-reasons-trump-was-right-pull-out-the-paris-agreement.

Even worse, hundreds of trillions of dollars more would be required to provide income equality for the hundreds of millions of foreigners entering the United States under the socialists' open border policy over the next few decades. Socialist elites would tax wealthy Americans, until they would have to reach into the pockets of the American middle class for more taxes. If socialists manufacture more money, they will devalue the dollar, which would soon lead to inflation with the dollar becoming worthless. An economic collapse would follow. The clueless socialists should know that no country can be taxed into prosperity, but rather, the wealthy and middle-class citizens of these countries revolt against big government that promises to benefit only immigrants, the lower class, and the ruling elites. This is oppression and taxation without representation, likely resulting in a second American revolution. Targets of the revolution will be socialists such as Kamala Harris, Bernie Sanders, Elizabeth Warren, Cory Booker, Alexandria Ocasio-Cortez, Governor Andrew Cuomo, Governor Gavin Newsom, Governor Bill de Blasio, and Kirsten Gillibrand, among other tax-thirsty Democratic politicians.

Soak the Rich, Destroy the Opposition, Make Tyrannical Laws

Global warming is about socialist elites going after the wallets and purses of the wealthy, the middle class, and businesses, to funnel their money to enrich leftist groups, companies, and institutions that support socialist politicians and socialist control, under the name of global warming. Corrupt Democrats could justify spending money on any item they claim that is associated with global warming. Global warming is *just the beginning* of *soaking the middle class* for more government spending.

Socialism never produces wealth, except for socialist elites in power, such as Nicolás Maduro of Venezuela and multibillionaire Vladimir Putin of Russia, who stole much money and amassed great wealth. Dictators and communists imprison or commit genocide against any citizens of their country who oppose their socialist/communist rule. Some examples are the Turkish genocide of Armenians, the Third Reich's genocide of Jews during World War II, the "Killing Fields" of Pol Pot of Cambodia, communist China after World War II, Joseph Stalin's mass starvation of millions of Russians, and Nicolás Maduro's oppression of Venezuelan citizens.

Questions News Media Hosts Never Asked of Democrats in the 2020 Presidential Debate

Question 1, regarding socialism in the United States: How are socialists, if elected, going to enforce their socialist laws and force their agenda on freedom-loving Americans who have never had a socialist government?

Answer: Socialists have to become tyrants if they plan to tax-oppress freedom-loving Americans and drive them into poverty or homelessness while socialist elites themselves live like royalty. To implement their spending plans, socialists have to collect enough money from wealthy Americans. States and local governments would also have to impose higher taxes on citizens and create new ways to increase taxes for every American. California and New York are good examples of states that tax-oppress their citizens. Socialists could print more money; raid Social Security or eliminate it; raid the VA or eliminate VA benefits to veterans for service-connected diseases or disabilities; confiscate part or all of your personal 401(k) retirement fund or part of your personal bank account; repossess your home(s); or repossess your business.

Question 2: How will socialist politicians enforce their tyrannical laws?

Answer: By first taking guns away from Americans, severely weakening or eliminating the Second Amendment, and hiring foreigners who don't know and don't care about the Constitution to enforce their tyrannical laws. When socialists pass laws to confiscate your assets and hire people to enforce their oppressive laws, the police will have become tyrannical stooges. Socialist tyrants cannot function without confiscating wealth. And the more they want to spend, the more money they will need to confiscate.

Question 3: How are socialist politicians going to tax the 1 percent or 2 percent they say are willing to pay taxes to give every oppressed American and every illegal alien the free stuff they so much deserve?

Answer: The top 1 percent to the top 20 percent of wealthiest Americans will pay little or no taxes to socialists. They are smarter than socialists. The rich 1 percent likely would have transferred all their millions or billions of dollars into foreign accounts *before* the 2020 election if they thought it was likely that a socialist would be elected president and if they thought Democrats would win a majority in both houses of Congress. The very rich planned to have all their money in foreign banks that socialists would be unable to touch. The rich know how to shelter their income from taxes through charity foundations. The very rich were even considering renouncing their citizenship and moving out of the country to save their wealth. Many likely sold their homes or have a sale pending. No part of their billions will be in the United States by the time a socialist gets into office. It is a myth, a lie, or erroneous for socialists to think billionaires will give away between 50 percent and 90 percent, or more, of their wealth in taxes to socialists so the latter can spend it on government investment scams, bridges to nowhere, and foreigners entering the United States. It is also a myth that the rich 1 percent actually trust socialists to manage their money or manage the United States, after they've seen how ineptly Democratic politicians have managed the homelessness problem in poop states such as California, New York, and Illinois. Rich Americans will not trust Democratic leaders who allowed rioters to destroy lives and properties in their liberal cities and who now seek to bail out these mismanaged cities to rebuild them after the destruction from the riots. All sensible Americans will see how corrupt socialists will become when they enrich themselves in office with lobbyists and donors, and how they mismanage health care, and how difficult it will be for them to tax-oppress the middle class and businesses, which will result in disastrous consequences for the economy.

Socialism will not work in the United States because the taking of much from great economic achievers and hard workers, and the redistributing of their wealth to causes such as illegal immigration, reparations for blacks, green energy, the bailing out of Democrat-run mismanaged states, Biden's health-care plan, climate change donations to foreign countries, and foreign aid, will only be met with opposition, tax evasion, and violence. Socialism and communism have never built prosperity for workers, but it does so for the ruling elites. Capitalism under current US laws and under the Trump economy resulted in the greatest economy in US history prior to the COVID-19 pandemic, providing jobs, opportunities, increased income, and the most industrial production in US history, along with enabling all to achieve the American dream.

Socialism Will Not Work in the United States

A socialist government strives for equality for everyone and sees a utopia where income equality is provided for all. But it never succeeds. Evidence to support this statement is found in the history of the human race, particularly in modern history, where socialists and dictators such as Adolf Hitler, Pol Pot, Joseph Stalin, Mao Tse-Tung, and Nicolás Maduro Moros of Venezuela have gained notoriety and failed their citizens. Some of them murdered or caused the deaths of hundreds of thousands, or even millions, of their citizens; I wouldn't call that a utopian dream. The mind of a socialist is distorted with a false sense of reality and is lacking in common sense. Such a person does not understand the nature of humankind and our need to be free. Real Americans do understand these things, as did our nation's founders.

Libertarians love freedom, but they expect to live in a reality where things will be fixed by themselves; they want no government intervention in the lives of citizens. How socialists often fail is that they allow crime and corruption to happen, and then they react after the damage has already been done. A lack of responsible government would prevent that, just as President Trump advocated preventing illegal immigration and unvetted mass immigration into the United States. Why? Trump and Republicans knew that we wouldn't have a country if we had open borders, and that to have open borders would bring about severe economic consequences for US citizens, raise a concern about public safety, and permit a culture change that would drastically revise our American customs and traditions, something that would leave the United States unrecognizable in the future. Corruption is common among socialist elites and their cronies, who all tend to be the main benefactors of socialism.

Left-wing crony capitalist elites in the Obama administration were the main benefactors of the economy. They enjoyed taxing the hell out of wealthy people and the middle class, and running businesses out of the country to avoid high taxes, resulting in massive job losses and unemployment.

Republicans advocate the economic policies of President Trump and Ronald Reagan, including limited government, tax relief, complying with constitutional laws, regulating immigration, and achieving peace through strength. Above all, Republicans enjoy the freedoms that the founders of the United States granted to us by way of the Constitution and the Bill of Rights. We do not seek to take over other people's countries. Instead, we urge them, help them, or fight with them to achieve freedom from tyranny and oppression. Republicans stand for God, family, and country; the freedoms we have; the strength to defend ourselves from tyranny and oppression; and the effort to keep making America great.

How Socialists Plan to Take Over the United States and Maintain Their Power

There is no doubt that if socialists, with their greed for power, pass laws to ban firearms in the United States, or if the president signs an executive order or declares martial law to this effect, there will be a bloody revolution in this country. This surely will happen if we elect socialists like Beto O'Rourke, Cory Booker, Bill de Blasio, Eric Swalwell, or Kamala Harris. Beto O'Rourke already said that if elected, he wants to go after every law-abiding citizen's guns. Cory Booker said he will create a federal anti–white supremacist agency to detect hate speech on social media and to investigate and go after white-supremacist terrorists.

Socialists will likely use a gestapo-like police force to go into the home of every law-abiding American who has registered an assault weapon in order to confiscate it. An existing Federal Agency, such as the Department of Homeland Security may be transformed to fill that function. Local police agencies have police officers who are patriotic Americans who cherish our Constitution and freedoms; most won't enforce confiscation of weapons and would likely quit their jobs. Those who remain employed will be mandated by socialist city administrators, in charge of states such as California, Oregon, Illinois, New York, and Washington State, to confiscate guns. There are three choices if one wishes to enforce confiscation of weapons:

1. A federal police agency would enforce confiscation of weapons and coordinate that effort with every state and local police department, or else police departments will fire all police officers who refuse to enforce these laws and will hire new police officers who will. Who do you think they will hire? Amnesty migrants who care little or nothing about the Constitution.

2. The federal government under a socialist president and Congress may hire a foreign police agency for assistance composed of officers who don't care about American freedom or the Constitution.

3. A tyrannical US president may use an executive order to hire UN Peacekeeping military forces to enforce socialist laws and prevent rebellions and uprisings, as is outlined in one of Obama's executive orders. This would mean a socialist federal government would likely hire mercenary forces and authorize them to put down rebellions by freedom-loving Americans, killing Americans on US soil if necessary.

There is no doubt that liberal Democrats and their lawyers have already thought of this, particularly socialists like Beto O'Rourke and Cory Booker. Freedom-loving Americans must never give up their guns or even register them with a federal agency to prevent socialist tyrants from knowing where these guns are located so as to confiscate them. Socialists already know that law-abiding freedom-loving Americans will oppose confiscation of weapons.

Who would be targets of gun confiscation? The answer should be easy and obvious: Freedom-loving Americans will not give up their constitutional freedoms, or allow oppression, or surrender to tyranny. Americans will fight for freedom. Socialism has been tolerated in Europe because Europeans are used to it; they were born into it, and it's their heritage. They are not like freedom-loving Americans. In the United States, socialist tyrants in Washington, DC, would likely come after our guns before passing ugly tax-oppressive laws that would likely drive hardworking Americans into poverty and/or homelessness.

Elimination of the Electoral College: What It Means, and Why the Electoral College Must Be Kept

The population of the thirteen colonies after the American Revolution was mostly concentrated in the state of New York. Leaders of other states refused to accept the Articles of Confederation to unify all states, where majority rule by population would elect the candidate every time. To remedy this, the Electoral College was designed to assign two senators from each state to make elections fair to elect a president and pass rules. One hundred senators make up the Senate, two from each of fifty states. The Electoral College decides the election of a president.

Each state is allocated two electors for its US senators plus one for each of its US Representatives, which number may change each decade according to the size of each state's population as determined in the census. The Electoral College consists of 538 electors. A majority of 270 electoral votes is required to elect the president. A state has the same number of electors as it does members in its congressional delegation: one for each member in the House of Representatives plus two senators.

If 75 percent to 90 percent of the US population lived in blue states, the election of a president would never be fair if decided by majority vote. That's why sleazy Democrats want to do away with the Electoral College and want open borders. They think Americans, especially ignorant millennials, will support majority-win elections. We have a republic, not a democracy. The voices of individual states count, not the voices of mobs from heavily populated blue states.

In 2019, Democrats opposed the census, which asks the state to list the number of noncitizens living within its borders. In doing so, a state like California records a false number for its population to inflate its allotted number of electoral votes.

Millennials and Socialism

Millennials are embracing socialism, and they don't have a clue what it will do to this country or to them personally. About 50 percent of millennials support the social engineering of culture, religion, the economy, moral values, and gender identity; the promotion of LGBT rights; the legalization of currently illegal drugs for recreational use; the weakening of the military; the movement to defund or reform law enforcement; increased immigration; and a reformed labor force. None of these things can happen without painful taxation oppression, which will bring the US economy to a collapse. The government's allowing of millions of immigrants into the United States and giving them amnesty will cause businesses to replace blacks and unskilled millennials with amnesty migrants who will work for cheaper wages. Rioting, looting, violence, and chaos will become a frequent occurrence. Destruction of our freedoms will lead to another bloody American revolution, making the United States vulnerable to Russia, China, and terrorists around the world. Open borders would invite criminals and terrorists into the United States. Socialists don't have a clue that they will ruin the United States, which is why they must never be elected to take complete control of the federal government.

Millennials Who Learned to Hate the United States Are Clueless about Its Greatness

Those embracing socialism have no idea that the United States has evolved into a land of opportunity for all and that every race now has a good opportunity to become prosperous. All clueless millennials hear about is getting freebies from big government for a living. They apparently never came to understand that nothing is really free. They don't realize the price that they will have to pay for socialism is the giving up of their freedoms. The free medical care one gets under a socialist regime will have many drawbacks, such as waiting for weeks (or even months) to see a doctor. When millennials get old, they may have no social security. More people will die from lack of treatment (as happened with some of our veterans). With all the illegal aliens coming into our country, we will have more diseases, such as the coronavirus, spreading and not enough vaccines or medicines for all. Ask yourself this question: Why do people come to the United States when they need an operation done or they need some treatments done in a timely manner? Why do they come for free college? What happens when all the colleges are full and a US citizen has to wait for his or her turn? The way things are looking now, our Democratic representatives in government are making laws to give illegal aliens priority status in terms of attending college. Free college and health care are already being granted to illegal aliens in some states.

Do millennials care where all the money is coming from to pay for all the free socialism stuff? The very rich know how to dodge taxes legally, or they may move out of the United States. Anyone who works will see less of their hard-earned money after taxes are taken out. Soon thereafter, people will stop working with the idea of letting everyone else pay for everything. Soon the United States will be gone! Socialism has never been successful in any country. Millennials were taught to hate the United States, and in so doing they ignore what our forebears worked so hard to achieve. Capitalism, ingenuity, industriousness, and hard work is what made the United States the greatest country on earth. Remember how our country was doing when Barack Obama was president—low unemployment. Look how much better the United States became under Donald Trump's presidency.

Voter Fear that Should Have Reelected President Trump: Repercussions of Socialism

Today we have the fear of socialism; tax oppression of the middle class; ridiculously high taxes (70 percent to 90 percent) on the wealthy; extremely high taxes on businesses to pay for free healthcare for all indigenous people and illegal aliens in the United States, free tuition for illegal aliens, and free housing for poor people and illegal aliens in the United States; increased taxes on purchased goods and services, on utilities, phone bills, and gasoline, and for clean air and water; an increase in taxes to pay for prisons, trials, police, and so on; and worse, open borders that will cause tremendous increases in taxes for everything the United States offers for free to the hundreds of million foreigners who will be entering the country over the course of a few decades, looking to claim *their* free government handouts. All this horrendous Democrat spending should have caused President Trump to be reelected in 2020.

Do any Democrat politicians currently in power have a clue about the repercussions of taxation oppression as mentioned above? Answer: No, they don't care how much it would cost because it's the wealthy who will be paying for it. Democrats ~~and they~~ do not want to talk about it because of the $trillions required for these expenditures are frightening, and these expenses will need to be siphoned from the pockets of middle-class Americans, wealthy Americans, and businesses.

Do Democrats know anything about what happens to an economy controlled by socialists?

Answer: No, they are clueless. Wealthy people will renounce their citizenship and quickly take their wealth out of the country before the socialists can confiscate their bank accounts. Corporations will have massive layoffs or declare bankruptcy, or they may again relocate their business overseas, as they did under the administration of the arrogant con artist Barack Obama, *before* their businesses are illegally confiscated by the socialist government. In some cases, corporations will pass on their losses from taxes on to the consumer with higher prices of their goods or services and may lay-off employees and replace them with people willing to work for cheaper wages. A major decline in the US economy will follow.

In a photo I found on the internet, Alexandria Ocasio-Cortez (AOC) is pictured with the idiotic caption, "To me, what socialism means is to guarantee a basic level of dignity."

But the four photos and the comments below her photo destroy her asinine theory. The four photos are as follows:

1. **A** photo of the Soviet Famine (1932)—very poor, malnourished children with bony ribs
2. **A** photo of the Chinese Famine (1959)—a mother and her children dying of hunger
3. **A** photo of the Cambodian Famine (1975)—malnourished children waiting in long soup lines for food
4. **A** photo taken in Venezuela (2018)—Venezuelan citizens eating cats to prevent starvation.

All these photos depict historical events caused by socialist tyranny, which degrades human life and causes deaths to the citizens of tyrannical socialist countries. Often, it is during the process of remaking a country by a ruthless tyrannical government that causes starvation and the genocide of people who oppose tyranny. If socialists fail to see the results of socialism in history, they are bound to repeat history. (The images mentioned in items 1–4, above, can be seen on bing.com.[1])

Pictures like these should be shown in history classes in public schools to show the devastation socialist and communist regimes bring to humanity. Viewing such images should drive Americans to oppose the treachery of socialism, communism, and fascism, and arm themselves against power-hungry elites who exploit, control, and oppress the masses for their own political and economic gain. What is not mentioned in the list of photos I found online is a picture of Germans eating out of garbage cans after the defeat of Fascist Nazi Germany in 1945.

Saul Alinsky, a socialist, in the early twentieth century described eight levels of control, or conditional requirements that must be obtained, before creating a socialist state. They are levels that contain information on the following:

1. Health care—use it to control people.
2. Poverty—increase poverty to control the poor and provide freebies paid to them by taxing the rich.
3. Debt—increasing debt and poverty to produce more poor people.
4. Gun control—ban or restrict guns to make people helpless in defending against tyranny.
5. Welfare—build a dependence to control people.
6. Education—control the media and what they say, and control what children learn in school.
7. Religion—remove God from government and schools.
8. Class warfare—divide the rich and poor to tax the oppressive rich with the support of the poor.[2]

---

[1] Bing, https://www.bing.com/images/search?view=detailV2&ccid=4I1jE4C 0&id=6B5DB3290295D79132FBB9AD76CB160B6965CD83&thid=OIP.4I1 jE4C0PifD6itJe-dFbwHaJQ&mediaurl=https%3a%2f%2flookaside.fbs bx.com%2flookaside%2fcrawler%2fmedia%2f%3fmedia_id%3d1152436 111586530&exph=960&expw=768&q=aoc+and+pictures+of+famines& simid=607994397986654853&ck=F77A0C5F96A70329AEB2E7DA 2B588725&selectedIndex=151&FORM=IRPRST&ajaxhist=0.

[2] *Saul Alinsky's 12 Rules for Radicals*, Bolen Report, https://bolenreport.com/saul-alinskys-12-rules-radicals/.

Socialists have twelve rules for radicals that can be implemented to deceptively, cruelly, and strategically outwit or destroy the opponents of socialism. These are included on the Bolen Report website, cited above. These rules are well-known to Democrats. Hillary Clinton wrote her college thesis on *Rules for Radicals*.

25

THE GREEN NEW DEAL AND CLIMATE CHANGE

Climate Change Is Merely a Tax-Hike Socialist Scam

Climate change is a socialist scam. Under the climate change umbrella, taxes can be allocated to any blue state, leftist organization or leftist contractor for any scams called climate change. Dishonest politicians feed countries misinformation and pose as alarmists of global warming. Politicians, mainly socialists, fund millions of dollars to dishonest environmental scientists and researchers to promote the idea of global warming in order to cause world hysteria about global warming and climate change. The objective is for politicians to tax the citizens of their country and to request donations from rich countries of the world to help them "prevent causes of global warming." The UN is one the biggest backers of this gimmick, requesting millions of dollars for global warming. What the UN and countries are not revealing to the public is the following:

1. It's a tax scam to establish a socialist slush fund.
2. Politicians then use the slush fund to spend on whatever they want. It's easy for dishonest politicians to spend tax money on anything they want and then justify it as a cause of global

warming, even giving themselves raises or giving money to organizations that contribute to their elections.

Climate change is just another scam to redistribute wealth and power from supporters of capitalism and their power to leftists who will support the socialist government. Climate change is a hoax, falsely propped up as fact, scientifically unverified, and merely an excuse to tax the wealthy and redistribute their wealth. For socialists, climate change is only a tool to institute socialism in the United States. The major polluters of the world, China and India, will not participate in throwing money into climate change programs. These two countries will expect ignorant politicians like Alexandria Ocasio-Cortez to alarm Americans and urge them to pay control the problem. The UN and the EU will desire that Americans put up most of the money as well.

Millennials and Climate Change

Millennials don't have a clue as to why socialist politicians want climate change to be a hot issue; it is to institute socialism and control, enable self-enrichment, and ensure they will stay in power. Young millennials don't realize they are being used as pawns by socialists and being sheared like sheep, as the naive victims they are. Liberal teachers also teach—and urge—naive millennials to "go out and protest" so they can make their feelings known to the press and to the world! Teens are double-sheared as sheep to advance the agenda of socialism. Were these bamboozled teens told how much climate change policies would cost taxpayers? Do they realize who will pay for climate change programs and what it will do to our US economy? Do these teens understand that corrupt socialists will enrich themselves? Check out Vladimir Putin in communist Russia. Why is he a multibillionaire? How about tyrant Nicolás Maduro of Venezuela? Why is he a billionaire? Worse, these millennials don't know if the United States spends trillions of dollars on climate change programs. China, Russia, and India, the worst polluters, will continue to pollute the earth, and the actions of the United States and the EU will have an insignificant effect on climate change.

AOC Predicts the End of the World by 2031

Socialist Alexandria Ocasio-Cortez says the end of the world is coming in 2031. Does she have any scientific facts to support this idea? She doesn't say how it will happen, what funding is required to control it, who will provide the funding, or if the United States will be the only nonpolluter in the world. Nor does she say how to make China, India, and other major polluting nations comply with her Green New Deal, before the world ends. Currently Biden plans a $3 trillion Infrastructure tax plan, loaded with pork, where part of it is for climate change.

26

GUN CONTROL AND CONFISCATION

As Democrats Move Closer to Socialism, the More They Want to Restrict or Ban Guns

Ronald Reagan is quoted as having said, "The gun has been called the great equalizer, meaning that a small person with a gun is equal to a large person, but it is a great equalizer in another way too. It ensures that the people are equal of their government whenever that government forgets that it is servant and not master of the governed."

FIGURE 1. Famous quotation by former president Ronald Reagan on the Second Amendment

Very well said. All Democrats, especially socialist members of the Democratic Party, want to take guns away from law-abiding Americans. Why? To tax-oppress the rich so they can fund their multitrillion-dollar spending plans. Socialists want to pass laws to confiscate the wealth of rich Americans, whom they hate, and the wealth of the middle class. Tax-oppressive laws cannot be enforced unless the government starts arresting people for tax evasion and confiscating homes from middle-class Americans, which will lead to a revolution. Democrats know this, so they, like Venezuela's politicians, need to take our guns to remain in power.

Freedom-loving Americans will not stand for tyranny and will not give up their guns. It's a choice between two things. The first is giving your wealth to a socialist government that knows better than you how to spend it and, as a result, being driven into poverty or homelessness. The other choice is to fight tyranny in an armed revolution—that's my choice.

Note that Venezuela was once a wealthy country until corrupt socialists took over the government and the citizenry surrendered all their weapons to the government. Now the socialist government has confiscated the wealth and the citizenry is starving. Why, in once-prosperous Venezuela, are citizens now eating cats to survive?[1]

Gun Restrictions and Confiscation Policies, and Socialist Goals

"Happiness is a warm gun," sang the Beatles, but Democrats are singing registration, then confiscation, of your guns. A firearm registration bill was introduced in the Pennsylvania Legislature on March 8, 2019.

Safety is the argument of antigun activists, but their claim of control is a means to their end goal of a gun-free society. This progressive policy

---

[1] Nandita Singh, "Why, in Once-Prosperous Venezuela, Its Citizens Are Now Eating Cats to Survive," the Print, dated January 29, 2019, https://theprint.in/theprint-essential/why-in-once-prosperous-venezuela-its-citizens-are-now-eating-cats-to-survive/184470/.

can be implemented only if there are compliant citizens. But political opponents, the "deniers," must be eliminated by way of social shaming or civil and criminal penalties. There are historical lessons of totalitarian governments that are free to rule because citizens have been deprived of weapons.

In *Nazi Firearms Law and the Disarming of the German Jews*, Stephen P. Halbrook observes as follows:

> The record establishes that a well-meaning liberal republic would enact a gun control act that would later be highly useful to a dictatorship. That dictatorship could then consolidate its power by massive search and seizure operations against political opponents, under the hysterical ruse that such persons were "Communist" firearm owners.

> It could enact its own new firearms law, disarming anyone the police deemed "dangerous" and exempting members of the party that controlled the state. It could exploit a tragic shooting of a government official to launch a pogrom, under the guise that Jewish firearm owners were dangerous and must be disarmed. ... This dictatorship could, generally, disarm the people of the nation it governed and then disarm those of every nation it conquered.[2]

The Fundamental Rights of US Citizens

"A well-regulated militia, being necessary to the security of a free state, the right of the people to keep and bear arms, shall not be infringed." This text is straight from the wording of the Second Amendment to the US Constitution.

---

[2] Stephen P. Halbrook, *Nazi Firearms Law and the Disarming of German Jews*, StephenHalbrook.com, https://www.stephenhalbrook.com/article-nazilaw.pdf, 536.

"In the 2008 case *District of Columbia v. Heller*, the Supreme Court held that the 'Second Amendment protects an individual right to possess a firearm unconnected with service in a militia, and to use that arm for traditionally lawful purposes, such as self-defense within the home.'"[3]

"The above experiences influenced perceptions of fundamental rights in both the United States and Germany," Stephen Halbrook explains. "Before entering the war, America reacted to the events in Europe in a characteristic manner. Seeing the Nazi threat and its policies, Congress passed the Property Requisition Act of 1941 authorizing the President to requisition certain property for defense, but prohibiting any construction of the act to 'require the registration of any firearms possessed by any individual for his personal protection or sport' or 'to impair or infringe in any manner the right of any individual to keep and bear arms.'"[4]

"Remember that registration of firearms is only the first step," stated the sponsor of the Requisition Act, Rep. Paul Kilday (D-TX). "It will be followed by other infringements of the right to keep and bear arms until finally the right is gone."[5]

Restrictive State Gun Laws

A secret Nazi Gestapo Order (1941) is compared to Pennsylvania's firearm registration bill (2019) in this side-by-side chart. Source: A pdf e-book entitled, NAZI FIREARMS LAW AND THE DISARMING OF THE GERMAN JEWS, by Stephen P. Halbrook taken from, Arizona Journal of International and Comparative Law, No. 3, 483-535 (2000), copyright 2000. Page 534 contains the chart cited. Before the chart are the words,

> *"...a secret Gestapo order in 1941 established a system of central registration of persons obtaining firearms other than*

---

[3] Legal Information Institute of the Cornell Law School.
[4] Halbrook, *Nazi Firearms Law and the Disarming of German Jews*, 536–37.
[5] Ibid., 537, fn. 289.

*military officers, police, and political leaders. An implementing
directive stated:"*

The website is: https://www.stephenhalbrook.com/article-nazilaw.
pdf, page 534.

Pennsylvania's bill has more requirements than the Nazis' order. In
Pennsylvania, if the bill becomes law, a gun owner will be required to
provide more information than a person who registers to vote.

For the right of self-defense, a person would be required annually to
self-report ownership of each gun and describe it in detail. A certificate
or renewal is not guaranteed, because the state police could deny the
application. Partisan bureaucrats may not appreciate an applicant's
conservative politics: allegiance to the Bill of Rights and limited
government. Far-fetched? Just ask Tea Party organizations who were
delayed or denied nonprofit status by the IRS under Barack Obama.

The state police database could be released for official or nefarious
purposes. The Pennsylvania Legislature may operate under the guise
of oversight.

Antigun zealots could dox persons who own guns. The names of
New York's permit holders for concealed weapons were posted via a
map on the internet. A multistate map was proposed. Liberal news
agencies and the social media mob have harassed law-abiding private
citizens. Identification of gun owners is not likely to deter criminals,
who may have a shopping list for gun collections.

An enemy could learn that you own a gun. A related "red flag"
law may be used for a fraudulent claim against you. The police will
confiscate your gun pending a court hearing. Meanwhile, an enemy
has an opportunity to cause injury to you or murder you.

Law-abiding citizens' registration of guns will not prevent criminals
from obtaining unregistered guns. No lives will be saved. Note the bill's
absence of "whereas" clauses of findings of facts to support unidentified
benefits. Also note the absence of redeeming press releases of the bill
being introduced by Democrats Angel Cruz, Mary Jo Daley, and Mary
Louise Isaacson; and Democrat cosponsors Joseph C. Hohenstein,
Joanna E. McClinton, and Benjamin V. Sanchez. The bill failed in
2009–10, 2011–12, 2013–14, 2015–16, and 2017–18.

This proposed law could be enforced only if the government is aware that you own a gun. Will the police conduct a search for guns, literally door to door?

If you are forced to use a gun for self-defense but fail to comply with registration rules, could your defense effectively be an infringement of the Fifth Amendment? Fail to register a gun, then risk a criminal penalty of ninety days in jail. The government likely will confiscate your gun; you likely will not be eligible to possess another gun; and you likely will be limited to lesser forms of self-defense.

Gun registries will lead to gun confiscation, as illustrated by Australia, Canada, and Germany, as well as the United States, including in California, Illinois, and the heart of liberalism, New York City.

National gun confiscation has been proposed by liberals including Rep. Eric Swalwell (D-CA; 2018); the NAACP (2018); and Hillary Clinton, presidential candidate (2016). Liberals want a total ban on firearms.

Speaker of the House Nancy Pelosi suggested that a Democratic president could declare gun violence as a national emergency.

Conclusion

Have we not learned the lesson of the Nazi policy to disarm its citizens and then control them? Nazi gun laws facilitated the murder of political enemies, specifically, the Holocaust, where more than six million Jews were murdered.

What part of the Second Amendment's independent status, "shall not be infringed," did these legislators, some of them attorneys, not understand? The US Constitution trumps a state statute.

Liberals ignore constitutional law in favor of an agenda of a gun-free society. Liberals use safety as a ploy for gun registration, leading to confiscation of guns.

The wisdom of our founding fathers was clear: The Second Amendment is a guard against tyranny, whether the enemy is foreign or domestic.

If They Can Take Your Guns, They Can Take Your Other Freedoms

Every combat veteran knows where all his or her guns are 24-7. If you don't have a plan in case of a home invasion or a potentially deadly crime about to happen, lives could be at stake. To avoid legal trouble, know the laws on the use of deadly force thoroughly before shooting someone. Always hide guns from children, in places where they won't find them, because they tend to play with them as toys.

Know that if the government wants your guns or plans to restrict the kind of guns you may have as a law-abiding citizen, then it is preparing to destroy more of your freedoms in the near future, and it doesn't want freedom-loving people to rise up against it with weapons.

Why Freedom-Loving Americans Need Guns

As in Venezuela, tyranny brings crime in the streets, fights for food, home invasions, lack of food and starvation, lack of medical care, riots, refugees fleeing the country, unjust imprisonment, illegal entry into private homes, taking control of your food, home, and transportation for government use, and the theft of your wealth. These are important reasons why we need both guns and brave men and women to use them—to fight against tyranny.

Socialists may use UN security forces as authorized by an Obama executive order to put down conservative rebellions of people whom the government is oppressing in many ways: taking their wealth, taking their property, imprisoning them, killing them, surveilling them, starving them, and disarming all people to make the United States into a Venezuela.

We Must Fight to Keep Our Guns to Deter Tyranny

Conservatives must prevent a shift in their wealth and power to leftist supporters of socialist tyranny.

We law-abiding Americans must keep our guns and be able to purchase guns whenever we want. We don't need the untrustworthy, dishonest, arrogant socialists in the Democratic Party telling us otherwise. Their reason for taking our guns is that Democrats want to confiscate the wealth of all hardworking Americans through taxation oppression, and with guns, taken away, law-abiding Americans will lose their power – wealth and power will have been transferred to the Democrat elites. Democrats anticipate violent opposition from conservatives, which could lead to a revolution. We must prevent the United States from ever becoming a socialist country, and we must fight to keep our guns. We must prevent a redistribution of our wealth to leftist causes and keep our power to defend against tyranny and the excessive control of our lives.

Never give up your guns. After a bill to confiscate semi-automatic weapons of law-abiding citizens is passed, and before government agents come to your home to confiscate your weapons, that is the time for an armed revolution against tyranny. Law-abiding Americans must never be oppressed like the defenseless citizens of Venezuela who have no guns to fight their tyrannical government with, and end up starving or eating dog and cats for food. The only ones who will eat well will be the tyrannical socialists in power. Hollywood leftists will continue to support the socialist tyrants in power and make ~~violent~~ negative propaganda movies against conservatives and Christians. The fake news media will slander all Christians and conservatives.

Gun Ownership: The Right to Self-Defense

Police officers tell victims that they have a right to defend themselves against gang members and other criminals using a gun, but only in self-defense because the shooting incident may end up in court. Not only will law-abiding police officers refuse to enforce any laws that are unconstitutional regardless of being told to do so by liberal city mayors and city administrators, but also many of them will resign if commanded to enforce unconstitutional laws. Many will also file lawsuits against the city. Officers fired or resigning will be replaced by people who are not patriotic and know little or nothing about the Constitution. That would mean the hiring of illegal aliens or foreigners given amnesty who will do what liberal political tyrants want. Hiring foreigners as police officers and accepting leftists and foreigners into the military will be one major way for a tyrannical government to get its laws enforced and put down any conservative rebellions. Who are the rebels opposing tyranny? They are as follows:

- patriotic active or former police officers
- patriotic active military personnel or veterans
- conservative families
- Christians
- all freedom-loving Americans.

To enforce tyranny, tyrants in power need to build their military and gestapo police agencies before they pass any law to abolish the Second Amendment.

Democrats use poor excuses to ban guns, leaving law-abiding Americans defenseless against gangs or home intruders and, especially, against a powerful socialist tyrannical government that oppresses them. Liberal fools should ask questions as to why millennials turn into mass killers. If criminals don't use guns, they will use cars to plow into crowds, use homemade bombs to blow up crowds, and so on. The problem is in the mind of the psycho. Psychologists, sociologists, law enforcement, and parents should have a conversation about the root cause of troubled millennials who have turned into cold-blooded killers.

How a Potential Secession of States and Bloody
Civil War Might Be Prevented

In 2022, if Republicans take the majority in the House, they may avoid a secession of states leading to an armed revolution against increasing tyranny from the Biden Administration, a Democrat-ruled Congress, and a leftist-led US Supreme Court. If Republicans take the majority in the House, further Democrat laws designed to consolidate their power forever may be stopped. Then it will be possible to avoid or delay a secession of states, since Democrats will still control the Senate and White House. However, if the economy collapses and enters into a recession or depression, Democrats will become very unpopular for their policies ruining the economy, and voters will have an opportunity to elect a conservative who can restore the economy. In general, Republicans now have to figure out how to:

1. Prevent corrupt Democrats from repeating the election fraud of 2020 from happening in all future elections.
2. Prevent H.R.1 from being passed
3. Prevent the Democrats from eliminating the filibuster in the Senate
4. Challenge Joe Biden in US courts for giving amnesty to millions of illegal aliens so they can vote Democrat and together with leftists, win all future elections
5. Prevent Washington DC from becoming a state (more Democrats in Congress)
6. Prevent Puerto Rico from becoming a state (more Democrats in Congress)
7. Prevent Joe Biden from packing the US Supreme Court
8. Prevent Congress from eliminating the electoral college
9. Start an impeachment on Joe Biden charging him with aiding and abetting illegal aliens to cross the border causing a crisis and ignoring and denying the crisis he caused with his dictatorial executive orders
10. Start an impeachment process to remove Christopher Wray for:
    a. failure to investigate the 2020 election fraud in a timely manner with no current results
    b. failure to conclude an investigation of Hunter Biden and Joe Biden for their Ukraine and China scandals
11. Snatch John Durham from the closet he is hiding in and get a status on his investigation of the origins of Russian collusion. He must be fired if he has no results to hold anyone accountable.

All border states should sue the Federal government for allowing hundreds of thousands of illegal aliens into the country and stopping border wall construction to keep America safe and to enforce immigration laws. All illegal aliens should be deported by law. All illegal aliens should be tested for COVID. Whosoever tests positive, should not be allowed transport into American communities. Border states should not bear the financial burden of caring for illegal aliens when it's the Democrats in Washington DC who are aiding and abetting their entry.

If President Trump runs in 2024, or another Reagan-style Republican runs for president, there is no chance any Republican will win the presidential election if the following occur:

1. Biden gives amnesty to millions of illegal aliens, who will vote Democrat, and with current leftists, will always win future elections over conservatives

2. Democrats stole the 2020 election once; they can do it again in 2024 with little or no opposition, and the Supreme Court again will refuse to hear election fraud cases

3. H.R.1 passes; elections will be rigged and no conservative president can ever be elected

4. Even if Democrats agree to require mail-in ballots to be properly signed with proper ID, to be submitted on-time to be counted, and all ballot counters are required to be observed, a GOP win will not be possible if Biden grants amnesty to millions of illegal aliens who will, as a result, be allowed to vote. The overwhelming majority of amnesty aliens will vote Democrat.

5. Biden packs the US Supreme Court and all Democrat legislation will pass unopposed

6. Democrats may eliminate the electoral college and always win votes with mob rules from the most populated blue states.

Every one of these six obstacles must be overcome for conservatives to win another presidential election. The GOP must challenge Item# 1 all the way to the Supreme Court. If they cannot be overcome, tyranny and loss of freedoms will increase and the only solution will be secession of states and an armed revolution against tyrants in Washington DC and states that support them.

PART 6
TYRANNY IN THE UNITED STATES: THE COMING SECOND AND THIRD US CIVIL WARS

27

HOW SOCIALISM BECOMES TYRANNY IN THE UNITED STATES

Irreversible Election Wins and No Checks and Balances Leads to Tyrannical Leftist Policies

A fraudulent election resulted in a win for Joe Biden as president, as well as a majority win and control of both houses of Congress. This means:

1. There will likely be no checks and balances between the branches of government.
2. If Democrats can commit election fraud once, they can commit it again in all future elections.
3. The US Supreme Court refused to hear 2020 election fraud cases; they have gone to support the dark side (the nefarious Democrats)
4. Congress can pass election laws to win all future elections.
5. Congress can allow Washington, DC, and Puerto Rico to become states to increase the number of Democratic senators.
6. Congress can give amnesty to tens of millions of immigrants to win all future elections; this alone will ensure that Democratic election wins in the future are irreversible.

7. If the Biden administration packs the Supreme Court, all laws passed by a Democrat-controlled Congress, tyrannical or not, will likely be upheld by the Supreme Court.
8. Creeping socialism begins as leftist policies are implemented to social engineer US culture and US institutions.
9. If H.R.1 becomes law, elections will be rigged and no conservative can be elected
10. More confiscation of wealth and shifts in power away from conservatives will increasingly weaken conservatives

Human needs, human rights, soaring immigration, the Democrats' greed for power and control, indoctrination of kids in public schools, the cancel culture crowd seeking to "deprogram" seventy-five million Trump voters, assertions of systemic racism in the United States, and our declining values and morals, is shifting conservative power toward socialism. As creeping socialism in the United States begins, customs and traditions will change. Social government as its laws are passed unopposed, policies implemented, and laws enforced on a persistently freedom-loving Americans. The cancel culture fears Trump supporters and their resurgence and control. That is why Democratic politicians are continuing to target conservatives, harassing them, doxing them, having them fired from jobs, urging businesses not to hire them, stifling/blocking their voices, and rigging elections so "Trump cultists" never win elections. Catholic doctrine conflicts with the false god of socialism; the Bible considers abortion and homosexuality as sins. The Democratic cancel culture will stifle religious voices and replace biblical morality on abortion and homosexuality with political morality.

An example of cancel culture: The Nazis called Jesus Christ an Aryan, but today, the Black Lives Matter cancel culture claims Jesus Christ was a black man, and calls for removal or vandalism of statues of a white Jesus Christ. A reporter from corrupt CNN called for the reprogramming of seventy-five million Trump voters; this is essentially urging a war perpetrated by the Left against Trump voters for believing in American greatness and for putting America first.

The leftist government grows stronger as it achieves leftist policy milestones over time and increases its power and control over its citizens, practically unopposed by any other political party. The Biden administration will shift power to the left by doing the following:

1. divide and label Trump supporters as racists, white supremacists, cultists, and capitalist oppressors;
2. control and utilize the media to publish or broadcast false propaganda to sway public opinion
3. indoctrinate youth in public schools, colleges, and universities about slavery, white privilege, and systemic racism, and educating them on protesting against white supremacists;
4. change election laws to stay in power forever;
5. stop deportations and grant amnesty to millions of DACA members for future votes;
6. stifle conservative speech and religious freedoms, and block conservative posts on social media;
7. offer trillions of dollars in government reparations to blacks whose ancestors were historically oppressed victims of slavery and Jim Crow laws;
8. heavily suppress or ban the Second Amendment to the Constitution;
9. increase the Democrats' power and control over time;
10. confiscate wealth through taxation oppression and distribute that wealth to strengthen the power and control of Democrats and their cronies
11. take eventual control of corporations and industry, including the means of production and manufacturing and the distribution of goods.

As a goal, leftist Democrats seek reforms of culture and institutions and a transformation of today's Federal government into a socialist-style government in America. To accomplish this, Democrats need to successfully pass laws and executive orders that will perpetually keep them in power forever.

Joe Biden Administration Executive Orders

As aforementioned, Joe Biden has signed off on at least thirty-seven executive orders; the first eighteen follow:

1. mandating use of masks and social distancing in federal buildings and on federal lands, and for government contractors, only urging states to do the same;
2. rejoining the World Health Organization (WHO) and pledging to donate millions of dollars to it;
3. granting amnesty to DACA illegal aliens once brought in as children or teenagers, most of whom are now adults;
4. including illegal aliens in the census counts to bolster Democratic representation in Congress in states with a hefty population of noncitizens;
5. ending the Muslim ban from known terrorist countries and allowing visas for Muslim immigrants;
6. halting the building of the wall along the southern border;
7. reentering the Paris climate accord and donating millions of dollars toward climate change efforts so as to move away from fossil fuels;
8. According to Breitbart, canceling the Keystone XL Pipeline project, cancelling building of the southern wall, and suspending oil and gas permits on federal land, costing an estimated 70,000 jobs. (this means the United States will no longer be energy independent; Saudi Arabia will become rich and will become the petroleum energy leader from selling oil because of Biden's executive order); Source: An article in Breitbart entitled, "Pollak: Biden Kills Up to 70,000 Jobs on First Day in Office", by Joel B. Pollak, dated 01/22/2021 at website: https://www.breitbart.com/economy/2021/01/22/pollak-biden-kills-up-to-70000-jobs-on-first-day-in-office-job/
9. reversing vehicle emission standards;
10. enforcing a temporary moratorium on oil and natural gas leases in the Arctic National Wildlife Refuge;

11. reversing Donald Trump's limits on having federal agencies, contractors, and institutions hold diversity and inclusion training;
12. increasing funds to maintain national monuments;
13. ending systemic racism and LGBT discrimination where the federal government may be involved with institutions, and assessing punishment for violations (Will the Catholic Church lose its tax-exempt status because it does not permit same-sex marriage or refuses to hire homosexuals to lead youth programs? Remember what happened to the Boy Scouts of America);
14. delaying student loan payments;
15. requiring White House staff to sign an ethics pledge;
16. provided billions of dollars to states suffering economically because of COVID-19 (which means California, Illinois, New York, and other badly mismanaged states **received** a bailout from taxpayers);
17. delaying evictions and foreclosures of federal mortgages on account of the pandemic; and
18. mandating prompt production and availability of COVID-19 vaccines and tests for distribution.

On this last point, note that President Trump made vaccines possible with his tireless negotiations with biotechnology companies, but the corrupt fake news media smeared him for inaction and blamed him for the pandemic. Now most Americans are desperate to get vaccinated. Democrat-run states such as California and New York are begging for enough vaccines to be distributed to their states.

The $1.9 billion COVID relief bill had little to do with COVID health relief but had more to do to bail out mismanaged states run by Democrats. Biden's executive orders raised taxes on hard-working middle class families and on corporations that will pass their tax losses to their consumers. The Biden Administration is still planning on raising taxes even higher to pay for infrastructure, climate change, and more "equity" spending. Biden killed about 70,000 jobs with his Federal action against oil and gas production, thus causing oil companies to raise prices on gasoline for the rich to the very poor; who do you think will suffer the worse economically? Answer: the hard-working taxpayer and the poorest people.

Raising more taxes will divert taxpayer funds to enrich Democratic politicians, increase their power, benefit primarily Democrat-run states, their lobbyists and leftist contract organizations, as in Barack Obama's crony capitalist administration.

An executive order and Congressional legislation on strict gun control are planned that will create much controversy and opposition from millions of law-abiding people. Leftists are currently indoctrinating law enforcement and the military to curb racism and white extremism in their ranks. Executive Order 13 will punish any police agency that is systemically racist in treatment of nonwhite suspects.

Democrats will fund the leftist-sponsored fake news media to manufacture favorable propaganda to prop up socialist elites and their great policies and speeches 24-7, and to manufacture hateful negative propaganda against the seventy-five million Trump supporters 24-7. House leaders and Senate leaders, including some traitor Republicans, tried to impeach Donald Trump again even though he already had left office, so that he could never run for president again—this is how much vindictiveness and fear Democrats have toward this powerful man. Fearful Socialist politicians and the propaganda news media will push lies and deception against "Trump cultists" because they pose a threat to the ruling Democratic elites.

Americans will be forced to comply with increasing tyrannical laws passed over time. Socialists will tax the middle class and the wealthy in order to use their money to care for the massive number of illegal aliens entering the United States. Open borders will attract caravans of foreigners into the United States, people seeking to get their fair share of government handouts and the other bones thrown at them by socialist politicians. Throughout history, only the socialist elites and their supporters have prospered by the confiscation of the wealth from large businesses, the rich, and the sheep they have exploited.

Democrats did not change the hearts and minds of Americans, they stole the 2020 election and they will likely steal future elections, unless a fraud-free voting system is designed. According to election machines,

Democrats won, and a peaceful transition of power occurred under a never before seen heightened level of armed police and military security.

The Democratic Party Has Already Declared Civil War on Trump Voters

Joe Biden's call for unity, plastered in the media during his inauguration and in the following days, was a call for Trump voters to join with the radical agenda of the leftist Democratic Party and reform the United States together, as in the days of Barack Obama's "Hope and Change" campaign message. House Democrat Mike Doyle (D-PA) was quoted as saying, "Now we're in charge, and maybe some of them [i.e., Trump-supporting Republicans] don't understand that yet."[1]

Democrats have no interest in collaborating on legislation with Republicans. The message is essentially, "We're the boss, you're the sheep. Get the hell out of our way." This is not unity. The transition of wealth and power from conservatives to leftists has begun.

Biden's unity is essentially a call for seventy-five million Trump voters to surrender to the socialist policies of the Left like sheep. Biden's unity is for the Democratic Party to bully Trump voters, not to unite the country. Nancy Pelosi created articles of impeachment against President Trump a week before he left office, to pass to the Senate, where the articles of impeachment were argued and a vote was taken to dismiss the articles or to remove Trump from office, even though Trump had already left office on January 20, 2021. This vindictive, spiteful ill will of Nancy Pelosi was only political theater. If two-thirds of the Senate had voted to impeach former president Trump, it also would have decided whether Donald Trump could run for president again. All Democrats feared Trump will would run again and win, which is why they were hoping the Senate would vote to disallow him from running for president again. This is another example of vindictiveness and hate violating Biden's farce call for unity.

[1] Melanie Zanona and Sarah Ferris, "Now We're in Charge: Dems Freeze Out GOP on Bipartisan Bills," Politico, March 25, 2019, https://www.politico.com/story/2019/03/25/congress-bipartisan-bills-1230293.

Another example showing that Biden's unity is a farce is Alexandria Ocasio-Cortez's comment on social media: "If you don't like the Green New Deal, then come up with your own ambitious, on-scale proposal to address the global climate crisis. Until then, we're in charge—and you're just shouting from the cheap seats."

Worse, the Left's vile hatred of Trump voters has been echoed by journalists in the corrupt Democratic propaganda fake news media, who pushed the need to reprogram seventy-five million Trump voters, saying they should be:

- fired from their jobs
- prevented from getting employment
- blocked, censored, or removed from social media websites
- reeducated in reeducation camps

The leftist news propaganda is designed to divide the United States and conquer conservatives. President Biden, other Democratic politicians, the corrupt news media, Wall Street, and high-tech corporations have joined together in unity to declare a nonviolent civil war on Trump voters and to incite more division with their spiteful ill will, vindictiveness, and disrespect. Democrats claim they are in charge now, so Trump supporters must become their sheep and their thoughts need to be "reprogrammed" in a United States that is supposed to think freely. The Democrats could care less about the First Amendment.

Since the 2016 election, Democrats have resorted to corrupt tactics and crime to win elections. Former president Barack Obama weaponized the agencies in his administration to spy on candidate Donald Trump in hopes of having him removed him from office and thereby rig the election for Democratic candidate Hillary Clinton. Obama's White House was also involved in monitoring the conversations of Donald Trump and his staff, and his family, with foreign leaders to see if any crimes were committed, in hopes of invalidating his election if he should win. Obama made use of federal agencies, included the DOJ, FBI, and CIA; his White House staff; UN Ambassador Susan Rice; and members of the State Department to try to achieve this end. Corrupt candidate Hillary Clinton even paid millions of dollars for a phony Russian dossier full of misinformation from Christopher Steele, a former UK intelligence officer, so she could leak it to the Democratic propaganda media to use to slander and embarrass candidate Donald Trump. It was hoped that US citizens would believe the lies and vote for Hillary Clinton—it was a news media war she conducted with the help of the DNC and John McCain, a phony Republican who helped her obtain a copy of the Russian dossier, distributed it to members of Congress and to leaders of the CIA, DOJ, FBI, and other agencies, then leaked it to the fake news media. When Democrats can't change the hearts and minds of their citizenry, they rig and/or steal elections, manufacture trash **news** to smear their opponent, and change election laws to win elections and obtain power.

Even after candidate Trump won the 2016 election, leaders of Obama's weaponized agencies continued to spy on Trump to try to invalidate his presidency to remove him from office. These agency leaders were labeled as a cabal known as the "Deep State," who targeted President Trump for at least three years into his presidency. Foreign intelligence agencies from Australia, Italy, and the UK were used to continue to spy on Donald Trump and his staff members, such as Carter Page, General Flynn, Roger Stone, Paul Manafort, George Papadopoulos, and Donald Trump Jr. The following personnel are the targets of John Durham's investigation:

FBI	James Comey, Peter Strzok, Lisa Page, and Andrew McCabe
CIA	John Brennan
Office of the Director of National Intelligence	James Clapper
DOJ	Loretta Lynch, Rod Rosenstein
Obama White House staff	Valerie Jarrett
Others	Sally Yates, Susan Rice, and Bruce Ohr and his wife
Members of Congress	Adam Schiff

Some references as to who is being investigated by John Durham can be found in the article "35 Key People Involved in the Russia Hoax

Who Need to Be Investigated," by Willis L. Krumholz.[2] Unfortunately, as of March 2021, John Durham appears to be hiding in some closet, as no one has heard from the man and his investigations.

Another strategy Democrats use to attain power is to manufacture hoaxes to impeach a president and remove him from office. President Trump was very much feared by Democrats in the House. As president, he brought the US economy to a record high level of prosperity, achieved never before trade deals with China, reformed NATO funding, continued building a wall along the US-Mexican border, and negotiated peace in the Middle East, for which he was nominated for a Nobel Peace Prize. Trump drew tens of thousands of supporters to every campaign rally he had. No wonder Jerry Nadler and Adam Schiff, under the direction and approval of Speaker Nancy Pelosi, tried to impeach Donald Trump after the 2016 election for Russian collusion. The Mueller investigation lasted almost two years (twenty-two months) and ended with no evidence of Russian collusion, which was a terrible disappointment to the Democratic progressives and socialists. Another possible reason why President Trump was impeached is that he suspected that Joe Biden and his son Hunter were involved in corrupt deals and money laundering with the Ukraine and in pay-to-play corruption deals with China. House Democrats wanted to suppress that investigation and prevent Trump from asking more questions about Biden's corrupt activity with the leaders of the Ukraine.

More hoaxes to remove President Trump from office were hatched by House Democrats such as Adam Schiff, Jerry Nadler, Alexandria Ocasio-Cortez, Maxine Waters, Al Green, and Rashida Tlaib. The Ukraine scandal was also tried and failed. The tactic backfired on the Democrats because it exposed a scandal committed by Democratic president Joe Biden and his son involving quid pro quo deals Joe Biden had forced on Ukraine officials when he was Obama's vice president. Money laundering was also involved. Trump was acquitted of all impeachment charges by the Senate. This was another failure of Pelosi's corrupt House Democrats.

---

[2] Willis L. Krumholz, "35 Key People Involved in the Russia Hoax Who Need to Be Investigated," the Federalist, March 8, 2019, https://thefederalist. com/2019/03/08/35-key-people-involved-russia-hoax-need-investigated/.

After three and a half years of trying to remove President Trump from office, Nancy Pelosi, Adam Schiff, and other House Democrats accused him of causing the deaths of Americans for not doing enough to contain the COVID-19 pandemic originating from China. The Democratic fake news media parroted the Democrats. Some of the despicable fake news media even accused President Trump of causing the COVID-19 pandemic. Nancy Pelosi and other House members and the hate-Trump media accused President Trump of being a racist when he disallowed travel from China into the United States while he was being impeached in January 2020. Using Operation Warp Speed, President Trump negotiated with US biotechnology companies to develop COVID-19 vaccines, which had already been given to various groups in December 2020, to the surprise of Democrats. In 2021, millions of Americans are eagerly waiting for enough vaccines so they can get vaccinated. The major conclusion that can be reached from President Trump's first term in office is that Democrats *do not* change the hearts and minds of Americans to win their votes, but rather, these greedy, vicious, corrupt, and dishonest politicians coordinate well to commit election fraud to win elections, disregarding honor, respect, and integrity, and angering more than seventy-five million people who have common sense and goodwill.

Socialists win support of some Americans with the aid of false propaganda from the fake news media by misinforming viewers and bashing Trump voters, causing widespread disunity. Democrats will win the support of millions of illegal aliens by them with free government assistance and amnesty. Democrats have used the race card to an extreme, attempting to cause widespread division and animosity between the white and black races. The race card is used to rile up blacks based on the United States' racist past, and to blame white people's ancestors in the United States for historical oppression.

Democrats also use the capitalist oppressor card to victimize people with low incomes and to indoctrinate young people to hate capitalist, racist America. Democrats have increased the suffering and poverty of business owners by lockdown mandates, preventing them from conducting business to make a living because of COVID-19. Democrats say that the unfair amassing of wealth of rich white oppressors is done at the expense of low-paid workers, and Democrats express the hope that these oppressed victims will rise in numbers to elect socialists, who will take wealth from oppressors and redistribute it to the oppressed classes. The problem with some of the socialists selling this theory of victim–oppressor is that they are hypocrite multimillionaires who made their fortunes under capitalism. This includes Bernie Sanders, Warren Buffett, and Elizabeth Warren. Even leftist Barack Obama, who was mentored by a communist (Frank Marshall David), is a multimillionaire who amassed his wealth under capitalism.

President Trump was expected to win the 2020 election by a landslide but lost by election fraud. So far, nothing has been done by either Democrats or Republicans to make election computers fraud-proof in all states. No reforms have been proposed to prevent corrupt ballot counters, corrupt election officials, and corrupt state politicians, uniformly in all states, from engaging in corrupt practices to win elections.

Divide/Label Black Americans as Victims of Racism and Economic Oppression

Under creeping socialism in the United States, socialists must create class conflict to divide and label Americans into groups, namely, oppressors and victims. The Left makes up names for allegedly hated and oppressed groups of victims so leftists can use these words as labels to revile anyone who stands against the oppressed underdog victims of the United States. Words benefit socialists as war tools to accuse conservatives of intolerance, racism, inhumanity, immorality, white supremacy, white nationalism, white privilege, Islamophobia, homophobia, toxic masculinity, sexism, a sense of being above the law, and a desire to wage a war on women. Such labels place Trump voters into oppressive-type groups the Left uses to bash and revile, and divide and destroy the opposition. Leftist politicians use these words and phrases, not only to win votes from the oppressed, but also to win the support of gullible people for reforming our culture, destroying the status quo, destroying conservative values, stifling the Christian religion, delegitimizing patriotism, and defiling the country in its present form. It's a nonviolent civil war waged against conservatives. When was the last time anyone heard of Democrats embracing patriotism and the greatness of the United States?

The fake news media is already using these new words and phrases invented by Democratic politicians and the media itself to label groups and to revile and slander anyone whom they define as a "Trump cult supporter" who stands against the poor, oppressed victims of the United States. Using these hate-speech tools, socialists will silence conservative expression and conservative speech and destroy the reputation of conservative candidates running for high government positions. Liberal high-tech companies have already silenced conservative thought and expression on their social media websites.

Open Borders Will Increase the Size of the Democratic Party's Voter Base

What if the number of oppressed victims in the United States were to be significantly reduced? What if blacks began escaping the Democratic plantation of welfare, food stamps, and other handouts in favor of getting an education and a good-paying job and becoming prosperous? What if there were more jobs than could be filled and opportunities galore in the United States? That would destroy the victim–oppressor class-conflict theory of socialist economics. So, what do socialists do? Answer: They remake the United States with a massive influx of illegal immigration to seed the country with future amnesty migrants to join with Democrats.

Biden has already welcomed millions of illegal aliens from all over the world to enter the United States illegally; hundreds of thousands have already crossed the southern border and it has resulted in a massive border crisis that the Democrats are unable to resolve without massive taxpayer expenditures. This is equivalent of the Biden Administration paying illegal aliens to come to the US free of charge. It's a Democratic scheme designed to increase the political power of socialists at some future time in the United States, when the migrant population, together with the progressive and socialist citizens, will outnumber conservative voters to elect a Democratic socialist president and elect leftists in both houses of Congress. Democrats need to import migrants to win all future elections. Without immigration reform including open borders, Democrats will have to rig and steal elections, or impeach a conservative president, and use the fake news media as a war machine to slander, defame, and smear conservatives, their families, and their policies.

The Hypocritical Socialist Strategy to Exploit Illegal Aliens

Crying Schumer and **fake news reporter** Rachel were seen on TV crying and pretending to care about illegal aliens being separated from their families at the border. Ocasio Cortez complained immigrants were ~~and~~ drinking water from toilets. The fact is that illegal aliens are being exploited by Democrats to attain future votes and cheap labor. Illegal aliens are only future investments to Democrats; Democrats never cared about illegal aliens and open borders before Donald Trump became president. It was former president Barack Obama who put children in cages at the border before deporting them. Why then blame Trump? He inherited the problem from the arrogant con artist. Anti-immigration speeches were recorded and shown on TV, airing remarks/speeches made by Bill Clinton, Chuck Schumer, Hillary Clinton, and other politicians who did not want immigrants coming into the United States illegally. But when Donald Trump became president, Democratic hypocrites began allowing open borders and massive illegal alien migration into the United States for the following reasons:

- They saw it as an investment to gain adequate votes to elect Democratic politicians in future elections
- They anticipate millions of illegal aliens would vote for members of Congress who would support a redistribution of tax wealth to illegal alien families and low income workers through "equity laws" passed by executive orders and by legislation from Congress

- They anticipated illegal aliens once given amnesty will support Democrat tyrannical laws
- They saw it as a way to supply cheap labor to industries to make up for the major tax losses industries will experience under socialists.

It is ironic that when ICE threatened to send illegal aliens captured at the southern border to sanctuary cities in California, Democratic politicians of California did not want them in their neighborhoods; they wanted to avoid them like the plague. This shows their true hypocrisy and the reality about nonacceptance of illegal aliens in the communities where they live. Did Chuck Schumer and Rachel Maddow ever cry about Kate Steinle, who was shot and killed by an illegal alien, or about any of the US children killed by MS-13 gang members, or about the women who are brutally raped by illegal aliens on their way to the United States border? They won't cry, because neither of them cares about decent US citizens and they want illegal immigrants to live in places other than where elite Democrats live.

Liberal Democrats, with the aid of illegal immigrants, will gradually dominate the United States, similar to how Muslims are slowly dominating Europe; Muslims are overpopulating Europe, including Scandinavia, and slowly taking over in these places. Immigrants from south of the US border are willing to assimilate into our culture over time; Muslims in the Europe or in the United States are not. Democrats plan to achieve power and control by changing our culture and institutions, our schools, and our religious institutions. Democrats will pass laws to radically remake the United States over time. It all began under the arrogant con artist Barack Obama with his socialist "Hope and Change" slogan. Social engineering = evolution of culture. Once in power, Democratic socialists will become tyrants, pass tyrannical laws supported by more massive migration into the United States, modify election laws so socialists always win, change or destroy the Constitution, and begin a series of deals and gimmicks to tax-oppress the wealthy, the middle class, large corporations, small businesses, and manufacturing industries. If large corporations attempt to relocate outside the United States, the socialist Democratic federal government will nationalize these corporations and run them. Lawsuits will have no merit against the socialist government, as the courts will all be appointed and packed by socialists in power. Only smart rich people who saw it coming will escape the United States with their wealth. Middle-class homeowners will be stuck with oppressively high taxes.

In short, if the encroaching socialist reform process is not stopped early enough, then confiscation of wealth will be enforced, in conflict with taxpayers. Although the Biden Administration will pass strict gun control laws and laws to confiscate assault rifles, these laws will not be enforced because: first, law-abiding citizens will not give up their assault rifles, secondly, state governors will threaten to secede from the United States or secede, and that may lead to a second civil war. May God help us.

Open Borders Is About Cheap Labor, Culture Change, and Votes

Democratic politicians cannot win elections without the help of illegal alien voters or without rigging or stealing elections, because they are desperate for power and they cheat to win. Democrats don't care about illegal immigrants who are criminals. They don't care if these immigrants murder, rape, burglarize, or assault Americans. They figure it's the job of the police to catch the criminals after illegal immigrants have already committed the crimes. Sick Nancy Pelosi once said that any crimes committed by illegal aliens were to be considered collateral damage. It's a reactive policy that Democrats have toward the safety of Americans, rather than preventing loss of US lives by illegal alien criminals or by legislating immigration reform. We don't want the following types of people in the United States:

• Muslim migrants who hate the United States and its culture and want to turn the United States into a Muslim country;
• any immigrants who hate our culture and want to impose their culture on the United States;

- lazy immigrants who refuse to work or else who come into the United States so as to rely on government assistance (we must not accept migrants who enter the United States only to claim their share of free government handouts offered by Democrats, thereby becoming a burden on taxpayers);
- migrants who refuse to assimilate into our culture and be productive;
- migrants who support Muslim terrorist groups such as Hamas, ISIS, and al-Qaeda, and Iranian terrorists;
- migrants who want to steal our technology, like the Chinese;
- migrants who have a background of being prosecuted for serious crimes anywhere in the world or previously in the United States;
- migrants who refuse to work because they do not speak English;
- migrants who commit entitlement fraud;
- migrants who refuse to take an oath to support or defend our Constitution, *or* people who agree at first, then renege, and later break their oath to defend the US Constitution; and
- migrants of immoral character.

As of March 2021, caravans of migrants are attracted by Joe Biden's immigration policies and immigration policies legislated by the House under Nancy Pelosi's leadership. Biden has created a massive crisis at the border and none of the Democrat politicians are willing to call it a crisis. Instead, Democrat leaders either remain tight-lipped, or label the thousands of illegal aliens illegally entering the US as a "challenge". ICE is overwhelmed as care-givers for over 18,000 migrant children who are separated from their families and living in large storage containers under squaller conditions, while the head of DHS Mayorkas, is asking for volunteers to help at the border. Nancy Pelosi gives kudos to the illegal aliens coming in, and the several fake news agencies and Democrat politicians are blaming the crisis at the border on former President Trump. ICE is transporting Illegal aliens across America. Immigrants are released to buses waiting for them without any checks to see if they are infected with COVID-19. Immigrants along border states are economically burdened by the amassed illegal aliens living in tents and large containers. As of March 2021, the Biden Administration has forbidden anyone to take photos of illegal alien campsites along the southern border filled with squalor and filth to be seen by any reporter or member of Congress.

The fact that a percentage of illegal aliens commit heinous crimes, or that a massive number of illegal aliens coming through in caravans will cause an economic burden on US taxpayers, or that a high number of them will take jobs from US citizens because they will work for cheap wages, is completely irrelevant to the Democratic elites. Democrats want illegal immigrants in the United States for their votes, so the Democrats can gain power. Does offering illegal aliens free health care, free tuition, and free government assistance and risking the safety and lives of Americans, so Democrats can get the illegal alien vote, a good policy? Answer: *No*, it isn't.

Since Democrats stole the 2020 election, the Biden administration has promised to give amnesty to millions of DACA illegal aliens so they can vote. Joe Biden has stopped construction of the wall at the southern border, and massive caravans are heading for the border already. This will add a significant problem to Biden's massive economic spending plans. How many millions of illegal immigrants, who now cannot be deported as mandated by one of Joe Biden's executive orders, will be given amnesty to be eligible for welfare, food stamps, unemployment, and social security as US citizens? Have Democrats assessed the burden on taxpayers?

Democrats know that letting millions of illegal immigrants into the United States will change the population in states and gain them additional federal representation in the House, also increasing their number of electoral college votes. Joe Biden now allows illegal aliens to be counted in the US Census as US citizens, that is, as part of the legal population of each state. Democrats will be elected thanks to the additional millions of amnesty migrants, who will always outnumber Trump voters, and enable Democrats, starting with President Joe Biden, to easily transition the United States into socialism. Since seventy-five million Trump voters were made irrelevant, they will not be represented; rather, their voices will be vindictively shunned and repressed. The lack of checks and balances between the branches of government has allowed the coming tyranny of the Democratic ruling class and the oppression of millions of Americans.

Millennials with college debt, unskilled workers, unemployed citizens, and the homeless, should be worried about the flood of illegal aliens Democrats are letting into the country. Democratic politicians always say that illegal aliens take jobs that no one else wants, usually farm labor. That may be true for some migrants, but what Democratic politicians aren't saying is that illegal aliens will take almost all unskilled paying jobs from college dropouts, millennials, unskilled blacks, seniors, and the homeless, and prevent many unemployed US citizens from getting jobs.

Illegal aliens will work for lower wagers in fast-food restaurants, in movie theaters, factories, in laundry shops, in department stores, as teacher's assistants, as nurses, as food clerks, as car mechanics, as trash collectors, as gardeners, as delivery drivers, as truck drivers, and so on. illegal aliens will replace unskilled and low-wage workers in their jobs because they will work for less. Unless displaced millennials are able to get new jobs, they must become accustomed to a life of welfare, unemployment insurance, and food stamps, and may well go back to living in mommy and daddy's basement. Forget about social security; there might not be any left in the fund when millennials are old enough to get it. American kids out of high school will also be unable to compete with illegal aliens and will have to accept the same wages as are paid to them.

Migrant workers who replace US citizens in the workplace with cheaper wages will create classes of the very wealthy and the very poor, as now exist in California. Very rich people live in mansions all along the coast, from San Diego to Northern California. Illegal aliens will work for these people for low wages, much like the corrupt rich Mexican politicians and business executives who live in Mexico, who hire peons for their cheap labor. California lawmakers want a state of rich landowners with peasants working for the very rich. In their lust for power, Democrats will have suppressed higher paying jobs opportunities for millennials and unskilled black workers.

David A. Herrera

Generalized Strategies of Socialism

The leftist agenda of the Biden administration has already begun unopposed. The agenda is a series of executive orders signed by Joe Biden. It is a continuation of former president Barack Obama's "Hope and Change" on steroids. Biden's existing executive orders, plus the coming leftist Congressional legislation, will reform all major institutions and affect our status. Executive orders and congressional laws will stifle free speech; weaken gun rights; weaken Christian institutions; weaken the military; promote cronyism-style enrichment. Democrats will weaken the US economy with immense spending on millions of immigrants, the Green New Deal, climate change, health care, COVID-19 relief, infrastructure, aid to the UN, aid to the World Health Organization; foreign aid to South America; and funds for salaries, pensions, healthcare, and travel expenses of members of Congress and workers in government agencies. Democratic strategies are designed to creep toward socialism, and they target Trump voters with reprisals in their unified nonviolent civil war against Trump voters.

First Socialist Strategy: Create a Socialist Agenda and a Spending Plan

Socialists must establish a spending plan; determine resources and personnel required to implement a socialist system of government, ensure economic development, and develop methods to continually increase and maintain power; and define sources of revenue. All planning is designed to achieve power and fulfill the socialist agenda. Here is the plan:

1. Organize and select socialists and other leftists to fill government positions.
2. Estimate a spending plan (not necessarily a budget) including income and expenditures. Expenditures include:
   * COVID-19 relief package with a majority of pork spending
   * the Green New Deal

- programs to combat climate change
- free health care for illegal aliens
- free college tuition for illegal aliens
- loan reduction or forgiveness for college students in debt
- raise additional high taxes on the upper and middle class Americans to pass an infrastructure pork bill that includes another bailout of blue states to resolve their homelessness, healthcare, housing problems, and aid to states for welfare recipients.
- bailout blue states with billions of dollars so they can use their local tax collections for black reparations
- billions of dollars for the arts and humanities and for Hollywood
- billions of dollars for Planned Parenthood and abortion clinics

3. Reverse all tax reductions of the Trump administration and raise new high taxes on corporations.
4. Find other ways to increase tax revenue.
   - Raise taxes across the United States by defining new graduated income tax levels.
   - Reimpose the individual death tax.
   - Impose a wealth tax on the wealthiest Americans.
   - Increase capital gains tax.
   - Increase taxes on all corporations and small businesses.
   - Increase costly new environmental regulations on businesses, particularly the oil industry.
   - Increase taxes on all Americans by charging taxes on miles driven
5. Determine resources and personnel to fill government staff positions.
6. Determine political initiatives to expand Democrat perpetual power and increase the socialist voting base by:
   - Eliminate the Electoral College.
   - Eliminate the Senate filibuster.
   - Grant Washington, DC, statehood to add two more Democratic senators to the Senate.

- Grant Puerto Rico statehood to add two more senators to the Senate.
- Continue with open borders to increase the immigrant population, then grant them amnesty so as to win elections forever. Provide illegal aliens free government handouts to draw them into the United States.
- Pack the Supreme Court with five more socialist Supreme Court justices.

7. Decrease the size of the US military and its budget.
8. Subsidize the socialist supportive corrupt news media to do the following:
   - disseminate favorable news for the socialist government
   - disseminate misinformation about seventy-five million Trump voters
   - slander, revile, and scandalize the opposition
   - modify public opinion toward the left.
9. Establish relationships with other world leaders.
10. Inflate salaries and pensions for top socialist government officials.
11. Curtail drilling and production of oil and gas, and other petroleum energy, thus putting millions of Americans out of work and risking the possibility of secession of rich oil states from the union.
12. Control the distribution of food.
13. Punish Christian churches for not hiring gay people or for refusing to officiate same-sex marriages.

The foregoing list of socialist agenda items is not all-inclusive.

Democrats will celebrate their stolen election win as a referendum on the plight of the oppressed and as a call to support and protect gender equality, income equality, government handouts, tolerance for Muslims, homosexuals, and transgender people, and to end systemic racism in the United States. Democrats will seek to save the planet from its upcoming catastrophic disaster brought on by the extraction, refining, distribution, and use of fossil fuels and release of carbon chemical emissions into the atmosphere. They will give amnesty to millions of illegal aliens and welcome them to join the United States and share in the wealth with promises of free government handouts and amnesty.

Second Socialist Strategy: The Cancel Culture and Censure of Conservative Expression

Bidens's socialist executive orders were passed and promptly approved in less than 60 days. Biden's COVID-19 relief bill was passed on March 12, 2021 and the tax monies are currently being distributed to the states. His executive orders are not to gain fame and build a legacy. His primary goal is with the Democrats to gain perpetual power, control, and enrichment for Democrats.

In the pursuit of power and declaration of war against Trump voters, socialist politicians will use the fake news media as a war machine against conservatives, will use high-tech giant corporations to silence and block conservative opinion and free speech, and will indoctrinate **youths** in public schools, colleges, and universities about the evils of capitalism, historical racism, and the victims who were oppressed. The liberal fake news media will continue to manufacture false propaganda against conservative politicians. Youth in public schools will be taught to hate the United States, with teachers citing racist and imperialistic events in US history. The fake news media and the Hollywood liberal crowd who hated President Trump the most were ecstatic and celebrated when President Trump was gone. Although Trump left office on January 20, 2021, vindictive Nancy Pelosi and the House of Representatives impeached President Trump, blaming him for instigating the violence during his rally at the Capitol on the day when the Senate certified Joe Biden's election win. The Senate reviewed the articles of impeachment against Donald Trump in February 2021 and voted against impeachment.

Social media giants have already been blocking conservative posts on their websites. Voices on social media that oppose socialists and their policies will be considered to be engaging in white-supremacist hate speech. High-tech companies will either block conservative posts or eliminate the accounts of conservatives from their websites, as some have already done. Federal agents will track and monitor Americans who express opposition to the socialist government, just as communist China is presently doing to its people.

Conservative journalist Tucker Carlson of Fox News was doxed, and leftist agitators protested and harassed him and his family in front of his home. Publisher Simon and Schuster dropped plans to publish Senator Josh Hawley's book entitled *The Tyranny of Big Tech* after the Trump rally on January 6, 2021, where protesters got just outside the doors of congressional chambers. Hawley's canceled book was to expose the tyranny of leftist high-tech companies in the United States.

House Democrat Alexandria Ocasio-Cortez proposed a federal commission to figure out who's telling the truth and who's spreading misinformation and fibs in the media. The commission would be a "Supreme Fact-Checking" or "Truth Commission" agency of the federal government, regulating free speech in the media, likely headed by evil corrupt Democrats like Adam Schiff or Jerrold Nadler. Any media that allows the dissemination of misinformation would be brought to trial under the "Truth Commission" court and, if found guilty of spreading lies, would lose its media license and be removed from TV, radio, talk shows, social media, magazines, and newspapers by the federal commission. Pro-Democrat high-tech company fact-checkers would have the authority to block whomever they please who are posting "fibs and misinformation" as their opinions.

On January 8, 2021, Twitter canceled President Trump's Twitter account permanently. The liberal fake news media was overjoyed with this action. Now high-tech giant Facebook is stifling free speech and threatening to block or revoke the accounts of anyone who posts what it thinks are false opinions. Apple prevented *Parler*, a conservative application, from being accessed on Google Apps on Apple cell phones by users. The fake news media was enthused when high-tech giants said they were going to target the more than seventy-four million Trump supporters in order to silence them and prevent them from expressing conservative thought and opposition to the Biden administration.

Leftists are some of the most intolerant people on the planet. Leftist hypocrites do not tolerate conservative speech on college campuses and in universities, especially in liberal states such as California, New

York, New Jersey, Oregon, Washington, and Illinois. Leftist students are intolerant to the point of using violence against people whom they disagree with.

The fake news media has remained silent on the corruption of Joe Biden and his son Hunter Biden. Although former President Trump and current GOP leaders requested a special counsel to investigate Hunter Biden for criminal allegations with China and the Ukraine, no council was ever appointed. It is likely that in the corrupt Biden administration, President Biden and his son will get away with the crimes they committed. Despite hard evidence of money laundering, the House remains mute on Joe Biden and has no interest in impeaching him. The FBI and DOJ are also ineffectual in investigating Joe and Hunter Biden's corruption. DOJ and the FBI are likely in Joe Biden's pockets, just as Attorney General Eric Holder and James Comey were in Barack Obama's pockets. The Biden administration will become the most corrupt administration in US history. Unfortunately, there is nothing the American people can do about it because corrupt Democrats who control the government are less likely to hold their own accountable.

The Biden administration will introduce legislation to allow the Muslim religion to be taught in public schools, funded by American taxpayers. Through CAIR, foreign Muslim countries will also fund public schools and universities to teach courses in Islam to convert US students or indoctrinate them. CAIR has ties to terrorist organizations in the Middle East. College students will be taught to hate the United States for oppressing Muslims groups both in this country and in the wider Muslim world.

Today, the reason liberals and socialists in the United States partner with radical Muslims is that they have the same enemy: conservatives, Christians, and Jews. Louis Farrakhan, a leader of the Nation of Islam in the United States, has preached hatred against "white devils" and "termite" Jews, but in October 2008, he called Barack Obama a "messiah". House member Ilhan Omar gave a number of anti-Semitic speeches in Congress, condemned Israel, and blamed white people for the problems in the United States. Democrats never criticized her for being a racist. Progressives and Muslim organizations subsidized by Saudi Arabia, Iran, and other rich Arab countries want to convert

American children to Islam. Together with progressives and socialists in the United States, they will seek to indoctrinate schoolchildren into believing the United States is a bad nation, the United States was never great, and the United States needs social change.

The strategy here is to successfully use Democratic socialists, the fake news propaganda machine, and high-tech corporations to wage a war on Trump voters 24-7 as they did with President Trump himself. The leftist fake news media, including high-tech social media, will work hand in glove with socialist politicians, funded by leftist billionaires, as a multiheaded dragon to demonize and attack conservatives, Republicans, Christian churches, Christian organizations, capitalists, rich white men, businesses that support conservatives, and right-wing organizations.

Obama weaponized agencies to allow intelligence officers, the FBI, the NSA, and intelligence contract agencies to use computers in secret to influence elections and to frame and blackmail anyone who may have committed a crime. *ShadowNet* is one such computer that tracks and monitors targets opposed by the Deep State to disable, blackmail, or destroy them. *ShadowNet* was designed under the Obama administration by General James Jones, an intelligence computer expert. John Brennan, James Clapper, John McCain, Lindsey Graham, and Sally Yates knew about *ShadowNet* and its use.

Socialist members of Congress on intelligence committees will be leaking any convenient misinformation and pro-socialist information to the liberal fake news media so the latter can use it for propaganda purposes. Information is created and disseminated on computers from intelligence agencies and the military that were designed to push false information to influence social media on the internet, to provide misinformation to fake news sources, to create a false characterization of politicians, to influence elections, and to blackmail politicians. The network of users were government contractors such as Dynology Systems, the Analysis Group, the Global Defense Group, and the Atlantic Council. These are all participants in what is known as *ShadowNet*. An article describing a video entitled *Transcript of the Film "Shadow Gate,"* by Millie Weaver, indicates in detail how clandestine operations were conducted against candidate Donald Trump with the Russian dossier to set up him and his campaign staff for Russian collusion, provide witnesses against him to impeach him, and assist the Mueller investigation. Millie Weaver indicates the same group of contractors are behind the fake news in mainstream media, to influence operations on social media, cause civil unrest nationwide, and push the "defund the police" movement.[3]

Third Strategy: Tax-Oppress Wealthy Americans

The third strategy of socialism is to pass tyrannical laws tax-oppressing Americans, including taxing the wealth of the middle class, small businesses, and large corporations. This is a major goal for socialists to run their government, but it will be a very long and troublesome strategy to implement as the very rich will have already outsmarted the socialist politicians by leaving the United States with all their wealth, or sheltering their wealth, or transferring their wealth overseas, and as a result will face little or no tax debt. As a result, the middle class will be significantly harmed as taxation oppression takes a significant chunk of wealth from them, driving them deep into debt, poverty, and even homelessness. Jobs will be lost and the stock market will crash like never before. To compound this problem, open border policies will allow massive immigration into the United States with immigrants running to claim their fair share of the government handouts such as free health care, free cash, free housing, free college tuition, and welfare. Unskilled millennials and blacks working low-paying jobs will likely be dismissed and replaced with amnesty migrants who will work for lower wages. Amnesty migrants and the lower class who are dependent on government assistance will support the socialist tax oppression on both the wealthiest Americans, the middle class, and on corporations.

---

[3] "ShadowGate—What They Don't Want You to See (Bitchute)," Vision Launch, August 17, 2020, https://visionlaunch.com/shadowgate-what-they-dont-want-you-to-see-bitchute/; Patrick Bergy, "Is the 'Deep State' Blackmailing Our Justice Department?," Victim of the Swamp, November 21, 2017, https://www.victimoftheswamp.com/2017/10/21/is-the-deep-state-blackmailing-our-justice-department/.

David A. Herrera

Fourth Socialist Strategy: Create a Police State

Socialist presidential candidate Cory Booker suggested that, if elected, he would create a special federal police force that would seek out, monitor, investigate, and apprehend any right-wing white people who commit hate crimes. This is not an agency to prevent racism; it is a racist agency bent on strictly targeting white people—a decision based solely on race. This is a Cory Booker's idea of a national gestapo force, reminiscent of the Gestapos of Nazi Germany who went after Jews and illegally entered the homes of German citizens looking for weapons. Such a thing will never fly in the United States. However, Joe Biden may, at some time, create a US police agency run by the DOJ with a police czar to head it. The job of this agency would be as follows:

1. Monitor and investigate civil rights violations, hate speech, revolutionary speech, hate crimes, and antisocialism dissent.
2. Leverage the power of nationwide arrest; work with other federal agencies; and hold local police agencies accountable for violation of civil rights.
3. Assist IRS agents and local law enforcement in evicting any Americans from their homes who are in tax arrears, and confiscate their homes.
4. Assist the Bureau of Alcohol, Tobacco, Firearms, and Explosives to confiscate weapons of conservatives who are opposed to the socialist government or for merely expressing antigovernment hate speech.
5. Reform states and cities in the United States to ensure police officers are not beating up or killing black people because they are racists. Federal police agents would coordinate with state and local officials to assist in the solving of crimes related to matters of state and federal law and involving national security.
6. Enforce all federal laws as directed by the DOJ and the president. If a socialist Congress passes tyrannical laws, the federal police agency will coordinate with local law enforcement to ensure these tyrannical federal laws are enforced, for example, laws that are passed by both houses of Congress, signed by the

president, and approved by the Supreme Court, such as taxation without representation, laws that violate civil rights, and laws that violate the First, Second, and Fourth Amendments. The federal police agency will convince states and local law enforcement to enforce these laws as well. In this case, the oppressed victims are the American people, and the oppressor become the socialist government bureaucracy.

The Biden administration and Congress will support the violation of Americans' First Amendment rights. Democrats will stifle conservative speech and continue to spy on US citizens for any personal opinions expressed as dissent on media or that could be interpreted as hate speech. Personal opinions expressed on social websites that encourage antigovernment dissent or protests or that propose a revolution against the Biden administration will be interpreted by the federal socialist government as hate speech, sedition, and/or a conspiracy to incite a revolution. To solidify power, socialists will monitor, track, and investigate any Americans expressing antigovernment sentiment, thoughts, and opinions, thus violating their First Amendment rights, using ShadowNet. This is exactly what the Chinese communist government is doing today in China—using artificial intelligence software in computers to identify antigovernment speech and spying on individuals who express it. In China, authorities will go after an antigovernment protester or dissenter, who subsequently disappears.

In summary: Socialism is already developing the United States with Joe Biden's executive orders and his call for Democrats to unite against Trump voters. Through legislation and executive orders, leftist Democrats will do the following:

- enhance their power in government;
- tax the rich to promote income equality for all, including the millions of illegal aliens;
- claim to end systemic racism in the United States;
- compensate blacks of today whose ancestors were oppressed more than one hundred fifty-five years ago;

- revive and expand Obamacare, and providing free health care for illegal aliens;
- support and fund abortions;
- save the United States from destruction with climate change reform and green energy; and
- draw a sufficiently large illegal alien population to the United States by offering free government handouts so as to add to the population of progressive and socialist US citizens to outnumber conservative voters. All it takes is for millions of illegal aliens to be given amnesty and voting rights only once, so they can elect Democratic Party politicians with a majority in both houses, and a Democratic president. Conservatives will be outnumbered from then on and will never win elections.

The cost to give away free stuff to citizens and illegal aliens is not free. Socialist politicians never revealed before the 2020 election details about what the total price tag of their spending items would be or how all their spending plans would be paid for. In the 2020 Democratic presidential debates, several socialists initially refused to talk about costs and only cited that only the richest Americans would be taxed. They had no credibility at all.

Democratic politicians advocating socialism in the United States are deceptive and extremely naive. Why? Answer:

1. Most Americans oppose paying high taxes, especially for tax monies going to illegal aliens.
2. Not one Democratic presidential candidate indicated how he or she would enforce collecting such high taxes amid massive opposition.
3. Socialist politicians think the wealthiest Americans will allow them to impose a "wealth tax" on them, confiscating 50 percent to 90 percent of their wealth. Rich Americans are not stupid. They are much smarter than socialists. Socialists will have much difficulty collecting taxes from the rich 1 percent or rich 2 percent, who know how to shelter and hide their money.

4. After Democrats are dumfounded as to how the very rich have escaped paying taxes on most of their wealth, naive socialists will resort to taxing the middle class, which will bring about horrific opposition.

5. If socialists print more money, the value of the dollar will be reduced, the cost of goods will increase (inflation), and demand for most goods will decrease because of lower affordability and, therefore, lower demand. In foreign trade, prices will increase for goods sold to the United States as the value of the dollar will decrease. It may decrease to the point where the World Bank removes the dollar as the world standard and substitutes gold or Chinese currency as the new monetary standard.

Under the leadership of great presidents like Donald Trump and Ronald Reagan, the United States became a great and prosperous country. Americans were proud to be Americans and loved the United States. These presidents lifted the human spirits of freedom-loving Americans, who sought opportunities to work hard, become prosperous, and achieve the American dream. It was a call to all Americans to "be all you can be" in a United States that offered ample opportunities to all for jobs, prosperity, and success. These presidents celebrated God, family, and country, seeking to raise the standard of living for all US citizens. Is it any wonder that millions of people want to get into the United States for opportunities to achieve wealth and prosperity in a land where freedoms are guaranteed by the Constitution? The conservative policies of these presidents won the hearts, minds, and hopes of sensible people, not by bribing illegal aliens to enter the United States, nor by offering free stuff and never achieving prosperity; not by big government stealing the wealth of wealthy Americans to give to foreign migrants, nor by rigging or stealing an election to win; but by promoting traditional American values.

In terms of a spending plan, a true socialist government will seek contractors to achieve the listed activities itemized in the spending plan. Instead of relying on supply and demand, socialists will assess the demand for products across the United States and order the distribution of products. Big government's role will eventually determine product output and pricing levels. Socialists will likely have a difficult time making proper decisions given the needs of consumers versus demand for products. However, by monitoring inventory levels of products in states and communities, socialist central planners can avoid major production distribution inefficiencies. Whenever stores experience a surplus of a product, this signals the need to cut prices, and vice versa.

One of the consequences of socialist control of the means of production is the lack of competition between producers or manufacturers; this reduces the incentive to adjust prices. Socialist control of production and adjustment of prices will cause gross inefficiencies and give rise to a bungling bureaucracy. Also, an environment can be created where political interests are put ahead of the basic needs of the citizenry. For example, a socialist federal government may desire to spend a majority of its funds on environmental cleanup, climate change programs, or green energy deals, rather than providing the basic needs of food, shelter, and medicine to the general population. Another example is the government providing illegal aliens with government handouts, while US citizens are homeless, living in poverty, suffering poor health, and going without sufficient soap, food, or TV sets.

Another misappropriation of funds in the socialist spending plan is the higher spending on health care, worker pensions, subsidies for illegal aliens, and reparations for historically oppressed groups, that are prioritized over adequately funding the US military, which can become very vulnerable and unable to protect the United States against aggression. In a pure socialist country, there is no stock market, no Wall Street. Communist countries like China have a free market system of supply and demand, as well as rigid government control. Therefore, China is not a pure communist country.

Fifth Socialist Strategy: Provide Government Handouts to Illegal Aliens Paid for by Rich Capitalist Oppressors

The aforementioned third strategy of socialism, is to launch a massive propaganda campaign advertising the "free" benefits of socialism to foreign immigrants made possible by tax-oppressing 50 percent to 90 percent of the wealth of rich people. These taxpayers will be left with 50 percent to 10 percent of their wealth and no benefits from their taxes. The total projected costs for the socialist spending plan are seldom revealed, and if they are, they are likely inaccurate. The objective is to redistribute significant portions of somebody else's wealth to "systemically racially oppressed victims" and foreign immigrants in order to gain their support in elections to office; this is corruption. This is taking lots of money from the rich to distribute freebies to immigrants to get their votes through future amnesty. This amounts to a corrupt pay-to-play scheme, using wealthy people's money to barter for political power. Socialists have been advertising government handouts to illegal aliens, but they have not been transparent about their estimated cost per year. Democrats must determine the following:

1. can the rich be taxed to pay for every expense item in the Biden Administration's tax plan?
2. what are the repercussions of high taxation and excessive spending on the economy?
3. how many millions of immigrants entering the United States each year will receive free taxpayer government assistance? Can taxpayers afford it?
4. how long will the Biden Administration ignore the mounting opposition of allowing millions of immigrants into the US each year and paying taxes to care for them?
5. how many millions of immigrants granted amnesty will apply for welfare, food stamps, disability insurance, unemployment insurance? What are the expected cost estimates, and do you have to raise taxes again?
6. how many millions of immigrants will receive free health care if they cannot get Obamacare?
7. what percentage of immigrants will be added to the homeless population, since most immigrants entering the United States will be destitute?
8. how is massive illegal alien entry into the United States fair to US taxpayers and what will they get out of it?

The intent of this strategy is to attract between one million and two million immigrants each year, some of whom are criminals, some of whom are terrorists, some of whom are disabled, and most of whom are destitute, without education or job skills. But the nefarious intent of open borders and amnesty is to eventually give illegal aliens voting rights so Democrats can win elections forever. That is not a policy that should ever be used to win elections at the expense and safety of US taxpayers.

Note that on July 7, 2020, Reps. Rashida Tlaib (D-MI) and Ayanna Pressley (D-MA) sponsored a bill in the House called the *BREATHE ACT*. The bill proposes to do the following:

1. Eliminate federal programs and agencies, such as ICE, DEA, and the Department of Defense, involved in the criminal justice system.
2. Defund the police and use the funds for social services (welfare, reparations for blacks, aid for homeless, etc.).
3. Eliminate life sentences, and permanently close prisons and border detention centers.
4. Abolish electronic monitoring of prisoners.
5. End gang databases (including gang members with records of murder, rape, gang violence, robbery, and other felonies)
6. Establish a commission to study reparations for blacks.
7. Establish commissions to study reparations for drug pushers, prostitutes, victims of police violence or border violence, and violators of Native American treaties.
8. Provide federal grants for disenfranchised communities.
9. Establish pilot programs for a universal basic income.
10. Allow convicts and ex-convicts to vote, and give amnesty to illegal aliens so they may vote.
11. Allow grants for the lifetime education of illegal immigrants and incarcerated criminals.

This ridiculous bill was taken from the Movement for Black Lives' 501(c)4 Electoral Justice Project by House members Rashida Tlaib and Ayanna Pressley, both Far Left socialist members of the Democratic

Party. The bill is nothing but a Christmas wish list, and is not expected to be approved in the House. For more information, contact policy@ m4bl.org.[4]

If the *BREATHE ACT* is ever passed, a secession of states would likely follow and a new union of states would be formed as quickly as possible. Democrats should be warned that people who are highly taxed are moving out of California and New York State, going to states with lower taxes. New York and California will be left with immigrants, freeloaders, the unemployed, drug addicts, criminals, welfare recipients, and the homeless, all to share the wealth from a reduced tax base.

The millions of illegal aliens given amnesty will join in the Democrats in unity in the nonviolent civil war against the seventy-five million Trump voters. Amnesty migrants will significantly enhance the power of the Democratic Party ruling class currently in charge, who will force conservatives into compliance with socialist tyrannical laws, or else they'll be punished economically or criminally. More power given to Democrats only emboldens them to continue stripping Constitutional rights of conservative Americans.

Sixth Socialist Strategy: Severely Restrict or Ban the Second Amendment to the Constitution

The Biden administration promised to sign an executive order to restrict gun sales. Socialists, now more than ever, will seek to severely restrict or repeal the Second Amendment of the Constitution for fear of an armed uprising of seventy-five million former Trump voters who wish to defend their civil rights and fight back against the nonviolent civil war the unified Democratic Party and President Biden have waged on them. The nonviolent civil war is described only as a series of legislation passed by Congress and signed by the president, along with executive orders signed by President Biden, to deprive Trump voters

---

[4] Black Lives Matter, "The Breathe Act," BreatheAct.org, July 2020, https://breatheact.org/wp-content/uploads/2020/07/The-BREATHE-Act-PDF FINAL3-1.pdf.

of their civil rights. An executive order and Congressional legislation on gun control are coming.

One bill introduced by Democratic members in January 2020 was H.R. 5717, which bans semiautomatic assault rifles, specific guns, specific shotguns, silencers, and high-capacity magazines; outlines weapon storage requirements; imposes a 30 percent tax on every gun owned in the United States; and imposes a 50 percent tax on ammunition—among other things. It has not been enacted into law so far, but it could be now that Democrats control two branches of the federal government.[5]

The Sixth strategy of socialism, which may be implemented concurrently with Strategy 4, is to create a police state so as to restrict, confiscate, or ban guns and ammunition for good reasons: tyrannical laws are coming, and the socialist-controlled federal government doesn't want a revolution or secession. This will be the most-opposed tyrannical law passed by socialists. Socialist political candidates of 2020 Beto O'Rourke, Cory Booker, Kamala Harris, and Eric Swalwell are well-known for supporting confiscation of weapons. To cite an example from the socialism era of Nazi Germany, to conquer a nation, Adolf Hitler is quoted in the book *Table Talk: Secret Conversations* as having said the following sometime between February and September 1942:

"The most foolish mistake we could possibly make would be to allow the subjugated races to possess arms. History shows that all conquerors who have allowed their subjugated races to carry arms have prepared their own downfall by so doing. Indeed, I would go so far as to say that the supply of arms to the underdogs is a 'sine qua non' for the overthrow of any sovereignty. So, let's not have any native militia or native police."[6]

Instead of "subjugated races," socialists in the United States would substitute "subjugated Trump voters" or "subjugated conservatives," who will become the hated enemies of socialists, progressives, and

---

[5] "H.R. 5717 (116th): Gun Violence Prevention and Community Safety Act of 2020," January 30, 2020, GovTrack, https://www.govtrack.us/congress/bills/116/hr5717/text/ih.
[6] Hugh Trevor-Roper, *Hitler's Table Talk, 1941–1944* (New York: Enigma, 2000), 425.

radical Muslims as evidenced by their political rhetoric. Within the "conservative" group would be subgroups such as evangelical Christians, Catholics, patriotic military personnel, patriotic law enforcement officers, capitalists, heterosexual married couples, and freedom-loving people. In a February 2018 interview with Al Jazeera English, House Congresswoman and radical Muslim Ilhan Omar said: "Our country should be more fearful of white men," regarding US domestic terrorism. She also said, "Right-wing extremists have been responsible for most of the deadly domestic terrorism in the U.S. in recent years, but nevertheless most of the focus of policies and law enforcement is directed at the Muslim community." She insinuated that most members of law enforcement focusing on Muslim communities are white supremacists, and therefore the focus is racist, Islamophobic, and invalid.

Quoting the second Amendment of the Constitution:

"A well-regulated Militia, being necessary to the security of a free State, the right of the people to keep and bear Arms, shall not be infringed."

Banning semiautomatic assault rifles by way of a Biden executive orders or a Democrat-authored legislation passed by Congress is a direct infringement on the rights of the American people, and will be a huge mistake. Militias have the constitutional authority to form and organize to oppose tyranny, be it from any police or military agency representing state, local, or federal, that seeks to take away the right of self-defense – the second Amendment. Law-abiding citizens will not allow police or military to confiscate their weapons. Secession of several states from the union is likely to occur to ensure free states, as states will become fed up with the socialist tyranny of the federal government interfering with their lives and freedom. If a bill like H.R. 5717 is forced on the seventy-five million Trump voters, most of them will refuse to comply with it. Police and military personnel will have difficulties enforcing that law. A percentage of law enforcement and military personnel will refuse to enforce that bill. Confiscating assault weapons and large capacity magazines from law-abiding Americans with or without a warrant, or banning the Second Amendment will bring the United

States closer to a violent and bloody civil war between seventy-five million conservatives and the tyrannical federal government. Banning the Second Amendment is a giant step toward causing freedom-loving Americans to become like the oppressed people of Venezuela, left completely defenseless, conquered, oppressed, and starved. Americans will be unable to rise up against tyranny.

Before strategies 7 and 8 (defined below) can be effective, socialists need to ban firearms or make firearms owned ineffectual to make US citizens completely defenseless against the tyranny that is to come. Following are some predictions in light of this claim:

1. If a secession of states occurs, or widespread militia revolutionary violence across the United States occurs, the socialist federal government may utilize Obama's Executive Order 13732, which allows UN Peacekeeping Forces into the United States to help the United States with law enforcement or military matters in a national emergency.

2. The socialist federal government will declare martial law to mobilize the police state and the military against a revolution by freedom-loving Americans fighting against socialist tyranny as individuals, militias, or from seceded states.

3. Laws to tax-oppress Americans and/or nationalize businesses in the United States will not be well received. Chatter on social media will convey the message to the FBI, DHS, and DOJ that a violent armed revolution has begun possibly between red states and blue states, **or** between conservatives and socialists. The civil war will be between those who choose to live free or die, liberty or death, and those who choose to side with corruption, oppression, and tyranny.

The possibility of secession of states will become a greater reality before an armed revolution occurs. But secession needs to be planned carefully, with militias ready and mobilized in each seceding state to protect its leaders and citizens from an invading federal government. Seceding states will establish their own armed forces, will unite, and will mobilize to protect and defend the Constitution and their states against the US socialist federal government and any foreign powers.

Seventh Socialist Strategy: Pre-Tyranny Mobilization for a Civil War

Concurrently, the Seventh strategy of socialists is "tyranny enforcement," which must be completed by preparing law enforcement agencies to enforce tyrannical laws. Strategy 7 has two parts. The first part involves setting up personnel and resources for DHS and/or a federal police agency to partner with the United Nations to bring about enforcement of US-passed tyrannical laws to keep the peace and to prevent or address any potential protests, revolutions, acts of terror, or antigovernment uprisings that may occur from armed, oppressed, freedom-loving Americans. The authority to perform the first part was previously granted by Barack Obama with Executive Orders 13629 and 13732, as defined below.

The second and last part of Strategy 7 is for the socialist government to recruit amnesty migrants as police officers at the local, county, state, and federal levels across the country. The goal is to ensure enforcement of tyrannical laws, which patriotic law enforcement personnel may likely refuse to participate in. The objective is to transform the Department of Homeland Security as a federal police force to coordinate with local law enforcement activities as per EO 13629 and, if necessary, invite UN Peacekeeping troops onto US soil to keep the peace. At this point, both seceding states and the socialist federal government will be mobilizing for a second US civil war.

Socialists will use amnesty migrants, as employees of US law enforcement agencies, to enforce tyrannical laws as directed by executive order. The same with the US military; preferential hiring of amnesty migrants will be carried out with the purpose of ensuring tyrannical laws are enforced and armed rebellions are put down. As in Venezuela, enforcement of tyrannical laws would be much easier to achieve if oppressors simply had no guns to defend themselves with. If seceding states had little or no guns, US military troops consisting of mostly amnesty migrants would quell rebellions of these seceding states with no means of defense. Seceding states would take control of all military bases in their states.

The first part of the Seventh strategy is to use Obama's Executive Orders 13629 and 13732:

Obama's EO 13629

This executive order establishes that the White House Homeland Security Partnership Council can be used as a federal police agency to partner with local law enforcement to provide national security within the United States. This EO would allow a socialist-controlled federal government to put down any rebellion of freedom-loving Americans by using the military. A socialist president could even amend this EO to provide additional peacekeeping duties by UN military organizations made up of personnel from other UN member nations on US soil.

This EO means a socialist-controlled federal government can use the Department of Homeland Security (DHS) as a special police force of the US government to partner with various foreign armed military and law enforcement organizations to put down rebellions, in the interests of national security, caused by conservatives and alleged white supremacists who are fighting against a tyrannical socialist federal government. Freedom-fighting militia groups will unite to plan a revolution against the US federal socialist government; these militia groups will not give up their weapons.

Obama's EO 13732

The text of this executive order reads, in part, "The protection of civilians is fundamentally consistent with the effective, efficient, and decisive use of force in pursuit of US national interests. Minimizing civilian casualties can further mission objectives; help maintain the support of partner governments and vulnerable populations, especially in the conduct of counterterrorism and counterinsurgency operations; and enhance the legitimacy and sustainability of US operations critical to our national security. As a matter of policy, the United States therefore routinely imposes certain heightened policy standards that are more protective than the requirements of the law of armed conflict that relate to the protection of civilians."

The "support of partner governments" means UN Peacekeeping troops from various countries can be summoned to US soil and used to put down conservative rebellions fighting against an oppressive socialist federal government so as to keep the peace (wink, wink).

A simple explanation of these executive orders is to suppress Americans fighting for freedom against a tyrannical socialist government. Objectives would be for a socialist-controlled federal government to have a ready and prepared federal police agency with the personnel and resources to address uprisings, attacks on police, and acts of domestic terrorism and, if necessary, call a UN Peacekeeping Force to enter US soil to quell any terrorism, rebellion, or major disturbance. The socialist federal government will say the rebellions are a violation of the national security interests of the United States. So, any patriotic freedom-loving Americans who keep their weapons and rebel against a tyrannical socialist government will face huge challenges. Freedom-loving Americans are unlike people in Europe (including Scandinavia), China, or Russia, and unlike people of the socialist theocracies of the Middle East. Americans will fight the oppressive laws of tyrants. In the near future, freedom-loving Americans will be outnumbered by US military at all levels and by foreign UN mercenary troops—not good.

Today, most members of law enforcement are patriotic Americans who enforce the laws objectively and uphold the Constitution. Most members of the US National Guard and members of the US military are also patriotic, freedom-loving Americans. These Americans will not betray the United States or the Constitution and will likely refuse to enforce any illegal tyrannical laws. If the socialist-controlled federal government succeeds in banning the Second Amendment, I predict most law enforcement officers will refuse to enforce gun ban laws and confiscation of firearms laws enacted to oppose law-abiding Americans. But the socialists in power will use a lot of excuses to ban firearms, and 100 percent of these excuses will be false.

US military and law enforcement agencies must never cave in or surrender to any laws that deprive Americans of their constitutional rights. The military and law enforcement should never allow the federal government, especially if it becomes socialist, to permit foreign troops on US soil to put down rebellions of patriotic Americans fighting for their freedom, and must never allow foreign troops to kill Americans on US soil. Our military and law enforcement agencies should resist federal social engineering of local, state, and federal government that would take freedoms away from individuals. If our military and law enforcement fail the citizenry, the United States is doomed and is on its way to becoming a Venezuela with the military and law enforcement supporting and protecting elite-class tyrants.

If the socialist government of the United States ever uses Barack Obama's executive order to call UN Peacekeeping Forces into the US to quell rebellions of freedom-loving Americans fighting the tyrannical government, these will be essentially mercenary boots on the ground who will be given the power to arrest Americans and the power to kill Americans. Where might these UN Peacekeeping Forces be from? More than likely, they will be from Latin America, which will be given amnesty and US property if these mercenaries are successful in putting down right-wing rebellions. This means American freedom fighters may lose their homes as booty to the mercenaries. The socialist federal government may even seize personal properties, bank accounts, retirement accounts, government checks, medical benefits, and investment accounts of patriotic freedom fighters by way of an executive order. If socialist tyrants confiscate guns prior to these actions, freedom fighters will be no match for the well-armed enforcers of tyranny.

In a socialist country led by tyrants, the food supply's production and distribution chains must be monitored by freedom-loving people to prevent the socialist government from confiscating and distributing food and necessities only to its socialist supporters and cronies. As repeated throughout history, socialist and communist tyrants sometimes control the ownership and supply of food to starve the opposition, for example, Joseph Stalin in Russia, Kim Jung Un in North Korea, and Nicolás Maduro in Venezuela.

Socialists do not want an armed civilian revolution as in Venezuela. So, the second part of the seventh strategy is to hire amnesty migrants to replace police personnel who refuse to enforce tyrannical laws. Socialists will also prefer to hire amnesty migrants over US citizens because the former will have no problem killing US civilians to put down a rebellion as in war. Amnesty migrant hiring practices will be promoted to ensure the "national security" of the tyrannical government.

Tyrant elites in government will use labels such as "war on the rich white oppressors of humanity" to describe people who refuse to give up their guns and a fair share of their wealth, or to preserve the national security of a great nation whose civilians are under attack by renegade oppressors bent on violating the laws of our country. The socialist-controlled fake news media will demonize the subgroups of oppressors, such as freedom-militias, Christians, conservatives, right-wing radicals, white supremacists, racists, those who are opposed to Islam, and greedy, heartless capitalists.

Eighth Strategy: Socialist Control of All Corporations and Industry, Including the Means of Production, Manufacturing, and Distribution of Goods

God forbid if socialists implement this strategy. If so, the United States as we know it will be in dire trouble with massive unemployment, nationalization of industry, no stock market, no capital investment for industry, difficulty obtaining enough tax revenue, a civil war going on, possibly a secession of states already having occurred, mercenary forces acting as UN Peacekeepers and killing Americans, socialist gross mismanagement of the United States, and rising widespread crime and lawlessness. Those who have guns will be criminals, the socialist military, freedom-fighters, or law enforcement. Immigration will be overrunning our country, homelessness will be rampant, food lines will be established to prevent starvation, the United States will be vulnerable to foreign nuclear attacks, socialist elites in government will become corrupt, and many people will die in the second US civil war. I hope this scenario never becomes a reality, but it is a likely possibility if something is not done to prevent this scenario of American horror.

At this point, Americans are technically at war, having experienced tyranny and oppression and having already mobilized and now waging an armed rebellion against the socialist federal government. Why a rebellion? The oppressive and unanswered list of grievances of American patriots who are part of the rebellion will be as follows:

1. the stolen election of 2020 and a defunct Supreme Court ignoring the heist;
2. loss of constitutional rights and freedoms;
3. taxation without representation;
4. oppressive and tyrannical laws passed without the consent of US citizens;
5. unjust confiscation of personal wealth, to be distributed to illegal aliens and as for black reparations;
6. unjust enrichment of the corrupt socialist elites within the tyrannical government;
7. unjust confiscation of homes and personal property;
8. a severe restriction or a ban on, and confiscation of, all firearms—a violation of the Second Amendment;
9. major loss of wages and prosperity from a ruined economy run by socialists;
10. increased homelessness, disease, and filth in practically every state and major city;
11. unavailability of food, leading to starvation, except in states that support the tyrannical government;
12. wrongful imprisonment and water-board treatment of freedom-loving American patriots;
13. UN Peacekeeping Forces used as "mercenaries" on US soil to kill Americans;
14. police agencies consisting of amnesty immigrants who imprison or kill rebelling Americans;
15. illegal entry of mercenary and police into personal homes without permission—a violation of the Fourth Amendment;
16. no due process or defense counsel for rebelling prisoners;
17. mandatory closure of churches across the country because police will round up Christians for suspected crimes;

18. allowing foreign immigrants to take over the United States and making it their home at the expense of US citizens (the remaking of the United States at our expense is unacceptable);
19. increasingly, cities in several states allowing sharia law for Muslims; and
20. needless death and destruction.

These grievances amount to pure and simple oppression by a tyrannical government. I predict these grievances will all become a reality because the freedom of patriotic Americans is incompatible with socialist tyranny in America. Worse, clueless elite socialist politicians want to destroy seventy-five million Trump voters and are not truly concerned with the well-being of the citizenry. They are concerned about themselves, their enrichment, and maintaining **perpetual** power.

The ironic thing is, socialists don't have a clue how horribly their tyranny will affect patriotic Americans. Socialists seek to maintain full control of the US government and control over everyone's lives, rather than caring about individual freedom, bloodshed from a civil war, or the Constitution. The most clueless are the reporters of the fake news media who dish out dishonest propaganda, fantasy and fiction reports to thrash their opponents for a living. The ones most responsible for this nightmare are socialist politician leaders in the United States who painted a rosy picture of a false utopia and had their supporters believing everything they were provided was free. Socialists bamboozled these poor fools, especially unskilled blacks and millennials, thinking everyone would be happily employed, with comfortable wages and equal pay, working for nationalized industry. Socialist elites who run the country will enrich themselves to become multimillionaires or multibillionaires just as Nicolás Maduro of Venezuela is now, or Vladimir Putin of Russia is now. Friends and families of these socialist elites will also become rich through corruption, similar to how Joe Biden made his relatives rich with corrupt foreign deals. Corruption among elites will continue under socialism, as did under a capitalist government. Government type may change, but human nature will be the same for greedy and corrupt humans.

Clueless socialists will realize one day that foreign criminal cartels will build their empires in the United States. Drug cartels from Mexico, Central America, South America, Russia, and Asia will form a foothold in US cities and will enrich themselves by selling drugs. They will smuggle guns into the United States exploiting Biden's open borders, and independently fight any socialist agency of the federal government or local police force that tries to interfere with their illegal business. Chinese and Russian criminal syndicates will establish roots in the United States under a socialist government. The US military under the US socialist government, and UN Peacekeepers, will battle conservatives, Christians, freedom-loving Americans, veterans, freedom-loving active military personnel, and patriotic former law enforcement officers. Drug cartels will kill anyone who stands in their way.

How Socialism Will Creep in the United States

I've mentioned that it would be a major hurdle for the United States to become socialist, if ever such a thing were to happen. How could the United States become socialist? Answer: If US citizens vote for Democrats, who go on to win the presidency and a majority in both houses of Congress, Democrats will grant amnesty to millions of illegal aliens who, together with American liberals, socialists, and communists, will always vote for Democrats, enabling them to win all future elections. Democrats will make further changes to election laws to maintain their power forever. Encroaching socialism occurs as Democrats implement leftist policies, which include the ability to do the following:

1. Silence or stifle free speech—a First Amendment violation
    Democratic socialists will oppose speech and protests against tax oppression; gun confiscation; a poor economy; rising poverty, crime, and homelessness; and filth in US communities. The socialist federal government will not allow conservative speech on university campuses, in public schools, in churches, or at public gatherings. They will have much more control in dealing with protesters than we currently have now. Hate

438

speech will be defined only by socialists, and anyone suspected of violating hate speech laws will be prosecuted. This has already occurred in the state of New York. Saying the phrase *illegal aliens* is an infraction with a $250,000 fine. Liberals in New York under Andrew Cuomo claim it's discriminatory to say this phrase. Referring to someone by gender in New York is also a violation of the law, punishable by a large fine. Social media companies such as Facebook will be controlled to detect hate speech defined only by socialists. Violators will be identified and investigated as potential terrorists or white supremacists. Watch what you say.

2. Stifle or reform US institutions
    Socialists will reform immigration; create government agencies to support socialist corruption; spy on private persons; spy on, monitor, and track conservative groups using artificial intelligence computers; spy on public schools, colleges and universities, health-care providers, places of worship, social media users, news and other communication media, law enforcement, the military, and abortion clinics; and monitor the elite pay and pension system.

    It is even more possible that no member of the Biden administration or member of Congress suspected of committing a crime or suspected of corruption will be held accountable for anything. If the economy fails, a long depression may develop that will put all socialists and the Biden administration in a lot of trouble. But it is even more likely that leftist Democrats will steal the next election even if the country goes into a long economic depression.

    Socialists will not tolerate the voices of religious opposition, which includes preaching morality against socialists, so they will stifle churches or pressure them to change their focus from biblical morality to "human rights" political morality, claiming the two are biblically the same, which is false. Liberals and socialists want churches to make homosexuality and abortion morally acceptable.

3.   Legalize open borders and give amnesty to millions of illegal aliens

Open borders and free handouts to foreigners will bring massive caravans of illegal aliens into the United States from all over the world, all seeking to claim their free stuff. Democrats will restrict ICE to stop only those suspected of drug trafficking and other crimes, and will limit deportations. This means taxes on US citizens and businesses must be increased to pay for caring for the millions of new immigrants who will enter the United States each year. Again, socialists will get amnesty migrant votes and strengthen their political power and control. Hence, the United States will become socialist.

4.   Increase taxes for the wealthy, the middle class, businesses, and industry

Socialists will advertise capitalists as rich white oppressors of the poor. Politicians will anger the poor with inaccurate political rhetoric, so the poor will back the socialist government in its bid to raise taxes on the rich and on the middle class to provide government handouts to the poor to gain their favor and dependence. Costly environmental regulations will be reimposed on businesses, and businesses will be fined if they don't comply with the regulations. The socialist-owned propaganda media will demonize rich people to gain favor with the poor, who will have become dependent on big government.

5.   Overhaul the military and law enforcement

All top generals and other military brass who do not dance to the beat of the socialist drum will be fired. Pro-freedom generals who oppose changing the status quo pose too high a risk for socialists. Socialists will appoint and promote only amnesty migrants, members of LGBT groups, and Muslims to the rank of general, as these are the groups that can be trusted to fight freedom-lovers. Along with the federal police, lesbian, gay, bisexual, and transgender people; the social engineered military in charge; and people who feel victimized by rich white people will support, protect, and defend socialist elites. Ironically, the rich will pay for all free handouts promised by socialists because it is the rich who allowed themselves to be robbed by the socialist politicians. But if the very rich and smart were to leave the United States with their wealth, the brunt of taxes to fund the military reforms would be on the shoulders of the middle class.

6. Restrict firearms, ban assault weapons and high-capacity magazines, tax existing firearms—Second Amendment violations
   Democratic politicians in some states have already pushed for heavy restrictions and high taxes on gun sales, purchases, and ownership, and in some states, Democrats have passed or are threatening to pass laws to confiscate weapons for illegal reasons. Some want to ban firearms altogether. This is a red flag, warning that socialists are planning to prevent a revolution in the future. Examples: Cory Booker wants a federal government registry of guns so the Feds know who owns guns, how many guns each person owns, and where to find owners if they need to confiscate guns. Kamala Harris wants to create an executive order to confiscate all assault rifles and large-capacity magazines. Beto O'Rourke wants to buy back weapons from gun owners, but if they refuse, he advocates entering their homes and confiscating their weapons—a violation of the Second Amendment.

7. Prepare the socialist government for a civil war
   As increased resistance mounts to taxation oppression, increased poverty, homelessness, and crime, the socialist elites in Washington, DC, will need to hire a federal police force, like the one Obama desired but failed to implement, to control all local police departments across the United States, the reason being that most police departments in cities across the United States will not support the coming socialist laws or the federal government's control of their police forces. Therefore, socialist

elites will hire only foreign migrants whom they can rely on to enforce their upcoming socialist laws. An executive order may be activated to call in armed UN Peacekeeping Forces.

The oppressive effects of socialism on freedom-loving Americans will become so great that the pressure will foment a second US civil war. Another revolution against tyranny will begin by freedom-loving Americans who, hopefully, have kept their guns and ammunition to fight the onslaught of tyranny and oppression of the socialists in Washington. Our only hope will be for all patriots and good people to unite and fight a bloody revolution against socialist elites and their foreign mercenaries who will assist them in putting down the resistance. The good guys will be our former military, our veterans, and all good folks who love freedom.

The only morality that socialists will embrace and live by will be the gospel of socialism, not the Gospel of Jesus Christ. Socialist morality will be preached and propagandized by the evil fake news media, which is full of communists and socialists. To prevent a massive exodus of corporations relocating to seceding states or overseas, the socialist federal government will change the Constitution by passing and ratifying amendments to allow the confiscation of property for the common good and the nationalization of businesses, making the socialist federal government the biggest employer in the world. Businesses and manufacturing will be nationalized and controlled, and the distribution of goods will be manipulated. This means that workers will be paid at government-dictated rates and that food will be distributed solely to socialist-supporting groups and organizations. Like Joseph Stalin, socialists distribute food only to those geographical areas and states that support socialism; those that don't will starve unless they grow their own food.

All one has to do is look at several examples of countries where socialism began as an idealized wonderful utopia and became an oppressive dictatorial government that took away freedoms of the individual.

Ask Vladimir Putin why he is a multibillionaire in communist Russia and how he and his Russian agents killed leaders opposing him in elections. Ask Nicolás Maduro how he turned a once wealthy, thriving democratic country into a dictatorial socialist country, where he stole all the wealth for himself and the military that protects him, whereas the majority of the population in Venezuela are eating out of garbage trucks and starving today.

Ask the religion of peace in Turkey how the Turkish socialist government gave meaning to the word *genocide* when they killed 1.5 million Armenians in their country and in areas of the Middle East under their control. The Turkish government ordered the Turkification and Islamization of the surviving Armenian Catholics.

In the United States, two Muslim members of Congress are also members of CAIR, a Muslim organization that wants to Islamize the United States. Given the rapidly accelerating rate of Muslim immigration to the United States and the fact that Muslims have the one of the highest birth rates of any group of people on earth, a likely date for the United States to become Muslim majority is 2060 or 2080.

On June 3, 2009, Barack Obama falsely called the United States a Muslim nation. He also said the United States was not a Christian nation, though there is an 80 percent demographic of people who consider themselves Christian. Something like the Turkish genocide of Armenians that occurred from 1915 to 1918 could happen in the United States if Muslims were to take over the government by the end of this century, *if* we patriots don't prevent it.

Look for Signs of Socialism and Tyranny; They Are Obvious

It is not difficult to see tyrannical laws legislated and passed by our federal government. One sign of the beginning of socialism in the United States is the gradual destruction of our constitutional freedoms we enjoy. More and more new laws designed to restrict or prevent citizens from exercising their constitutional rights are passed. Taxation oppression of Americans, the directed distribution of wealth to cronies, and the enforcing of tyrannical laws with a brutal police force and a ruthless military under tight control are signs of the tyranny to come.

Note that most all Democrat-run states want to severely restrict or completely eliminate ownership of firearms in the United States. It's only Democratic politicians who redefine hate speech in order to stifle the free speech of whomever they disagree with. Note that it's mostly socialist Democrats who are anticapitalistic and are doing everything in their power to remove a successful capitalist president who made capitalism successful and brought record-level prosperity to the United States.

Today, leftist Democratic politicians are pushing California closer to socialism by oppressing their constituents with high taxes and by passing laws that heavily restrict the carrying and use of firearms in the state.

Socialist Tyranny and Division in Steps after a Stolen Election

After stealing the 2020 election, Joe Biden has picked his cabinet and has already indicated that he would approve tyrannical laws that will impact hardworking Americans.

1. Congress will create and pass oppressive tax laws to meet spending plans.
2. The Biden administration will decide who will be taxed and at what tax rates.
3. The Biden administration will plan how to deal with tax resistance and tax evasion.
4. Congress will pass a law to allow open borders so as to flood the United States with a massive number of immigrants from all over the world, expecting these immigrants, after given amnesty, always to vote for socialists. Immigrants will be exploited for their cheap labor.
5. A federal police agency will be established under the DOJ to coordinate with all cities across the United States and their police departments to enforce gun laws and to confiscate guns from law-abiding citizens if necessary. The federal police force will be used by the DOJ to investigate conservative uprisings,

militias, pockets of rebellion, right-wing domestic terrorists, and those posting any opposition to tax laws on social media. (Note that passing tax laws without being able to enforce them is useless.)

6. The Biden administration will reduce the size of the US military and remake it into a force composed primarily of immigrants with socialist military leaders who will do what the socialist government demands, not the will of the people. The Biden administration will again allow homosexuals, transgender people, and cross-dressers into the military.

7. The socialist government may pack the Supreme Court with an additional number of liberal justices to override any decisions by conservative judges already on the Supreme Court.

8. Congress will eliminate the Electoral College. The reason for eliminating the Electoral College is to maintain socialist power by mob rule, that is, only the most populated states, which contain a majority of liberals and socialists, will vote for leftist candidates for president.

9. An established federal police agency will enforce all tyrannical laws passed by executive orders and by Congress, jointly with local law enforcement.

10. The Biden administration will repeal or heavily amend the Second Amendment to the Constitution to prevent citizens from using weapons for self-defense and from opposing the upcoming tyrannical laws. Federal and local law enforcement will have the resources to enforce tyrannical laws and arrest citizens on charges of tax evasion, conspiring to commit treason, or participating in a rebellion, or who are guilty of weapons violations.

11. Given that Americans love their freedoms, their US Constitution, and their prosperity, resistance to socialism started just after the election of Joe Biden. But the moment the Second Amendment is repealed, together with tax oppression, a violent armed revolution will begin against the tyrannical government.

12. As in Venezuela, the tyrannical government will use the military, composed of amnesty migrants, to put down pockets of resistance and right-wing militias, and will enter anyone's private home to arrest members of the resistance. The military may join local and federal law enforcement to occupy red states in order to maintain law and order.

13. Alternatively, the central government may use an executive order to call UN Peacekeeping troops to put down freedom-fighter rebellions on US soil. This action will expand the second US civil war into a bloody one.

14. As in Venezuela, and as in the Soviet Union under Joseph Stalin, the distribution of food will be controlled by the socialist government. Food will only be distributed to blue states in order to starve conservative pockets of resistance in red states. Many patriotic freedom-loving Americans will suffer and die.

In the end, socialists are never about God, family, or country. They are only about themselves, obtaining power, wealth, and control. For socialists, it was never about humanity, dignity, respect, morals, tolerance, or economic or racial equality. It is all about power, control, and riches for themselves as history has repeatedly shown.

The shortened version of the steps listed above is as follows:

1. Plan the socialist structure and operations of government; determine resources needed, agencies, budgets, functionality, and agency leaders; outline plans for the military and law enforcement; determine a new system of taxation.

2. Pass an open borders law for support, votes, and cheap labor.

3. Create a federal police agency and remake law enforcement with immigrants.

4. Remake a military composed of immigrants.

5. Pack the Supreme Court and eliminate the Electoral College so as to forever win votes.

6. Repeal the Second Amendment and confiscate guns to prevent armed rebellions against tyranny.

7. Pass oppressive tax laws to confiscate wealth from the rich and the middle class. Use the media to manufacture propaganda to justify tax oppression and proclaim its alleged benefits.

8. Use coordinated local and federal law enforcement agencies to enforce tax laws and confiscate wealth by force, if necessary; and use the military to put down rebellions.

9. Should a civil war begin, control the distribution of food as a weapon to starve the opposition.

10. Create prisons and concentration camps for conservatives, Christians, and any patriotic freedom-loving Americans who have been captured in the United States' second civil war. Use mostly immigrants to run these prisons and camps.

Capitalism in the United States and individual freedom and prosperity are incompatible with socialism. The Democratic Party *will* pass laws to levy high taxes on Americans to siphon the wealth of rich people and the middle class in order to give government handouts to illegal aliens and poor Americans and to meet their own socialist spending agenda. If tax-oppressive laws are passed, along with gun confiscation, the resistance will not allow the socialist government to enforce any of these oppressive laws. By January 20, 2021, when Joe Biden was inaugurated president, most rich people probably had sheltered or hidden their wealth. Massive amounts of money will have been transferred to foreign banks by millionaires and billionaires prior to, or shortly after, the results of the election. Tax evasion will be rampant.

Socialist politicians will have to enforce the tax collection laws they passed for all citizens, who may refuse to pay high taxes or who may be unable to pay their taxes because of the COVID-19 pandemic. Who will enforce these tax-oppressive laws? Answer: Leftist city administrators will reform and reshape police departments, directing them to enforce tyrannical laws by hiring amnesty migrants who don't care about, or know little or nothing about, the US Constitution but who will do their jobs as requested. There is no doubt that if leftist mayors are elected in cities across the United States, they will force their police departments to enforce tyrannical federal laws, firing any police officers who refuse.

To put pressure on cities, the socialist federal government will withhold federal funding from any city that refuses enforce socialist laws.

Watch for socialist federal government to do the following:

- Allow terrorist groups such as Antifa and Black Lives Matter to target and terrorize conservative protesters and Christians, silence conservative politicians and prevent their speeches from being heard, and vandalize churches.
- Severely restrict the First Amendment for conservatives and the Second Amendment for everyone.
- Eliminate the Electoral College.
- Pack the Supreme Court with leftist socialist justices.
- Grant Washington, DC, statehood to increase the number of Democrats in the Senate by two and gain control of the National Guard.
- Grant Puerto Rico statehood to increase the number of Democrats in the Senate by two.
- Oppress US citizens with high taxes over the next ten years without representation.
- Control the distribution of goods, favoring liberal states loyal to the tyrants.
- Place costly regulations on large corporations and small businesses.
- Continue to use COVID-19 as an excuse to shut down businesses and to use the pandemic as a tool to dictate assembly for free speech, limit attendance at church services, and reduce interstate commerce. This will have very bad consequences for the economy and will lead to higher poverty, higher debt, homelessness, loss of homes, loss of tax revenue, and an increase in crime.

What Tyrants Don't Understand

All socialist tyrants feel much better when they pass laws to ban guns before they confiscate the wealth of the citizens. Tyrants will be confronted with a revolution if citizens have guns.

Transforming a freedom-loving country that is used to prosperity earned by hard work into a socialist United States will indeed be difficult for socialists to accomplish. Worse, taking guns away from freedom-loving Americans, that is, their right to self-defense and their ability to fight tyranny, will be a formidable task, if not an impossible one in the United States. But socialists don't care what conservatives think; they say they're in charge. Conservatives will be ignored, "canceled," or "reprogrammed." Conservatives must be sheep that either obey or are forced to obey.

Socialist politicians in the United States don't understand that taxation oppression drives the very rich to hide and protect their assets. No sensible rich person, including Democratic millionaires and billionaires, will gleefully be robbed of 50 percent to 90 percent of their wealth so socialists can give it away to illegal aliens and spend it on climate change, use it to enrich themselves and their cronies, and use it to achieve other spending dreams. Socialists don't understand that taxation oppression will be shifted to the middle class, since insufficient taxes will be collected from the very wealthy. The wealth of the rich will have escaped their claws—they will be outsmarted by the rich. Then the middle class will be driven into debt, poverty, or even homelessness because of their inability to pay high taxes and pay off their debt. As hunger, poverty, and homelessness increase, resentment against the government will grow. Soup kitchens across the United States to feed the homeless will grow in number and size as seen only on conservative TV media. Martial law will be declared to control demonstrators and violent protesters. Armed militias will increase across the United States as resistance to socialist government tyranny.

28

TYRANNY CANNOT SUCCEED WITHOUT UN "PEACEKEEPERS" AND MASSIVE IMMIGRATION

UN Peacekeeping Forces Called to Defend Tyranny in the United States

An executive order (EO) signed by Barack Obama gave the UN authority to bring armed peacekeeping forces into the United States to help local US law enforcement authorities maintain law and order in fights against freedom-fighting rebels. This is a good example of the UN meddling in US internal affairs. This executive order, which was signed by former president Obama, authorizes the exact substitute that Obama was seeking for a federal police agency overseen by the federal government. Since his idea wasn't well received and would not be approved, he signed an executive order, wording it very cleverly and deceptively as an order for the UN to intervene in US domestic conflicts labeled as a "national security crisis." This would include putting down rebellions by white supremacists, and putting down rebellions by freedom-loving Americans if they were oppressed by a tyrannical US government. In this case, local law enforcement agencies across the United States would not have to necessarily hire illegal aliens as police officers, but a tyrannical US government would authorize UN soldiers to fight against conservatives and put down their rebellions against tyranny. Such a law could only be signed and approved by a despotic or dictatorial government oppressing its people. This EO is an even stronger reason for Americans to keep their guns.

The UN took control of the "compound" it was allotted as temporary UN property during a Civil Society Conference held in Utah. In 2019, the UN under Barack Obama took temporary ownership and control of US land and the buildings on it, and considered it as their own property. This is tyranny by the United Nations. If UN Peacekeepers are ever invited into the United States, they will take over land, buildings, and facilities and may not work with the US military to run its peacekeeping operations. What if the UN uses communist troops from China or radical Muslims from the Middle East as "peacekeepers"? To resort to summoning UN Peacekeepers to fight in the United States, the federal government must be losing the second US civil war, or else it considers the current level of discontent to be a sufficient threat to national security. In its peacekeeping duties, the UN can temporarily take over US land to house its troops.[1]

UN Peacekeepers will take over US properties as they did in 2019 in Utah, to house their troops and fight to put down conservative rebellions. The UN will claim this is international territory.

An important conclusion is that the United States needs to get out of the UN and kick the UN headquarters out of New York City, to some other country. The UN's agenda is to govern the nations of the world, including the USA, and it wants to distribute part of the United States' wealth to share with selective poor countries that support the UN by way of tyrannical socialism. To the UN and the cabal that runs it, they do not want any nation making itself great again, making itself

---

[1] Enoch More, "United Nations Shuts Down Free Press at Salt Lake Conference," Defending Utah, October 24, 2019, https://www.defendingutah. org/post/2019/10/24/United-Nations-Shuts-Down-Free-Press-at-Salt-Lake-Conference. More information is found in an article by DC Clothesline entitled "Battling Tyranny Worldwide," October 28, 2019, https://www.newswars.com/watch-un-takes-over-utah-taxpayer-funded-venue-claims-its-international-territory/.

prosperous through hard work and ingenuity, without sharing that wealth as they see fit. China wants to rule the UN New World Order (NWO), along with the NWO cabal.

Government should never submit to any control by the UN or to its laws. The UN is part of a New World Order conspiracy to take control of every developed country in the world with socialist rule to control the economy, the education of children, and law enforcement agencies; to control the militaries of subservient nations and disarm the civilians; and pick and choose the leaders of these nations. The UN conspiracy is very similar to the New World Order cabal conspiracy; they are very much alike. But there are conspiracy theories on the internet claiming that the Communist Party of China wants to take control of the UN or offer its services. In February 2017, Chinese president Xi Jinping vowed to lead the New World Order.[2]

One can rest assured that if there is a civil war in the United States between the blue states and the red states, and if socialists are in control of the federal government, then the socialist leaders in Washington, DC, will call UN troops to fight against the freedom-loving red states to put down their rebellions. The UN will quickly and gladly pounce on the opportunity to control the remnant of Trump voters who are fighting for their freedom. If the UN offers Chinese communist troops, US socialist politicians will summon millions of Chinese "peacekeeping" troops to kill and/or capture Americans on US soil, defeat the red states, secure their own control, and disarm the civilian population. Death, destruction, and starvation will follow for the red states, and a free United States of America will no longer exist.

The US socialist government should ask the UN the following questions before it accepts Chinese UN Peacekeeping troops into the United States:

1. Will the Chinese Communist Party withdraw its UN "peacekeeping troops" from the United States willingly, or

---

[2] Zheping Huang, "Chinese President Xi Jinping Has Vowed to Lead the 'New World Order,'" Quartz Media, February 22, 2017, https://qz.com/916382/chinese-president-xi-jinping-has-vowed-to-lead-the-new-world-order/.

will they seize an opportunity to make excuses as to why China should remain in the United States?

2. Will China demand billions of dollars in remuneration for their fighting efforts, or will China proceed to defeat the socialist US regime in Washington, DC, that hired it and replace it as a "protective state" under UN control and UN globalist leaders?

3. Would socialists in positions of power in the United States government naively trust the Chinese troops to withdraw from US soil? Or perhaps the communist Chinese will forcefully keep their troops in the United States for a prolonged period of time under UN authority, to ensure a "secure and proper transition of rule" for the socialist US regime, and to further assist them militarily in enforcing tyrannical US laws and aid them in the remaking of the United States?

4. Another opportunity to be seized: Chinese or Muslim peacekeeping troops sent by the UN may want to seize US oil wells in Texas, Oklahoma, and other red states for remuneration for their "peacekeeping efforts." The UN will sanction that move so it can get its share of the American pie.

A corrupt, incompetent old man with intermittent memory loss who frequently refuses to answer hard questions in interviews and is handicapped in his articulation of the English language, who is owned by the Chinese Communist government—that is, Joe Biden—would be the perfect stooge to naively let UN Chinese communist troops into the United States to fight conservative rebellions. If Joe Biden frequents his basement again to recover from dementia, his socialist vice president will surely select either Chinese or Muslim UN Peacekeepers to assist in putting down "Fight for American Liberty" insurrections.

It's ironic that, in their quest for power, Democrats don't ask permission from taxpayers to pay for all the stuff these politicians want to give "free" to illegal aliens. Democrats will not ask for taxpayer permission to confiscate their wealth or ask how much they may take.

Socialism Failed in Russia, Venezuela, and Cuba. Socialist EU and Scandinavian Economies Are Suffering because of Massive Muslim Immigration

The Soviet Union ran out of money to support its vast control of Soviet Bloc territories, its funding of its own military, and its communist control over its territories. The reason for the Soviet Union's failure was not war, famine, revolution, or a coup; it was purely economics. Cuba, ditto; no one can brag about Cuba's economy. The entire country has remained a Third World country since Fidel Castro took it over in 1959–60. Cuba has rotting old buildings, has poor people everywhere, and has accomplished nothing to coax people to move there.

Venezuela was a democratic country that turned socialist because of corruption. Hugo Chavez, followed by Nicolás Maduro, took over the government by way of election fraud. Then the two of them rewrote Cuba's constitution and stole billions of dollars to enrich themselves. Hugo Chavez died, but Maduro continues to pay off his military with high wages, several of whom he promoted to the rank of general. Venezuela is a failed country formed purely from tyranny, corruption, and oppression, the same as Cuba and the USSR. Why do you think Vladimir Putin is a billionaire in a communist country?

The European Union and Scandinavian countries are suffering economically because of the massive number of Muslim immigrants from the Middle East and North Africa flooding their countries and overwhelming their free-handout economies. Muslim immigrants are using the free handouts of *socialism* to survive and overpopulate the countries so they can one day gain control of these countries.[3] Socialist countries such as France, Germany, the UK, and Belgium took allocations of Muslim immigrants from the European Union and are now regretting it. The old Europe is slowly dying. Why did the EU allow these Muslims into European countries? The immigrants were allocated to European countries who agreed to accept them as cheap labor. The socialists' fatal flaw: they never realized foreigners would be a tool to change their culture and reform their institutions. Even though

---

[3] Douglas Murray, *The Strange Death of Europe* (London: Bloomsbury, 2017).

cheap foreign labor has helped European countries' economies, the Muslim overpopulation soon became a burden on these economies, with added crimes committed by immigrants, and the refusal of Muslims to assimilate into each country despite the efforts to have them contribute to its success and prosperity.

29

GENERAL TACTICS AND STRATEGIES OF TYRANNY

Once radical Democrats take full control of all three branches of the federal government, they will pass oppressive laws to confiscate wealth. It will be necessary for the socialist federal government to do one of the following things, indicating which r of the following enforcement agencies under the DOJ it would be relying on:

1. Use DHS and IRS agents to coordinate with state and local governments to enforce tax laws. This means these federal government agencies will seize private assets because of unpaid taxes and may imprison tax evaders.
2. Create a federal police force that will *pressure* every local law enforcement agency to *enforce* tyrannical laws.
3. The DHS or a new federal police agency with the IRS will seize and nationalize businesses that refuse to pay taxes or cannot pay them.

Immigrants who know little or nothing about the US Constitution, or ignore it altogether, will be hired and used as members of "socialist gestapos" paid by taxpayers to enforce tyrannical laws.

Power-hungry socialists will be unable to collect sufficient tax revenue from wealthy Americans to spend on their utopian wish list.

Wealthy Americans will oppose oppressively high taxes. It's taxation without representation; what are wealthy people getting from paying 50 percent to 90 percent of their income as taxes?

No wealthy American will trust socialists investing in bungling, fraudulent, or ineffective green energy companies such as Solyndra, as incompetent former president Barack Obama did during his presidency in 2012. After receiving $527 million in loans from the US government, Solyndra paid back only $24 million after filing for bankruptcy. Into whose pockets did the $503 million go? Can anyone imagine multiple Solyndra-type green companies going bankrupt with billions of dollars lost in waste, fraud, and abuse of taxpayer money? Who will be held accountable for such gross mismanagement and incompetence?

Who in their right mind would allow the federal socialist government to steal 50 percent to 90 percent of their wealth so that part of their money may be given to illegal aliens from all over the world entering the United States illegally? Wealthy Americans are smart enough to know that giving money away to illegal aliens is a future vote-getter for the very socialist Democratic politicians who are robbing them of their wealth. How would the socialist federal government collect taxes from the very rich if *all* of them transferred all their money overseas?

A newly "transformed" police agency with gestapo-type powers can legally force its way into homes to confiscate guns, thus violating the Fourth Amendment of the Constitution. If law-abiding people refuse to give up their guns, the local gestapo police department will put such people in prison. Some law-abiding citizens may even be "Roger Stoned" in a predawn raid, with helicopters overhead, with law enforcement busting down doors and arresting senior citizen couples in bed who refuse to give up their guns.

Why would socialist politicians fear freedom-loving, law-abiding citizens with guns? Answer:

Politicians *must* levy extremely high taxes on the very rich, the wealthy, middle-class homeowners, small businesses, and large corporations if they are to be able to achieve the items on their socialist utopian wish list. There will be severe opposition, tax evasion, and a lack of cooperation from citizen who would prefer not to get robbed by the socialist IRS. If businesses or corporations refuse to pay taxes, the government will confiscate the businesses or nationalize the corporations and hire its own people to run them. Cheap labor from peasant migrants will replace US workers, formerly in high-paying jobs, in the running of these corporations. Such migrants will be trained by remaining loyal executives who bow to socialism. Unions will be outraged at Democrats, especially union workers. Socialist elites have no choice but to control unions, which demand high wages, as is the case in Mexico. Radical Democrats will offer free handouts to all US citizens, debt relief for millennials with high college debt, and free handouts to the massive number of illegal immigrants they have allowed into the United States for at least the last four decades. Illegal aliens are "seed investments" for Democrats as they expect the illegal alien population to vote Democratic. The "seeds" of investing in an illegal alien population will sprout when illegal aliens are given amnesty and voter eligibility, making it possible for socialists to stay in power forever.

Another goal of socialists is to destroy the Electoral College, which currently determines who gets elected president. This means states' rights don't matter anymore and only the most populated states in the United States will determine who wins the presidency via the popular vote. Note that today the majority of the US population lives in blue states. This may mean, for example, that votes from only four or five states out of the fifty that make up the union may determine who wins every presidency; all other states will be ignored. This is pure and simple mob rule. The Supreme Court will likely be packed with socialists to approve every law the tyrannical Democrats want. The result: The federal government, installed only by the few most populated states, will become the supreme authority of the land and states' rights will no longer exist. But this will not be done easily or overnight.

As Democrats accumulate more power, a revolution will begin before the federal government eliminates the Second Amendment and demands law-abiding Americans surrender all their weapons. This and taxation oppression will cause the second US revolution, because our freedoms will be slowly and methodically destroyed. By continuing to *replace* patriotic Americans such as police officers with amnesty migrants to enforce socialists' unconstitutional laws, and by replacing patriotic members of the military with mostly amnesty immigrants to protect and defend the tyrannical government, the socialist government is in effect mobilizing for war against and oppression of its opponents. Who else will enforce unconstitutional laws? Answer: foreigners, *not* patriotic Americans. Patriotic law enforcement officers and members of US military love our freedom and love our country; they would refuse to violate our existing Constitution and would refuse to illegally arrest or imprison US citizens. Foreigners who don't care about US laws will enforce any illegal executive orders signed by the president or any laws passed by congressional tyrants. And there will be a lot of foreigners to choose from, including Muslims.

If a federal police force and local law enforcement from states, counties, and cities are still ineffective in enforcing laws, the socialist federal government may activate Barack Obama's executive order that calls for foreign peacekeeping forces to aid the United States in times of a crisis. That is, UN–US peacekeeping military forces will be called, with US national security cited as the reason, to US soil to put down freedom-fighter rebellions and civil protests. These "mercenary" UN Peacekeeping Forces will likely kill American freedom fighters on US soil to defend tyranny.

Patriotic military members, law enforcement officers, US veterans, and able-bodied families will keep their weapons, will rise against Democratic tyranny before tyrants become powerful enough to make the United States into a Venezuela, and will win, but it may be a bloody civil war.

The Democrat Goal of Perpetual Power and Conservative Opposition

The purpose of the Democrats is to accomplish their goal of being in power forever. This is how they plan to do it:

By advertising free stuff to foreigners from all over the world handed to them by the federal government and by government in states such as New York, New Jersey, and California, Democrats plan to enable/allow the trafficking of foreigners into the United States from all over the world by proposing open borders, eliminating ICE and DHS, and allowing unvetted immigrants to enter the country with no background checks to detect terrorists, murderers, child molesters, and rapists. Democrats want amnesty for all foreigners who come into the United States. Once hundreds of millions of foreigners are in the United States, these immigrants will change the racial, cultural, and religious landscape of the country. Traditional America will be no more; this is also a goal of the socialist Democrats. Since the American people rejected Hillary Clinton in the 2016 election, the same population, unless illegals significantly populate the United States, will reelect President Trump and reject Democrats again. As a result, the current patriotic population who voted for Donald Trump will be reduced to a minority, and the Democrats expect foreigners to vote for them forever so they can maintain power and control.

Another part of the Democrats' strategy is to increase taxes on goods and services. This will cause an increase in prices and in the cost of living, thereby causing illegal aliens to move to other states. For example, illegal aliens working for minimum wage in California will not be able to afford the higher taxes for gasoline, housing, or utilities; car registration fees; car insurance premiums; fees for driver's licenses; increased traffic fines; and so on. The rise in the price of food will also cause them to move to other states where taxes are not high and the cost of living is much lower. This means the Electoral College in any red states illegals move to will also change the political landscape of those states. It also means flipping a red state to a blue state because of immigrants moving to red states. Blue states will intentionally raise taxes to increase the cost of living and drive out illegal aliens, who will move into other, red states to overpopulate them and flip them to blue states in order to increase and win congressional votes. Red states can prevent illegal aliens from migrating from blue states to red states by using ICE to check interstate migration and apprehend any noncitizen migrants.

Democratic politicians in states such as California are even letting illegal aliens run for elected state government positions and for positions in city and county government. This strategy will also help Democrats maintain forever control in California. Once Democrats attain "forever" power and control of states and all three branches of

The Coming Tyranny

the federal government, they will then try to change or destroy the Constitution to model a socialist, tyrannical-style government. That completes their strategy.

But the Democrats' strategy is flawed; it's already opposed by patriotic and powerful Americans. A second US revolution will very likely occur if all the aforementioned Democratic government handout policies are implemented, putting illegal aliens first rather than taxpaying American citizens. American citizens:

- will not accept taxation without representation
- will not be bullied by tyrants into paying high taxes and will not be oppressed by tyrants
- will not give up their guns to tyrants or to police agencies consisting of foreigners acting as gestapos to enforce the destruction of the freedoms and rights of individuals
- will refuse to give this country away to illegal aliens
- will refuse to pay for free stuff Democrats are handing to illegal immigrants who will be granted amnesty to get votes, which goes against taxpayer interests
- will take up arms against federal government socialist tyrants and blue states like California
- may prevent a red state from flipping to blue. Laws in red states should propose that if states such as New York and California serve as funnels of massive illegal aliens into other states, then red states should sue California, New York, and other blue states for care and expenses incurred for each illegal alien crossing from those blue states into their red states. Each illegal alien should be returned to his or her state of origin. All Democratic lawmakers in California should be sued as well. California and New York bear costs when they allow illegal immigrants into their states and cannot take care of them because of their intentional policies of inflating the already high cost of living, causing undue burdens on illegal aliens, causing them to leave the state.

461

Mayor Bill de Blasio of New York City has already allowed New York City payments to the homeless to relocate to other states without the states' knowledge. All illegal aliens coming from California and other blue states into red states should not be allowed to collect welfare and food stamps, unless California, New York, or the other blue state where they came from foots the bill. A wise plan in red states is to stop illegal aliens from crossing over from California and to deport them or charge California an "interstate migrant tax" for each migrant. Why should taxpayers in the rest of the country foot the bill for illegal aliens flooding out of California and New York? California caused the problem, so it should be held accountable for massive migration coming out of its blue state into a red state or another blue state, neither of which can handle the immigrants either.

The Socialist Revenge of Democrats on Trump Voters in 2021

Conservatives have lost all representation in government because the 2020 election was stolen and now Democrats control both houses of Congress. Loud voices have been heard from both houses of Congress, expressing the hate, ill will, contempt, and disrespect that Democrats have for President Trump. Democrats had demanded Mike Pence remove President Trump from office using the Twenty-Fifth Amendment. The alternative was that the House threatened to impeach the president.

Democratic members of Congress are hell-bent on canceling anyone they disagree with. They are hell-bent on canceling any discussion of issues in debates; Democrats are not interested in winning the hearts and minds of the people. Never before has there been such viciousness; just listen to what the Speaker of the House Nancy Pelosi says, or the remarks of Senate majority leader Chuck Schumer. Many traitor Republicans, such as Mitt Romney, have joined the contemptuous Democrats in suggesting Trump be removed in office with only two weeks left before Trump's term was up. And Joe Biden had the nerve to lie to the American people about running on a campaign of unity of the country?

In a letter to President Trump, Archbishop Viganò from the Vatican signaled what good leaders in the Vatican were concerned about—the "Great Reset." Socialist governments are funded by corrupt billionaires, backed by the New World Order, to rule every aspect of human life, using the COVID-19 pandemic as a tool to arrest people for having COVID-19, dictating when people can assemble or not assemble, dictating when they can or cannot go to church, and mandating lockdowns that ruin lives and drive people into poverty or homelessness. Socialists will deprive humans of their freedom and their God-given rights, and the citizenry will be governed by tyranny. But the forces of good, with God on the side of those who stand against evil, will expose their corruption and immorality, which is why they hate President Trump. Watch for the coming tyranny, and stand with God to do the right thing. We may lose battles, but we must win the war.[1]

FIGURE 2. The scale of injustice

Since the Democrats captured a majority in both houses of Congress, the Biden administration will be able to change election laws so Democrats can win all future elections. They will have no

---

[1] Archbishop Carlo Maria Viganò, "Archbishop Viganò Warns Trump about 'Great Reset' plot to 'Subdue Humanity,' Destroy Freedom," Life Site News, November 30, 2020, https://www.lifesitenews.com/news/abp-vigano-warns-trump-about-great-reset-plot-to-subdue-humanity-destroy-freedom.

checks and balances between the branches of government, especially if Biden packs the Supreme Court. With open borders and millions of illegal aliens entering the United States, the scale of injustice will be tipped when the illegal immigrant population is given amnesty. With liberal votes combined, Democrats will outnumber conservatives and therefore will win elections. It's called "the scale of injustice" because liberals and socialists cannot attain power by debating issues or by winning the hearts and minds of citizens, but rather by their corrupt, abrasive, manipulative remaking of the United States, rigging and stealing elections, and changing our culture and institutions to attain power at the expense of others.

With President Donald J. Trump's mandate to build a wall along the southern border of the United States, and thanks to the teamwork of ICE, the Department of Homeland Security, US Citizenship and Immigration Services (USCIS), the coast guard, and other federal agencies, we have significantly reduced the flow of illegal immigration into the United States and prevented the scale of injustice from being tipped by liberals and illegal immigrants.

Additionally, President Trump crippled Democrats and diminished their opportunities for attaining power. With Trump's veto power, House Democrats had little or no chance of passing any legislation, such as giving COVID-19 checks to illegal aliens, bailing out mismanaged blue states to puff up their civil servants' salaries and pensions, and giving stimulus money to Hollywood moguls.

A Prelude to Socialism: Details on Why the Left Wants Illegal Aliens in the United States

It's logical to conclude that Democrats oppose gun ownership by law-abiding American citizens because they fear a future a revolution against future socialist elites attaining perpetual power. Democrats also want to protect *all* illegal aliens from deportation, including any criminals among them. Democrats already advocate that illegal aliens should be permitted to buy guns. Liberal Democrats and socialists, by placing *illegal aliens* into a category as victimized people who are hated because of their race, make illegal immigrants think that rich white Americans are responsible for their economic misery. Lazy, irresponsible, freeloading millennials will vote for, protect, and support liberal Democratic socialist policies in future elections. Democrats plan to take power by allowing more illegal aliens into the United States to get their votes under amnesty, as they presently continue to offer free government handouts to illegals.

Worse, illegal aliens are desired by the Left for the following reasons:

1. Cheap labor
    Americans with high-tech degrees making between $100,000 and $200,000 per year will be replaced in high-tech companies by computer developers from India and other countries who will work for between $30,000 and $50,000 per year, thus displacing highly paid American workers. Why?

    *   Corporate profit—and high-tech company executives will make huge profits.
    *   Socialism requires cheap labor as it nationalizes part or all of its manufacturing industry and consequently has to run these industries with no experience whatsoever. But socialist elites will have to hire contract workers from foreign countries who provide cheap labor to engineer and manufacture their products, which used to get done by American brilliance, innovation, and engineering, but at cheaper wages.

    Democrats also want illegal aliens to enter the country as unskilled servants to provide cheap labor for liberal billionaires such as the ones who live along the coast of California. Democrats in many states are advertising free government handouts for illegal aliens to draw them toward the United States like a magnet.

2. Votes
    By allowing open borders, the United States will see one massive caravan after the other entering the country, mostly from indigenous countries around the world, with people

who have no skills, no education, and no wealth. Very poor unskilled migrant workers will seek jobs from employers who will hire them, causing a displacement of the American workers, particularly blacks and millennials who are used to working for higher wages.

3. Destruction of unions
Open borders do not help unions. With the abundance of cheap labor from the caravans of foreigners coming into the United States, there will be no need for strikes and the socialists will cause unions to dissolve. Example: The Mexican government has so much cheap labor from South and Central America, and within Mexico itself, that manufacturing industries can hire anyone they want for cheap labor and labor unions will never succeed in bargaining for higher wages. In the United States, socialist politicians are no friends of labor unions.

4. No incentives will be offered for innovation and invention
Given that socialist elites don't know how to manage industrial manufacturing, or how to manage homelessness in their poop cities, or how to reduce crime in their communities, they will hire an expert "industrialist czar" who, they hope, will run various manufacturing industries in the United States that are nationalized by the socialist federal government. And given that low-skilled foreigners and high-tech foreign workers can be hired and paid low wages to run US industries, there will be little or no incentives or rewards to develop better-quality products or find strong *demand* for the products as in a capitalist system, where competition, innovation, and invention can create and increase profit. The wages of all workers will be the same no matter how productive or brilliant they are; wages must be held down for all employees for socialism to work.

5. Free Higher education for everyone, including immigrants
The cost of a college education today is tens of thousands of dollars per student, which can be obtained from college loans.

Currently there is about $1.6 trillion in debt owed by college students in the United States. Socialists in power will hire teachers to educate students and provide them with skills to enter the workplace, while socialists are ruining the country. Socialists are already suggesting free tuition for everyone, paid for by the taxpayer, and the forgiving or reducing the amount of college loan debt. Socialists expect taxes paid by wealthy Americans to pay for a free education in the United States. Socialists are betting on students getting the same level of education that was provided under capitalism. Naive socialists think that the level of education will remain the same or even improve—quite the contrary. Great reductions in tuition means that all the left-leaning liberal, socialist, and communist professors in college will have their salaries slashed. Social elites in power can't pay these leftist professors high wages, as their colleges and universities are subsidized by the government. That will reduce the quality of the professors hired. If the massive numbers of foreigners who enter the United States are given free college education in addition to existing US citizens, how much will that cost? No socialist politician will estimate the cost of education under socialism. It is too scary to talk about, on top of other spending items socialist politicians are afraid to talk about. College professors' salaries will be significantly reduced by the very liberal socialist system these leftist professors were indoctrinating high school and college students with. They will have to get used to the low wages or else quit.

6. Taxation
    Socialists will confiscate the wealth of American individuals, not only 50 percent to 90 percent of the wealth from rich people (the top 5 percent), but also at least 50 percent of the wealth from the middle class, consisting of hardworking Americans and homeowners, thereby driving them into deeper debt, poverty, or homelessness. But the top 5 percent may give up their US citizenship and/or transfer all their millions

or billions overseas so their money will never be robbed by socialist politicians. Socialist politicians never conduct surveys or speak about public sentiment toward paying high taxes.

What is the sentiment of Americans who may be asked to give their hard-earned money, by way of taxes, to illegal aliens and welfare recipients, to fund free education for all, to pay employee wages in nationalized industries, to fund free health care for everyone, including illegal aliens, to fund pensions of members of the military and law enforcement, to pay reparations for blacks, and to enrich socialist elites? Answer: Taxpayer sentiment will be extremely negative, and these actions *will* result in a major revolution or in massive protests against paying out any taxes to socialist elites in Washington. What will the socialist elites' response be? Answer: They will ban the Second Amendment or severely restrict the freedoms it guarantees to make law-abiding citizens defenseless if they should revolt against the coming tyranny. The socialist government will establish a national police force as an arm of the federal government that will enforce IRS laws to confiscate properties of people avoiding taxes or significantly in arrears. A federal gestapo-style police force has already been suggested by Barack Obama and Cory Booker. Cory Booker wanted a federal agency to go after "right-wing terrorists," who are white people suspected of using liberal-defined hate speech or of committing hate crimes. It's essentially a war on any white people who express dissent, and is a violation of free speech. Booker obviously seeks to make his racist buddy Louis Farrakhan very proud.

7. To nationalize industry
   Will workers be paid enough to allow them to make their mortgage payments and support their families with the wages that a nationalized industry will provide? How many millions of people will become unemployed by the canceling of a government-subsidized project such as the Keystone XL Pipeline, which brought oil from the United States and Canada?

What will happen to the economy? Will anyone have a pension left? Will social security for seniors be raided by socialists? Will the IRS confiscate homes? Will VA compensation for service-connected disabilities be canceled? Will retired military members have their pensions honored, or will their pensions be reduced? Will 401(k) accounts be partly or fully confiscated if the owners owe taxes? In time, socialists will methodically get their dirty hands into every conceivable money pie there is and break the Social Security and VA piggy banks for money to spend on the common good. After homeowners and the unemployed find themselves unable to pay their debts to banks, the banks will seize whatever assets they have in savings and retirement to make up for their losses. Only federally insured savings will be compensated to the customer out of his or her bank savings.

Will we see soup kitchen lines in major cities across the United States, with many people lining up for food? Answer: yes, because of the increased poverty and homelessness generated by socialist policies. Democrats will weaken the United States and make it vulnerable to our enemies, and may cause the defeat of the United States by foreign enemy nations. In 1956, Nikita S. Khrushchev of the Soviet Union said about the United States, "We will bury you." He meant that the United States would die from within and be finished off by its enemies.

8. Homelessness
Homelessness exists in the shamelessly neglected poop cities of California such as San Francisco and Los Angeles. These cities are living proof that Democrats cannot manage major cities in the United States, in addition to mismanaging crime-ridden cities. With California taxpayer money being spent on free health care for illegal aliens as a priority, it is no wonder that these clueless Democrats can't reduce their massive homeless problems by spending more. California lawmakers and Governor Gavin Newson prefer to fund free health care

for illegal aliens over funding care for the homeless and veterans of California; this will put California and the rest of the nation under the potential danger of the spread of communicable diseases such as tuberculosis, typhoid, bubonic plague, and COVID-19, and skin diseases caused by a combination of trash, rats, and fleas, which the incompetent leftist politicians of California cannot adequately or consistently prevent or clean up. Just what are these shameless politicians in California doing to benefit the citizens and taxpayers of California? Answer: High taxes imposed on businesses and individuals do little or nothing to benefit the people who live in ghettos, and will fail to prevent homeless people from loitering and defecating in and around businesses in many city areas. High taxes, homelessness, high crime, and poverty are driving the middle class out of California into nearby states.

9. Crime

Crime-ridden cities such as Detroit, Chicago, Baltimore, and Los Angeles are proof that liberal Democratic politicians cannot manage a major city in the United States. Leftist groups like Antifa and Black Lives Matter only add to the crimes committed in these cities when mayors and their city administrators order police to stand down and let their cities be looted by criminals and burned to the ground. Liberal politicians are so antipolice when it comes to the sensitive issue of race that they allow mob rule in their cities and stifle police action against mobs. In Portland, Oregon, the liberal mayor allowed a conservative journalist to be beaten up by a mob, caught on camera and shown nationwide on TV. Antifa cowards in masks were videotaped beating up a helpless old man. Antifa was videotaped destroying Confederate monuments just because they disagreed with the actions of historical US leaders represented by these monuments. Has the FBI labeled Antifa as a terrorist group? No, but if a white supremacist group were to beat up an old black man, or tear down a statue of Barack Obama or Joseph Lenin in the State of Washington, or one of

Che Guevara in Florida, then Joe Biden's administration would label these people, using his slew of executive orders, as hate groups and terrorists who should be arrested. Members of Black Lives Matter (BLM) advocate killing police officers and attack them during riots. A member of the New Black Panther Party (NBPP) shot and killed five Dallas police officers. Why hasn't FBI director Christopher Wray labeled BLM and the NBPP each a terrorist group?

10. Terrorism
Liberal socialist members of Congress do not want to vet illegal aliens. Democratic leftists have sanctuary laws to prevent released illegal alien criminals from being deported by ICE. Crying Senator Schumer and Rachel Maddow, the latter being a member of the hate-Trump media, cried crocodile tears about videos taken of children in cages at the border who had been separated from their families. But no one ever shows their crocodile tears on TV when US citizens are murdered or raped by illegal aliens, or when MS-13 gang members torture and kill a student in high school with a machete. Why the hypocrisy? It turns out that the video shown on Fox News about children in cages was taken during former president Barack Obama's term in office, but the fake news never revealed this fact to the public when they showed the video. Both Schumer and Maddow teared up on TV about the wrong president, but blamed it on President Trump.

How Democrats Will Use Immigration to Attain Socialism

Democrats today appear to represent and benefit foreigners more than they do citizens because not enough US citizens support Democrats. So, the Democrats' plan to gain power is to offer free stuff to draw foreigners into the United States from all over the world, even from countries whose citizens want to kill us, so they can also vote to support them and their socialist agenda. Taxes will increase as prosperous Americans are ripped off to pay for foreign immigrants, who will have the socialists to thanks for giving them free stuff paid for by tax-oppressed US citizens.

Wealthy taxpayers get *nothing* in return for paying higher taxes. This is tyrannical taxation without representation. Under a socialist regime in United States, if the economy declines for any number of reasons, then poverty and crime will increase and Democratic socialists will become desperate to ban and confiscate guns in fear of a revolution. As people resist giving up their weapons and police officers refuse to enforce the ban or confiscation of guns, a plan to hire amnesty migrants to a federal police agency will be promoted to enforce confiscation of weapons. Part of the plan is to fire high-ranking patriotic soldiers and replace them with leftist officers or amnesty immigrants. Foreigners may be offered amnesty if they join the military. A trusted military will enable socialists to have better control of the military to protect and defend socialist elites.

A Secession of States under the United Constitutional States of America

A new secession of states may occur as our Constitutional rights are being taken away and our ability to have fair elections is destroyed. A new Bill of Rights and a new Declaration of Independence may be written, signed, and submitted to the US Federal socialist government as reasons to secede from the Union. If Federal police agencies, with the help of local law enforcement, try to take guns away from citizens, a secession of states may occur, and a new bloody American revolution may occur. At this point, Democrat socialists in Congress will debate on preventing a secession of states or negotiating the tyrannical policies they have imposed on the seceding states. But the union of seceding states, which could be called the "Constitutional United States of America" (CUSA), will have a full list of state grievances against the tyrannical government, citing oppression, loss of states' rights, and lack of representation for the seceding states, along with their citizens' loss of constitutional rights and freedoms. Former patriotic police officers, veterans, and soldiers will join good folks to take back the United States from the socialist elites. American patriots and freedom fighters will never allow socialism to rule the United States or control their lives.

If the socialist USA decides to mobilize the US military in non-seceding states and declare war on the CUSA, then American patriots will also mobilize and declare war on socialist USA. Patriots will live free or die, and socialists will be forced to surrender or die. After many foreigners are killed in a bloody war, patriotic Americans will also suffer casualties. This is the scenario I see, as I also see red flags and hear the alarms of tyranny set by members of the Democratic Party.

A Declaration of Independence from the Socialist Government of the USA

Seeding states will file the following grievances about things affecting their states:

1. Severe restriction or banning of firearms, which violates the right of self-defense and the Second Amendment of the Constitution, causing undue cost burdens on law-abiding gun owners.
2. The declaring an unarmed civil war by the socialist USA on seventy-five million Trump voters through a series of oppressive dictatorial executive orders and oppressive socialist legislation.
3. Socialist leaders, partnering with big business, stifle conservative speech on social media, which violates the First Amendment.
4. Socialist leaders partnering with Black Lives Matter and Antifa, which are domestic terrorist groups, are vandalizing church statues and church buildings. Those are personal property crimes and trespassing on personal property.
5. Socialist leaders, partnering with the corrupt socialist propaganda media, stifle religious freedom and Christian voices. This a violation of the First Amendment of the Constitution.

6. The socialist US government, by executive order, is unfairly punishing churches in an effort to get them to violate their Christian morals by taking away their tax-exempt status, which otherwise is granted to religious institutions, if they refuse to hire homosexuals for church activities or allow homosexuals to lead youth group activities, and if they refuse to allow same-sex marriages in their churches.

7. The socialist US government, by way of executive order, is unfairly using oppressively high taxes to fund abortions at organizations such as Planned Parenthood, when the performing of abortions violates their Christian morals.

8. Socialist leaders, partnering with the corrupt socialist propaganda media machine, have declared a news war against conservative Americans, demonizing them, urging and celebrating retribution for their being Trump voters, urging oppression, showing vindictiveness, and calling for a "reprogramming" of conservatives and people with conservative thinking.

9. No southern border security causes serious safety and COVID-19 concerns. Joe Biden's executive order halted building of the southern border wall. This executive order aids and abets illegal aliens and facilitates their entry into the United States, which is a violation of immigration law and constitutional law.

10. Refusing to deport illegal aliens entering the United States is a violation of immigration laws, violates constitutional law, and risks American lives given the high number of foreign criminals transporting illegal drugs, which kill some of the Americans who use them.

11. Levying large taxes without offering requisite representation is a problem. Additionally, conservatives have little or no representation in a socialist system of government where there are no checks and balances and where the Democratic Party controls two of the three branches of the federal government.

12. High taxes on income and property causes undue economic hardship.

13. The federal-run education system is flawed. Children in public schools are being taught to hate the United States, are being

forced to hate the history of the United States and its founders, and are encouraged to have a negative image of white people. Public schools do not focus on real education and do not promote patriotism or a love for the United States.

14. Wealth is unfairly distributed to people based on race.
15. High taxes are used to create funds to provide government assistance to immigrants, granting them amnesty in exchange for votes so as always to keep socialists in power.
16. Election laws are unfairly changed to keep socialists in power permanently.
17. Democrats will pack the Supreme Court so as always to have their socialist legislation approved.
18. Distributing the federal taxes of seceding states, disguised as COVID-19 relief, to bail out mismanaged Democrat-run states is irresponsible and unfair.
19. Sanctuary cities protect criminal illegal aliens from being deported.
20. Oppressive laws require transgender men to use female dressing facilities and showers in public schools, and allow them to compete unfairly with females in sports.
21. Police agencies are criticized as being racist and using excessive force.
22. Elected Muslim members of Congress will likely partner with Hamas and other terrorist groups for future US mercenary needs to assist in resolving strife/rebellions.
23. Killing the Keystone XL Pipeline project, which helped the United States to achieve oil independence, will affect seceding states negatively and has caused one thousand workers to lose their jobs.
24. There is a proposal to tax the rich and businesses at a rate between 50 percent and 90 percent and to raise the taxes of other hardworking people to benefit immigrants, pay for global warming and green energy programs, and maintain socialist power and control.
25. The Christian religion has been stifled. Socialists define the new morality and impose taxes on churches because the socialist

government wants religious institutions to allow immoral actions, such as same-sex marriage, that violate Christian beliefs.

26. The socialist government uses its own definition of hate speech to accuse conservatives of being racist and of continuing systemic racism if they use such words as deemed hateful. Conservatives object to being monitored, tracked, and spied upon by the socialist US government so as to be targeted for retribution. Their privacy is invaded when they express dissenting opinions of the government, and they face possible arrest for free speech and thought that advocates in words a revolution against a tyrannical socialist government and/or advocates a secession of states.

27. Hollywood liberals denigrated, harassed, and threatened to harm or assassinate President Trump, or to kidnap his son, and they denigrate Trump supporters, partnering with Antifa, Black Lives Matter, the corrupt news media, big corporations, and the socialist US government. This is unacceptable.

28. The evil fake news media slandered, lied about, and defamed President Trump and his family 24-7 for four years, a practice that continues even now, after Trump has left office. The socialist corrupt fake news media has joined the socialist government, Wall Street, and high-tech corporations in that it is being used by corrupt politicians.

29. Democratic politicians urge people to run Trump-supporting employees and Trump supporters wearing MAGA hats out of restaurants and other places of business, also suggesting that Democrats get in these people's faces and shout profanities at them. Joe Biden preaches unity, but to achieve unity is impossible with all his executive orders and with Democratic members of Congress threatening conservatives with violence, harm, disrespect, hate, and deprivation of their civil rights in places of business.

These are oppressive actions on the part of a socialist government that degrades conservatives and stifles their lives, thoughts, religious rights (including the right to worship God), speech, and opportunities to work for a living and to sit in a diner or at a lunch counter without repression or harassment. At risk is the right to work hard and achieve economic prosperity to accomplish the American dream; the right to life, liberty, and the pursuit of happiness; and the right to live a healthy economic life without being punished for being a member the white race, which has committed sins in the past. To lose these things would be a travesty of justice, an attack on our constitutional freedoms and our way of life. Therefore, it is our right, as the Constitutional States of America, to secede from the union to be free from tyranny and oppression.

A Prelude to the United States as a Third World Country: Immigration and Liberal-Run Poop Cities

The importance of preventing illegal aliens from entering the country cannot be stressed enough. It is crucial we do this if our nation is to survive. If we have open borders, the political power will shift from freedom-loving conservatives to the socialist members of the Democratic Party, who will destroy the US economy and many of our constitutional freedoms, which *will* eventually lead to a second bloody American revolution. We will be fighting either the mercenary UN Peacekeeping Forces or our own local, state, and federal police forces and the US military, consisting of mostly immigrants hired by socialist elites at all levels of government to enforce their tyrannical laws—if we American patriots let them.

If We Trust Socialists and Embrace Their Free Stuff, Then We've Allowed Ourselves to Be Snookered

The UN is reporting that since last year, Venezuela has been killing people who protest against Nicolás Maduro's dictatorial government, on top of starving its citizens. That's what banana republic dictators do who usurp power illegally: steal the country's wealth, and pay their crony police and military friends large sums of money to allow death squads to arrest, torture, or kill opposition leaders, control redistribution of food to friends in order to starve the opposition, and allow Cuban and Russian troops onto Venezuelan soil to protect the regime against US intervention. Guns had already been taken away prior to all the extreme repression of Venezuela's citizens, and death squads had been created. The first thing Maduro's regime did was to pull a Hillary Clinton—rig the election in their favor, but without the use of Russians.

Don't think this could happen in the United States? Given the massive support and power of former president Trump, patriotic police, active military members, veterans, conservatives and their families, and Christian organizations, such a thing won't happen here. But by chance, in the future, if a socialist is elected by our country with a majority of illegal aliens, freeloaders, and leftist Democrats, it could happen. Early stages of the process have already begun in California. For example, there are harsh law restrictions on guns and ammunition, confiscation of specific weapons and magazines in many cases, increased taxation without representation, open borders, and ads to draw illegal aliens into states such as California and New York State. Illegal aliens are allowed to hold state government elected positions; foreigners are hired as police officers to enforce socialist tyrannical laws; illegal aliens are protected from deportation in sanctuary cities; entire law enforcement departments are politicized; homosexuality is taught to kids in public schools; and the middle class is being eliminated with many, slowly, moving out of California, leaving only the very rich and very poor. More power and control are the goal of California Democrats, which will lead to undesirable tyranny. If the federal government becomes infested with socialists, the United States will initially become like California, and soon thereafter it will be like Venezuela, including making use of a gestapo agency and/or death squads. Civil war will break out bigtime before that happens. Prediction: In the end, freedom will prevail and the socialists will be brutally defeated because Americans will have kept their guns. But all this will have come at a huge price.

Joe Biden Will Continue to Weaponize Federal Agencies to Destroy His Opposition

Joe Biden will likely continue to weaponize all federal agencies, as happened under the Barack Obama administration, to weaken, blackmail, or destroy his opposition by any means possible. A Deep State II will be developed to destroy the reputations of political opponents and remove them from office. If suspected of being guilty of a crime, a political opponent or staff member will be "Roger Stoned" in predawn raids, arrested, and charged with the crime or even with bogus charges. This kind of government corruption and tyranny will result in a major civil war.

The Deceptive and Naive Socialists

Following are some reasons why I believe socialists to be both deceptive and naïve:

1. Socialists will refuse to publicly reveal the estimated grand total of their spending policy costs.
2. Socialists will always push the idea to the poor and immigrants that everything is free, which is false.
3. Socialists will never be accurate on who all will be taxed, how much they will be taxed, for how long they will be taxed, or what other surprise taxes are being considered or manufactured to tax the very rich, the middle class, and businesses.
4. Socialists will not reveal how they will deal with people who cannot afford or who refuse to pay taxes, how they will collect taxes from tax evaders, and what tyrannical laws they will enact to enforce taxation oppression.
5. Socialists don't realize that they will be unable to collect sufficient taxes from the rich, who will escape with their wealth to other countries or have their money hidden or sheltered from taxes. As a result, socialists will have to hit the middle class and businesses harder with taxes.

6. Socialists don't realize taxation oppression will drive a great number of middle-class Americans into poverty, high debt, and even homelessness.

7. Socialists don't understand that high taxes and costly regulations will cause businesses to go bankrupt, or relocate overseas to avoid taxes, or lay off a massive number of workers. As a result, socialists don't realize that the stock market will drop like never before or cease to exist if the economy fails.

8. Socialists don't realize taxation oppression will lead to another bloody armed civil war.

9. Socialists don't realize that millions of illegal aliens will come into the United States each year to get their free government handouts offered by socialists. This will bring down the US economy under the socialists' open border policy.

10. Socialists don't understand human nature or the unalienable rights of humankind, not getting that the following things are true about human beings—

    a. They want to be free from tyranny and oppression.

    b. They want to be free from big government control over their lives.

    c. They want to be prosperous from their hard work, rather than conform to government-mandated wealth redistribution for income equality.

    d. They will never give up their inalienable rights, given by God, to seek life, liberty, and the pursuit of happiness without government intervention or tyranny.

    e. They never want to be slaves in chains serving a master, that is, the socialist government.

30

THE SOCIALIST INDOCTRINATION OF YOUTHS IN PUBLIC SCHOOLS

The Indoctrination of Our Youth in Schools and Misinformation by the Media Have Caused the Majority of Students to Oppose American Values and Embrace Socialism

Many youths in schools do not learn about the US Constitution, patriotism, citizenship, how our country became great, the challenges our nation faces in the world, why we are a great country, the value of freedom, or what our military personnel died for on the battlefield in past wars. Most teachers today are leftists who think the United States and its founders were racist and the US Constitution was written for white supremacists. This is the garbage kids are currently taught by liberal teachers across the United States—a false indoctrination of our youth. From the 1960s to the end of the twentieth century, most high schools taught US history and civics. But all that changed in the twenty-first century for millennials, especially during the Obama administration.

Racism wasn't invented in the United States; it had been a practice for thousands of years in the history of humankind. Europe, the Middle East, and Africa have a long history of slavery. North America was colonized when slavery was still an acceptable institution. Black African merchants sold blacks to Europeans and North American merchants. Colonists brought slaves to North America. The United States has a history of racism, particularly in the South, where slaves were used to work in agriculture. Slavery ended in 1863 after the US Civil War by President Abraham Lincoln's Emancipation Proclamation. But the United States also had many people in its early years who were against slavery, particularly in the North. In early America, parts of the United States and specific members of Congress in various US administrations were racist. After the US Civil War ended in 1865, it was tallied that approximately three hundred thirty thousand troops from the North had died fighting the Confederacy and to free slaves.

The United States evolved; this is one important fact that deceptive Democratic politicians who play the race card always omit. Today the United States is *not* a racist country, nor is there any systemic racism in the United States as President Joe Biden and his staff claim and want you to believe. It's all about getting elected and increasing the power base by way of black support. Christian values and the consciences of white people saw the unfair plight of those suffering from racism and discrimination. Civil rights laws were passed, and since the 1950s, as the United States evolved, the justice system was reformed. Just as genes mutate and dominate, with old bad genes dying and better genes propagating, American values evolved into the culture we have today. Racism in the United States today is nowhere near what it was during the 1950s and 1960s or earlier. Although racism has to do with the personal beliefs and choices that come from the hearts and minds of people, leaders throughout US history, whether black, white, or other people of color, were agents of change who transformed the United States into a nation of dignity, respect, and tolerance for one another with justice, law and order, and the promotion of Christian family values.

The United States was founded on Christian values and not by any other religion. The Bible's morality can never be changed; it is the human race that has often interpreted biblical scripture for its own convenience, for its own exploitation of others. Some politicians have tried to align biblical morality with their own false political values and have used it to justify their own personal prejudices or crimes. The United States has always been a great nation, as mentioned earlier when responding to Governor Andrew Cuomo, and to Eric Holder, Obama's stooge for attorney general. There can be no doubt that the United States has been and continues to be the greatest nation on earth. Educators in high schools, colleges, and universities must come to grips with reality and must educate youth on the United States' great accomplishments since its founding. The truth must be taught to kids in school of the evolution of the United States to its status of greatness today, instead of politicizing US history to defend any party.

Failed schools, poor teachers, poor education curriculums, poor student discipline, and bad school administrators are the root causes of poor education. Biased leftist political beliefs, which debase our history, slander our values, and thrash our culture, should have no place in schools.

Liberal-biased teachers are not concerned with US history. They resent it and hate the United States. Students are indoctrinated in liberalism, progressivism, socialism, or communism. Then they become the most intolerant human beings after they graduate from school. They are taught not to tolerate any free speech they disagree with. They create their own definition of hate speech; any speech not fitting with their definitions comes from people they deem to be haters. Indoctrinated students do not tolerate the Christian religion, ICE, rich white people, capitalism, or those who oppose illegal aliens, and above all, they did not tolerate President Trump or his staff. The irony is that even though these biased chump teachers and indoctrinated bamboozled kids hate the United States, they never leave the United States, so we're stuck with them.

History about leaders who committed mass murder and transformed their governments into fascist entities, communist entities, or dictatorships is apparently kept a secret from millennials by liberal Democratic teachers who teach and glorify socialism and big government to indoctrinate students. World history repeatedly shows that death comes to those who love freedom and oppose tyrannical rule by military force, by police action, through starvation, or by a lack of medical care. In each case, the millions of victims who possessed weapons had their guns confiscated prior to their demise. Those in this country who fought and gave their lives so Americans today could be free were brave men and women who died in honor. It's better to die fighting for freedom than to die in chains under tyranny.

There are many sick-minded millennials in the United States who have no parents, or parents who neglect them, or parents do not discipline them. God is missing in their lives. Teachers in some states are not allowed to discipline kids. In California and other liberal states, politicians have passed laws to introduce kids to homosexuality and teach them about a genderless society so as to promote homosexuality to kids at a young age. Democratic lawmakers pass bills, as in California, to prevent teachers from disciplining kids who curse at them. Some kids come from single-parent families or are missing both parents; they have no moral guidance, which allows some of them to create a culture of evil where anything goes, even mass killing without a conscience.

When I was in civics class at Los Altos High School in 1965, my teacher Mr. Nichols once said, "In the future, you will be the ones to defend our constitutional government and explain the difference between communism and capitalism and why our capitalist government is a better form of government." Mr. Nichols, a conservative, was so right.

Today, only eight or nine states require teaching civic classes in public schools. This is why there is a lack of knowledge about US government, how it works, and the meaning of good citizenship. Topics such as the best of the United States, defending and fighting for its freedom, the reason for forming our constitutional government, and how we justify our form of government versus other forms of government are not taught in public schools.

Why Some Americans Hate the United States

Most liberal Democratic teachers, particularly professors in universities, do not think the United States is great and prefer to ignore or despise US tradition and culture. Some students coming out of universities even hate the United States. This is one root cause of the loss of our customs and traditions. Liberal indoctrination in schools is part of the reason why California is failing. It also explains how liberal Democratic elites can control and "groom" uneducated young students to support leftists in their attainment of power. We now have more socialists in Congress than we did in 1965.

According to Alexa (voice activated), the number of registered Democratic voters in the United States is 48,408,000 (40 percent), and the number of registered Republican voters is 35,142,000 (29 percent). The population of the United States as of July 2020 was 325,719,000. So, there are more Democratic voters than Republicans in the United States, and the political affiliation of 31 percent is unknown. One can only infer from this data that 31 percent of the population of the United States are new residents, unregistered voters, people who are not affiliated with either the Democratic or Republican political party, or people who do not vote. There is a high probability that a significant portion of this 31 percent of the US population are illegal aliens. Illegal aliens cannot legally vote in federal or state elections. Unfortunately, we do not know how many thousands or even millions of them voted in the 2020 election. Many illegals who obtained false IDs or were granted driver's licenses over the years were able to use them for identification, including for voter registrations. At the federal level, we see why Democrats believe in open borders and why they prefer mail-in ballots, which are often fraudulent.

31

HIRING IMMIGRANTS AND USING THEM TO ENFORCE TYRANNICAL LAWS

Leftists Will Run Police Agencies and Hire Amnesty Migrants to Enforce Laws

If socialists are ever elected to control the federal government for the first time, they will create a federal police force and pack it with migrants, thugs, and leftists who will pledge to, and be trusted to, enforce all socialist tyrannical laws. A federal police force will essentially be a politicized leftist police agency or a mostly *mercenary* police force to arrest violators of socialist tyrannical laws, a gestapo force that over time will be authorized to enter the homes of US citizens to take their guns away and/or incarcerate them without trial or due process, forcing a second American revolution.

Hiring migrant foreigners as police officers should be a red flag to all indicating that the government at the federal, state, and local levels are preparing to enforce some upcoming oppressive tyrannical laws that many police officers may not want to enforce.

Local, state, and federal socialist and Democratic politicians and civil rights organizations are changing the hiring standards and composition of police agencies, beginning in blue states. Instead of hiring well-qualified police candidates in cities such as Denver, Colorado, or parts of the country such as California, New York, and Illinois, socialist

Democratic politicians will continue to use racism, discrimination, and intolerance as socialist tools to hire more foreigners whose backgrounds cannot be checked and who are much less qualified than US citizens. Liberal Democratic politicians don't want to hire the best-qualified people for police work; they want to pack police agencies with foreigners whose political views are consistent with their own socialist views. Their socialist goal is to hire police officers who are capable of enforcing socialist tyrannical laws and to create police departments whose members can be molded to ignore or oppose the Constitution and to care less about patriotism, and are trained to enforce all laws socialists pass as "reforms."

As big government violates the constitutional rights of Americans. The United States has been remade and become lost. Given the current state of affairs, a second American revolution will be necessary to take the United States back from tyrannical control.

The second reason that liberals favor foreign immigrants over US citizens is that foreign immigrants provide cheap labor and can be employed for lower wages.

In the socialist-run United States, more foreign immigrants would be needed by a tyrannical government as police officers and members of the military. The military would be tasked to put down rebellions and right-wing militias. Police officers would be tasked to enforce tax laws and gun laws, to prevent and stop hate speech, to enter homes to confiscate guns without warrants, and to assist IRS agents in confiscating private homes and nationalizing industry and manufacturing businesses if homeowners or industrial companies are in tax arrears.

How Law Enforcement and the Military Will Be Controlled

If a Democratic president is elected in the United States someday, that president will not hesitate to declare gun violence a national emergency and therefore will restrict gun sales and the carrying of guns, ban guns, or confiscate guns based on their twisted socialist excuses, which in the end would be the beginning of the tyranny of the

US government. Over time, the United States will end up in the same situation as Venezuela with people stripped of their weapons and their wealth and therefore no longer able to fight the tyrannical socialist elites in power. Who will be the equivalent of Nicolás Maduro's military defending him? Answer:

1. socialist Democratic mayors controlling police departments;
2. police departments consisting only of supporting socialists and foreign immigrant workers hired as police officers;
3. an overhauled US military composed of only higher-paid socialist supporters;
4. perhaps a contracted foreign military force from a Muslim country hired to defend and support socialist elites in the United States;
5. perhaps UN Peacekeeping Forces authorized by a socialist executive order to put down freedom-loving American rebellions opposed to the tyrannical socialist US government in power.

As a prelude to socialism, the hiring of foreigners as police officers has already started, and a gestapo force has already been suggested by presidential candidate Cory Booker. Elizabeth Warren has already suggested replacing the function of the DHS with "something else." That something else will be a federal police agency.

On July 7, 2016, Micah Xavier Johnson, a member of the New Black Panther Party (NBPP), ambushed and killed five Dallas police officers and injured nine others. Two civilians were also wounded. Johnson, an Army Reserve Afghan War veteran who was angry about the police shootings of black men, stated that he wanted to kill white people, especially white police officers. The shooting happened at the end of a protest of the police killings of Alton Sterling in Baton Rouge, Louisiana, and Philando Castile in Falcon Heights, Minnesota. Dallas police finally killed Johnson. It's because of terrorists such as the NBPP that all police departments must be armed with special military weapons and resources to take out these racist killers who hate white people.

In August 2018 presidential candidate Beto O'Rourke expressed his antipolice sentiments: "Black men, unarmed, black teenagers, unarmed, and black children, unarmed, are being killed at a frightening level right now, including by members of law enforcement without accountability and without justice."

Failed socialist Democratic candidate Beto O'Rourke said that a "frightening level of unarmed black teenagers" are being killed by police; this was fact-checked by the *Washington Post* as statistically false.[1] Beto O'Rourke resigned as a Democratic presidential candidate because of a lack of support and funding. He had a criminal record of burglary and DUI in El Paso, Texas. He expressed his anti-ICE rhetoric, and said he wanted to tear down any walls Trump built along the southern border if elected. O'Rourke joined antipolice socialists Cory Booker and Kamala Harris in advocating using police officers to confiscate guns from law-abiding citizens.

Los Angeles police officers are trained in the academy to deal with antipolice mobs such as those they had faced during the Watts riots of 1965 and the Rodney King riots of 1992. Police officers are supposed to call for backup to confront a mob of thugs and arrest them for failing to disperse, for purposes of officer safety, to prevent assault or battery of a police officer, or for interfering with police duties. The only way mobs today will succeed with their crimes is if police departments are ordered by liberal mayors or city administrators to stand down and take this kind of harassment and ignore the riots. Daryl Gates, the LA police chief during the onset of the Rodney King riots, was fired for dereliction of duty in preventing the riots and for failing to order an organized police mobilization against rioters and looters, who caused more than fifty deaths, with more than four thousand injured, and cost $1 billion in property damage in Los Angeles. Mayor Tom Bradley, once a police officer himself, was ashamed, not of black thugs burning the city, but of Daryl Gates and the LAPD for ignoring it.

In October 2018, in Portland, Oregon, Antifa protests turned violent, the result of a twenty-seven-year-old black man who had been

---

[1] Glenn Kessler, "Beto O'Rourke Claims on African Americans and Police Shootings," *Washington Post*, August 30, 2018, https://www.washingtonpost.com/politics/2018/08/30/beto-orourkes-claims-blacks-police-shootings/.

shot and killed by police in the previous month, after allegedly shooting two people and approaching officers with a gun. Antifa activists blocked traffic, shouted profanities at drivers, threatened violence, and damaged cars.

But the liberal city mayor, Ted Wheeler, ignored the lawlessness of the Antifa mob and allowed a conservative journalist to be beaten up, which act was caught on camera. Antifa cowards in masks were videotaped beating an elderly man bloody with a crowbar. As another man attempted to help, he was also hit in head with the crowbar, then sprayed in face with mace. Ted Wheeler is still mayor of Portland, Oregon.

On July 23, 2019, two NYPD officers were seen on video making an arrest. They were ambushed by several individuals, doused in water, and then struck in the head with the buckets. Another video showed two NYPD officers walking away with their heads held low as a mob also dumped water onto them. Antifa was declared a terrorist group by President Trump after they were observed rioting, and they believed responsible for organizing the rioting from May 28 to June 1, 2020, in various cities across the United States as a result of police brutality against George Floyd, who was black.

Antifa and Black Lives Matter are funded by George Soros, who should be arrested as a coconspirator in funding, aiding, and abetting these domestic terrorist groups that commit violence. More examples of antipolice behavior could be cited.

Respect for law and order has remained relatively unchanged from the twentieth century to the twenty-first century when it comes to apparent police brutality in black neighborhoods. But disrespect for law enforcement has increased in the United States by white people who beat up people they disagree with, or break statues or monuments of people from US history whose actions of philosophies they disagree with. These are not Antifascist groups, but rather a bunch of anarchist mobs who mimic Nazi racist brownshirt mobs in Germany, who burned books they didn't like and beat and persecuted people they didn't like.

Congress should fund contracts with think tanks to find root causes of antipolice hatred for purposes of police reform and prevention of police violence, profiling, and discrimination against nonwhite people.

Politicians should assign a commission to determine the root causes of disrespect and hatred of police officers in the black community. Blacks must understand the necessity and legality of police officers shooting a black person in self-defense in the pursuit of law enforcement and justice. Threats and attempts to kill police officers must never be tolerated.

Police officers should understand the only legal choice for firing their weapons is for self-defense when they fear their lives are in imminent danger. Many police officers, especially white officers, avoid policing and enforcing the law in black communities because they fear they might cause a race riot and be fired.

City administrators and politicians at the state and federal levels are supposed to make laws to prevent mob lawlessness and enforce laws it, not ignore it. They should not "hand the keys of the city" over to mobs so they may riot and destroy the city by ordering police to stand down. Teachers in public schools should influence the attitudes of people from a young age to respect police, instead of disrespecting police. Psychiatrists should offer advice to recommend keeping violent offenders incarcerated. There should be statistics from studies conducted that indicate weak, moderate, strong, or very strong correlations between different kinds of violent criminals and the likelihood they will shoot and kill police officers. Judges should then give these violent offenders longer prison terms for good reason, for purposes of common sense, and because of the high risks such offenders pose to law enforcement.

The Lawlessness of Antifa and Black Lives Matter—Domestic Terrorists

The Antifascist organization known as Antifa is a violent and lawless organization that does not function as an Antifascist peaceful protest group but, rather, as an armed paramilitary domestic terror group of extreme leftists supported by the Democratic Party. Antifa are not actually Antifascist; they are fascists themselves, who want changes made by using force and terrorism against anyone they do not agree with. Antifa labeled US historical leaders who were slave owners as fascists and destroyed their monuments. Antifa labeled the Trump administration as fascist without any logic or common sense. Antifa is a violent terror organization prepared with a variety of weapons designed to be used to silence free speech, beat up conservatives, tear down historical monuments, and beat up people they don't like in public. Antifa mimics the Taliban in Afghanistan and ISIS in the Middle East, who tore down non-Muslim religious artifacts they opposed. Antifa is a watered-down US Taliban composed of radical leftists, among whom are black Muslims, white liberals, homosexuals, brainwashed millennials, socialists, communists, and anarchists. In the past, they have vandalized Christian statues during protests, destroyed or stifled free speech in public, and protested in and around city offices or buildings that allow ICE to arrest illegal aliens. Some Antifa members are:

- inexperienced young hooligans, nerds, and opportunists who are cowards when they aren't wearing their mommy-pressed black Ninja-style outfits they wear during protests and riots
- radical millennials who hate the United States and can't assimilate into the current culture
- paramilitary revolutionaries who train in anti-USA militia groups.

Their leaders communicate with and are funded by representatives of the New World Order cabal to plan nefarious acts of terrorism in the United States.

President Trump declared Antifa a domestic terrorist organization on May 31, 2020. Antifa is composed of radical leftists who support socialist and communist Democrats. Their mission is to terrorize conservatives, join with peaceful protesters as a pretense and opportunity to riot, clash with right-wing protesters, attack ICE, attack police officers, and commit violence against conservatives speaking in public places. Members of Antifa were seen on TV beating up a handicapped old man in public wearing a MAGA hat. They are essentially cowards hiding behind masks to prevent their faces from being recognized. They obstruct passageways and destroy property.

Evidence surfaced, as indicated by DOJ Attorney General William Barr, that Antifa played a major role in planning, coordinating, and participating in the Minneapolis, Minnesota, riots and in several riots in other cities across the United States, causing the destruction, burning, and looting of businesses, government monuments, churches, and buildings. Never before in US history has any police department in the United States abandoned a police building, leaving it to be burned by rioters, as has the Third Precinct of the Minneapolis Police Department. Their abandonment of their police building was a misguided retreat, giving a victory to Antifa, who had set the Third Precinct on fire. Since Antifa is a terrorist organization now, if any of their members are caught organizing, directing, or participating in riots again, they can be attacked or captured by the military or arrested by the police as terrorists.

Currently, leftist mayors in primarily Democrat-run cities such as Portland, Oregon; Seattle, Washington; Minneapolis, Minnesota; and Washington, DC, have ordered police to stand down and let protesters-cum-rioters burn and loot businesses, rather than ordering police to pressure-hose rioters to disperse them along streets and to prevent them from destroying property or causing potential harm to police and other citizens. Note that all protesters must disperse when the police declare an illegal assembly when a crowd forms in a specific location, whether the crowd is peaceful or violent. Protesters who refuse to disperse, or any who toss feces, urine, bricks, or gasoline-filled bottles at police, will be arrested and taken to jail.

During the riots, it was reported that some leftist Hollywood celebrities publicly funded the Minnesota Freedom Fund and the NAACP to bail out protesters arrested by police. Leftist judges in Minneapolis, New York City, and other Democrat-run cities were quickly releasing protesters after they had been booked. Some well-known celebrities who contributed to the Minnesota Freedom Fund are Steve Carell, Ben Schwartz, Chrissy Teigen, Patton Oswalt, Janelle Monae, and Seth Rogen.

Some professional sports players and Hollywood actors even cheered rioters and encouraged them to commit more sadistic rioting as indicated from their Twitter accounts, such as John Cusack, Michael Moore, rapper/actor Ice Cube, Trevor Noah, and Colin Kaepernick.

Failed presidential candidate Julián Castro, socialist New York City Rep. Alexandria Ocasio-Cortez, Rep. Ilhan Omar (D-MN), Rep. Ayanna Pressley (D-MA), and Rep. Rashida Tlaib (D-MI) have all solicited donations to *ActBlue*, a charity that enables donations be made for "bail funds," according to the *New York Times*. But after looking up **ActBlue** online, I think it may be a fraudulent website, according to reddit.com.[2]

At least thirteen Biden campaign staff members posted on Twitter that they had made donations to the Minnesota Freedom Fund. Failed presidential candidate Kamala Harris promoted the Minnesota Freedom Fund on Twitter.[3] One list of relatively unknown petty actors who supported the fund is found at https://www.hollywoodintoto.com/stars-fund-protesters-not-victims/.

Why Is the First Amendment Important?

The First Amendment is important because it's the constitutional right of every American to *safely* express their opinions in public places, in social media, in government forums, in the news media, and at schools, colleges, and universities. No US citizen should be silenced for being a conservative or for standing up for God, family, country, conservative values, and the freedoms the US Constitution provides.

This amendment also allows all Americans the freedom to worship God the way they see fit and express their religious beliefs without government interference or violent retribution. The beliefs of every American who is Christian shall not be trampled by atheists or other self-interest groups, or by any level of government in the United States.

---

[2] See https://www.bing.com/search?q=actblue+site%3awww.reddit.com.

[3] Collin Rugg, "Here Is the List of Celebrities Paying Bail for Violent Rioters and Looters," Trending Politics, January 2021, https://trendingpolitics.com/here-is-the-list-of-celebrities-paying-bail-for-violent-rioters-and-looters/; Christian Toto, "Hollywood Stars Douse Riots with Digital Gasoline," Just the News, June 2, 2020, https://justthenews.com/nation/culture/hollywood-stars-douse-riots-digital-gasoline.

32

THE NEW WORLD ORDER AND THE GEORGE FLOYD RIOTS OF 2020

Riots occurred across the United States after a forty-six-year-old black man, George Floyd, was arrested in Minneapolis, Minnesota, on May 28, 2020, for paying for store items with a counterfeit twenty-dollar bill. As Floyd appeared to be complying with arresting officers while handcuffed, Derek Chauvin, a white police officer, was videotaped pinning him on the ground with a knee on his neck, subsequently causing his death by suffocation. This incident was interpreted as police brutality, which caused protests across major cities in the United States, and subsequent rioting, which caused more than $55 million in damage in property loss and multiple injuries to police in Minneapolis alone. Rioting also caused tens of millions of dollars of damage mostly in the cities of blue (Democratic) states.

Likely Conspiracy Analysis and Scenario

Just after the police brutality incident and the killing of a black man by a white cop, wealthy members of the New World Order cabal such as George Soros, and other elite globalists, saw perfect opportunities:

1.   for House Democrats to pass a law to fund trillions of dollars in bailouts for Democratic states;

2. to make the crisis all about race and the ongoing oppression of the black race (for example, anger blacks and cause them to incite riots);

3. to organize the effective tools of the Democratic Party, Antifa, and Black Lives Matter (BLM) to provide them the resources they need to conduct riots, for example, crowbars, fireworks, water bottles, bricks, gasoline, and explosives, and pay them to effectively plan riots in the most vulnerable cities in blue states across the United States;

4. to coordinate allowing the destruction of cities mismanaged by leftist mayors and governors so as to allow Antifa and BLM to loot, burn, destroy property, and kill or injure police in a conspiracy with Democratic governors to destroy businesses and patriotic American monuments and symbols, and lead and entice other people, including blacks, to loot, burn, and destroy property as well;

5. to cause significant burning, looting, and destruction across blue cities, before incompetent governors finally call in enough resources to quell the riots and examine the damage.

Democratic governors and mayors demand trillions of dollars in emergency disaster relief from leftist Democrats in Congress and they got it as part of the COVID-19 relief bill.

The Conspiracy of the New World Order Cabal Using Antifa and Black Lives Matters in Riots

The leftist New World Order (NWO) cabal are rich socialist elites who want to create a socialist world government, which they want to control by internally destroying the status quo of world powers as necessary and/or reforming the institutions of all world powers, including the United States. In the United States, these institutions include colleges and universities, public schools, federal, state, and local governments, the economy, law enforcement, the military, immigration policies, churches, religion, social services, elections, and the justice system. The NWO cabal seeks to bribe, fund, employ, and influence leftists like themselves to redefine biblical morality in major religions in Europe and the United States to justify their socialist agenda using their new morality for humankind. The New World Order elites seek to end economic injustice, along with bringing an end to racism, Islamophobia, sexism, homophobia, and xenophobia. The cabal expects everyone to live in peace, singing "Kumbaya" together in a happy utopia controlled by big government. This is the new world order they seek under their leadership and control.

The New World Order is opposed to nationalism, heralded by any nation to achieve its greatness; they were appalled by President Trump's agenda to make America great. Cabal socialists want to be the only big government that creates greatness and shows how to control it. The cabal socialists would like to see the United States subservient to and regulated by the United Nations. Cabal socialists such as George Soros, world bankers who control large sums of wealth and economies, high-ranking members of churches who are corrupt or homosexuals, leaders of the European Union, and the elite European Rothschild family would all like to see socialism internally implemented in the United States to strengthen their global power and control; they would have done anything in their power to take down President Trump and his Republican voters in the United States, to benefit US Democratic leftists and help put them into positions of power and influence across the United States. Members of the cabal may likely have already funded useful and trusted leftists and prospects running for office in the United States who could affect the social reforms they need to cause insurrections in the United States against leaders like President Trump, for example, to impeach President Trump, using tools such as Antifa and Black Lives Matter (BLM) to stir up a sense of victimization, fear, and anger in the black population and to drive many blacks into rioting in order to destroy, weaken, or cause reforms to law enforcement and government leadership positions.

Tucker Carlson, a Fox News reporter, claims BLM pressured many businesses to pull ads from his show. Papa John's Pizza, Disney, and T-Mobile are just a few businesses that have been extorted by threats of protests, violence, and rioting against their businesses if they didn't comply, so they were promptly forced to comply with the demands of BLM, an organization that has joined Antifa as a domestic terrorist organization. How many other businesses across the United States will these lawless domestic terrorists extort in order to get what they demand?

Reforms are more possible when triggered by a crisis, such as the death of George Floyd, a black man, caused by a racist white police officer. A US president who inspires American nationalism and pride in the greatness of the United States, and who succeeds in making America great, goes directly against the desired goals of the socialist cabal and socialist elites in the United States. Democratic politicians who said America was never great are governor of New York Andrew Cuomo and former attorney general Eric Holder under the Obama administration. The sentiment is shared by liberal public schoolteachers who indoctrinate our youth.

Note that globalist socialists, when approaching today's economic reforms, will use the same tactics as the socialists in the United States. They will strip the wealth from the wealthiest countries, for example, the United States, to give it to less unfortunate developing countries to create economic justice by implementing convenient policies such as those related to climate change. They will say underdeveloped countries are more affected by climate change to justify allocation of taxes to those countries. This is the same strategy US Democrats use to offer free government handouts to immigrants, to draw them into the United States to gain their votes and to support passage of their tyrannical socialist laws specific to the wealthy in the United States. By weakening the United States and propping up the economies of other countries, the NWO cabal gains the support of a multitude of underdeveloped countries and also gains increased power and control.

After having allowed liberal cities to be destroyed or burned, blue states will likely apply for hundreds of millions of dollars in federal disaster relief to rebuild the cities that liberal mayors and governors irresponsibly allowed to be destroyed by rioters. The police brutality crisis gave Democrats, particularly socialists, and the NWO cabal opportunities to weaken law enforcement, defund law enforcement, get rid of police officers, or possibly replace them with some leftist organization to do social work instead of police work. The Minneapolis City Council, some of whom support Antifa and BLM, considered abolishing or defunding their police department. Cities such as New York, Los Angeles, Phoenix, and San Francisco proposed significant cuts to the funding of their police departments. To appease protesters, Muriel Bowser, the black mayor of Washington, DC, ordered a city street leading to the White House to be renamed as Black Lives Matter, painted in yellow, which extended for blocks. Socialist politicians continue to champion the evil work of Antifa and BLM organizations and allow them to riot, put down conservative speech, stifle religious freedom, and attack police officers. They allow Democrat-biased news media to spread fake news against conservatives 24-7, and hey demand trillions of dollars in reparations for blacks. They destroy capitalism in the United States by destroying businesses and making jobs less available, and turning the United States into an anarchic chaotic nation with no regard for the safety of US citizens or enforcement of constitutional law—all socialist goals.

Peaceful protesting is a right granted under the First Amendment to the Constitution. But the cabal and phony religious US Democratic politicians knew and disregarded the fact that peaceful protests during the George Floyd riots would always bring with them bad people whose acts to destroy the livelihood of others, rob their stores, and beat and shoot people—all sins and the work of the devil. Grossly inefficient mayors of Democrat-run cities who failed to protect their citizens and failed to prevent local businesses from destruction aided and abetted the work of the devil. But that's what the NWO cabal wanted, in concert with its associated hierarchy of supporters. Blacks and whites alike know that the slogan "No justice, no peace" means city police and businesses are going to experience burning, looting, death, and destruction since the people are not getting the justice they are starving for. That is, no peace is cause for rioting, death, and destruction to effect change. The man whose shoes no one has ever filled since his assassination, who would be totally opposed to this slogan, is none other than civil rights leader Dr. Martin Luther King Jr., who changed the hearts and minds of many people to achieve important and significant civil rights victories.

The failure of the Minneapolis protests was that these protests were overshadowed by rioting, which got more attention in the media, as many black young thugs were seen on TV breaking windows along many city streets, looting the businesses, and setting them on fire. How will carrying cases of liquor out of liquor stores bring about justice? How will young fat white women carrying merchandise out of a Target store in a cart accomplish reform against police brutality or honor the death of George Floyd? Why didn't Barack Obama fix the problems with the police during his eight years as president? But he's got suggestions now. What makes city mayors or members of city councils think that by dismantling or defunding their police departments, they will bring either justice or peace to black communities? What makes blacks think that after the riots are over, business owners will be able to rebuild or remain in the same neighborhood?

Some black leaders are calling for "economic justice," asking that corporations donate to the NAACP, BLM, or other black causes. As a first step, they are also calling on mayors of cities to provide funds for rebuilding riot-destroyed businesses, whether these funds come from city, state, or federal government. Funding the rebuilding of businesses that have been destroyed should not be the responsibility of taxpayers from outside the states that are led by incompetent Democratic mayors and governors who mishandled the rioting and allowed the businesses in their jurisdictions to be vandalized, destroyed, or burned.

Notice there was not even a peep out of Speaker Nancy Pelosi or Senate Minority Chuck Schumer, who did not condemn the rioting, burning, and destruction of Democrat-run cities by leftist domestic terrorist organizations. But after the riots were over, Pelosi appeared on TV announcing offering trillions of dollars in emergency aid relief largely to Democratic states, but the Senate and President Trump rejected their bill because of their incompetence in handling the riots. Democrats sought to make President Trump's rejection of the House's Emergency Relief Bill a campaign issue, blaming Trump for the riots and for refusing to help riot-torn cities in need, which incompetent state and city Democratic politicians allowed.

Note that the rioted areas in Detroit in 1967 and Los Angeles in 1965 and 1992 were never significantly rebuilt; riot-torn areas are today still mostly empty fields or dilapidated ghettos where little or no businesses returned. These cities and states lost their tax base as businesses moved out of the area, afraid to serve black neighborhoods. White flight occurred because no white person wanted to live in or near dangerous areas where blacks rioted or lived. As a result, blacks were left segregated, welfare surged, and crime and poverty increased. It is easily predictable that blue states today will have areas of their cities end up the same way after the riots. For more about the Detroit riots, see under "Then and Now" at http://ss.sites.mtu.edu/mhugl/2015/10/13/detroit-riots-1967/.

On June 5, 2020, the truthful news reported that the month of May had seen the highest employment increase within one month in US history; 2.5 million jobs were gained. But employment decreased in failed Democrat-run cities such as New York, Boston, Washington, DC, Los Angeles, and Chicago. All these Democratic cities in May and early June 2020 had been mandated with stay-at-home orders by Democratic politicians because of COVID-19. But during the riots over the death of George Floyd, the same politicians suddenly authorized peaceful protesters to assemble close together in the streets, with most wearing masks, to protest police brutality without harassing them, arresting them, or ticketing them.

Even former president Obama put his two cents in on George Floyd's death by telling protesters to "make people in power uncomfortable," also saying that this crisis is "politically advantageous for protesters who are calling for widespread reform of police departments and large-scale institutional change." This simply means tyrant politicians seek to defund, weaken, restrict, and limit policies and procedures of law enforcement agencies in Democratic states such as California, New York, New Jersey, Minnesota, Washington, Oregon, and Illinois. It is understandable why former president Obama wanted fewer police and more violence. Obama's mentor was socialist Saul Alinsky, who was a huge proponent of violent revolution in the United States. Obama encouraged rioters and looters to continue protests and rioting, equating the violence to the American Revolution to make progressive change. Additionally, Obama said the widespread protests were just another way the United States was paying for the "original sin of our society" that began with slavery. Saul Alinsky taught that leftist violence in the streets could overtake the US government—an insurrection by revolution.[1]

With their executive orders, Democrats in blue states ordered everyone to stay at home because of COVID-19. But they were completely silent when rioters and protesters joined closely together in their states. Democratic politicians didn't fine protesters in large groups or individual rioters as these tyrant mayors and governors ordered the police to fine people in churches, ticket vehicles parked in church parking lots, fine people inside restaurants, and threaten police, also saying they would pull people from the water on beaches. That's hypocrisy and unequal justice.

---

[1] Rebecca Diserio, "Obama Recommends 'Protestors' Continue Mayhem on Streets, Gets Epic Smackdown," Mad World News, June 4, 2020, https://madworldnews.com/obama-protesters-mayhem/.

33

ATTEMPTS TO RESTRICT, BAN, AND CONFISCATE WEAPONS

Why Is the Second Amendment So Important?

Because it's the constitutional right of every American who may need to prepare to defend himself or herself, and his or her family, against criminals, government tyranny, and wild beasts. Americans should never give up their guns and instead should die fighting with dignity—which is better than being incarcerated or made a slave in chains. American patriots must defend their freedom and prevent the United States from turning into a socialist country.

There may come a day when we will need our guns to deal effectively with tyrannical politicians and their gestapos who will terrorize and brutalize US citizens. There are already Democratic politicians who want to take guns from law-abiding people and liberal Democratic judges who hold gun manufacturers liable for shootings committed by insane career criminals. These judges ignore the fact that guns are designed to *legally* protect and defend the innocent. Therefore, no one should not be sued by any person or any organization for the misuse of guns.

_____

David A. Herrera

Socialist Tyrants in Power Will Confiscate the Best Firearms for Fear of a Revolution against Them

If tyrants and socialists know who own guns through a federal gun registry, then the federal government can gather intelligence data on whomever they want, surveil anyone they want for any reason on social media and on our cell phones, interfere with our freedom and our privacy, and spy on us all they want. It's another form of abuse of power for the elites, just as Barack Obama weaponized his government agencies to spy on candidate Trump prior to the election of 2016. Democrats who want to restrict, outlaw, or confiscate guns, prevent the sale or purchase of guns, stifle the carrying of weapons, or restrict the number of bullets in a magazine become tyrants who take away our right to bear arms.

As the elites in Washington, DC, become more socialist, they tend to pass laws to take away the freedom and rights of the individual for what they say is the common good. They also fear a revolution that will take their control and power away. Many ignorant people in the United States are completely unaware that Democratic state legislators have been proposing and passing very restrictive gun laws in California because these Democratic elites in California fear a future revolution.

In Washington, DC, the Democrats are also beginning to pass laws to store information on any law-abiding Americans who own guns. Only terrorists, illegal aliens, and criminals will not comply with *any* gun laws. So why would Democrats pass them? Answer: to target conservatives and white people who cling to their guns and Bibles.

How the Socialist Tyrants Plan to Enforce Laws to Confiscate Specific Firearms

As of January 29, 2021, the Biden administration had signed forty-two executive orders. Non-COVID-19 executive orders should be unconstitutional. Joe Biden is governing like a banana republic dictator. Congress should be discussing and debating issues addressed by these executive orders, such as immigration, equity, the economy, and the

504

environment. The Speaker of the House knows many of the issues in these executive orders would not pass the House if made into a bill, and some would not be passed in the Senate. The arguments and debates on the issues addressed by the executive orders, in the form of proposed House bills, would cause a major embarrassment for the Democrats, so Nancy Pelosi is allowing Joe Biden to legislate from the White House, bypassing Congress and distracting the American people with the Trump impeachment.

After the January 6 assault on the White House, Nancy Pelosi and other Democrats blamed Trump for instigating it, and impeached him for a third time. The second impeachment hoax (the pay-to-play scheme with Ukraine) failed in the Senate. Democratic members of Congress distrust the National Guard and think troops linked to white supremacy might commit mass murder against President Biden and members of Congress. Democratic members of Congress think Republican members of Congress who take guns with them into congressional meetings will murder Democrats during these congressional meetings. House Democrat Alexandria Ocasio-Cortez thought that Republican senator Ted Cruz was going to murder her. The Department of Homeland Security was warned to look out for white supremacists who will start a revolution. Democrats are absurd in their fear and paranoia. The real reason for the Democrats' alarmist, unfounded accusations of US troops and Republican members of Congress being untrustworthy is that Democrats want to ban the Second Amendment.

There is no doubt that if socialists, with their insatiable greed for power, pass laws to ban firearms in the United States by executive order or martial law, then a bloody revolution will likely occur in this country. Beto O'Rourke had said that if elected, he would go after every law-abiding citizen's guns. Cory Booker said he wanted to create a federal anti–white supremacist agency to detect hate speech on social media, investigate hate crimes, and go after "white supremacist terrorists." No Democratic politician, including Joe Biden and the Democratic politicians of Congress, ever mentioned dealing with the violence of Black Lives Matter and Antifa.

Tyrannical socialists will use a gestapo police force to enforce gun laws. If law-abiding citizens are not compliant with gun laws, then tyrant-supporting police will go into the home of every American who registered a weapon in order to confiscate their firearms. Police officers who are patriotic Americans and support the Constitution will not enforce confiscation of weapons. Law-abiding citizens may shoot and kill police officers who have become enforcers of illegal tyranny, trying to force their way into the homes of law-abiding citizens who own guns. This will be the beginning of a revolution across the United States. There are four ways socialists may enforce confiscation of weapons:

1. By creating a federal police force to enforce gun laws with coordinated efforts with local law enforcement.
2. By police departments across the United States firing all police officers who refuse to enforce these laws, and hiring new police officers who will.
3. By President Joe Biden declaring martial law in the United States and using the military to assist law enforcement to confiscate firearms from law-abiding citizens.
4. If gun confiscation still fails under martial law, Joe Biden may authorize UN Peacekeeping troops with an existing executive order to assist police and the US military in unarming American citizens by force. This would mean a socialist federal government would likely use mercenary UN Peacekeeping Forces to put down rebellions and kill law-abiding freedom-loving Americans on US soil as necessary.

All attempts to confiscate assault rifles, large capacity magazines, and other Democrat-banned firearms from US citizens will likely trigger a secession of states, which will eventually lead to an armed revolution against the socialist federal government.

Freedom-loving, law-abiding Americans must never give up their guns or even register them with the Federal government so federal tyrants may one day knock on our doors demanding our guns. Guns should always be an issue of states' rights under constitutional authority, not under a fascist, socialist, or communist government dictating authority.

Under what conditions would socialist tyrants come after our guns? The answer should be easy and obvious: Freedom-loving Americans will not give up their constitutional freedoms or yield to oppression and tyranny. If Americans ever give up their guns, Americans will become like the oppressed citizens of Venezuela, who are unemployed, have lost their homes, and are starving. In the United States, socialist tyrants from Washington, DC, would come after our guns for the following reasons:

1. to prevent a rebellion opposed to the oppressive taxes on the very rich and middle-class Americans;
2. to prevent a rebellion of people opposed to taxation without representation;
3. to prevent a rebellion of Americans who are driven into poverty and homelessness by the incompetence and tyranny of the socialist ruling elites;
4. to prevent rebellions by Americans whose homes have been confiscated by the IRS thanks to taxation oppression, leading to their inability or refusal to pay;
5. to prevent rebellions when the economy fails, causing massive unemployment and sharp increases in crime, lawlessness, homelessness, starvation, and chaos all over the United States.

Because socialists are anti-capitalists, they will wage an economic war on hardworking people, small businesses, and large corporations; a collapse of the US economy is highly probable. Elizabeth Warren and Bernie Sanders are two clueless failed presidential candidates who said they would declare economic war on the wealthy, the middle class, and all businesses across the United States. US stock markets will fall sharply to the lowest levels in history, causing panics, in turn causing people to take money out of their bank accounts. Large and small businesses will begin massive layoffs of employees. Many companies will declare bankruptcy. Rich people will have had hidden or will hide their money overseas and/or renounce their citizenship to avoid paying the very high taxes; that would leave the Biden administration unable to collect adequate taxes from the rich 2 percent, whom they always attack. Rich people are not stupid as most socialists and Democratic liberals think;

surely the rich made their plans to take their money and run by January 20, 2021.

Let's address another aspect of socialism. Another horrible scenario that many Americans may not be aware of or understand is that a socialist government typically can and may eventually take over major businesses and manufacturing in the United States. That is what socialism does—it takes possession and control of all manufacturing companies and their methods of product distribution for reasons of national security or on account of lack of production. But the socialist government then has to hire workers who will run their nationalized companies, such as those involved in the energy industry. President Biden has already canceled the Keystone XL Pipeline, causing gasoline prices to go up. The purpose of the plot to attack the petroleum industry is to make petroleum products unaffordable and force a transition to clean energy in transportation, home energy production, air travel, and so on, no matter how many millions of jobs are lost, no matter how many oil and gas companies go under, and no matter how many states are devastated by this move. Biden's plot to destroy the oil industry will lead to a secession of states unless laws are passed to protect oil, gas, and coal jobs until a sensible transition to clean energy can be made. Oil-producing states will resist nationalization of the oil industry by the socialist government. That's another reason Biden wants to destroy the petroleum industry. High-tech companies such as Facebook, Google, and Apple will be taken over and managed by the federal government; all profits will go to the socialist government and not to stockholders, as there will no longer be any public capital investments for US companies as an incentive to create wealth.

The federal government will use social media to promote its agenda and propagandize how successful and productive it has become. That is exactly how the Soviet Union falsely propagandized its successes with agricultural crop growth in the newspaper *Pravda* during the 1950s. It was a well-known fact that during the 1950s, agriculture and crop growth in the United States under capitalism was far superior to that in the Soviet Union, which had a communist-style government. Should the socialist government be allowed to nationalize the petroleum industry in the United States, oil and gas production may continue until a complete transition is made to clean energy. During the transition, socialist elites will capture a percentage of the immense oil profits to enrich themselves. It boggles the mind how one man, Vladimir Putin, can become a multibillionaire in a formerly communist country, Russia, where income equality in theory is emphasized and even boasted about. But in practice it is not for elite rulers.

One flaw of socialism is that the incentive for workers to be more productive, to compete with other businesses for profit, to work harder, to find innovative ways to increase production, or to seek improvement in the quality of the product will be significantly diminished as the pay will be the same. In other words, why work harder and be inventive if one doesn't have to? Under socialism, no one will make more money unless they work longer hours.

If the day comes when a socialist federal government nationalizes industry and manufacturing in the United States with profits that *are not enough* to pay for all the socialists' utopic spending items, the socialist government may raid funds from Social Security, or reduce or eliminate veterans' benefits. What do you think veterans will do about this? I know exactly what they will do, and they will do it well. This means the elderly and veterans will receive reduced income to pay for the large socialist government spending plan. The extra funds trimmed from reduced Social Security and VA benefits will have been actually stolen.

Unions might be dissolved as workers are paid the same and no greedy capitalist is abusing them or depriving them of raises. With socialism, you get what you get, and you like it. There's no bargaining for raises or for health benefits. Why should there be? All workers are treated equally and are paid equality in the jobs and professions they're working in; no one should ever be treated unfairly. A union retirement fund or pension will no longer be needed. There will also be no need for 401(k)'s as there will be no investments in a socialist economy and no incentives for companies to be more profitable. There is no sense for a company to try to save money from wages since the wages likely will not be enough to pay all one's personal expenses. Banks will still exist under socialism. A good example is China, which has gotten very rich by selling cheaply made products to the United States at lower prices, making billions of dollars per year. China uses banks owned by the government for profit from capitalist transactions in foreign countries. US workers will have no benefits from banks, although banks may still exist in the United States to do transactions with foreign countries.

If the federal socialist government cannot collect enough tax revenue from the rich 2 percent of Americans, most of whom will have already transferred their own wealth to other countries, then the government may decide to raise taxes on the middle class or print more money.

If the socialist government prints more money to pay for the trillions of dollars in government assistance to illegal aliens and other spending sprees, the value of the dollar will be reduced. The World Bank will seek to make gold, or another foreign currency that is stronger and more stable than the US dollar, the standard of exchange. This means the cost of goods and services will increase in the United States, causing inflation. Americans will need more money to pay for these higher-priced goods and basic necessities; therefore, workers will demand higher wages. If the socialist government can't meet workers' demands, there may be protests, riots, or other lawlessness. Labor unrest and economic chaos are two more reasons why socialists would take guns away from the nation's citizens: to prevent rioting, protests, and lawlessness because of their economic failure to curtail spending, inflating the cost of goods with their bad economic policies that impact the livelihoods of workers and their families.

A desperate last resort, after failing to collect money from rich and middle-class Americans, and after printing has caused runaway inflation, is for socialists to attempt to confiscate a percentage of existing bank assets, directly affecting the personal savings and checking accounts of US citizens. Additionally, the IRS will target all Americans who are in tax arrears and evading taxes, and confiscate their personal property, garnish their wages, and put the tax evaders in jail. This will only make matters worse for the socialist ruling elites.

When banks lose money because of debt and bad investments, or the when the stock market falls sharply and never recovers, banks lose any money that is not guaranteed by the government. If depositors deposit more money into a bank than what is guaranteed by the US government, then bank losses can cause banks to seize from depositor accounts any monies that are not federally insured. That occurred in

Cyprus in 2013. Bank losses can affect the very wealthy with their large deposits possibly not being guaranteed. Cypriot banks recovered their losses with depositor money that was not guaranteed by the government of Cyprus. Worse, the government of Cyprus couldn't even return the guaranteed deposits to depositors, so depositors lost all their savings. What Cyprus did was to shut down its banks so depositors couldn't take any cash out of their bank accounts—a nightmare. However, the EU bailed Cypriot banks out, and Cypriot depositors were able to recover about 47 percent of their original deposits on average. If such a thing happens in the United States under a socialist regime, Americans will be driven to overthrow the socialist government and try to get their money back from the wealth of enriched socialist elites. This cannot be done without guns, particularly privately owned semiautomatic assault rifles, and magazines carrying more than ten rounds.

These are good reasons Americans may be driven into a second bloody civil war in a United States of America that was traditionally used to prosperity and freedom. In socialism, first they come after your pocketbook, then they come after your guns. Then they come after all your possessions when you're left vulnerable and can't fight.

Why We Must Never Give Up Our Guns to Socialists or Liberals

Democratic leftists have already stolen an election, and now they control two branches of the federal government. Joe Biden has signed at least forty-two oppressive executive orders, many of them reversing former president Trump's executive orders to lower taxes for economic growth. In addition, Americans paying the overwhelming majority of taxes are opposed to giving their tax money to an ever-increasing population in the form of government assistance to illegal aliens, reparations for blacks, and bailing out financially mismanaged Democratic states under the guise of COVID-19 relief funds. Tax oppression will lead to revolts. Democratic politicians will become tyrants and come after your guns, your wealth, and your possessions, leading to another major civil war.

Law-abiding citizens own guns for self-defense and the protection their families. It is difficult to understand why government would take away the necessary tools that otherwise protect us from home invaders, killers, or gang members, which are commonplace in many regions of the United States today. It is a tragedy to lose family because one hadn't the proper tools to defend them. Worst of all is for law-abiding citizens to surrender their guns to a tyrannical government by decree, a government that is oppressing its citizens. And if we refuse, the government resorts to Nazi-like gestapo tactics to enter homes, in violation of the Fourth Amendment of the Constitution, to confiscate weapons, using lethal force if necessary. If this occurs, tyrannical government will be hell-bent on making its citizenry defenseless, except for those who manage to hide their weapons. Socialists who confiscate firearms from law-abiding citizens will risk the loss of innocent lives because criminals will certainly have guns. The United States must never become like Venezuela.

The question then becomes, why would socialists take our guns away? Socialists will quickly say it's for our own good, for public safety, and to prevent mass shootings in public places. Don't believe it. Socialists think Americans are stupid—and many are, especially millennials. The truth is, socialists want no resistance from the US citizenry when they enact oppressive economic and social laws. Their goal is to eliminate resistance to remake the United States by way of social engineering of culture, religion, the economy, moral values, gender elimination, promotion of LGBT and pedophilia, legalizing illegal drugs for recreational use, politicizing the military, politicizing law enforcement, and reforming the labor force. Socialists know that imposing high taxes on the rich and on the middle class will meet with opposition. As Bill de Blasio said in the Democratic debate without any other Democrat challenging him, "We need to tax the hell out of the wealthy." Without their permission? What benefits will the taxpayer gain? What taxpayer? How much income will be taxed for the wealthy on a graduated tax scale? Even if it's detrimental to your business, or even if you are unable to support your family or pay your debt, you will be taxed at whatever rate the government dictates, without your permission.

In order for socialists to pass laws that violate the Constitution, such as banning free speech or banning guns, Democrats first have to vote to amend the Constitution by a 75 percent majority in both houses, the president must sign the law, and the Supreme Court has to approve or reject the new amendment. To get around that, corrupt socialists like Joe Biden or Kamala Harris may ban any amendment by executive order; this is outright dictatorship and unconstitutional. If Republican members of the House or Senate challenge any unconstitutional executive order, a stacked Supreme Court will rule on the side of President Joe Biden. If the Supreme Court, by chance, rejects a bill, a simple 75 percent of both houses of Congress can override the Supreme Court's rejection to see that the law is passed. Unethical and corrupt socialist politicians will radically change the rules of government to gain an advantage and power for themselves.

Socialists are very aware that any unconstitutional laws they pass will take away our long-held traditional freedoms. In order for any new amendments that are successfully passed to be enforced, socialists will need remake the military and law enforcement agencies across the United States so they become capable of enforcing their tyrannical laws. Before passing unconstitutional laws, they will need to "reprogram" the opposition, which is made up of conservative and patriotic citizens who are any of the following:

- law enforcement officers
- active military personnel
- veterans
- families with traditional family values
- Christians
- Republicans
- Trump voters.

Politicizing Law Enforcement and the US Military.

If we give up our guns to tyrannical socialists running the country, then the socialist government will feel comfortable passing laws to levy oppressively high taxes on wealthy individual Americans and on businesses. Federal agents will confiscate land, farms, and homes because of unpaid taxes. If we are left defenseless, we will lose our freedoms, our homes, and maybe our lives. We should never give up our guns; we must unify as patriots to defeat tyranny. If we ever allow the United States to become a socialist country, it will lead to a bloody revolution. If we keep our guns, there's a chance freedom-fighters can win. If we surrender our guns, we cannot fight, we cannot win, and we will lose our freedoms, our homes, and our lives. We will be left starving and defenseless as in Venezuela, with no chance of winning a revolution.

Before socialists confiscate guns, they need to know who has them. Socialists will demand federal registration of all guns belonging to all law-abiding Americans. They will call it gun control. The purpose of registering guns with the federal government is for the FBI, DHS, ATF, and US Marshals to go after those weapons anytime they want in the future, pass laws to impose arbitrary taxes on weapons already owned and new ones purchased, restrict which types of firearms can be owned, decree how firearms must be stored, and require costly licenses to own firearms. Socialists will also pass laws that punish violators of gun control laws with jail or fines. These laws would cause undue hardship for gun owners and would restrict the right of defense. Plus, they are oppressive laws that are unconstitutional. This is too much interference by big government into states' rights to allow their residents the right to own and carry firearms.

Law enforcement will be politicized, retrained, or fired. Cities, counties, and states will be run by elected socialists and liberals who will make policies to replace law enforcement personnel who refuse to enforce tyrannical laws with people who have no problem illegally entering the homes of law-abiding people to confiscate guns and/or rifles, with or without warrants. Why foreigners? Most likely hired as police officers will be amnesty migrants who are not familiar with traditional US values or the Constitution and will take orders to enforce tyrannical laws without hesitation. Many law enforcement personnel will resign or be fired. However, fired law enforcement personnel will unite with underground militia groups to fight the tyrannical government.

Social engineering of the military will be similar. A socialist commander in chief will replace high-ranking officers who will not follow orders to defend and protect the socialist government of the United States. Patriotic active military personnel will retire or leave the military because of the changes they oppose. Branches of the military will prefer to hire amnesty migrants who will defend tyrannical laws. The military may evolve into a military of foreign migrants who may be called by an executive order declaring martial law to put down right-wing rebellions or conservative groups that may be labeled or suspected as white supremacists or terrorists. Foreigners hired into the US military will not hesitate to kill conservative US citizens in a rebellion, particularly if the former are Muslim.

Veterans will be the deadliest force the military of migrants and the law enforcement agency of foreigners will ever encounter. US veterans of foreign wars will have more experience and skills in warfare than most of the active military consisting of essentially foreign migrants. But the FBI, DHS, and intelligence agencies will again be weaponized to identify, track down, and go after veterans who have weapons and who may become potential revolutionary leaders or terrorists. Veterans will unite and form armed militias to protect their homes and the areas they occupy.

At some point when innocent law-abiding citizens are killed by the US migrant military, a second American revolution will begin. The destruction of the First, Second, and Fourth Amendments, together with taxation without representation, will be the cause of the revolution. States will likely secede from the union, claiming their states' rights have been violated by the tyrannical socialist government. Governors of those states will seize all federal armed forces bases in their own states and control them. Seceding states will form their own central government and adopt the original unamended Constitution of the United States as their own. A military draft will occur, and a military will be established and mobilized to protect the new Constitution and states against aggression from the socialist federal government. Military personnel from non-seceding states will be assumed to be on the side of the US socialist government, so they will not be allowed to enter the seceding states. Members of all weaponized federal agencies of the socialist United States will not be allowed into seceding states. Regardless of secession, almost every state in the USA will have pockets of armed patriotic citizens opposed to the socialist government tyrants in Washington, DC.

Socialists will encourage open borders so more foreigners can enter the United States and be given amnesty to join law enforcement agencies and the US migrant military. There may be a point where there are so many immigrants getting these jobs that prior law enforcement officers, veterans, and conservative families joining the revolution will be outnumbered.

Because of the ongoing preparation for civil conflict, our US military composed mostly of migrants will be too weak to deal with foreign aggression or to prevent the building of nuclear weapons by North Korea and Iran. US military forces around the world will weaken, and Muslim terrorist groups will be emboldened to commit terrorist acts of aggression against Israel and other allies. The United States will become vulnerable to foreign enemies such as Russia, China, Iran, and North Korea.

Giving Up Your Guns Means Submitting to Oppression and Tyranny

No freedom-loving law-abiding American citizen will allow big government to take guns away from him or her, including assault weapons. If you're a homeowner (even with a mortgage), know that the Biden administration is already oppressing these homeowners by raising income taxes and property taxes, reimposing death taxes, and collecting higher capital gains taxes on the sale of homes. Higher income taxes results in a lower income. Your state and local governments will raise your state taxes to spend the money on free health care and free college tuition for illegal aliens, on black reparations, on climate change, and will also increase gasoline taxes, utility taxes, tourist taxes, internet taxes, phone taxes, automobile registration fees, and traffic ticket fines. If all these taxes become a financial burden on homeowners and you can't pay your mortgage, you may lose their home due to foreclose.

Renters may also may not be able to afford increased rent passed by the owner to the renter due to the owner's higher property taxes. Where will the renter live? How oppressive would that be?

Given that corporations will pay higher taxes under the Biden tax plan to provide Infrastructure spending, corporations will pass their corporate tax losses to the consumer. This means their products will cost more and you will pay for higher prices for common goods. Corporations and small businesses may also dismiss employees and hire illegal aliens, who will work for cheaper wages. The American low-wage worker will be easily be replaced due to the plentiful illegal aliens available under open borders. If business gets worse, businesses may reduce employment and not rehire. Some companies will declare bankruptcy. Some corporations may relocate outside the US and dismiss all working employees in a given location in the US. Under Joe Biden, I predict the economy will fail and Biden and the Democrats in Congress will have a bleak future in government leadership after nearly after the homeless population in the US increases and lives in poverty due to Biden socialist spending policies. There will be mostly the very rich and the very poor with a much reduced middle class. Nancy Pelosi will retire and spend her days eating her expensive ice cream she showed off in her refrigerator on TV, while hundreds of homeless people are outside her gated mansion in San Francisco are almost starving. But not to worry, Biden will throw some bones at the unemployed, the homeless, and illegal aliens such as healthcare aid, childcare aid, and welfare through his Infrastructure pork spending bill.

If mass rioting, looting, chaos, and confusion come to your community, be prepared if you own a gun. If gestapo law enforcement comes to your home looking to take your guns, fight them or you will become like the starving, defenseless masses of Venezuela without weapons.

The lessons of Venezuela should have sunk in the American mind. You cannot revolt against tyranny without weapons. Venezuelans gave up their guns, so now they can't fight or eat. Only elite socialist Venezuelan politicians and their military cronies will eat and prosper. Nancy Pelosi will be eating her expensive ice cream from her refrigerator while hundreds of homeless people are almost starving outside her mansion in San Francisco.

34

FREEDOM-LOVING LAW ENFORCEMENT WILL NOT ENFORCE A REPEAL OF THE SECOND AMENDMENT

Patriotic Law Enforcement Officers Will Not Enforce Violations of the Second Amendment

Patriotic and honest US law enforcement personnel will *not* violate the Second Amendment of the US Constitution, even if told to do so by their police commission, their country board of supervisors, or their mayor. If they were to enforce gun control laws, that would be a violation the Second Amendment, meaning they would be committing a crime and therefore be subject to criminal referral, arrest, trial, and possibly prison.

The only condition under which police departments are likely to enforce gun control laws that violate the Second Amendment to the Constitution is when a police department is politicized to align with the Left and is composed mostly of foreign migrants and socialists with an agenda to support socialist laws. In particular, the most harmful foreign migrants to be hired by police departments would be Muslims who hate Americans. Given gestapo powers, they would easily violate the Fourth Amendment rights of US citizens.

Militias that oppose gun control by the leftist state government of Virginia have already formed; they are opposed to tyrannical antigun laws passed by the Virginia State Legislature and approved by the leftist governor. Virginia antigun laws violate the Second Amendment. Lawmakers are withholding pay from all law enforcement agencies that do not enforce their tyrannical laws. Militias are already preventing tyrannical lawmakers from oppressively reacting to police who refuse to enforce their tyrannical laws.[1]

When a state in the United States, or the federal government, is taken over by despotic tyrannical socialists, they will always pass tyrannical laws, such as one permitting the confiscation of our firearms to make us vulnerable. Then, they will pass oppressive tax laws to confiscate our wealth, driving us patriots and our families into poverty or homelessness. I call on law enforcement, military veterans, and active military personnel to resist and oppose any laws that violate our constitutional freedoms or any laws that try to oppress us by taking away our pay for protecting the rights of law-abiding citizens, and our means to survive. Socialism will always lead to tyranny, and tyranny will always lead to another revolution in the United States. We American patriots must never allow government lawmakers and other bureaucrats to take away our freedoms and turn us into Venezuela, whose people are being starved and left without arms to fight tyranny.

As a Vietnam veteran, I wish all the militia freedom fighters in Virginia the best of luck. Go strong and resist tyranny. May God bless you in your righteous endeavors. Go to Washington, DC, to make your case for the defense of freedom in your state, and to make known your efforts to protect the constitutional rights of law-abiding citizens, standing with former president Trump. I am confident he will assist in dealing with socialist tyrants who oppress the citizens of Virginia.

---

[1] Gregory Hoyt, "It Begins: Virginia Forms Active Militia to Protect Sheriffs, Citizens from Unconstitutional Laws," Law Enforcement Today, December 16, 2019, https://www.lawenforcementtoday.com/it-begins-virginia-forms-active-militia-to-protect-sheriffs-citizens-from-unconstitutional-laws/.

David A. Herrera

The Pillars of Our Defense Are Patriotic Law Enforcement and the Military Supported by Freedom-Loving Americans

We support our patriotic and brave men and women of law enforcement and the military, and veterans, who defend our freedom, who provide justice, and who love the United States. The main lines of defense for our country are patriotic military personnel and law enforcement officers who love our country. When he was in office, President Trump was fighting to preserve our freedoms, sustaining the economy, dealing effectively with the coronavirus epidemic in the United States, and making the United States a great country once again.

In Venezuela, citizens made a bad choice to give up their guns. Then they chose a wolf in sheep's clothing as their socialist leader, Hugo Chavez, who, followed by Nicolás Maduro, disarmed Venezuela's citizenry, stole all the wealth from Venezuela, starved many people, and killed many dissenters. Venezuela has a corrupt military and corrupt law enforcement officers who protect a ruthless dictator rather than protect the freedom of the people.

Abolishing ICE would allow a multitude of crimes committed by members of drug cartels to endanger the lives of Americans and would allow illegal criminals to go back into communities to endanger Americans again. House Democrats even want to defund or abolish ICE, so how will they be able to stop the flow of drugs, MS-13 gangs, and human trafficking? Then Democrats vote against preventing an illegal alien from buying a gun. There's only one conclusion: Democrats want illegal immigrants into the country for votes; human life and misery are of no concern, but people are mere collateral damage on the socialist path toward gaining control and power

Drug Racketeering between Drug Cartels and the Mexican Government

It's sad that Mexico has become even more corrupt than before on account of the violent drug trade and human trafficking, the heinous murders committed by Mexican drug cartels, and the greed of corrupt Mexican politicians and their corrupt rich cronies. Corrupt Mexican officials from local Mexican police stations, Mexican border guards, and state and federal Mexican politicians are on the take from drug cartels, which profit off illegal drugs and human trafficking. If any of the drug cartels get out of line or assassinate the "wrong" government official, the federal government will send the Mexican marines to wipe out the specific drug cartel involved, so there's a mutual understanding between corrupt government officials and leaders of the drug cartels.

The high murder rate in Mexico is the result of warfare between rival drug cartels for control of drug trafficking and human trafficking in their territories. Mexico continues to be a country of the very rich and the very poor, just as the state of California is becoming. Over-taxation of the middle class by California state officials is forcing the middle class to leave the state, as is happening in another populous blue state, New York.

The Importance of ICE

A young incompetent Democratic House member, after visiting ICE detention camps where apprehended illegal aliens are detained, made inaccurate allegations comparing them to Nazi concentration camps. Illegal alien detention camps don't even compare to Nazi concentration camps used by Adolf Hitler in Germany. It's attempted sensationalism and pushing lies that only gullible, naive, low-IQ, and uneducated people will believe without knowing the facts.

ICE's job is to arrest illegal aliens crossing the border and detain them at available facilities. Democrats in Congress refuse to fund facilities, so ICE is stuck with the overcrowded facilities they have now. ICE is confiscating heroin, cocaine, and other drugs from drug traffickers at the border that kill thousands of Americans each year. ICE provides apprehended illegal aliens the necessities, such as food, clean water, showers, and toiletries, they need to survive. ICE provides medicine and medical treatment for the sick and injured. ICE has rescued some children and adults from drowning when crossing the

Rio Grande in Texas. ICE does not round up innocent people who are citizens or noncitizens and send them to gas chambers then burn their corpses in ovens, or execute people in horrible ways as the Nazis did in World War II.

35

SIGNS OF THE COMING TYRANNY IN THE UNITED STATES

Signs of the Coming Tyranny in the United States

A prelude to tyranny is becoming more apparent, and realistic, by the socialist positions and policies taken by Democratic members of Congress that will lead to tyranny, as follows:

- State governments will confiscate property, as stated by Mayor Bill de Blasio of New York.
- In case of inadequate or failed tax collections or tax deficiencies, socialists will likely confiscate 401(k)'s, seize bank accounts and investment funds, get into the Social Security slush fund, tax all pensions at a higher rate, increase taxes on the sale of any sale of gold or silver, and reduce or stop all tax refunds.
- Ban and confiscate firearms, and punish those refusing to surrender weapons—all designed to prevent a massive revolution against socialist tyrants.
- Enact oppressive tax laws at the federal level to deprive hardworking people of their wealth. Accumulated taxation at all government levels may reach 90 percent on the wealthy, and 50 percent to 70 percent on the middle class; it's taxation without representation again for redistribution of wealth.

- Provide free health care and college tuition to illegal aliens.
- Revive Barack Obama's "shovel-ready jobs" or LBJ's Great Society program to make work guaranteed for people.
- Open borders—let hundreds of millions of foreigners from all over the world come in and enjoy the free government handouts paid for by wealthy Americans and hardworking middle-class people. Democrats hope to benefit from cheap labor as California is now doing from illegal aliens, while the rich Democratic elites living all along the California coast grow richer.
- Prevent corporations and the manufacturing industry from relocating overseas—socialist Democrats would seize corporations to keep them in the United States, then regulate them and control them.
- Create massive spending plans to pay for the Democratic politicians' "Alice in Wonderland" utopia of income inequality, climate change programs, the Green New Deal, black reparations, homosexual reparations, college loan debt forgiveness, and the use of taxpayer money to enrich the socialist elites in power.
- Implement massive nationalization, control, and management of manufacturing, industry, high-tech, and energy companies, other businesses, the production and distribution of goods and services across the United States. The socialist government may choose to distribute food only to blue states and starve red states as communist Joseph Stalin starved millions of people in Russia and neighboring countries who did not support him.
- As in Venezuela, only the socialist elites in power will be the only rich benefactors of the economy protected by law enforcement and military personnel who are loyal to the elite Democrats.
- Assuming that capitalist Americans are freedom-loving people, socialist elites will likely pass tyrannical laws, use gestapo tactics, impose martial law, and even contract foreign troops to quell rebellions from American freedom fighters within the United States, whom wannabe tyrants like Cory Booker and Beto O'Rourke will label as "white supremacists" or "right-wing

terrorists." Tyrant elites in government will starve any pockets of resistance in red states, bringing about another bloody civil war in the United States.

We must never give up our guns to a tyrannical government that I sense is coming. Signs will indicate danger before tyrants start proposing and passing laws to ban or confiscate weapons. It's makes smart It's common sense for all law-abiding Americans to refuse to give up their guns. If socialists win the 2024 election with the aid of are elected by a growing population of illegal aliens given amnesty as police officers to enforce their tyrannical laws. Patriotic police officers will not enforce illegal laws such as the confiscation of the weapons of law-abiding citizens. We must never be bamboozled by a corrupt tyrannical government like the people of Venezuela were. If we do not take up arms against tyranny, or if we give up our weapons, we will starve or flee the country like the helpless citizens of Venezuela.

Another prelude to tyranny is that a US socialist government will take freedoms away from individuals by passing only enforceable laws. When they hire foreigners as police officers willing and able to enforce tyrannical laws, or when mayors who support socialists in government get elected across the United States, they will direct police departments to either enforce tyrannical laws or stand down and not enforce laws, which will enable terrorist groups such as Antifa to beat up conservatives without consequences. This is how the United States will be controlled by socialist tyrants. It starts with a socialist federal government destroying constitutional freedoms, remaking the United States with a massive number of foreign migrants, and offer these migrants jobs in state government and in police agencies to support the tyranny of the Left.

Warning Signs of Tyranny

Some things to look out for include the following:

- Actions by mayors who allow domestic terrorist groups such as Antifa to take over several blocks of city streets, as happened in

Seattle, Washington, which taken-over area anarchists called the "Capitol Hill Autonomous Zone," or CHAZ, and who set up barricades and armed checkpoints declaring city blocks a "cop-free zone."

- Actions by police who do nothing while violent protest mobs attack or beat conservatives giving speeches in public or at universities.
- Actions that allow leftist mobs to use violence against conservatives or Christians in public rallies.
- A president of a leftist federal government who creates a federal police agency specifically designed to surveil and target conservatives and right-wing opposition.
- A president who weaponizes personnel and federal resources to create another "Deep State" cabal.
- The hiring of primarily immigrants in law enforcement and in the military to enforce leftist tyrannical reform.
- The repeal or significant restriction of the First Amendment to punish leftist-defined conservative hate speech and to stifle antisocialist government speech.
- The stifling of religious freedom and the removal of the tax-exemption status of Christian churches accused of giving political speeches rather than proclaiming Christian doctrine.
- The severe restriction or altogether banning of the Second Amendment to make US citizens powerless to defend themselves against criminals, domestic rioters and terrorists, and socialist tyrants.
- The passing by socialists of open border immigration laws with the intent of giving all illegal aliens amnesty (automatic citizenship) without vetting them. These people will join with liberal US citizens and will overwhelm conservative voters so that Democrats always win elections.
- The ability of Democratic leftists to steal any election if necessary as long as corrupt Democrat-run states conspire with corrupt election officials, corrupt ballot counters, corrupt mail carriers, and fraudulent election computer companies.

- The option for Joe Biden of packing the Supreme Court with additional socialist or communist justices to enable approved passage of all tyrannical laws. Democrats will never be challenged in the rigged court system.
- The elimination of the Electoral College to rig elections in favor of mob-ruled elections. For example, blue states have the highest populations, and only the popular vote will determine elections.
- The imposition of high taxes on wealthy American citizens, including the middle class, without commensurate representation.
- The imposition of harsh environmental regulations on businesses, particularly the petroleum and petroleum-run transportation industries, to comply with new leftist-defined standards for a clean environment, which will economically weaken or destroy these industries. These leftist environmental standards will also create jobs for leftist-supporting companies whom targeted businesses must hire to help them meet costly regulations and standards.
- The control of the distribution of goods by socialists to flow only to leftist states that support tyrants, while at the same time reducing distribution of food and other necessities to red states that oppose tyrants in office Joseph Stalin style, for example, starving the opposition.
- The practice of high-tech giants canceling accounts or blocking the free speech of a conservative politician for any reason, and blocking speech from a president's conservative supporters. The corrupt fake news media and socialist politicians will applaud these high-tech companies.
- The printing of a lot of dollars by government to fund its socialist spending plans, resulting in a devaluation of the dollar, causing massive inflation and the refusal of other countries to accept the US dollar as standard currency.
- The usurping of, or significantly reducing the funds for, Social Security and VA disability checks. The seizure of private bank accounts from citizens without warning, the seizure of pension

funds and a reduction in pension payments for all employees, and the seizure of insurance annuities and 401(k)'s in order to fund socialist spending scams out of desperation because of lack of funds, similar to what happened in Cyprus.[1]

Americans will see the beginning of the end of the stock market when the economy begins to collapse, caused by failed socialist economic policies. Confiscating wealth through oppressive taxation will eventually collapse the economy; only the rich elite socialists and communists, and the rich who escaped taxation, will have everything they need.

Tax-evading Americans will be punished by confiscating their homes, their personal wealth, and/or their businesses. Millennials and low-skilled blacks will be the hardest hit economically as cheap foreign migrant labor will drive them out of their jobs. This is a betrayal of millennials and blacks by the ruling socialist government. Young millennials have been indoctrinated to embrace socialism in public schools, and they voted for Democrats, but then they learned that immigrants, who will work for lower wages, would replace them in the workforce. Now they realize that if they don't work, they won't eat under socialism, and they will be dependent on what bones the socialist government throws at them.

Socialism is an experiment in the attainment of power by a few ruthless, corrupt, and dishonest elites who will say anything to offer a false utopia to anyone who is a sucker to embrace it. Finally, millennials and low-skilled blacks will find that they will have to work for low wages, will never prosper as in capitalism, and forever will be sheep of the socialists.

---

[1] Mike Adams, "Cyprus Government Raids Private Checking and Savings Accounts as Citizens Panic," Natural News, March 17, 2013, https://www.naturalnews.com/039522_Cyprus_government_looting_bank_accounts.html.

Red Flags to Watch for in Terms of a Socialist Agenda for the United States

Note: That the US Supreme Court allowed the election theft of 2020 to be unchecked and unchallenged will be known in US history as the mother of all blunders. The US Supreme Court should be stripped of its "justice" function because it refused to hear lawsuits from the state of Texas and seventeen other states claiming they had evidence of election fraud. This means a handful of key states can illegally change their election rules and commit election fraud and nobody will care, thus affecting the outcome of the presidential election impacting other states; that is not justice. As a result, it will be extremely difficult to stop or reverse any tyrannical legislation passed by Congress and approved by a socialist president. Fraudulent elections have bad consequences for the United States. Red flags to look for include the following:

1. The corrupt Democrat-run media will continue to vilify the rich as oppressors of the poor to gain support of the poor and illegal aliens to justify tax-oppressing the rich and the middle class.

2. Democratic socialists will begin discussing reparations for blacks, involving up to $6.2 quadrillion.

3. Governors and mayors of Democrat-run states will continue with their despotic unconstitutional lockdowns of business that will kill US businesses and drive business owners into bankruptcy, debt, poverty, or homelessness.

4. Socialist Democrats will consolidate power by providing tax breaks to their loyal supporters from private industry, funneling taxes to reform conservative institutions in the United States, and declaring war on wealthy Americans. The tax booty collected from the war on wealthy Americans and businesses will be needed to meet the enormous socialist spending plan of tens of trillions of dollars.

5. Immigration reform will allow foreign migrants to "share the wealth of the United States"; free government handouts will

be paid for by taxing capitalists. The goal is to exploit foreign migrants to remake the United States.

6. Weaponize government agencies to establish Deep State II to spy on political opponents in order to destroy them in future elections; use dirty tactics to smear opponents using the socialists' supporting media, and rig elections.

7. Reform, politicize, and control police agencies across the United States to enforce tyrannical laws.

8. Fire US military generals and brass incompatible with socialist ideals, and replace them with dependable liberals, socialists, homosexuals, transgender people, cross-dressers, and foreign migrants who are willing to defend a "more just and tolerant socialist United States."

   Note: The goal here is to prepare the US military to put down any future anticipated rebellions by conservative freedom-loving Americans who oppose tyrannical taxation laws and to assist police agencies in disarming the US citizenry.

9. Legislate gun control, ban guns, or confiscate guns from private homes. At this point, patriotic freedom-loving Americans begin forming secret armed militias to oppose the tyrannical socialist federal government. States will likely secede from the United States. The intent of socialists will be to disarm the citizenry and make them defenseless as Hugo Chavez did with Venezuelan citizens.

10. Watch your wallets and purses, as socialists will confiscate your wealth to spend on the Green New Deal, climate change programs, and free health care for illegal aliens as more migrants enter the United States in massive numbers. Socialists *dare not* provide any estimates of the *total cost* of their plans or how these plans will be paid for, who will pay, and how much the taxpayer will pay.

11. Redistribute wealth, collected from taxing the wealthy people remaining in the United States, the hardworking middle class, and businesses, to freeloaders and foreign migrants to achieve income inequality.

Note: Socialists in power will begin overtaxing the wealthy without providing them any benefits in return. Freeloaders who think they deserve everything free will vote for socialists in future elections, as will foreign migrants who come to the United States to claim their share of American wealth, as soon as they are given amnesty. Prosperous Americans who were highly taxed to pay for it all will still undeservedly be advertised as capitalist oppressors who deserved to be robbed—no pity for the rich white racist capitalist. An increase in armed freedom-fighter militias will battle the police and federal agencies. The IRS will confiscate more personal wealth and more homes of US citizens.

12. Eliminate the Electoral College.
13. Pack the Supreme Court with extreme leftist judges.
14. Legalize marijuana to keep millennials lazy, dumb, happy, and drugged to get their votes.
15. Legalize prostitution to get the pervert and Hollywood vote and their donations; Vice President Kamala Harris supports legalized prostitution.

This all will lead to a full-scale American revolution, the red vs. the blue, conservatives against US tyrannical government elites and against their politicized gestapo police departments. The US military, also politicized, will likely be packed with foreign migrants who will be called to put down rebellions of patriotic Americans fighting for their freedom and their lives. The corrupt tyrannical socialist elites in power will be the main targets of patriotic freedom-fighting Americans.

Worse, if the socialist law enforcement and the politicized US military cannot put down freedom-fighting American rebellions effectively, socialists will activate Barack Obama's executive order to call UN Peacekeeping Forces into the United States to aid the US military and law enforcement in stopping insurrections and defeating the freedom fighters on US soil. This means UN Peacekeeping troops will be authorized to kill Americans fighting for freedom on US soil. This is not the scenario Americans should have, but it's the most likely one that policy tyrants will create. The United States has failed to prevent "the mother of all blunders" caused by the US Supreme Court. Americans will now suffer the consequences of a socialist government that will control every aspect of their lives. Conservatives no longer have representation in government now that President Trump is gone.

Will Freedom-Loving Americans Ever Surrender to Tyranny?

Do we want theocracy, fascism, socialism, or communism in the United States? Do we want to surrender our constitutional freedoms to communist or socialist elites? Do we want socialists to plan what products we need, control the manufacture of products, and distribute them to whomever and wherever socialist planners prefer, at the set prices they want? Do we want Muslims immigrating to the United States to change its culture, overpopulate it, and gradually take over the government to remake the United States into a theocratic Islamic fascist nation? Do we want a dictator who rules with executive orders to bypass Congress to abolish or diminish amendments to the US Constitution? Answer to all these questions: Absolutely not, because of the American character.

1. The majority of Americans by nature love freedom.
2. Americans will never give up the constitutional freedoms that they and their forebears fought and died for.
3. Americans will never surrender to tyrants; they will go to war rather than be enslaved.
4. Americans will not be silenced.
5. Law-abiding Americans will never give up their guns to tyrants.
6. Americans will resist tax oppression without representation by a tyrannical socialist government.
7. Americans will not stand for their Constitution to be shredded.
8. Americans opposing tyrannical laws will never allow themselves to be rounded up and imprisoned by gestapo-type police who enforce tyrannical laws.

9. Americans will not live under a system of government that provides no opportunities for wealth, prosperity, or reward, or reasonable pay for merit, innovation, creativity, invention, and a good work ethic.

10. Americans will resist giving up any family inheritance wealth to the state so the government can give it to foreigners.

11. Americans will not tolerate socialist control of the media, government-sponsored propaganda, or control of social media to spy on and block opponents of the socialist government.

The seeds of socialism in the United States have already been planted. Democrats stole the election, and they plan to implement their radical socialist agenda. Tyranny is coming to the United States; it is already expressed in the policies announced by President Joe Biden.

36

THE COMING SECOND US CIVIL WAR BETWEEN THE RED AND THE BLUE

The Refusal by Oppressed Freedom-Loving People to Comply with Socialist Laws

Trump supporters know that socialist Democrats have already begun violating their constitutional rights in the state of Washington, for example, stifling free speech in universities and restricting Second Amendment liberties. Anarchists are still trying to take over parts of major Democrat-run cities in the United States by force. Antifa and Black Lives Matter (BLM) are destroying and burning churches, statues, monuments, and the symbols of capitalism—businesses. This is equivalent to the sacking of Rome and the end days of the Roman Empire, when tribes from all over Europe, such as the Visigoths, Vandals, Anglos, Saxons, Franks, Ostrogoths, and Lombards, ravaged Italy, each taking its turn, eventually carving out areas in which to settle down. The Anglos and Saxons populated the British Isles, and the Franks ended up in France. This is equivalent to the destruction of religious artifacts and Christian churches in the Middle Eastern countries by ISIS and in Afghanistan by the Taliban. It's already happening.

Twitter has already banned former president Trump from using their site, and other tech giants such as Apple, Google, and Amazon are preventing *Parler*, a conservative alternative to Facebook, from being accessed on their internet servers by the millions of people who are registered users of the site. Freedom of expression of seventy-five million Trump voters is being banned, stifled, and violated by Democrat-leaning high-tech companies, with the support of the fake propaganda news media and the corrupt, vile, and vindictive Democratic politicians. Freedom of speech is already being destroyed in the United States. These high-tech companies have a monopoly on social media and internet servers.

Americans must refuse to obey tyrannical laws and defend our constitutional freedoms. The Democratic Party wants open borders to stifle voices of freedom, to allow BLM to destroy businesses while preventing police from stopping them in Democrat-run cities, and to eliminate the right of law-abiding citizens to bear arms. To strip freedom away from patriotic Americans, socialists want to create a federal police agency, like Obama wanted but failed to implement, and like 2020 presidential candidate Cory Booker wanted, in order to enforce oppressive tax laws and disarm citizens before they can rebel against socialist tyranny. The only two ways socialists can enforce tyrannical laws is to hire illegal aliens as federal police and/or hire UN Peacekeeping troops on US soil to fight freedom fighters. In such a scenario, civil war is inevitable.

How Socialist Tyrannical Laws Will Lead to a Bloody Civil War

Democrats today appear to represent immigrants more than they represent US citizens because not enough citizens support Democrats. Democrats were rejected in the 2016 election, and since that time, Democrats have done nothing to win the hearts and minds of the majority of Americans, except engage in violence, burn and destroy US institutions, and attempt to remove President Trump from office. The sacrilegious Left even burned several Catholic churches in July 2020; one in San Gabriel, California, was burned to the ground, and one in Florida was rammed by a nutcase who set the church on fire while parishioners were holding Mass. Democrats plan to gain power by remaking the United States with a massive increase in the illegal alien population. This means allowing an open border policy and offering free stuff to attract foreign immigrants into the United States from all over the world, even from Muslim countries whose citizens want to kill us, so they can, once given amnesty, vote for and support the socialist agenda. Taxes increase as prosperous Americans are ripped off to pay for the free stuff to foreigners, who will come in massive caravans to get their free stuff. But there is no such thing as free stuff, and socialists know it. "Free stuff" will be paid for by tax-oppressed wealthy American citizens who, after losing a portion of their wealth, will get *nothing* in return for paying high taxes. This is already happening in some states hit hard by the COVID-19 pandemic, which are seeking to raise the already high taxes on homes and businesses, especially in Democrat-run states like New York, California, New Jersey, Minnesota, Illinois, and Washington.

As the economy declines and police departments in many cities across Democrat-run states are defunded or disbanded, poverty and violent crime will significantly increase and Democratic socialists will become desperate to ban and confiscate guns in fear of a *revolution*. As people resist giving up their weapons, and given that current police officers will not enforce the banning or confiscating of guns, Democratic politicians will hire foreign immigrants to serve in a federal police agency and work with local police forces to enforce confiscation of weapons. Obama tried to establish a federal police agency to control all police departments across the United States during his administration, but he *failed*.

As they replace high-ranking patriotic soldiers with foreigners in the military, socialists will also have political control of the military to protect and defend them and their policies. As this immigrant-composed federal police force, or new gestapo, tries to take guns away from citizens, a new bloody American revolution will occur. At this point, there will be no other recourse but war. Former patriotic police officers, veterans, and soldiers will join good folks to take back the United States from the socialist elites. American patriots and freedom fighters will never allow socialism to rule the United States or control their lives. Socialists will be forced to surrender or die after many lives have been destroyed on both sides in the bloody war. Americans will see a series of red flags planted, warnings given, and alarms set by encroaching socialism as it becomes tyrannical. Plans that should raise the red flag include the following:

1. obstruction of the building of border security;
2. the offer of free stuff to illegal aliens to draw them into the United States like a magnet;
3. the use of sanctuary cities to protect criminal illegal aliens from being deported;
4. the use of Black Lives Matter and Antifa as an arm of the Democratic Party to fight conservatives, attack police, and remove monuments and statues that represent racism, slavery, or a threat to socialists and communists, also using these domestic terror groups to effect reforms championed by Democratic socialist politicians who, along with the fake news media, will propagandize such groups as a justified revolutionary effort against fascist Trump supporters, as peaceful protesters, and as tools to loot businesses and burn them down to destroy capitalists;
5. the election to Congress of Muslim members representing Hamas and other Islamic terrorist groups for the future mercenary needs of our military, police agencies, or federal agencies;
6. the passing of laws to tax wealthy Americans and businesses up to a rate of 90 percent, and to raise the taxes of other hardworking people, to pay for free immigrant benefits, global warming projects, green energy, and socialist reform;
7. the stifling of the Christian religion by defining socialism as the new morality and proposing taxes on churches. Redefine/reinterpret biblical morality to make it be 100 percent in agreement with political socialism, and justify liberal policies and beliefs, such as abortion and homosexuality, as the "new morality." The Democratic LGBTQ crowd will enthusiastically promote same-sex marriages in churches, view same-sex marriages as normal behavior, and claim the

practice is morally justified in the Bible. The LGBT crowd will mandate homosexual education in all public schools for young children across the United States to promote male pedophilia and homosexuality;

8. the redefinition of hate speech as speech that Democrats/ socialists disagree with, making it so their high-tech partners can stifle free speech or so their gestapo police can target and prosecute any conservatives whose speech the Democrats disagree with;

Democratic politicians have urged people to run Trump employees and supporters out of restaurants and other public places, to get in their faces, and to shout profanities at them. Democrats also composed a list of doxed journalists so Black Lives Matter and Antifa could be dispatched to homes of conservative journalists to harass them and protest against them on their own property merely for expressing conservative thought—an outright violation of civil rights and a violation of First Amendment rights.

The Democratic Party is the party of jovial enthusiasts of homosexual perversion and the LGBTQ lifestyle. They want to introduce children to homosexuality at a young age in public schools using a bunch of phony political criteria, such as tolerance of others, eliminating gender, and the teaching of the "alternate lifestyle" to young kids; they are already doing this without parental consent in some states.

Joe Biden will weaken the US military as former president Barack Obama did in his administration. Biden will let China become the world's most powerful economy, surpassing that of the United States, and will let China rule the world. Biden will fire generals who oppose his policies, reduce funding for the military, leave them with inadequate resources, and again allow cross-dressers, people who have had a sex change, and homosexuals into the military to further weaken it.

Some of these actions have already occurred, some are promised by the Biden administration, and all will continue to occur.

A Prelude to Tyranny: Reasons Why Tyranny Will Lead to a Bloody Civil War in the United States

The seeds of socialism have been planted by the Democrats in their stolen election of 2020. For seventy-five million freedom-loving Americans, a civil war will eventually be very likely for the following reasons:

- taxation oppression and confiscation of wealth from the wealthy and the middle class;
- the loss of our constitutional freedoms;
- elimination of the Electoral College;
- reparations for blacks;
- the banning and/or confiscating of firearms;
- the IRS being empowered to go after your home, your savings, and your pension if your taxes are in arrears;
- the use of your taxes to pay for "free stuff" given to illegal aliens in a United States with open borders (socialist politicians will steal from the rich and give the money to lazy freeloaders and millions of illegal immigrants so, once given amnesty, they will vote for socialist Democrats forever);
- massive unemployment and layoffs from industry because of socialism and high taxes;
- millennials and low-skilled blacks being replaced by illegal immigrants because the latter offer cheap labor;
- $1.6 trillion in college debt being forgiven for all college students;
- tens of trillions of dollars needed to pay for climate change, the Green New Deal, and Medicare for All;
- socialist elites enriching themselves with your tax money;
- the more than seventy-four million Trump voters not being represented well by the Biden administration.

There will be a socialist takeover of manufacturing industry when the economy collapses. A new Deep State will spy on anyone opposed to socialists in power. Speech will be stifled, or the right to free speech will be lost altogether. The rights of Christians will be stifled, or Christianity will be entirely destroyed. Children will be indoctrinated in classrooms.

Freedom-loving people will refuse to be tax-oppressed or driven into poverty or homelessness with their voices diminished, their weapons confiscated, or their freedoms taken as happened in Venezuela. We will have the bloodiest civil war ever before such a thing is ever allowed to happen in the United States.

Socialist Tyrants Are Enemies of Freedom

Socialist elites will be declared as enemies of the state when their gestapo police go into people's private homes to seize their firearms. That's the time for a massive revolution against the socialist elites; it will become the United States' second civil war—a war caused by evil, cunning socialists in the Democratic Party as they mobilize their army to take firearms away from law-abiding citizens. *Don't give up your weapons.* When tyrannical laws are passed and freedoms are destroyed, create or join a militia to fight tyranny.

Democrats will establish a federal police agency, which Barack Obama tried to create but failed, to control all local police departments in the United States. A federal police force will become the gestapo of the socialists that will enforce the destruction of freedoms of the American people.

Historically, the only ones who get rich and fat from socialism are the elite tyrannical rulers who often destroy the opposition with every means possible to keep a tight rein on their government. Why is Vladimir Putin, a part of the ruling elite in Russia, a multibillionaire? Why is Nicolás Maduro a multibillionaire? Why are the mullahs of Iran multibillionaires? Why are the king of Saudi Arabia and his royal family multibillionaires?

37

THE MASSIVE ELECTION FRAUD OF 2020

The Worst Concerted Massive Election Fraud Committed by Democrats in US History

The 2020 election in the United States was the most corrupt and most elaborate concerted effort to commit election fraud that has ever occurred in US history. It was designed, planned, and implemented by members of the Deep State at the federal level with computers and software manufactured by high-tech companies well-known to commit election fraud. The fraudulent computers, flash drives, and computer software were vulnerable to user manipulation and were capable of secretly and illegally flipping votes from one candidate to another without arousing suspicion. These fraudulent election computers were sold to approximately twenty-eight states, with Democratic-biased election officials in Democrat-run states, and perhaps some election officials in red states, for the purpose of manipulating the vote count to change the outcome of the presidential election fraudulently. State, county, and city leaders, ballot counters, elections officials, the US Post Office, and high-tech companies all conspired to commit election fraud on a massive scale.

Joe Biden winning this election does not make any sense. The massive election fraud of 2020 was intended to add enough votes for Joe Biden, whose policies were nebulous at best and not explained in detail. Joe Biden was said to have received the most votes of any presidential candidate in US history. It doesn't make any sense for the following reasons:

- Joe Biden hardly campaigned at all; he was stuck in his basement most of the time.
- Joe Biden ran on the soul of the United States, on being a nice guy, and on family history.
- His policies were nebulous and lacking detail to the American people.
- He hardly answered any questions that were not pre-scripted for him.
- Most all reporters were biased Democrats who lobbed soft, easy questions at him.
- He became hostile and angry when asked about his and his son's corruption.
- He never accomplished anything significant in forty-seven years as a politician.
- He has often been seen and heard on TV as incoherent; he appears to be senile, dazed, and confused with memory loss
- He had a reputation of being a creep around women and little girls.
- He had very low turnouts at his rallies, compared to tens of thousands of supporters at each of Donald Trump's rallies.

How can a man characterized as such, win an election? It all points to election fraud.

As of November 20, 2020, twenty-eight states had certified their elections for Joe Biden. Democrats won the race for the Senate in Georgia and now control the Senate in 2021.[1]

Lawyers for the Trump administration filed lawsuits against six states for suspicion of voter fraud, backed by some ballot counters who swore in affidavits under penalty of perjury that they personally saw irregularities in the ballot counts. Sidney Powell and Rudy Giuliani are

---

[1] Liam Doyle, "US Election 2020: Which States Have Certified Election Results?," the *Express*, November 29, 2020, https://www.express.co.uk/news/world/1366212/US-election-2020-which-states-have-certified-election-results-evg.

attorneys who investigated election computer and software fraud and claimed they had shocking evidence that massive fraud was committed. The evidence gathered in six key states was submitted to the Supreme Court of the United States to prove massive election fraud and to show that because ballots had been illegally omitted, President Trump should be reelected. Links to the evidence are found in the article "Defending the Republic" by Sidney Powell.[2] More evidence is addressed by the *Conservative Daily Post* in an article entitled "Evidence! More Than 'Double' Vote Margin in Swing States Is from Illegal Ballots."[3]

If Democrats can rig elections or steal them, then a president like Joe Biden doesn't need to take care of his "constituents." What if the economy tanks? Blame it on COVID-19 and Trump. What if there are massive layoffs for American workers? Illegal aliens would merely replace laid-off workers for cheap wages and lift the economy again. Like Obama said when the economy was bad, "It's going to get worse before it gets better." But it never got better. Stolen elections also mean a president can be senile and incompetent and con his way through the presidency for four years, letting his staff do all the thinking, budgeting, and worrying. Then Biden can pick and choose which of their policies to implement. It also means he can cover up scandals, corruption, and mistakes, or blame others for them. It means he can flail along without consequences, continue with corruption and self-enrichment without accountability, and use the fake news media to spread nothing but favorable propaganda to make himself look good. It means the media can portray a president who is loved by everyone and show him on TV being treated like a pet poodle, as Barack Obama was treated on *The View*. Elections have consequences, especially if they are rigged or stolen.

---

[2] Follow the link to see a list of Sidney Powell's evidence: https://hereisthe evidence.com/.

[3] G. Walrath, "Evidence! More Than 'Double' Vote Margin in Swing States Is from Illegal Ballots," *Conservative Daily Post*, November 20, 2020, https:// conservativedailypost.com/pennsylvania-court-orders-2300-votes-thrown-out-in-senate-race-state-counts-them-anyway/.

The Democrats Now Successfully Control
Two Branches of the Federal Government

President Trump was overwhelmingly expected to win reelection in 2020, but Joe Biden was confirmed as president on January 20, 2021, after a stolen election. Democrats won both houses of Congress. This means there will likely be no checks and balances between two branches of government. Democrats will pass all laws unopposed. Joe Biden may pack the Supreme Court with additional judges, and if so, in that case, Supreme Court will surely be in the pockets of the Democrats and Democrats will control all three branches of the Federal government. Democrats will strengthen their power to win all future elections by admitting Puerto Rico as a state and granting statehood to Washington, DC, from which Democrats will pick up four additional seats in the Senate. The Electoral College will be gone, and mob rule from heavily Democrat-populated states will always elect a Democrat as president in future elections. Red state votes will not matter. By passing unopposed tyrannical laws, Democrats will transform the United States into a country we could never imagine. Freedoms will be taken from millions of Americans as some states likely secede from the union.

The Growing Tyranny Will Intensify

Tyrannical laws will include taxation and wealth confiscation, gun confiscation, censorship and control of free speech, stifling of religious freedom, nationalization of industry, new forms of taxation, and open borders to allow massive numbers of immigrants into the United States, including radical Muslims, terrorists, and horrific criminals. Cartels will establish roots in the United States for control of drugs and sex trafficking; crime will increase; homelessness and poverty will increase; Social Security will slowly be phased out; and veterans' benefits will be significantly reduced or eliminated. Socialists will continue to mismanage the economy, resulting in increased homelessness, poverty, and crime in major cities.

Confiscated wealth will be the first to go, lining the pockets of socialist elites with their salaries, perks, and pensions, then to fund their crony friends to make the socialist government a success and more powerful—a form of redistribution of wealth to socialist supporters only. Police agencies will be politicized and reformed to enforce tyrannical laws of the socialist regime, whether corrupt or not.

Socialists will increase Muslim immigration into the United States from the Middle East and Africa. Muslims will seek to overpopulate the United States and will probably be granted sharia law so that they may practice it in their communities here in the United States. Congress will abolish the Electoral College and the Senate, so the United States will be run primarily by mob rule, the mob coming from blue states such as New York, Illinois, Washington, and California.

Congress will pass laws to control the news and social media to give the socialist government favorable press and issue favorable propaganda to prevent dissent and opposition. Recall that some Democrats said the United States was never great. Based on the extremism of the socialist regime, the socialist government may amend or repeal some constitutional amendments or create a new constitution, justified by their alleged humanitarian rights, tolerance, new morality, and nonracist form of government with equal wealth for all.

Over time, the United States will be transformed into Venezuela with all banks controlled by the government. Smart billionaires will have long escaped with their wealth as they planned prior to the election when socialists reared their ugly heads in our government.

As a result of mounting red state opposition to Democratic socialist rule, the socialist federal government will likely establish a federal police force, as Barack Obama and Cory Booker once suggested, consisting of trusted leftists, Muslims, and amnesty migrants willing to enforce tyrannical laws passed by the socialist government. The Fourth Amendment to the Constitution will be violated as federal police enter homes to confiscate weapons. Tax dodgers will have their properties and/or bank accounts seized. Tax oppression will lead to increased poverty and even homelessness in the United States. In conclusion, conservative Americans will be pushed to reject socialism, its failures, its oppression, and its tyrannical laws, leading to an armed revolution and, eventually, a major bloody civil war.

The Socialist Fantasy Utopia

Socialists want to transform the racial, culture, and political landscape of the United States, and our major institutions, from traditional conservatism, valuing God, country, and family, into a godless fantasy and nonracist utopia. Socialists hate the United States and its slave-owning founders. They reject and revise US history to justify their socialist policies and to destroy all historical landmarks, statues of historical figures, and historical monuments as a means to erase history. The leftist fantasy utopia will require a redistribution of wealth to produce income equality for all, except for the socialist elites in power. The socialist utopia requires high taxes imposed on the rich and costly environmental regulations on businesses for the sake of slowing climate change. Taxes will also be donated to world global member nations who are united to end world pollution and control climate change. The utopia will require government assistance and government handouts to shelter the homeless and millions of indigent immigrants entering the United States, all paid for by rich white people, who will be portrayed as historical oppressor capitalists.

Conservative values do not serve socialists well. Socialists detest the patriotism of a free and prosperous capitalist United States because it conflicts with their socialist ideology of controlling Americans like good little sheep. The utopia requires that socialist elites enrich themselves, their crony friends in big government, their business donors, and the leftist organizations that support them, such as the socialist propaganda news media. To build the fantasy socialist utopia, socialists need to advertise "free stuff" to attract foreign migrants to the United States from all over the world, giving them handouts in exchange for loyalty. Granting amnesty to tens of millions of illegal aliens will increase the power base of socialists forever. This is how the utopia is initiated and built. Socialists in government will build a socialist network of personnel who will develop a spending plan for their pet projects and submit costs for each of their spending whims. Socialists will seek contractors, industries, businesses, and organizations that can implement their plans to try to make their utopia a reality. Socialists will change election laws to enhance their power in government. The "free stuff" socialists give away will come from the hardworking taxpayers who are *forced* to pay for it, and worse, the taxpayer's interests will not be represented. For example, street repairs in their communities will be neglected, cities will become dilapidated, city infrastructure and repairs will be neglected, and major cities likely will be plagued with homelessness, filth, trash, and disease. California as run by Democrats serves as a good example.

A Scenario under Government Tyranny

Socialists typically do not understand the benefits that a capitalist state like the United States brings to its citizens. They do not understand the value of freedom and the Constitution, and why it has made the United States the greatest power in the world. But most of all, socialists do not understand that Americans will never live like sheep. They would rather die than live without the freedom they have been accustomed to.

Blacks who think they are victims of systemic racism should know that today is a different world in the United States today than fifty, one hundred, one hundred fifty, or two hundred years ago. They should never again think they will be put back in chains and live without freedom. But liberals know that blacks have vulnerable minds so that their egos can be easily exploited. Socialist politicians and race-agitators are always quick to point out the past, instead of saying how lucky black people should feel themselves to be living in present-day America. Liberals use US history as a weapon to cause people to hate the United States, to hate oppressive capitalism, and to hate the Constitution because it was created by our founders who were slave owners. Psychologically, it may be devastating to many blacks to find out in public schools that their ancestors were slaves, bought and sold as property, because today's blacks live in an entirely different world. They now live in a free and powerful country that allows their voices to be heard, not silenced. The elephant in the room is what liberals and socialists always omit or refuse to talk about—the fact that the United States has evolved. It's a new America, and all Americans of every race under current laws already have opportunities to prosper and achieve the American dream. President Trump praised blacks and people of other ethnicities, urging them to seek a good education. He also created jobs and opportunities for them to work hard at and, thereby, achieve the American dream. Trump's legacy for blacks is "be all you can be"— that is, do well for yourself and your family.

Democrats, on the other hand, are still lobbing bombs at blacks to inspire historical hatred, to remind them of the past sins of slavery and Jim Crow laws to create resentment in them. Democratic politicians claim blacks are still victims of oppressive white rich people instead of urging them to seek job opportunities to escape the plantation that Democratic politicians create for them. Liberals further entice them with reparations for historical oppression.

Not until recently have many blacks realized that they have been lied to by Democratic politicians, who only sought to anger them and to stir up their resentments to portray them as victims in today's United States, when in reality, white people are not oppressing them. On the contrary, white people can benefit blacks. Blacks now realize they also fought for this country in World War II, Korea, Vietnam, Afghanistan, Iraq, and other areas of the world to defend our freedom. They fought to keep the United States safe and their families safe, and they fought to ensure the freedoms of not only the people of the United States but also our allies across the world. Blacks should love their country and be proud to have served it with honor, not disgracing it and disrespecting it like people in the NFL and other sports are doing.

Historically, the US military loved American freedom and fought and died to preserve it. Today's military would never enforce tyrannical laws that destroy American freedom. Under a "remade America," however, the US military will be required to defend tyrannical laws that encroach on the constitutional rights of Americans and destroy their freedom. That is why socialists need to transform the military into a new cadre of personnel consisting of liberals and amnesty immigrants, to protect and defend the country from a future second American revolution perpetrated by patriotic freedom-loving Americans bent on defeating a tyrannical, oppressive government.

Lazy millennial freeloaders will also be suckers who will be taking the free bait offered by the socialist elites, some of whom will work, while others will refuse and will laze around the socialist plantation.

Our millennials will turn out to be very disappointing to the United States. They have been indoctrinated to hate the United States based not on what the United States has become, but on a fictitious foundation that claims today's United States is systemically racist; that rich white people oppress poor people and minorities; and that institutions such as law enforcement agencies, the military, schools, and churches, as well as our culture and our morality, must be changed to remake the United States. A percentage of blacks even go a step further and demand that the white people of today provide reparations to black people today for white oppression and discrimination against blacks in US history. That is, whites must be punished for their ancestors' sins. There are four major characteristics of freedom-loving Americans that socialists never understood. Such Americans will:

1. never be forced to accept or live under a socialist tyrannical government,
2. never be tax-oppressed to give up most of their hard-earned wealth to socialist elites,
3. oppose control of their lives by big government; they will not be treated like sheep, and
4. never give up any of their freedoms; they will live free or die.

It will take millions of strong voices to stand against tyranny, oppression, and a corrupt big government that has been creeping toward socialism and disrespecting America. The voices must be heard from freedom-loving patriotic Americans who will lead to make America a great country once again with opportunities and economic prosperity for all, and with a love and respect for our country. The ever increasing redistribution of our individual and capitalist wealth and the insidious and corrupt shifting of power by Democrats into bigger government must be stopped.

David A. Herrera

Veterans, Police Officers, and Military Personnel, Hang on to Your Firearms

Who will stand up to tyranny? Evil succeeds when good people do nothing, hear nothing, and say nothing. Good succeeds when brave men and women stand up to fight for God, family, and country to destroy evil.

A day will come when the military will have to decide whether they will be led by a tyrannical and oppressive government that is hell-bent on destroying our families, our family values, our Constitutional rights, our safety, guided by tyrants who disrespect our country, silence and cancel our voices, who are currently representing millions of unvetted immigrants from all over the world over many American citizens. Every member of the military will have to decide if they will stand on the side of freedom or stand on the side of tyranny, oppression, and corruption.

A day will also come when all members of law enforcement must decide whether they will stand for freedom or tyranny. They must decide if they will be forced to enforce tyrannical and oppressive laws affecting millions of law-abiding citizens. They must decide what to do if their local city, county, and state governments will admonish or defund them for respecting and protecting the rights of law-abiding Americans, or for standing up against mobs who terrorize our communities.

The military and police must independently decide who is the criminal, who is the enemy, who is the tyrant, who is the oppressor, and who is on the right side of justice. May God guide the conscience of every member of the military and law enforcement to choose wisely and to protect and defend our country and our citizens from domestic oppression and injustice and from foreign enemies.

More militias will be created and stand against tyranny. Veterans, trusted law enforcement officers, and military personnel will also unite to use military tactics to overcome and defeat the socialist armed forces and their police.

Law enforcement is the first level of defense of our citizens. The job of law enforcement is to defend and protect the status quo by enforcing laws in effect. For some lawless individuals and organizations, being unable to change laws, change the status quo, or protest laws is not enough. They advocate changing the status quo, changing existing laws, and remaking the United States through violence and terrorism. This is a Maoist, communist-style revolution. Enforcing current laws makes police officers a target of violence. Hooligans get in the faces of police officers, cursing at them and threatening them, and riot as a form of lawless "protest expression." Domestic terrorist organizations such as Black Lives Matter and Antifa want to remake the United States in their own image; they could care less about law enforcement, whether personal property is burned or destroyed, about collateral damage, or who suffers, as long as they get their way. These thugs who cover themselves with the cloak of justice are nothing more than thieves, vandals, and domestic terrorists. They cause the decay and decline of civilization. Unlike Dr. Martin Luther King Jr., these thugs justify violence as the best way to remedy social injustice, racial hatred and discrimination, and income inequality for the oppressed.

Patriotic US citizens should always keep their weapons to ensure socialist politicians never take away our constitutional freedoms, which many throughout US history have fought and died for. In unity, veterans will lead the charge against tyranny, if it ever happens. This country needs to educate our young to produce less of these socialist-loving millennials infected by the disease of socialism and communism.

Civics and US history are not being taught today to teach our young students lessons about how the United States became a great nation under the Constitution with rugged individuals who pioneered and became innovative, industrious, and highly technical. Students are not taught world history or taught about the evils of communism and socialism. Look where Venezuela was, and look what socialism did to its people today. Look at how people in Cuba, North Korea, China, and Russia live under communism. Look at how Joseph Stalin starved millions of people in Asia under communism, and why. Look at the death and destruction Nazi Fascism brought to millions of people in World War II and how freedom-loving people defeated the Nazis. Look at the atrocities created under Islamic theocracies, for example, in the Ottoman Empire of Turkey against the Armenians, and the atrocities committed by ISIS against Christians in Syria. Schools have failed to teach comparative government, including its benefits and disadvantages. School curriculum needs to be reformed across all states.

Preparation for a Revolution and Civil War

If another civil war against tyranny is necessary, God forbid, then able-bodied veterans must once again step up to serve another tour of duty in the defense of our country, to defend it against all enemies, foreign and domestic, and bring the enemy to justice. Only a percentage of freedom-loving law enforcement and military personnel will unite with patriotic veterans to organize the resistance against a tyrannical government that will keep its power by way of corruption. The freedom resistance must never give up their weapons, because the signs of the coming tyranny from big government are here. Big government has been encroaching our on our economic well-being, our constitutional rights, and our freedoms.

Under the Biden administration, criminals and terrorists can enter the United States undetected and unvetted. Such people can potentially cause great harm to Americans; President Trump had been trying to prevent that. We rely on our brave and patriotic law enforcement personnel at the local, state, and federal levels, and on our strong military, united with law-abiding patriotic families, to stand up to the armies of tyrants, criminals, and domestic and foreign terrorists.

Should Joe Biden's brain ever malfunction and become dysfunctional, with Kamala Harris becoming president, and should socialists ever gain total control of Congress and pack the courts with liberals, socialists, and communists, the tyrannical laws they pass and approve will only be enforced by traitors to our country who want to thrash the Constitution. Democrat-run states, cities, and counties will rely on the new reformed police to enforce Democrat-passed tyrannical laws and to defeat freedom-loving Americans to in order to keep their greedy, self-aggrandizing selves in control of government.

Well-planned *security* saves Christian lives. Unfortunately, that's where we are in the world today. Peace is what we need in the world today, and all wars and conflicts should end. But radical Muslims want to make Islam the *master religion* of the world by way of immigration, overpopulation, terrorism, and genocide. This should be a wake-up call to the protectors of freedom and our families so our children will *never again* become easy victims of fascist theocracy. China wants to be the dominant power of the world, threatening its neighbor countries in the Pacific Ocean and the United States. North Korea threatened its neighbor countries and the United States until former president Trump stopped by threatening North Korea with military force. President Trump used Ronald Reagan's "Peace through Strength" doctrine. Iran has often called the United States "the great Satan" and has threatened to wipe Israel off the face of the earth. But thanks to incompetent politicians such as Barack Obama and John Kerry, billions of dollars were gifted to Iran, a country that uses that much US taxpayer money to spread terrorism in the Middle East, Africa, and elsewhere.

As long as patriotic and law-abiding Americans keep their guns and fight the oppressive Democratic politicians trying to take our guns away or restrict their use, we will defend our freedom, our country, and our families. Too many events in world history show that the confiscation or voluntary surrender of weapons before a country is ruled by tyranny is what enabled dictators to suppress and oppress their people without any means to defend themselves.

38

THE SECOND AMERICAN REVOLUTION LEADING TO A SECOND US CIVIL WAR

On January 20, 2021, Joe Biden was certified as the president of the United States. The first revolution was the War of Independence, fought against England because of English tyranny and lack of taxation representation. The second revolution has already started and will accelerate under the Biden administration, eventually leading to a second US civil war. The US Supreme Court failed to hear election fraud evidence and rejected Donald Trump's election fraud lawsuit, as well as a lawsuit brought by Texas and seventeen other states challenging the results of the 2020 election. It's difficult to win against an elaborate election fraud scheme. It's not that conservatives failed to win the hearts and minds of Americans, but it's that the Trump administration were refused justice to present evidence of election fraud in key state supreme courts and in the US Supreme Court. The DOJ and the FBI failed to investigate the biggest election fraud in US history; that will never be forgotten. What the hell do taxpayers pay DOJ and FBI for? Unable to reverse the presidential win, we are now faced with Democrat leaders with the vilest and most vindictive among them having impeached President Trump for a violent rally against both houses of Congress that they accused Trump of causing.

David Atkins, a twisted-mind member of the California Democratic National Committee, was quoted as saying that removing Trump was not enough, adding that all seventy-four million Trump supporters had to be "deprogrammed," that is, reeducated in thought and mind. Atkins labeled seventy-four million Trump supporters as "cult members" who should all be reeducated to become the sheep of the Left. This simply means fascist-like David Atkins is a "thought police" officer who advocates seventy-four million Trump voters were violating the law by supporting the "Make America Great" polices of President Trump. He suggested all Trump supporters should gleefully and compassionately follow socialists and their agenda. What a sick California Democrat. California DNC member Atkins detests conservative free speech, but it is not enough to stifle and censure their free speech to "fix" Trump supporters; deprogramming their minds is his socialist science-fictional solution.[1]

Now at the beginning of the Biden administration, conservatives have diminished voices. High-tech giants canceled President Trump's Twitter account and his supporters' accounts, censored conservative posts on social media, and denied conservative social media websites access to the internet servers that these liberal high-tech giants own. Vindictive Democratic politicians are urging high-tech giants, the fake news media, and members of Congress to target Trump supporters to silence their thoughts, voices, and expressions on social media, ensure they cannot get employment, and fire them from their jobs, along with punishing conservative institutions with high taxes. Biden will likely threaten to take away tax exemptions for Christian churches if they do not hire homosexuals or allow same-sex marriages, which is something that violates the moral beliefs of traditional Christian churches and the Bible and increases the risk that gay male pedophiles will associate themselves with youth groups. Biden says nothing about taking tax exemptions away from mosques. Muslims also believe homosexuality is immoral; under sharia law, homosexuality is punishable by death.

---

[1] "Biden's America? California Democrats Demand to Put All Trump Supporters in Concentration Camps after Biden Takes Office," Conservative and Free, November 20, 2020, https://conservativeandfree.com/2020/11/20/bidens-america-california-democrats-demands-to-put-all-trump-supporters-in-concentration-camps-after-biden-takes-office/.

Looking back over US history, I believe we ignored the coming signs of tyranny that President Ronald Reagan warned us about: big government always seeking to control our lives and deny us the freedoms we as a nation fought so hard for. Additionally, Democrats failed to heed the words of Martin Luther King Jr. in his peaceful fight for freedom. Conservatives failed to ignore the signs of the Democratic leaders' lust for power and their evil schemes to create a one-party system forever. Conservatives failed to drain the swamp, failed to bring corrupt officials who were responsible for spying on candidate and former president Trump to justice, failed to indict Joe Biden and his son for corruption, and failed to instill American and Christian values in our youth both in schools and at home. Even though President Trump strengthened our economy like never before, and even though he addressed the issues of poor blacks and enabled them and other minorities to become prosperous like never before, President Trump was defeated in a fraudulent election. The Deep State, which began under the Obama administration, was too strong to defeat; they, together with state and local Democratic politicians, perpetrated the biggest election fraud in US history to put a senile and inarticulate old man in the White House as president and to remove a presidential candidate the Deep State didn't like. It was treason. The Biden administration will become inundated with high-tech giants who stifle conservative voices. Congress is already infiltrated by socialists and with Jew-hating Muslims with ties to Middle Eastern terrorists and who are supportive of domestic terrorists. All checks and balances between branches are lost. As a result, the United States is lost.

Even worse, if freedom-loving Americans fail to prevent the confiscation of wealth, the confiscation of our guns, the loss of our constitutional rights, the remaking of the United States with millions of foreigners, the culture and institutional changes socialists are trying to make happen, and the potential use of UN Peacekeeping Forces on US soil to kill freedom-loving Americans, then such freedom-loving Americans will lose the second civil war.

As a result of taxation oppression and excessive business regulations, the top 1 percent to 20 percent of the wealthiest Americans will be the first ones intelligent enough to renounce their US citizenship, or transfer their wealth overseas, and/or move to a business-friendly capitalist country with all their wealth. As the Biden administration imposes high taxes and costly regulations on businesses, look for many small businesses to go bankrupt, laying off their workers and replacing them with cheap labor immigrants. Look for large corporations to relocate overseas or for corporations to be nationalized.

Additionally, at least 25 percent of the middle class will probably relocate outside the United States, thus significantly reducing the tax revenue. As a result, the socialist government will be forced to raise taxes even more on the middle class to make up for the losses incurred by the rich, who escaped with all their wealth to other countries. Socialists know that 90 percent to 100 percent of Americans will resist giving up their guns, so common sense will drive socialists to hire police officers whom they can trust and who will enforce tyrannical laws. The 2020 election fraud was a checkmate for the USA. A revolution will begin and will strengthen over time: more than seventy-four million people with guns against the eighty-one million people who voted for Joe Biden. Every tyrannical law passed by the Democrats will add fuel to the fire in favor of an insurrection against the socialist federal government that is already burning.

Sometime at the start of the second US civil war, many patriotic Americans will form militia groups, hide their weapons, hide their wealth, and establish secret underground places to meet and plan strategies to overthrow the tyrannical government in a fight against the loss of our freedoms and constitutional rights, and against an entirely new corrupt socialist United States. A collapsing economy caused by high taxes and regulations imposed by the federal government will makes citizens more vulnerable, which in turn will force them to be dependent on big government for running their lives. Being deprived of our freedoms as Americans is worse. It's better to fight tyranny than to live in chains. The Biden administration will put people back in chains. Instead of leaving the United States, many Americans will choose to fight the tyrannical government. Police officers loyal to Democrat-run states and local governments and to socialist politicians in Washington, DC, who enforce tyrannical laws will all be considered enemies of freedom. They will also become targets of the new American revolutionaries fighting for freedom.

These revolutionaries will come from patriotic American families who believe in God, country, and traditional family values. If police and the military cannot quell the revolution, the US socialist government will likely call UN Peacekeeping Forces, as a matter of national security, to "keep the peace" on US soil, which means foreign mercenaries will be called to help police and military personnel to fight against patriotic freedom-loving Americans. They will kill them as necessary on US soil under the authority of the socialist tyrannical government. The United States of America will be the new USSR, or the United States Socialist Republic.

The question is, what country will the UN Peacekeeping Forces be from? The most plausible answer to this question is the following:

1. They may be Muslim troops from the Middle East, Africa, or Asia who may have connections to radical members of Congress who are Muslims themselves.
2. They may be Chinese troops.

If China volunteers to send millions of troops as UN Peacekeepers to the United States, then the US military, run by socialists and the Chinese troops, will easily defeat freedom-loving Americans. But the Chinese UN Peacekeepers may not leave the United States after a victory unless the United States pays them and the UN a hefty amount of compensation for the work done. The UN New World Order leaders will approve of this remuneration. US socialists will have no choice, being vulnerable, but to pay trillions of dollars in remuneration to China. If US socialists refuse to pay, they will be forced into a war with China, backed up by the UN. China will force the US socialist government to pay trillions of dollars in remuneration unless China decides to conquer the United States with its troops, missiles, and ships and take it over; the Chinese will know the US is more vulnerable than at any other time in history. This scenario will not end well for the United States unless Muslim troops from the Middle East or Africa are invited by pressured US socialists to fight against Chinese troops, complicating the conflict and the existence of the United States. In the end, the scenario to use Chinese troops as UN Peacekeepers will not be a good idea for the United States, which likely will end up a divided country under complete control of the UN.

Let us now assume Muslims from the Middle East or Africa, instead of Chinese troops, were summoned as UN Peacekeepers into the United States. It will be a bloody war in which the freedom-fighting militias will be defeated by the US socialist-run military and Muslim UN troops. After a conservative defeat or a defeated secession of states, US socialists retain power. The Constitution will be revised by socialist elites and no more freedom will exist in the United States.

As a reward for their peacekeeping duties and partnership, US politicians will allow more Muslim immigrants into the United States, who in a few decades will overpopulate the United States with Muslims, as they are doing now in Europe. When Muslims gain sufficient power in the United States, they will attempt to make the United States a Muslim nation and betray the US socialists who trusted them and allowed Muslim immigrants to populate the United States. Muslims will unite and resent socialists, whom they will see as godless infidels without morals. As a result, a third bloody civil war will occur between Muslims and non-Muslims in the United States.

Lessons That Should Have Been Learned Prior to the Second Civil War

The lesson learned from this hypothetical scenario is that Republican leaders lacked the wisdom, the common sense, the insight, and the courage to do anything about the culture change by leftists leading up to 2020. Most Republicans who were too complacent, tolerating social engineering by the Left, did little or nothing to prevent pervasive pornography, homosexual marriages, taxpayer-paid abortions, genderless bathrooms, male transgenders participating in female sports, and stifling free speech and religious rights, unable to stop leftists playing the race card and economic inequality card from dividing America. Above all, they were unable to prevent socialist politicians from taking over the United States in a fraudulent election and allowed the Biden Administration and a Democrat majority in Congress in both houses to accelerate the remaking of America and take Constitutional rights away from Americans. Conservatives should have done better in curbing leftist changes. Culture and institutions were changed in front of conservatives' noses because most were too snugly complacent, too tolerant, and/or too weak to do much of anything about it. The failure to prevent, reverse, or counter the leftists' social engineering of our culture yielded the following results:

- Legalization of same-sex marriages
- Homosexuality is introduced and taught in public schools. Protection and promotion of homosexuality in public schools.
- Male transgenders competing and winning every female sporting event.
- The Biden Administration reversing former President Trump's executive orders, raising oppressive taxes on the wealthy and middle-class Americans, allowing millions of illegal aliens into the US as an open border policy, and bailing and enriching blue states under the guise of COVID relief and Infrastructure bills, and unable to prevent the Biden Administration from banning assault weapons and severely restricting gun laws.
- The inability for conservatives to prevent all laws that allowed socialists to keep perpetual power and control of the US government.
- Progressive teachers are indoctrinating millennials in public schools to be hell-raisers as protesters against perceived injustices: systematic racism, police brutality, and free speech they disagree with. Students are indoctrinated to hate the United States, teach students to disregard the Pledge of Allegiance and the flag, to embrace socialism over capitalism, and to prohibit talk of Jesus Christ in public speeches and in classrooms. Some students are even taught that only violent revolution, such as that of Che Guevara or Mao Ze Tung, can only bring about social justice in America. Our schools and universities are infiltrated with these socialists and anti-American teachers and professors.
- In many US cities, people can't even wear a MAGA cap without getting attacked.

- Conservative speeches are forbidden on several liberal campuses.
- Most liberal and socialist members of the Democratic Party are trying to severely restrict gun sales or confiscate guns from law-abiding citizens.
- A longtime illegal drug, marijuana, was made legal to use for recreational purposes in some states, in violation of federal law.
- In cities controlled by liberal politicians, violent organizations such as Antifa and Black Lives Matter are allowed to riot, damage property, assault police, and beat up defenseless old men.
- Progressive politicians, along with Catholic progressives in the United States, want to change Catholic doctrine on abortion and homosexuality to state these are moral human rights.
- Members of Congress who are reelected to multiple terms are allowed to enrich themselves by cutting deals with lobbyists and engaging in pay-to-play schemes and bribes. We have allowed the Democratic Party to hold seemingly endless impeachment hearings to impeach a president whom Democrats hated, without passing any laws to benefit the American people in any way.
- Members of Congress may borrow money from Social Security to pay for anything they want and without paying the money back. Republicans in some states have failed to call for a Convention of States to put an end to congressional corruption and enrichment from lobbyists and donors. Issues need to be discussed to put an end to members of Congress who fail to perform their elected duties and neglect their districts, term limits, perks, and so on.

A Secession of States Will Be Justified by States' Rights and No Representation in Washington

Another secession of states may occur as, or before, a bloody armed civil war begins, led by Texas, Oklahoma, and several other red states. These will represent the Independent Freedom States of America (IFSA). These states will unite to form a central government and mobilize their own troops for their national defense. The secession will be justified by states' rights and a lack of representation from the USSR in Washington, DC. That is, the interests of each seceding state are not represented by socialists in Washington, DC. Secession will cause a great conflict, a national crisis, and a national emergency. Congress will debate sending military troops into seceding states, who will be met with heavy gunfire and guerrilla attacks by armed state militias to repel them. Acts of war begin.

During the coming second US civil war, socialists in power will send their USSR troops to seek and attack militias and militia training centers across the United States, mainly in red states. UN Peacekeepers will be authorized by executive order to fight alongside USSR military to put down state secessions, freedom-fighting rebellions, and militia camps, and to target Americans who sympathize with the freedom fighters.

Freedom-representing states will target tyrants, including Democratic federal politicians, state governors, and mayors; federal agencies; UN Peacekeepers; and any police agency on the side of tyranny. There will be a lot of bloodshed and mass shootings, perhaps genocide, execution, starvation, and refugees; prisons and prison camps will be full. The United States will become a war zone, vulnerable to enemy attack from China, Russia, North Korea, or Iran. What will the anarchists, protesters, and rioters who protested against social injustice during the Trump administration do? Answer: The cowards will likely escape to Canada or Mexico. Some will join the tyrannical government's military to fight freedom-loving Americans.

Unfortunately, many Americans will die. The socialist elites in government will not give up their power because they know that if they do, they will lose everything unless they inflict great harm upon patriotic rebels. This means that tyrants having control of manufacturing, supplies, and food will deprive areas in states known to have pockets of resistance, thus starving American families, just as Joseph Stain starved millions of people in Russia and surrounding countries who did not support him. Since radical Muslim immigrants and corrupt socialists have mutual respect for one another, Muslims will join the side of socialists against conservatives.

The following Democratic politicians who will be responsible for leading the United States into a civil war with their tyrannical socialist policies are Nancy Pelosi, Joe Biden, Alexandria Ocasio-Cortez, Eric Swalwell, Jerry Nadler, Adam Schiff, Chuck Schumer, Richard Blumenthal, Bernie Sanders, Kamala Harris, Beto O'Rourke, Julian Castro, Elizabeth Warren, Cory Booker, Ilhan Omar, Rashida Tlaib, Maxine Waters, Al Green, Sheila Jackson Lee, and Peter Buttigieg. Former leftist Democratic politicians who will support a socialist United States are Barack Obama, Hillary Clinton, and Bill Clinton. There are many Democrats in blue states, including mayors who will oppose the red state conservatives. The corrupt leftist propaganda news media, high-tech giants, and the Hollywood liberal crowd, all of whom support socialists and a remake of the United States, will also be responsible for the decline of the United States and the blood and carnage of the second US civil war between the red and the blue.

Examples of state and local officials who support extreme leftist policies are Governor Gavin Newsom, Governor Andrew Cuomo, and Mayor Bill de Blasio. These leftists are combined liberals and socialists who will cause the decline and destruction of the United States. Other leftists who support socialism and its rigid power structure are members of the Deep State and all members of the corrupt, propaganda-spewing fake news media.

Joe Biden ran on scaling down the oil industry and transitioning to green energy. If President Biden's administration attempts to destroy the oil industry with high taxes and costly environmental regulations, then states that benefit from gas and oil may secede from the union; these states will not allow a socialist federal government to nationalize or destroy an industry they have long relied on for their livelihoods.

White Americans will become a minority in the United States because of an increasing population of foreigners entering the country from all over the world through Joe Biden's open borders. The leftist endgame: End white oppression, power, and influence with taxation oppression. Transfer the wealth to an increasing population of nonwhite citizens, to include all foreigners. It's essentially a redistribution of wealth from alleged oppressive white capitalists to nonwhites, who will be made more powerful; this is the leftist goal of a remade United

David A. Herrera

States. Any citizens who don't comply with the socialist tyrannical laws like sheep will be identified, monitored, arrested, and prosecuted by police departments and federal agencies. Law enforcement policies will use new aggressive policies and brutal tactics to control the conservative "criminals."

Exceptions That May Prevent a Secession of State and Civil War

Exception# 1:
This is a weak exception. Republicans in 2022 may take the majority in the House of Representatives only and try to rescind some Democrat-passed election laws that will always guarantee Democrats a win in all presidential races. But the Senate and President Joe Biden may prevent the House from passing any legislation. The biggest obstacle to America and to this exception is not being able to overcome all aforementioned ways corrupt Democrat will pass laws to consolidate their power forever.

Exception# 2:
This is a strong exception. If the US economy tanks into a recession or even a depression, in which all Americans suffer due to the leftist policies of the Biden Administration and a Democrat-led Congress, voters will become very angry. American citizens may see the error of Democrat socialist ways and in 2024 elect Donald Trump for president if he runs, or another strong conservative that runs for president. Americans may also vote to put a majority of Republicans in both houses of Congress in response to the failed policies of Nancy Pelosi and Chuck Schumer. Then by Devine Intervention again, perhaps former President Donald Trump might get elected president with an all Republican control of Congress, pull us out of an economic crisis, and make America great again. This great miracle will save the US from future secessions and future civil wars and save many lives.

A Developed Socialist United States

A more developed and more powerful socialist government will nationalize and control businesses, create a police state that will enforce tyrannical laws, have a socialist-friendly military to defend the tyrannical government, severely restrict rescind amendment(s) to the Constitution, modify election laws so Democrats win every future presidential election, and continue to redistribute wealth to organizations and contractors, which strengthens socialism. And no one will be able to get a job without government approval. US citizens who are identified as conservative dissenters or protesters of socialism will be tracked by artificial intelligence software and be put into a "skunk list" database. If an American's name is in that database, the individual will be denied a job. The related information in the database will become part of an American's résumé. Retirement accounts will be heavily taxed, and Social Security will be significantly reduced or eliminated, its funds diverted to free health care for all. Veterans' benefits and pensions may be reduced or eliminated.

The US socialist government will never achieve income inequality, as every socialist country in history has failed to do. Only the hierarchy of elites and their strong supporters will prosper from socialism or communism. Those opposing the government, such as Trump supporters, may be sent to reeducation camps or may be forced to live in poverty. As an example, demonstrated in the history of the Russian Revolution, people opposed to the revolution were starved because food was diverted to only the supporters of communism; Stalin controlled the distribution of food. In Venezuela, only the ruling hierarchy have access to food; citizens who opposed the government did not. In Russia, communist Vladimir Putin is a multibillionaire who controls the nation. No newspaper is allowed to print unfavorable news that denigrates Putin or his policies. Many truths can never be reported. The same will apply to news media in the United States to journalists who attempt to slander socialist leaders. In Venezuela, socialist leaders arrest and torture members of the press who report "truths" that are considered "negative propaganda." In a developed socialist United States, any voices of dissent against the ruling elites will be censured or impeached without evidence or cause, and without legal representation, as was done a second time to President Trump seven days before he was due to leave office. The corrupt fake news media will demonize seventy-five million American citizens as cultists whose thoughts need to be reprogrammed. High-tech corporations in bed with the socialists will censor conservative speech on the internet and fire people from their jobs for advocating the making of the United States as a traditionally great nation.

In summary, developed socialism will advance to such a powerful stage that it will control the life of every American. The United States was not made for socialism; socialism won't work in the United States. If Americans resist, they will be imprisoned or killed, unless another major American revolution occurs. Does anyone think law enforcement under a socialist government will allow peaceful protesters mixed with rioters to throw bricks, water bottles, and firecrackers at police in major US cities? Does anyone think a police force under socialism will allow right-wing extremists to take control of city hall and surrounding city blocks away from police, while the police retreat and abandon their job of ensuring the safety and protection of the citizens in that area? Does anyone believe that a socialist United States will allow buildings to be burned, looted, or destroyed by white supremacist rioters in any major city while the government's gestapo police force idly stands by?

39

MUSLIMS VS. NON-MUSLIMS—
THE THIRD US CIVIL WAR

Muslims Join Support of the Socialist Agenda

It is interesting to note that most Muslims from the Middle East and Africa refuse to conform to US customs and traditions and fail to assimilate into US culture. The same is happening in Europe. Many Muslims dislike the United States and Americans, but they migrate to the United States to leech off its wealth instead of staying in their own mismanaged, tyrannical Third World countries. Many Muslim migrants refuse to obey US laws. Most Muslim migrants settle in neighborhoods with large Muslim populations containing several mosques, which are built with money from Muslim countries. Their goal is the same: make the United States Islamic as they have been making Europe Islamic for decades. Following is an example of a radical Muslim elected politician from a Muslim neighborhood in the United States:

Ilhan Omar, Who Wants to Transform the
United States into an Islamic Nation

House Democrat Ilhan Omar is an immigrant from Somalia, Africa, who became a US citizen and was elected to Congress in 2016 from her district in Minnesota. She is a member of CAIR, an organization that advocates a Muslim caliphate in the United States, leading to Islamic domination of our country. This is according to an article in *Loomered* entitled "FBI Warrant: Ilhan Omar–Linked Terrorist Owns Jihadi Training Ground Discovered in Alabama."[1]

"Despite the fact that CAIR has been directly linked to terror financing and is recognized as a terrorist organization in the majority Muslim United Arab Emirates, Omar has not denounced CAIR, and has instead chosen to work alongside the terrorist organization to push for more Islamic influence in American politics."

Ilhan Omar is a socialist who hates the US status quo, US culture, US institutions, conservatives, and the US Immigration and Customs Enforcement Agency. Omar is a racist who hates Jews and white men. She has radical Muslim contacts in the Middle East and in Africa.

Rashid Tlaib and Ilhan Omar are agents of Islam; their goal is to Islamize the United States. To accomplish this, they have to join US liberal Democrats as partners or "change agents" so as to methodically eliminate and reform the US status quo, including long-held customs, traditions, and institutions of our culture that patriotic Americans love. These Muslim women seek to destroy American nationalism, patriotism, and traditional conservative values. They seek to significantly reduce, marginalize, or force reforms upon the Christian and Jewish religions and their practices. Above all, they and the Democratic Party know President Trump once stood in their way. The stolen election of 2020 enabled Joe Biden to become president and removed President Trump from office. For three years, President Trump stood as an ominous force against radical Islam. He fought to make the traditional, conservative United States great by strengthening its economy, restricting illegal immigration, and strengthening its military to fight radical Islamist aggression. These two radical Muslim congresswomen supported the impeachment of President Trump and support socialist policies they hope will lead to the destruction, decay, and demise of traditional

[1] Laura Loomer, "FBI Warrant: Ilhan Omar–Linked Terrorist Owns Jihadi Training Ground Discovered in Alabama," Loomered, May 12, 2019, https://loomered.com/2019/05/12/fbi-warrant-ilhan-omar-linked-terrorist-owns-jihadi-training-ground-discovered-in-alabama/.

America. Their goals include the marginalization or destruction of Christianity and the replacing of the United States' constitutional republic with sharia law via a Muslim theocracy.

The Third Civil War in the United States

The remaking of the United States will have been done with of a partnership between non-Muslim socialists in the Democratic Party and Muslims in the United States. The Biden administration had lifted a ban that will allow increased Muslim immigration into the United States, as the European Union did with European countries.

If one looks at the last forty years of the history of Europe, one will see how millions of immigrants from the Middle East and Africa have affected Europe, as the European Union accepted millions of them to be allocated to specific European countries, who would in turn accept them for cheap labor and allow them to establish settlements there. Refer to *The Strange Death of Europe*, by Douglas Murray, published in 2017, to see how massive Muslim immigration has affected Europe and is currently killing its culture, instead of Muslims assimilating to contribute to the greatness of Europe. Muslim religious leaders (imams) are urging Muslims migrating to Europe to overpopulate each country so that, in the end, Muslims can attain government participation and control and establish a caliphate without firing a shot.

The second bloody civil war, between a socialist United States and freedom-fighting seceding states, will conclude with a victory for socialists with the help of UN Peacekeeping troops. Let us further assume that socialists and UN Peacekeeping–assisted socialist elites with their law enforcement and military will put down right-wing rebellions and the underground resistance effectively in blue states as well. Muslims, foreign and domestic, will have partnered with the socialists to defeat a common enemy—conservative freedom-fighting rebels and right-wing militias. The second civil conflict will no longer pose a significant threat to the US socialist republic's government, but the revolution by the underground freedom-fighting militias will still go on. UN Peacekeepers may stay in the United States for an extended time to keep the peace if the US socialist government does not have enough resources or personnel to fight the resistance freedom fighters. Freedom fighters will never give up fighting. The second civil conflict may not end until freedom fighters bring the Constitution and freedom back to the United States; they would rather live free or die. While the United States recovers from the second civil conflict, tensions and conflicts will begin between the increasing Muslim population and non-Muslim population.

Rich Muslim countries will offer the socialist United States economic aid for its post–civil war reconstruction efforts, in exchange for increased Muslim immigration into the United States from the Middle East and Africa. Muslims will argue these immigrants will also provide cheap labor to the United States.

The civil war between conservative Americans and socialists and their UN Peacekeepers will give rise to the socialist tyrannical theocracy of Islam, or "Islamofascism," in the United States. Up to this point, clueless socialists have partnered with Muslim immigrants who never assimilated into US culture but retained their strong belief in sharia law and the jihad, joined the fight to destroy conservatives, Jews, and Christians. Another revolution in the United States will occur between radical Muslims and non-Muslims. Muslims will betray the non-Muslim socialist ruling class. Muslims have always considered clueless liberal progressives and socialists as immoral atheistic enemies; this will be a complete shock to socialists. Good examples of what Muslims think, are immoral characteristics of liberals and socialists are the following:

- adultery
- rape
- selling, using, or legalizing illegal drugs
- theft and other serious property crimes
- excessive body exposure for women
- insolent women and insolent wives
- pornography
- prostitution
- homosexuality

- blasphemy against Islam
- atheism or secularism
- the adopting of Western customs
- protesters, anarchist thugs, and rioters
- their incompatibility with the Islam faith
- the fact that many liberals/socialists are nonbelievers of the Islam faith.
- any cartoons, artwork, speech, or propaganda from the news media that demonizes Muslims, their customs, and/or their religion

Liberal cities today, such as San Francisco, California; New York, New York; Los Angeles, California; Hollywood, California; Chicago, Illinois; Portland, Oregon; and Seattle, Washington, are being mismanaged by progressives. These cities have the highest crime rates and the highest rates of homelessness. Muslims will consider these cities as major centers of immorality and see them as a failure of American socialists.

Islam is incompatible with US secularist socialists and their debased morality. Muslim organizations will be funded by rich Arab countries, and more mosques will be built in the United States. Muslims will use the very same tactics socialists and progressives use to indoctrinate children. Muslims will require all children in public schools to learn about Islam, and Islamic courses will be taught in public schools for elementary schoolteachers. Muslims will have private schools that eliminate education about homosexuality

As the Muslim population in the United States grows, Muslim theocrats will demand sharia law and demand that the socialist government allow Muslims to have their own police forces in their own communities. Non-Muslim police brutality in Muslim neighborhoods will result in riots and violence. CAIR, a Muslim organization that promotes Islam in the United States and has ties to Hamas, the Muslim Brotherhood, Hezbollah, Iran, al-Qaeda, and ISIS, will have a larger voice in Muslim communities. Muslim members of Congress will also voice opposition to Muslim discrimination and will propose legislation to allow sharia law in all Muslim communities.

Muslims have always been aware of how perverted, nonreligious, and immoral their Democratic partners were in their struggle to jointly transform the United States from conservatism to socialism. Non-Muslim progressives and socialists were always naive and unaware of the methodical destruction that Islamic religious leaders had planned for them in the future; it will be a Muslim betrayal. Should socialists and Muslims jointly succeed in destroying conservatism and remaking the United States, Muslims will overpopulate the United States as they have been doing for many decades, to countries in Europe. Over the course of a few decades, Muslims will overpopulate the United States with Muslim men having up to four wives, and the Muslim birthrate will exceed the non-Muslim birthrate. More Muslims will run for elected office in the states they populate so as to gain more seats and power in the socialist federal government. Muslim-populated states will pass sharia law in their states.

A third US civil conflict will eventually develop between Muslims and non-Muslims, as Muslims gain positions in government—and in numbers. Many American black extremists will most likely join with Muslims against socialist non-Muslims. Since socialists have control of law enforcement and the military, and since non-US Muslims lack armed resources, US Muslims will accumulate arms, explosives, and dirty bombs from rich Arab countries such as Saudi Arabia and Qatar, and also from with Iran and Pakistan, to conduct acts of terrorism throughout the United States. To help the United States destroy itself, the Chinese may even release all their Uyghurs (Chinese Muslims) from internment camps into the United States, many of whom may be infected with COVID-19, to cause another wave of the pandemic to further weaken the United States.

The US socialist government may be forced to close borders and curb Muslim immigration using DHS and non-Muslim UN Peacekeepers to prevent further escalation of armed conflicts from Muslims. Suicide bombers will be used against law enforcement, UN Peacekeepers, and the US military. Terrorists will engage in widespread terrorism, killing innocent people, setting car bombs in populated areas, attacking police and the US military, and destroying government buildings and property. The biggest target prizes for Muslims will be socialist elites in Washington, DC, whom they will seek to assassinate or behead. In addition, the US Muslim government may accept the imprisoned Muslims of China, who will be given freedom and asylum in the United States to fight American militias.

While Muslims and socialists were engaged in the second civil war, Arab countries were urging millions of Muslims from the Middle East and Africa to join forces and enter the jihad with Muslims in the United States against infidel American socialists. If there are any conservatives still left, they will have to fight both tyrannical socialists and Muslim fascist theocrats. Unless patriotic US citizens expose, stand up against, and fight against the threats of encroaching socialism and Islamic fascism in the United States, and their partnership against conservativism, they will lose the United States, our great institutions, and our livelihood.

The Muslim population will grow faster than the non-Muslim population because of Muslim US births and Muslim immigration from Middle Eastern and African countries. Muslims who fought alongside socialists against conservative freedom fighters will betray non-Muslims whom they will consider godless and evil infidels. Muslims will resume training for warfare in militia training camps in Muslim communities and Muslim areas of the United States. Muslim terrorists from the Middle East will migrate into the United States to prepare for a catastrophic revolution against non-Muslim infidels.

Assumptions for an Islamic State in the United States of America: How Would It Begin?

A brokered UN peace agreement may occur to cease hostilities between Muslims and non-Muslims in the third US civil war. The war will end with Muslims gaining control of states mainly populated by Muslim immigrants. Non-Muslims will keep states with a dense population of non-Muslims. The United States will be divided between a US socialist republic and a US Muslim caliphate, the latter established in Muslim-controlled states. Muslims will run their US Islamic country as Saudi Arabia, Iran, Syria, Turkey, Pakistan, and Iraq.

After the brokered peace deal, the moral cleansing of the US Islamic American states will begin, with the gradual elimination of the following:

- non-Islamic religions
- feminism
- homosexual marriage
- pornography
- prostitution
- adultery
- antigovernment speech
- blasphemy.

The Muslim theocracy will outlaw the following:

- homosexuality
- the sale and use of illegal drugs
- firearms, except for police and military and high government officials
- anti-Muslim speech, protests, and rebellions
- many other crimes listed in US law, for example, theft, robbery, larceny, murder, and rape.

The culture of immoral leftists, consisting of homosexual practices, prostitution, pornography, and gang violence, will be targeted for cleansing and reform. California, home to the liberal and socialist perverts of Hollywood, and home to the US capital of homosexuality—San Francisco—and cities with perpetual gang violence such as Chicago, Baltimore, Detroit, and Los Angeles, will not be the places that are dominated by Muslims. Muslims will be repulsed by those states and their constituents. Muslims will not want to take over cities or states with notorious Western gangster violence and high crime; they will leave it to socialists to keep on mismanaging them.

Homosexuals will flee Muslim US states. Actors and actresses who voice their dissent against Islam will be given a chance to relocate outside Muslim US states. If they remain and continue their perverted practices, their heads will be put on a chopping block and they will be executed. Instant death will be given to gang members who commit gang violence and drive-by shootings. Instead, the Muslim police force will conduct a genocide of members of black, Hispanic, and Asian gangs. Non-Muslim religious institutions will be shut down or ordered to relocate. Honor killings and child brides will be permitted under sharia law.

The new Muslim states of America will declare their Muslim American country as a historical triumph and one of their most prized caliphates among those they control all over the world. The theocracy will use the religious police force to enforce sharia law, and establish mandatory Muslim control of education, the news media, and the internet in their states. Muslim police agencies and the military will be required to enforce Islamic laws, disarm the citizenry as necessary, enforce collection of taxes, fight crime, and put down rebellions, protests, and riots from non-Muslims who opposes the Islamic government. Immigration into Muslim America will soar.

Punishment required for certain crimes, such as the use and sale of illegal drugs, adultery, rape, murder, or blasphemy, may end up with one or more individuals' heads on the chopping block, Muslim or not. Adulterous or disobedient wives, and prostitutes, may end up in prisons run by Muslim guards, who may sexually abuse them. There will be no attorneys to defend them and no Miranda rights read to them. Women must wear clothes to cover any exposed skin so as not to invoke lust in men. Women must be chaperoned by a husband, father, son, or brother when they go out in public. No woman will be permitted to go anywhere unaccompanied by such a male family member so as to prevent prostitution or adultery. Muslim men may have up to four wives if they can reasonably support each wife. Up to four wives may share one husband, the wives all living apart. Non-Muslims will be treated like second-class citizens and will have difficulty finding work with high wages; they will have to work at laborious or menial jobs or be urged to leave the Muslim federation. However, men with brilliant minds and extraordinary talents and skills in technology, medicine, engineering, or some other field, who are willing to work, will be spared and will be offered job opportunities to benefit the Muslim economy.

A Muslim United States will be seen as a major historical failure and the result of the incompetence of American socialists. Socialists who naively trusted and partnered with Muslims for control and power will find themselves betrayed and living in a United States split into two countries. The United States of America, once a great country, will be weak and less powerful with a failing economy and with non-Muslim citizens left without weapons to defend themselves. Socialists may now see the horrific failure of their own socialist actions. Freedom fighters fought for God, family, and a free country as a way of life, and prospered. Socialists fought for power and control with little or no regard for the well-being of US citizens or the country. Muslims fought for a fanatical religion oppressing its people with draconian rules as a way of life, characterized by past events of genocide and religious cleansing, and forcing the conversion of any conquered victims to a fanatic religion by the sword, to attain a fascist theocracy.

All constitutional freedoms are gone. There is no Constitution; it was destroyed, the country's socialists replaced by Islamic caliphate states. Muslim immigration into the United States from the Middle East, Africa, Malaysia, Pakistan, and other Muslim countries in southern Asia will eventually overpopulate the Muslim federation of states in the United States.

Sharia law will be rigidly enforced in Muslim states. Those who practice homosexuality, promiscuity, or prostitution; get or perform abortions; use or make pornography; use or sell illegal drugs; or practice pagan rituals will suffer punishment under sharia law. Blacks who riot because of Muslim police brutality will *not* be treated like they were by the utter failures of Democratic governors and mayors in cities such as Minneapolis, Minnesota; Atlanta, Georgia; Portland, Oregon; Denver, Colorado; Washington, DC; Los Angeles, California; New York, New York; and Charlotte, North Carolina. Instead of retreating and abandoning a police station for rioters to burn, so no police would be present to protect the more than one hundred seventy businesses from fires set by rioters, Muslims would just machine-gun people belonging to any protest group, such as Antifa or Black Lives Matter, be they men or women, black or white, looting stores for TVs, pillows, vacuum cleaners, and liquor, as seen on TV. Muslim police will use "super-brutality" to contain anarchy and criminal events by mobs.

Muslim government rulers will frustrate and anger any US blacks who commit crimes and complain about police super-brutality. American blacks will seek help from the United States Nation of Islam, which once was headed by Louis Farrakhan, to unite black Muslims against the Muslim caliphate in the United States. Blacks will be shocked to learn they no longer have the freedom to protest, loot, block traffic, burn police cars, or throw projectiles at police who do nothing and let rioters burn the city without a police presence. The choice of action for blacks who are victimized by Muslim police in Muslim states will be as follows:

1. The Nation of Islam will try to negotiate a solution to Muslim police brutality against black people with the Muslim caliphate.
2. Black protesters and rioters will be forced to succumb to Muslim oppression, lest they be mowed down by gunfire or beheaded in a public area for everyone to witness.
3. Blacks may leave the Muslim federation to live in the non-Muslim American states, where socialists allow rioters to get away with anything.

There are rarely any protests to voice dissent in the Middle East, as members of Muslim governments such as Iran and Syria capture troublemakers, incarcerate them, torture them, and/or kill them. ISIS is notorious for decapitating the men in communities they capture and for holding Muslim women as sex slaves.

40

CONCLUSION

The United States evolved into progressivism during the presidency of Barack Obama. The Obama administration's "Hope and Change" policies were all about redistributing wealth to the low-wage earners, unions, high-tech companies, and leftist organizations to increase their power. The Obama administration was riddled with corruption and scandals, with Democratic elites enriching themselves from lobbyists and with pay-to-play schemes. Unemployment was high, and the national debt rose to $10 trillion in just eight years. Obama divided the people of the United States according to racial, economic, religious, and gender differences. Obama's staff went farther to the left than did previous Democrat administrations by weaponizing his domestic and intelligence agencies in an attempt to remove leaders from power both domestically and internationally.

Donald Trump was spied upon and was targeted for removal by the agencies that former president Barack Obama had weaponized to try to disqualify Trump from holding office because of a crime he may have committed. Trump shocked the Democrats in 2016 by being elected president. Still, the weaponized Deep State attempted to remove President Trump by a series of impeachment hoaxes, all of which failed. President Trump grew one of the strongest economies in US history with high incomes, record low unemployment, and opportunities for prosperity for all. SARS-CoV-2, originating from China, slowed the

US economy, but President Trump managed to get biotechnology companies to create vaccines ready for use by late 2020.

President Trump was, in modern times, the most hated president by Democrats—hated for his successes, for the promises he kept to the American people, and for his great accomplishments. He was nominated for a Nobel Peace Prize multiple times. The election of 2020 was the biggest instance of election fraud in US history. In a well-planned, concerted, and united effort by Democrats, and by using their resources, Joe Biden was elected president. President Trump and his investigators were given no chance to present their evidence of election fraud to key state supreme courts or even the US Supreme Court. Refusing to hear evidence of election fraud was the biggest miscarriage of justice ever committed by the Supreme Court of the United States.

Still, House Democrats feared and hated President Trump so much, they tried to impeach him seven days before he left office so that if he were impeached in the Senate, he would not be able to run for president again. More than seventy-four million Americans who voted for President Donald Trump had benefited from the greatest prosperity and the most job opportunities in US history. The United States under President Trump was the greatest country in the world.

Joe Biden became president on January 20, 2021, as Trump left office. Democrats won a majority in both houses of Congress with no checks and balances between the executive and legislative branches of government. Oppressive socialist policies have already been imposed on the American people. In less than ten days, Joe Biden signed forty-two executive orders, several that reversed the executive orders of President Trump. Joe Biden picked socialist Kamala Harris as his vice president. He also picked extreme leftists to work in his cabinet.

The Democratic socialist machine under Joe Biden has already declared a nonviolent war against Trump voters. The Democratic elite ruling class, the corrupt propaganda news media, giant high-tech corporations, and Wall Street have already begun to stifle the First Amendment rights of Trump voters and church groups. Tyrannical laws will be passed to "retrain" or "reprogram" Trump voters into compliance through fines, jails, doxing, stifling their opportunities for employment, and censure. Black Lives Matters (BLM) and Antifa may participate in violence against Trump voters or supporters, and even against Republican members of Congress. The socialist strategies listed earlier will be implemented to strengthen power among Democrats by changing election laws. Open borders and stopping the building of the southern border wall will allow massive illegal immigration into the United States. Joe Biden plans to grant amnesty to more than six hundred thousand DACA migrants who entered the United States as children in the Obama administration, and millions of other illegal aliens may be given amnesty by the Biden administration to increase the voting power base of the Democrat Party in order to win all future elections. As a backup, Democratic states with their fraudulent computers, mail-in ballots, corrupt election officials, and corrupt ballot counters can duplicate what they did in this most recent election to steal future elections, if necessary. The Supreme Court will again refuse to hear any evidence of election fraud. The beginning of the end of the United States has already come under the Joe Biden administration, sprung by the biggest fraudulent election in US history, committed in a conspiracy by Democrats and their corrupt supporters, all of whom are motivated by arrogance, greed for power, control, and self-enrichment.

Socialists will enhance their own police state to enforce tyrannical laws, particularly ensuring the rich, the middle class, and businesses pay their taxes. The Biden administration will pass an executive order and/ or Congress may pass legislation to restrict firearms and impose taxes on all existing guns and new gun sales, mandating gun registration with the federal government and confiscating certain types of semiautomatic assault rifles. Opposition to tyrannical gun laws across the United States will cause deadly confrontations between gun owners and federal agents and local police. If the United States Supreme Court ever rules that law enforcement agencies can confiscate assault rifles from private homes with or without a warrant from law-abiding citizens, there will be massive opposition to Biden gun laws, which will draw sales and ownership of these weapons underground.

A secession of states will likely begin, and a union of the Constitutional United States of America (CUSA) will be established. The socialist federal government will have no jurisdiction in the states seceding. CUSA will mobilize for probable war with the socialist federal government. Since the socialist elites want power and control and do not care about states' rights or constitutional law, a second civil war will likely occur. It will be a bloody one. Unfortunately, the predicted outcome will not be good for patriotic, freedom-loving Americans, as the socialist federal government will mobilize a large military force of leftist-indoctrinated amnesty migrants for war, who will overwhelm the military forces of the seceding states. In addition, if seceding states are lucky enough to force a stalemate, where neither side is winning, then the socialist federal government will pass an executive order requesting UN Peacekeeping troops enter American soil to assist it in putting down the rebelling seceded states or from pockets of resistance. The likely outcome is that freedom-loving Americans will be defeated and the socialist government will strip every seceding state of its wealth and firearms. Then it will turn seceding states into a Venezuela.

After the second civil war, another reconstruction period will begin under the supervision of the amnesty migrant military and UN Peacekeeping troops. During the war, the United States will be vulnerable to enemy attacks from China, Russia, Iran, or North Korea. China may take over Taiwan, and/or Iran will develop nuclear weapons and may use them against Israel. In either case, the United States will be powerless to do anything about it. The socialist government will be unable to protect its allies.

As reconstruction occurs, Muslims will continue to immigrate to the United States from the Middle East and Africa in massive numbers. They will join Muslims in Muslim-populated states. As Muslims begin overpopulating the United States, as they have done in Europe, more Muslims will take control of the government of the state in which they live. They will pass sharia law in all Muslim-populated states.

Since most socialist Americans are atheists or nonreligious, Muslims will betray socialists as immoral infidels who commit adultery, use drugs, legalize prostitution, promote and defend homosexuality, support transgender people, and who show pornography on TV. Muslims will themselves secede from the socialist United States. This will result in a third US civil war, this one between Muslims and non-Muslims. Islamic Middle Eastern countries will provide terrorists, weapons, and bombs to Muslim states and will fight against socialist non-Muslim states. The third civil war in the United States will likely be ended by peaceful negotiations led by the UN, whereby the Muslim seceded states will retain sovereignty because these states will be few. The United States, once a great country, will no longer be great; socialists will have ruined it with their greed, corruption, and lust for power. The United States will be split into two countries, a Muslim country and a non-Muslim country. Sadly, *The Coming Tyranny* predicts the end of the United States as we now know it. Only a miracle from God can prevent this horrible ending.

May God help our good people, and may God save our country.

AFTERWORD

My Relatives and I Fought to Protect and Defend the USA

As a Hispanic, I served my country in the US Army in Vietnam. My dad served our country fighting against Japan in World War II, and his brother (my uncle) served under General Patton fighting against Germany in World War II. One of my cousins was killed in action by rogue Nazis in Germany just after the end of World War II. My brother served in the US Air Force. My first cousin served our country well. We all were proud to defend the country we love, the freedoms we cherish, our faith in God, and our families against all domestic and foreign enemies.

APPENDIX

My Prayer

I Believe in God through Faith and in His Plan for Our Lives

Jesus, I see things that are good and bad in the world of politics in our country. I see loving families working hard to survive; I see the homeless in major cities in the United States hopeless and helpless; I see massive amounts of poor immigrants trying to enter the United States illegally to find a better life here; I see people who will never abandon you voicing their love for you; I see the love, kindness, and beautiful harmony between people, and between people and animals; I know of and see the hardships that the good people of law enforcement endure to protect us and our families; I know of and see the courage of good people in the military and the hardships they must endure to protect us and our country from bad people; and I see the sincerity, peace, patriotism, goodwill, and honesty of some government leaders who are trying to guide us with good laws and good leadership. As a man of faith who is a fighter defending your Word, our families, and our country, I have often failed in my deeds; in my thoughts; in choosing the right words about people I have called evil, incompetent, dishonest, and enemies; in being kind; and in forgiving others. Jesus, forgive me for my sins and give me a kinder heart, relentless strength, and the wisdom to choose the right words in responding to and dealing with what evil men and women do. Make me an instrument of change so that you will look favorably upon me and assure me that I have chosen my actions, deeds, and words wisely to effect good change. I will never abandon you, my Lord Jesus Christ. Amen.

ABOUT THE AUTHOR

David A. Herrera is a US Army veteran who served in Vietnam as a combat infantryman in 1967. He attained the rank of sergeant E-5.

After his three-year military duty, David A. Herrera attended California Polytechnic University, Pomona, in 1970, earning a bachelor of science degree in mathematics in 1974. His work experience includes working as a software programmer at the Jet Propulsion Laboratory, Pasadena, California, and as a software engineer at Lockheed Aircraft Service, Ontario, California, and at General Dynamics, Pomona, California. David was a subcontract manager who reviewed software, technical documents, and software testing for multiple subcontractors with Northrop Grumman in Pico Rivera, California. He became a software lead at Hughes Aircraft Systems International in Saudi Arabia. He worked as a software quality manager at Science Applications International Corporation in San Diego, California, and as a software quality control engineer lead at Raytheon Missile Systems in Tucson, Arizona. He also worked as a software engineer on missile software projects until his retirement in 2013. David received a monetary reward for his design of new statistical software on industrial statistical control processes.

He earned a master of science degree in systems and industrial engineering from the University of Arizona in 2006.

David A. Herrera is a traditional Roman Catholic and has been a member of the Knights of Columbus from 2008 to the present. He has been a registered Republican since the presidency of Ronald Reagan, and he voted in 2020 to reelect President Donald Trump. He is a conservative Hispanic who supports good education, patriotism, a strong economy, and opportunities for all to become prosperous and achieve the American dream. He strongly believes in in God, family, and country.

With his professional systems analysis skills and quality engineering expertise, along with his skills in creating systematic software and testing, writing and reviewing software documentation, conducting audits, and understanding how government and economics work, David A. Herrera is able to analyze and find defects in government political policies, processes, and procedures, find root causes of failures, and express remedial action for the resolution of such failures. David reveals that the biggest defects in US politics are liberal/socialist ideologies and policies. With his professional knowledge of probability and statistics and his studies in world history and US history, he is able to logically and analytically predict and explain how socialism, with its government interference and tyranny, will strategically and negatively affect American life and the US economy as we know it. Predictably and inevitably, a corrupt tyrannical government will lead the United States into a second civil war. With his research on executive orders, David predicts that the civil war will not go well for freedom-loving, patriotic Americans. After the second civil war, David predicts a 3rd civil war between American Muslims and non-Muslims in the US, which will end by negotiations and a divided America. Only miracles from God can save our country.

INDEX

Printed in the United States
by Baker & Taylor Publisher Services